Sovereignty and the New Executive Authority

The Oxford Series in Ethics, National Security, and the Rule of Law

Series Editors
Claire Finkelstein and Jens David Ohlin

Oxford University Press

About the Series

The *Oxford Series in Ethics, National Security, and the Rule of Law* is an interdisciplinary book series designed to address abiding questions at the intersection of national security, moral and political philosophy, and practical ethics. It seeks to illuminate both ethical and legal dilemmas that arise in democratic nations as they grapple with today's highly complex security challenges. The synergy the series creates between academic researchers and policy practitioners is designed to protect and augment the rule of law in the context of post 9/11 armed conflict and national security.

The book series grew out of the work of the Center for Ethics and the Rule of Law (CERL) at the University of Pennsylvania. CERL is a nonpartisan, interdisciplinary institute dedicated to the preservation and promotion of the rule of law in twenty-first century warfare and national security. The only Center of its kind housed within a law school, CERL draws from the study of law, philosophy, and ethics to answer the difficult questions that arise in times of war and contemporary transnational conflicts.

Sovereignty and the New Executive Authority

EDITED BY

CLAIRE O. FINKELSTEIN

AND

MICHAEL SKERKER

OXFORD
UNIVERSITY PRESS

OXFORD
UNIVERSITY PRESS

Oxford University Press is a department of the University of Oxford. It furthers the University's objective of excellence in research, scholarship, and education by publishing worldwide. Oxford is a registered trademark of Oxford University Press in the UK and certain other countries.

Published in the United States of America by Oxford University Press
198 Madison Avenue, New York, NY 10016, United States of America.

Library of Congress Cataloging-in-Publication Data

Names: Finkelstein, Claire Oakes, editor. | Skerker, Michael, editor.
Title: Sovereignty and the new executive authority / Edited by Claire Finkelstein and Michael Skerker.
Description: New York : Oxford University Press, 2019. | Series: Ethics, national security, and rule of law | Includes bibliographical references and index.
Identifiers: LCCN 2018016550 | ISBN 9780190922542 ((hardback) : alk. paper)
Subjects: LCSH: Executive power—United States. | War and emergency powers—United States. | Sovereignty. | War and emergency powers. | Executive power.
Classification: LCC KF5065 .S68 2018 | DDC 342.73/062—dc23
LC record available at https://lccn.loc.gov/2018016550

9 8 7 6 5 4 3 2 1

Printed by Sheridan Books, Inc., United States of America

Note to Readers

This publication is designed to provide accurate and authoritative information in regard to the subject matter covered. It is based upon sources believed to be accurate and reliable and is intended to be current as of the time it was written. It is sold with the understanding that the publisher is not engaged in rendering legal, accounting, or other professional services. If legal advice or other expert assistance is required, the services of a competent professional person should be sought. Also, to confirm that the information has not been affected or changed by recent developments, traditional legal research techniques should be used, including checking primary sources where appropriate.

(Based on the Declaration of Principles jointly adopted by a Committee of the American Bar Association and a Committee of Publishers and Associations.)

CONTENTS

PART THREE Vertical Sovereignty: Presidential Powers and National Security

PART FOUR Horizontal Sovereignty: International Relations and War

FOREWORD

Ever since the Westphalian Era the concept of "sovereignty" has emerged to be one of the truly important foundational ideas in history, helping define the authority of a ruler, the internal and external legitimacy of his power, and the norms governing the relationships among often-competing sovereigns. Notions of sovereignty underlie and have helped shape the formation of states and their frontiers, national identities, state conduct, the international order, the definition of rights, and keystone principles of both domestic and international law. The concept is venerable, complex, and fluid, and carries extensive descriptive and proscriptive weight.

But the idea of sovereignty and the debates that swirl around it are not merely of historical, academic, or legal interest: they are also potent, vibrant issues and as current and relevant as this morning's newspaper. As we are reminded on an almost daily basis, the concept of sovereignty possesses explosive political implications around the world, not least in the United States. Evidence of this is legion. Donald Trump—an unlikely and unconventional candidate as ever ran for the U.S. presidency—was unexpectedly elected in 2016 on a popular "America First" platform that he and his team asserted was grounded on the principle of "national sovereignty." The decision of the United Kingdom to exit the European Union, dubbed "Brexit," hinged on the British electorate's conclusion that too much sovereignty had been ceded to the supranational organization. Both Russia's occupation of the Crimea and China's assertion of control over the South China Sea rest on claims of sovereignty, albeit highly contested ones. So, too, Palestinian, Kurdish, Scottish, and Catalan calls for independence, to cite but just a few such examples, are couched in claims of sovereignty, as are the rationales of the nations that oppose such separatist efforts.

All these claims or visions of sovereignty are significant, but arguably the most novel and ultimately noteworthy of these could prove to be President Trump's. "In foreign affairs," he stated in his maiden speech to the United Nations, "we are renewing ... [the] founding principle of sovereignty."[1] Although Trump's

1. Donald J. Trump, "Statement to the United Nations General Assembly," Sept. 19, 2017, accessed at http://www.politico.com/story/2017/09/19/trump-un-speech-2017-full-text-transcript-242879.

sovereignty doctrine lacks detail and coherence, his administration's words and actions point to a reduced U.S. emphasis on human rights as a countervailing exception to a nation's claim to exercise unchallenged rule over its inhabitants under traditional sovereignty principles. If this is indeed to be the back-to-the-future path of U.S. foreign policy under the Trump administration, it could signal a marked change of course for a country that, since the Nuremberg trials, has slowly but unmistakably given greater and greater deference to the fragile but established trend to protect human rights, even at the expense of state sovereignty. This trend, labeled the "Responsibility to Protect" doctrine, was articulated as follows by former UN secretary general Kofi Annan: "State sovereignty is no longer an absolute shield behind which governments may hide to do what they please."[2] President Trump seems to disagree with Annan's bold assertion, and we may come to learn that in the crevices of this disagreement will lie the fate of nations, peoples, and individuals.

In the end, the parties to all wars, indeed, almost all conflicts, seek to legitimize their conduct in the language of right and wrong because it is understood that success in doing so enhances the prospect of ultimate victory. In instances of conflicts between nations, that legitimacy will often be found in competing interpretations of sovereignty. Whose interpretation should prevail? This book provides an excellent place to start in seeking to answer this question.

Sovereignty and the New Executive Authority, a splendid volume of essays ably curated by Claire Finkelstein and Michael Skerker, provides a highly sophisticated, broad, and timely survey of the current sovereignty literature. The book is a welcome contribution to our understanding of the multiple political and international controversies involving the issue and to the debates surrounding them.

July 10, 2018

Alberto Mora,
Executive Director of the ABA Rule of Law Initiative,
Former General Counsel of the
U.S. Department of the Navy

2. Koki Annan, "Prevention, Promotion, and Protection: Our Shared Responsibility," April 24, 2012, accessed at http://www.kofiannanfoundation.org/speeches/prevention-promotion-and-protection-our-shared-responsibility/.

LIST OF CONTRIBUTORS

Claire O. Finkelstein, Algernon Biddle Professor of Law and Professor of Philosophy, University of Pennsylvania Law School; Faculty Director of the Center for Ethics and the Rule of Law (CERL), cfinkels@law.upenn.edu.

Professor Finkelstein writes at the intersection of moral and political philosophy and the law. She has published extensively in the areas of criminal law theory, moral and political philosophy as applied to legal questions, jurisprudence, rational choice theory, and the ethics of national security and war. She is the editor of *Weighing Lives in War* (Oxford University Press, 2017) (with Jens Ohlin and Larry May), *Cyberwar: Law and Ethics for Virtual Conflicts* (with Jens Ohlin and Kevin Govern) (Oxford University Press, 2015), *Targeted Killings: Law & Mortality in an Asymmetrical World* (Oxford University Press, 2012) (with Jens Ohlin and Andrew Altman), and of *Hobbes on Law* (Ashgate, 2005). She is the founder and currently the faculty director of the Center for Ethics and the Rule of Law (CERL) at the University of Pennsylvania, an academic center devoted to protecting the rule of law in 21st Century armed conflict and national security practice.

Charles Fried, Beneficial Professor of Law, has been teaching at Harvard Law School since 1961.

Professor Fried was the Solicitor General of the United States, 1985–89, and an Associate Justice of the Supreme Judicial Court of Massachusetts, 1995–99. The author of many books and articles, his Anatomy of Values (1970), Right and Wrong (1978), and Modern Liberty (2006) develop themes in moral and political philosophy with applications to law. Contract as Promise (1980), Making Tort Law (2003, with David Rosenberg) and Saying What the Law Is: The Constitution in the Supreme Court (2004) are fundamental inquiries into broad legal institutions. Order & Law: Arguing the Reagan Revolution (1991) discusses major themes developed in Fried's time as Solicitor General. During his time as a teacher he has also argued a number of major cases in state and federal courts, most notably Daubert v. Merrell Dow Pharmaceuticals, in which the Supreme Court established the standards for the use of expert and scientific evidence in federal courts.

David Gauthier, Professor Emeritus of Philosophy, University of Pittsburgh, dgaut@pitt.edu.

Professor Gauthier's main philosophical contributions have been in ethics and moral theory, the theory of practical rationality and the formal theory of rational choice, political philosophy, and the interpretation of early modern moral and political philosophy, especially Hobbes and Rousseau. He was one of the principal theorists responsible for the revival of contractarian theory, and one of the first philosophers to introduce decision and game theory to moral theory. He is widely known for his seminar work, *Morals by Agreement* (OUP 1986), and has written widely in political theory and on a number of topics in politics, such as secession, nuclear deterrence, democracy, public reason. He is also the author of a number of important essays on the work of different contemporary philosophers.

Alexander A. Guerrero, Assistant Professor of Philosophy and Assistant Professor of Medical Ethics and Health Policy, aguerr@upenn.edu.

Professor Guerrero's research focuses on a number of different topics in political philosophy, moral philosophy, and philosophy of law, and topics in epistemology that relate to those three areas. His work has appeared in a number of leading philosophical and legal journals, including *Philosophy and Public Affairs, Philosophical Studies, Public Affairs Quarterly, Georgetown Journal of Legal Ethics, Criminal Law and Philosophy*, and *Jurisprudence.*

Aaron James, Professor of Philosophy, University of California, Irvine, aaron.james@uci.edu.

Professor James works in ethics, where he focuses on rationalism and the foundations of moral and practical judgment, with particular interest in constructivism (what it is, how it might explain objectivity, and whether it could provide a foundational theory). In political philosophy, he has recently written a book on fairness in the global economy, from a social contract perspective (*Fairness in Practice: A Social Contract for a Global Economy,* Oxford University Press, 2012). He has also written about Rawls's constructive method, its neglected realist and interpretive aspects, and its application to social structures within and across major domestic institutions (such as international trade). He has plans for a book on practice-based justification and global justice.

Sanford Levinson, W. St. John Garwood and W. St. John Garwood, Jr. Centennial Chair in Law.

Professor Levinson joined the University of Texas Law School in 1980. Previously a member of the Department of Politics at Princeton University, he is also a Professor in the Department of Government at the University of Texas. Levinson is the author of approximately 400 articles, book reviews, or commentaries in professional and popular journals—and a regular contributor to the popular blog Balkinization. He has written six books: *Constitutional Faith* (1988, winner of the Scribes Award, 2d edition 2011); *Written in Stone: Public Monuments in Changing Societies* (1998); *Wrestling with Diversity* (2003); *Our Undemocratic Constitution: Where the Constitution Goes Wrong (and How We the People Can Correct It)* (2006); *Framed: America's 51 Constitutions and the Crisis of Governance* (2012); and *An Argument Open to All: Reading the Federalist in the 21st Century* (forthcoming, November 2015). Edited or co-edited books include a leading constitutional law casebook, *Processes of Constitutional Decisionmaking* (6th ed. 2015, with Paul Brest, Jack Balkin, Akhil Amar, and Reva Siegel); *Reading Law and Literature: A Hermeneutic Reader* (1988, with Steven Mallioux); *Responding to Imperfection: The Theory and Practice of Constitutional Amendment* (1995); *Constitutional Stupidities, Constitutional Tragedies* (1998, with William Eskridge); *Legal Canons* (2000, with Jack Balkin); *The Louisiana Purchase and American Expansion* (2005, with Batholomew Sparrow); *Torture: A Collection* (2004, revised paperback edition, 2006); and *The Oxford Handbook on the United States Constitution* (with Mark Tushnet and Mark Graber, 2015). He received the Lifetime Achievement Award from the Law and Courts Section of the American Political Science Association in 2010.

Matthew Lister, Visiting Assistant Professor of Law, University of Denver Sturm College of Law, mlister@law.du.edu.

Professor Lister's research employs the critical and normative tools of moral and political philosophy to analyze the law of immigration, citizenship, and cross-border economic movements, as well as criminal law. He considers the doctrinal and institutional structures of immigration law, public and private international law, and, in a slightly different context, criminal law, and uses the tools of moral and political philosophy to provide a normative account of these areas. In looking at immigration and the movement of peoples, trade and the regulation of cross-border economic activities, and the development of international legal bodies, he explores the question of how these institutions should be ordered if they are to be just, legitimate, and fair to all involved. He has published in leading law journals including *Philosophy and Law, Chicago Journal of International Law,* and *Stanford Journal of International Law.*

S.A. Lloyd, Professor of Philosophy, Law, and Political Science, University of Southern California, lloyd@usc.edu.

Professor Lloyd works in the history of political philosophy, with special attention to the moral and political theory of philosopher Thomas Hobbes. Trained and mentored by John Rawls, Lloyd's scholarly interests in political philosophy and its history, contemporary liberalism, and liberal feminist philosophy reflect that tutelage. She has particular interest in the moral and political theories of Machiavelli, Mill, Hobbes, Marx, and Rawls. Lloyd's work in philosophy has attracted the interest of legal scholars and is often published in law reviews. Lloyd is regarded as an important voice in the current generation of liberal feminists.

Duncan MacIntosh, Professor of Philosophy, Department Chair, Dalhousie University, duncanm@dal.ca.

Professor MacIntosh works in metaethics, decision and action theory, metaphysics, philosophy of language, epistemology, and philosophy of science. He has written on desire-based theories of rationality, the relationship between rationality and time, the reducibility of morality to rationality, modeling morality and rationality with the tools of action and game theory, scientific realism, and a number of other topics. He has published in leading philosophy journals including *The Journal of Philosophy*, *Ethics*, and the *Australasian Journal of Philosophy*.

Larry May, W. Alton Jones Professor of Philosophy, Professor of Law, Professor of Political Science, Vanderbilt University, larry.may@vanderbilt.edu.

Professor May is a political philosopher who has written on conceptual issues in collective and shared responsibility, as well as normative issues in international criminal law. He has also written on professional ethics and on the Just War tradition. Over the course of his career, Professor May has published 24 books and 100 articles, and his books have won awards from the American Philosophical Association, the North American Society for Social Philosophy, the International Association of Penal Law, the American Society of International Law, and the American Library Association. In addition to holding the W. Alton Jones Chair of Philosophy and serving as a professor of law at Vanderbilt, Professor May is a Professorial Fellow at the Centre for Applied Philosophy and Public Ethics at Charles Sturt University in Canberra, Australia.

Alberto Mora, Associate Executive Director for Global Programs at the American Bar Association and director of the ABA Rule of Law Initiative (ABA ROLI).

Mr. Mora is currently the Executive Director of ABA-ROLI and a senior fellow at the Carr Center for Human Rights Policy at the Kennedy School at Harvard University. He retired in 2013 as vice president, secretary, and general counsel of Mars, Inc. He is the former general counsel of the United States Navy where he led an effort within the Defense Department to bring an end to the use of torture and official cruelty in the treatment of prisoners in military custody. He began his career as a foreign service officer at the U.S. Department of State. He has also served as international general counsel to Wal-Mart.

Mr. Mora was honored with the John F. Kennedy Profile in Courage Award in 2006. Under the administration of George H. W. Bush, Alberto served as the general counsel to the United States Information Agency. President Bill Clinton nominated him to serve on the Broadcasting Board of Governors.

Christopher W. Morris, Professor of Philosophy, Department Chair, University of Maryland, cwmorris@umd.edu.

Professor Morris's interests are in moral and political philosophy, practical ethics, legal theory, and the theory of practical rationality. Some of his current research develops the implications of his book *An Essay on the Modern State* for international affairs and world order and, in particular, legitimacy. Other topics include justice and reasons for action and a number of questions about moral standing. He is a faculty member of the Committee on Politics, Philosophy, and Public Policy, and was an Affiliated Research Scholar of the Institute for Philosophy and Public Policy.

Chris Naticchia, Professor of Philosophy, California State University, San Bernardino, cnattich@csusb.edu.

Professor Naticchia's research focuses on domestic and international justice and human rights. He has received two Faculty Research Awards from the National Endowment for the Humanities and was recently a visiting scholar at National Chung Cheng University in Taiwan. He is currently at work on a book project entitled "A Theory of International Recognition." Professor Naticchia has served as a referee for *Social Theory and Practice, The Journal of Social Philosophy, Res Publica, Political Studies,* and The *American Political Science Review,* and is a contributor to the forthcoming *Rawls Lexicon* (Cambridge), edited by David Reidy and Jon Mandl.

William E. O'Brian Jr., Associate Professor of Law, University of Warwick, W.Obrian@warwick.ac.uk.

Professor O'Brian joined the Law School of the University of Warwick in 2001 following 17 years as a practicing lawyer in the United States, specializing in commercial litigation. He teaches Tort Law, International Business Transactions, Law & Economics, and Evidence. His research interests include private international law, evidence, torts, and legal theory. His recent papers include "The Hague Convention on Jurisdiction and Judgments: The Way Forward," (2003) 66 *Modern Law Review* 491; "The Right of Confrontation: US and European Perspectives," (2005) 121 *LQR* 481, "Equality in Law and Philosophy" (2010) 53 *Inquiry* 257–84, "Distributive Justice and the Sovereignty Principle," (2011) 31 *Oxford Journal of Legal Studies* 1–21; "Confrontation: The Defiance of the English Courts," (2011) 15 *International J Evidence & Proof* 93–116, and "Fresh Expert Evidence in CCRC Cases," (2011) 22 King's Law Journal 1–26. He is currently writing a book on legal and political theory, with the tentative title "Live and Let Live."

Michael Skerker, Associate Professor in the Leadership, Ethics, and Law Department of the United States Naval Academy.

Professor Skerker's interests are in military, police, and intelligence ethics. He has published articles and book chapters on those subjects as well as on the topic of collective responsibility. He is the author of *An Ethics of Interrogation* (University of Chicago, 2010). His most recent book *The Moral Status of Combatants* is currently under review. The manuscript won the American Philosophical Association's 2013 Charles Sharp Prize for best unpublished manuscript on military ethics. He is the co-series editor for a series of books on military ethics published by Howgate Press. Prof. Skerker serves on the advisory committee to the High Value Detainee Interrogation Group Research Unit and consults with Southern California police departments. The views expressed in this chapter are his own and do not necessarily reflect those of the Naval Academy or any branch of the U.S. government.

Jacob Weinrib, Assistant Professor, Queen's University Law, jacob.weinrib@queensu.ca.

Professor Weinrib's research lies at the intersection of legal philosophy and public law. His overarching aim is to formulate a unified theory of the normative, institutional, and doctrinal dimensions of public law. He graduated from the Combined JD/PhD Program in Law and Philosophy at the University of Toronto, where he studied as a Vanier Scholar and received the David Savan Dissertation Prize. Before joining Queen's, he held a SSHRC Postdoctoral Fellowship at the New York University School of Law as a Global Hauser Research Fellow in the Center for Constitutional Transitions (2013–2014) and as a Dworkin-Balzan Fellow in the Center for Law and Philosophy (2014–2015). Weinrib is the author of *Dimensions of Dignity: The Theory and Practice of Modern Constitutional Law* (forthcoming, Cambridge University Press).

INTRODUCTION

CLAIRE O. FINKELSTEIN

I. THE CRISIS OF EXECUTIVE AUTHORITY

The controversies surrounding the authority and legitimacy of executive authority have moved front and center since the election of Donald Trump in November of 2016. No aspect of executive authority has been spared reexamination in light of this administration's rejection of the legal and ethical boundaries that have traditionally constrained the U.S. presidency. From basic questions about the legitimacy of political authority in the face of sharply divergent values; to questions of transparency in democratic governance; to the scope of the commander-in-chief power, both in and outside of armed conflict; to relations with foreign sovereigns and the duty to protect domestic interests; to confronting corruption and self-dealing among political leaders; and even to the integrity of the process by which presidential candidates come to power and their legitimacy in the face of pernicious foreign interference, critical questions about the philosophy and structure of democratic governance have come to the fore. A similar experience has gripped Europe and the U.K. in the past several years, with a surge in populist and right-wing sentiment, increasing isolationism, increased fear of immigrants, and a rejection of traditional liberal values. Some might say that democracy is now experiencing a midlife crisis, or worse, that it is on life-support and struggling for survival. Others might see democracy as showing grace under pressure, as doing precisely what democratic institutions were set up to do in times of crisis. They might argue that the current crisis demonstrates that democratic institutions are well designed, since they are self-correcting in precisely the way their European and American progenitors hoped they might be.

This volume addresses many of the perennial questions faced by the United States and the democracies of Western Europe relating to political authority, questions as ancient as the beginnings of political unions and so fundamental that they affect every political regime regardless of political orientation. Other questions addressed here are of more recent vintage and arise because of new and unusual factors in the current political environment. Whether old or new, all bear critically on the preservation of the rule of law in democratic governance, and all have been thrust into public consciousness with the events surrounding the 2016 presidential election to a degree that is unprecedented in our history.

Despite its particular relevance to current events, this volume has been a long time in the making. Most of the essays were first drafted for a conference held at the University of Pennsylvania Law School in 2013 bearing the same name as this volume. As the nature of the questions we were addressing appeared to be perennial ones, we took our time preparing our essays for publication. Little did we know when we held that conference that a short three years later no subject would seem of greater importance to understanding threats to the rule of law than executive authority and its role in sustaining or threatening democratic values. How prescient our 2013 conference truly was.

This volume will contribute to the public conversation on the nature of executive authority and its relation to the broader topic of sovereignty in several critical ways. First, it will help readers to understand that the current vital questions surrounding the nature of executive authority, and presidential power, have their intellectual roots in historical and philosophical writings about the nature of sovereignty, going back to the earliest writings in political philosophy. Second, sovereignty has historically been a complicated topic, and this volume will help to identify the terms of the debate. How does the intellectual history of the topic of sovereignty relate to the current crisis in executive authority we are collectively addressing at the present moment? Is the traditional notion that it is the people that are sovereign in a democracy and that their sovereignty is exercised through the constraint of our elected and unelected officials according to law still a viable idea? Does it still shape modern political governance? Third, and most critically, understanding the concept of sovereignty is essential to grasping the available options for confronting challenges to the rule of law in democratic societies, both from within and without: political leaders pose the greatest threat to the rule of law at the same time that wise and lawfully constrained sovereigns are best able to combat such threats and secure our freedom. Whether we will be a society that adheres to the rule of law or one that thwarts that value depends to a very great extent on the approach to law of our own sovereign leaders, as well as the responses we make toward threats from foreign powers.

Still, it must be understood that the concept of sovereignty reflects the core attribute of a particular political tradition: the concept of the modern, Westphalian state. Sovereignty has an internal, and we might say "vertical" aspect, namely the relation of the state to its citizens. It also has an external, or we might say "horizontal" aspect, namely the relation of states to other states. The concept of internal sovereignty first emerged in the seventeenth century, resulting in a rethinking of state authority and the relationship between individuals and the state. As clearly expressed in Thomas Hobbes's idea of the political leader as a *Leviathan,* the sovereign of the civil state was understood as having absolute authority over its citizens. By the eighteenth century, the Hobbesian conception of sovereignty as absolute authority had started to give way to a conception that bore a greater resemblance to modern democratic governance, namely the idea that sovereigns wield limited power, and that imposing such limitations on our political leaders is rational from the standpoint of individual self-interest. For John

Locke, for example, the sovereign was a substantially weaker figure than the omnipotent monarch Hobbes appears to have sketched in *Leviathan* and defended in real life. The constraints on the Lockean sovereign are a product of constraints on power built into the natural order, which are in turn a reflection of the limited power of the people to confer autonomy on any political leader in the face of implicit moral constraints. With Jean-Jacques Rousseau we find sovereigns yet further limited in relation to their subjects: sovereignty is now subordinate to the general will of the community, rather than the reflection of an abandonment of sovereignty on the part of the individuals governed.

In later writings in political philosophy, the topic of sovereignty became fused with the question of the authority of law and the exercise of coercion by sovereigns in the governance of their subjects. Jurisprudential writers, such as John Austin, H.L.A. Hart, Lon Fuller, Ronald Dworkin, Joseph Raz, and others, addressed in detail the nature of the relationship between legal and sovereign authority. In these writings, the topic of sovereignty became inseparable from the question of how to maintain a society of rule of law values in a world in which law is not always adequate to ensure effective governance. With regard to the external facet of sovereignty, the strong conception of states as sovereign came to define international relations. This strong conception, however, came under significant pressure during the second half of the last century, when skepticism about legal authority was inevitable in the wake of Nazi perversion of law and hence destruction of the rule of law as a political and moral concept. The result among many authors was a jaded view of the role that law can play in governing relations among world sovereigns, and law was seen by many as a fig leaf spread over the raw exercise of political might. That skepticism may indeed be the modern source of the rejection of the concept of the rule of law as an essential feature of democratic governance.

Today we have come full circle with our Hobbesian antecedents: defenses of absolutist conceptions of sovereignty, both internal and external, are now ubiquitous. The expansion of executive authority in times of emergency was a central theme in the Bush administration's defense of the use of certain interrogation techniques. This same theme was an important component in arguments for the legitimacy of drone strikes under the Obama administration. It has also been echoed by the judicial branch in its deference to the executive's ever-broadening discretion over matters of war. The District Court of the District of Columbia, for example, invoked the "political question" doctrine to refuse jurisdiction over a case involving the targeting of Anwar al-Awlaki, a U.S. citizen, in a case brought by his father, Nasser al-Awlaki, claiming the lack of a judicial procedure prior to a sentence of death violated his son's due process rights. The court stated that matters such as these lie solely within the purview of the political brances, and that there is no "carve out" based on the fact that al-Awlaki is an American citizen. Outside of the United States, other states are increasingly appealing to state sovereignty to justify the use of force in military confrontations. Russia, for example, has consistently invoked the concept of sovereignty as a basis for the use of force beyond its borders, despite the fact that often the use of such force violates international law and has not been authorized by the UN Security Council.

These developments show that traditional problems about sovereignty are of both theoretical and practical significance. The conception of sovereignty as absolute, unconstrained authority from a domestic standpoint appears to carry over to the domain of foreign policy. The connection between vertical and horizontal sovereignty appears to go at least as far back as Hobbes, who, living in a time of political turmoil, famously offered a regress argument intended to show that unless sovereignty is undivided and unlimited, stable and effective government is impossible. The difficulties within the United States in maintaining the equality of its three branches of government lend credence to Hobbes's argument. Given the role played by the concept of sovereignty in these debates, it is important to be clear about what states claim to possess when they assert the concept of sovereignty.

By contrast with the questions about vertical sovereignty discussed above, questions about horizontal sovereignty are in play when, for example, states attempt to impose restrictions on one another through binding agreements, or international law purports to constrain a state's actions with respect to its domestic affairs. Does the freedom enjoyed by a sovereign state give it the power to restrict its own freedom through treaties with other state parties? How should violations of treaties be remedied? Can agreements between states be analyzed under the same framework as contractual agreements between individuals? Do states possess sovereignty solely in virtue of their relations to the individuals within their jurisdictions, or is a state's right of sovereignty grounded to some extent in its relation to the larger system of states? How might the answers to these questions bear upon the further question of whether states enjoy an absolute right of sovereignty against the constraints of international law? Are there any conditions under which a state may take unilateral action against a terrorist group located within the borders of another state without violating the sovereignty of the host state? Does it matter whether the host state is unwilling or simply unable to respond to the original threat? Though the extent of foreign interference with fundamental democratic institutions such as we experienced during the 2016 election was unprecedented in its scale and intent, the actions of the Kremlin in attempting to influence the outcome of the election in Donald Trump's favor present merely an extreme variant on many years of attempted manipulation on the part of hostile foreign powers.

The rise of the internet and the transformation of war from open clashes between nations to conflicts involving international terrorist organizations have fundamentally changed the nature of war as well as the role of government leaders in responding to military threats. The executive branch, first under the Bush and Obama administrations and now under the Trump administration, has given itself an unprecedented level of discretion over life-or-death decisions in the national security arena. The details of these executive decisions, the legal arguments used to justify them, and even the nature of the conflicts in which these decisions are made are taking place by executive fiat, often in secret, rather than by reasoned arguments among the different branches of government and the public. These developments raise a host of questions. For example, judicial deference to the Central Intelligence Agency's decision not to disclose its procedures and criteria for putting an individual on its target list has resulted in a body of secret law determining which killings are consistent with the Fourteenth Amendment's requirement that no person shall be deprived of life without due process of law. Can these secret legal norms be valid, and are secret laws and courts ever justifiable? If principled reasons can be given for sometimes holding defendants criminally liable even though they were ignorant of the relevant law, might such reasons also determine the conditions under which states may justifiably conceal information from citizens? When the executive branch's responses to national security threats and the nature of the threats themselves are kept secret, can citizens hold elected officials meaningfully accountable for their policies? Even when we know some of the details about use of force by the executive branch, what are the appropriate conceptual tools for thinking about these actions? Are they really "acts of war," or are they different in morally and legally relevant respects? How might such differences bear on the executive's obligations in carrying out these relatively small-scale attacks? What are the implications of these changes in national security policy for the rule of law? To address these and other critical questions, this volume seeks to bring together philosophers, legal theorists, political scientists and others from a wide variety of academic disciplines, together with practitioners to consider the nature of sovereignty and its implications for current democratic governance.

II. A LOOK AHEAD

The first set of essays addresses foundational questions about the nature of sovereignty and attempts to trace the ways in which the traditional concept of sovereignty laid the foundation for the modern conception of executive authority. Who is the sovereign? What gives him or her legitimacy and the right to rule over others? What are the crucial elements or characteristics of sovereignty? From the Enlightenment on, there is a rich tradition of thinking of the sovereign as the representative of the people. Is the fact that the people authorize the sovereign to act on their behalf important for understanding restrictions on the nature of sovereign authority? This Part of the volume draws on a number of rich historical traditions in political philosophy, particularly the Hobbesian and Kantian contract traditions.

In "Hobbes on Sovereign Authority," David Gauthier addresses a central difficulty for the Hobbesian theory of sovereignty having to do with punishment. In a contractarian theory of punishment, individuals are thought of as authorizing the sovereign to act in their place, and in doing so they give up the right to rely on their own judgment and their direct promotion of their preservation. The reason they do this, of course, is that they view authorizing the sovereign to act on their behalf, which allows for cooperation with others, as leaving them better off than they would have been in the absence of sovereign authority. In light of this rationale for abandoning their original and expansive right of nature, however, the legitimacy of punishment requires explaining, since it is challenging to understand how human beings are acting in their rational self-interest when they authorize their own punishment.

Jacob Weinrib's essay addresses a tension within the Kantian theory of sovereignty between the core Kantian idea that individuals have a right to equal freedom and the idea that the sovereign is able to coerce individuals into meeting certain obligations. Weinrib offers a resolution to this difficulty within Kantian theory, one that allows him to elucidate the essential difference between the Kantian and Hobbesian conceptions of sovereignty. His account provides a Kantian justification of the sovereign's right to exercise public authority over subjects, one that incorporates a duty on the sovereign's part to respect the rights of the ruled. In so legitimizing sovereignty, Weinrib implicitly also establishes a duty on the part of the subjects to obey their legitimate sovereign ruler.

William O'Brian's contribution, by contrast, makes an argument against the duties of subjects to obey the sovereign. In particular, he suggests that most Kantian arguments in defense of sovereignty trade on some notion of fairness. But on his account, subjects are obligated to obey the sovereign on the basis of fairness only insofar as they are being asked to bear their fair share of the costs of the state, without needing to carry the weight of supporting those who are free-riding on the efforts of others.

The second Part examines the theory of sovereignty as it presents in debates about the nature of modern executive authority, with particular attention to the question of whether sovereignty should be unified or divided. In "Defining and Constraining the Sovereign," Charles Fried explores the original intent of the Anti-Federalists, as they echoed the sentiments of Jean-Jacques Rouseau and Immanuel Kant in opposing the idea of a unitary executive and the consolidation of executive power. He argues that the Federalists largely won in this debate, and that this has implications for how we understand the nature of executive authority today. Chris Morris's chapter addresses the foundations of the concept of sovereignty for modern executive authority. It correctly points out that there is often confusion in contemporary theoretical discussions of sovereignty, in which it is assumed that the head of the executive branch is the purveyor of the historical conception of sovereignty. He points out that the "sovereign" in a modern democracy is the entire government, and that the forerunners of modern democratic theory were laying a case for divided sovereignty, rather than conceiving of the president or prime minister as him- or herself the repository of sovereign authority.

Sharon Lloyd's essay takes up the theme of divided versus unitary executive authority through a Hobbesian lens. She presents Hobbes's argument that unless sovereignty is undivided and unlimited, stable and effective government is impossible. From the standpoint of our current constitutional structure, Hobbes's argument poses a dilemma, namely that modern sovereignty will be either unstable or unchecked and autocratic, and that we are faced with an ineliminable choice of evils. Lloyd responds to Hobbes's claim, however, by arguing that in modern democracies, if our governmental structure and legal system are determinately rule-governed, they may evade the dilemma Hobbes poses. A system of divided government, she argues, may be stable if sufficiently saturated by rule of law values.

Sanford Levinson appears to disagree. In addressing the issue of divided versus unified sovereignty in modern democracies, he takes up the perspective of the infamous Federalist Paper Number 41, in which "Publius" appears to argue for what we might call a "constitutional dictatorship" as necessary to the end of protecting the republic. Levinson suggests that though it is difficult for us to admit, we must recognize the necessity for occasional constitutional dictatorships in the name of national security. Levinson then asks: Given the inevitability of a dictatorial element within democratic leadership, does the U.S. Constitution present the most desirable model, especially when we consider Publius's claim that a high degree of political ambition is attached to all institutional power? Levinson suggests that we consider alternative models of executive authority in a democracy, such as that provided by ancient Rome.

The third Part focuses on the nature of modern presidential authority, with a focus on the expansion of executive authority as well as the increasingly secretive nature of sovereign authority in modern democratic nations. Since 9/11, there has been a profusion of secret national security programs, in addition to those pertaining to the interrogation, rendition, and detention of terror suspects, such as the metadata analysis program of the NSA and the cyber-intelligence and cyber-interference programs. The revelation of the conduct of these agencies shook Americans to the core shook to and caused many to question the legitimacy of executive power in this arena. The question this Part raises is how expansive presidential authority must be in order to ensure effective national security, and whether secrecy is a necessary part of sovereignty and strong national defense. Does a government that conducts so much without the endorsement and participation of its citizens forego its claim to legitimacy?

My own essay considers the expansion of executive branch authority over time, with a particular focus on the doctrine of the "unitary executive" and the increasingly broad powers of U.S. presidents in the face of national security challenges since 9/11. I argue that the most recent trend toward expanded executive power took place in conjunction with the enhanced interrogation program, as a byproduct of the effort to provide a legal justification for that program. This was accomplished through the identification of violent nonstate actors as "unlawful combatants." The same structure was then used by the Obama administration to justify the use of drones outside of zones of hostility. The Trump administration's abuse of executive prerogative is a more extreme version of the preceding two administrations' failure to follow legal constraints in the war on terror, and such expansion is a regrettable but logical next step in the changing conception of modern executive authority.

Michael Skerker's chapter addresses precisely the foregoing question. His argument is that as a general matter, transparency is not necessary for legitimacy since legitimate government actions are indexed to the hypothetical consent of a generic person rather than the explicit consent of particular people. Transparency is critical, however, for subjects of a democracy to ensure against corruption in the pursuit of otherwise legitimate aims. Where some security-seeking functions of government are at issue, the generic need to ensure against corruption is outweighed by the need to protect individuals as well as the country at large.

Chris Nattichia, in addressing the very same question, points out that social contract views such as Locke's generally reject secrecy, and that most such accounts insist instead that laws must be public. Recent American experience flies in the face of the traditional contractarian wisdom. Nattichia argues that what is both striking and shocking in recent years is the tendency to create not just secret intelligence operations, but secret *laws* governing those operations. He maintains, however, that it may be possible to account for these practices within contractarian paternalistic principles, whose scope is itself determined through contractarian reasoning, and thus might be able to account for some government secrecy that extends beyond classifying information and protecting intelligence methods and capabilities to maintaining secrecy in some governing laws themselves.

Larry May's chapter seeks to justify at least some secret, or private, laws by making use of the work of Lon Fuller and Thomas Hobbes. One might suppose, he argues, that the traditional "promulgation" requirement is the jurisprudential obstacle to justifying the use of secret laws, but that promulgation does not require that every citizen possess and understand the complete set of laws that may be enforced against him. The use of secret tribunals, however, is more difficult to argue, as the presence of the defendant at trial and the general transparency of tribunals is key to their legitimacy.

The fourth Part explores questions relating to "horizontal" sovereignty, meaning the nature of sovereignty when considered in relation to other sovereign nations. While most of the volume focuses on issues relating to "vertical" sovereignty, the international context helps us to illuminate a different aspect of the concept of sovereignty, namely the fact that the authority of one sovereign nation poses a limitation on the sovereign authority of other sovereign nations. This is particularly apparent where actions that a state feels necessary to protect itself are forbidden or limited by international law, because, for example, the state's adversaries receive more or different protection under international law than they do under domestic law. The chapters in this Part address whether the limitations posed by the various forms of international law are consistent with the concept of state sovereignty, and how conflicts between the two should be resolved. In addressing these issues, the essays also revisit fundamental issues addressed in Part I through a different lens.

Duncan MacIntosh argues that there are some laws that not only are permissibly private, but that can only be efficacious if they are private. These he calls "logically private laws." After proposing some general conditions under such laws ought to be enacted, MacIntosh then addresses both moral and practical objections to the existence of such laws.

Aaron James's chapter addresses the tension between state sovereignty and international law through a jurisprudential lens. Against the traditional view that political authority can only have a domestic source, the social contract tradition offers a contrary perspective. James's chapter outlines a defense of international law from the standpoint of a social practice of global scope. From this perspective, it is much easier to reconcile individual state sovereignty with the constraints of international law.

Matt Lister's chapter addresses the interpretation of treaties among sovereign nations, and proposes an approach to interpretation that helps to resolve the above dilemma by ensuring that treaties are sovereignty-enhancing for states in a way that is similar to the way that contracts may be autonomy-enhancing for individuals. He argues that importing an interpretive framework from domestic contract law will strengthen, not undermine, the legitimacy and fairness of international law, and treaty law in particular in that it minimizes conflicts with state sovereignty.

The last chapter in this volume, Alex Guerrero's, deals with the tension between electoral democracy and popular sovereignty, and argues that the two are fundamentally incompatible. Moreover, given that popular sovereignty is a necessary condition for political legitimacy, a system of electoral democracy would appear to be illegitimate. The incompatibility arises due to five distinct but interrelated factors: confidentiality, voter ignorance, voter psychology, electoral pathology, and money. The end result of these five factors is that national security policy created by elected officials is not reflective of real popular sovereignty.

Together, the chapters of this volume span the topic of sovereignty from its first self-conscious conceptualization in the seventeenth century to a detailed discussion of modern executive authority, and finally to issues of international sovereignty and national security policy. As the progression of topics in this volume unfolds, it becomes clear that we continue to grapple with the same dilemmas and conceptual puzzles surrounding the allocation of state power with which political philosophers began over four hundred years ago. As globalization increases, along with ever-more complex threats to national security, the strains in our intellectual tradition surrounding the concept of sovereignty become increasingly apparent. We may look back at the present moment as the period in which the traditional approach to sovereignty failed us: It failed us because it no longer enabled us to keep the executive branch in check; it failed us because the vertical concept of sovereignty turned out to be stronger than the horizontal concept, and finally it failed us because it damaged the foundations of all authority in democratic governance, namely the authority of the people whom sovereigns are designated to serve.

PART ONE

The Intellectual Roots of Sovereignty

1

Hobbes on Sovereign Authority

How the Right of Nature Becomes Sovereign Right

DAVID GAUTHIER

I. INTRODUCTION: FROM THE RIGHT OF NATURE TO SOVEREIGN RIGHT

How does Hobbes do it? How, beginning from the weakest of normative premises, does he derive the strongest conclusions? Or in other words, how does he derive sovereign right from the right of nature? The derivation, which I shall outline shortly, may seem surprisingly simple, until we come to the right to punish, which lies at the core of sovereign right and distinguishes the political from the moral. Here, as we shall see, Hobbes encounters a problem that leads him into setting out two mutually contradictory accounts of punishment. Can we rescue Hobbes from this predicament?

The issue raises questions about the viability of any contractarian theory of punishment. So our problem here is not a historical curiosity. If we can't rescue Hobbes, then it would seem that we can't rescue ourselves. And that would be an unwelcome result for those of us whose larger concern is to defend contractarian political thought, Let us then begin with the right of nature, explain the derivation of sovereign right, and the problem of punishment will face us.

"The RIGHT OF NATURE, . . . is the liberty each man hath to use his own power, as he will himself, for the preservation of his own nature, that is to say, of his own life, and consequently of doing anything which, in his own judgment and reason, he shall conceive to be the aptest means thereunto." (L.79, 14.1) So begins chapter 14 of *Leviathan*. And so begins Hobbes's account of the normative space in which human beings interact. All living beings seek to preserve themselves, but only humans represent their actions to themselves as conforming (or failing to conform) to normative standards.

Sovereignty and the New Executive Authority. Claire O. Finkelstein and Michael Skerker.

In *Leviathan* Hobbes offers no explanation for his introduction of right. In his earlier political writings, (DC I.7, 27) he had tried to relate the right of nature to the idea of right reason, but this seems to me confused and confusing.[1] The right of nature stands in need of neither explanation nor justification, although it does invite *explication*. Think of it as imposing an initial structure on normative space (cf. the initial sentence of Kant's *Grundlegung*, which treats the *good will* as playing a similar role). The right of nature is Hobbes's moral primitive; we proceed from it to spin out the normative story of *Leviathan*. As I have said, my concern is with only one part of this story—how the right of nature leads, for Hobbes, to sovereign right, and whether it provides adequately for the sovereign right to punish.

I have called the right of nature "Hobbes's moral primitive." The idea here, which I can only sketch,[2] is that the normative constitutes a distinct "space," emerging when living beings become capable of critical reflection on their own actions, so that they take considerations as providing reasons for and against, and are motivated by this reflection. And then they take the further step of critical reflection on their reasons, so that they ask whether what they take as reasons are properly taken to be reasons. Normative primitives are then those considerations that serve as justifiers without needing justification. For Hobbes the primitive is the right of nature, which expresses at the normative level the concern with preservation that Hobbes supposes characterizes life. The Kantian good will, the utilitarian greatest happiness principle, and the economist's utility-maximization (when understood substantively and not as tautological) are moral or normative primitives. They enable us to answer "should" or "ought" questions in ways that avoid arbitrariness without threatening an infinite regress.

Hobbes's argument in *Leviathan* has seemed to me to be best interpreted as employing the right of nature as the sole moral primitive. But towards the end of this essay, I shall introduce an alternative interpretation, in which both the right and the laws of nature constitute primitives. Hobbes mentions the laws of nature at the end of chapter 13 of *Leviathan*, before the right of nature makes its appearance. But the normative argument that Hobbes wants to present begins, not with this mention, but with the introduction of the right of nature in chapter 14. To which I now return.

The right of nature is purely permissive. It says, in effect, that what one can do, one may do. *Whatever* one can do. Hobbes is not squeamish about this. He says that since there is "nothing {a person] can make use of that may not be a help unto him in preserving his life ... it followeth that ... every man has a right to everything, even to one another's body." (L.80, 14.4) He speaks of "this natural right of every man to everything" and that "every man holdeth this right of doing

1. Some part of the right of nature can (and must) be given up. But Hobbes does not tell us to give up any part of right reason.

2. I hope to do more than merely sketch the idea of a moral or normative primitive in a further paper on Hobbes's moral theory.

anything he liketh." (L.80, 14.4) In such passages as these, Hobbes represents the right of nature as containing all normative space within its permissive scope, so that nothing is forbidden, and nothing required.

Hobbes's argument for the unlimited scope of the right of nature is not without its critics. Grant that any act and (possession of) any thing may (in some circumstances) be conducive to one's preservation. It does not follow that every act and every thing is actually so conducive. Hobbes makes every person the judge of what is conducive to his own preservation. But this does not affect the objection. A person may have the right to do any act or possess any thing that he believes conducive to his preservation; he does not thereby have a right to everything. Nor does it follow that he has a right to do "anything he liketh," unless we suppose that what he likes must be what he deems conducive to his conservation.

Nevertheless the objection seems misplaced. Hobbes takes conservation broadly, so that it covers "the security of a man's person, in his life and in the means of so preserving life as not to be weary of it." (L.82, 14.8) Later, in discussing the role of the sovereign, he defines it as "the procuration of *the safety of the people,*" where "[b]y safety is not meant a bare preservation, but also all other contentments of life." (L.219, 30.1) We shall see that the role of the sovereign is tied to the right of nature, so that what he may do cannot go beyond what the right of nature would permit the individual to do prior to society. So the right must cover what Hobbes calls contentments. The right thus permits whatever acts or possessions a person may view positively. It is in effect a right to do whatever one wants to do. Or as Hobbes puts it, "anything he liketh."

Hobbes's use of "right" differs from what we ordinarily understand by the term, in that the right of nature involves no correlative duty on the part of others. My right to life, as part of the right of nature, is only to do whatever I can to maintain my own life. It gives me no claim on you. Nothing you can do would violate my right. Advocates of "the right to life" do not understand "right" as Hobbes does. But his meaning, that "right" is purely permissive, is clear enough. And it does not lack normative force—to say that each person may do whatever he can do is to relate right to power in a quite particular way.

So we begin with an effectively unlimited permissive right. Hobbes does not find this a happy state of affairs. "as long as this natural right of every man to everything endureth, there can be no security to any man . . . of living out the time which nature ordinarily alloweth man to live." (L.80, 14.4) The details of Hobbes's argument here need not delay us. He establishes, or claims to establish, that men bent on their own "conservation and . . . delectation," (L.75, 13.3) recognizing no constraints on their actions but exercising to the full their natural right to all things, must find themselves in a condition of universal war that denies them the very conservation and delectation they seek. The remedy requires a change in the contours of their moral space, a change that must be effected by the persons themselves, for Hobbes recognizes no natural authority to balance against the right of nature. The unlimited must become self-limiting. When this is accomplished, the familiar concept of sovereign authority will have been given new foundations.

II. THE RIGHT OF NATURE

The right of nature, like any right, can be exercised. But its unlimited exercise is fatal. "For as long as every man holdeth this right of doing anything he liketh, so long are all men in the condition of war." (L.80, 14.5) How can limits be imposed? Hobbes's answer is not quite as clear as it should be. It seems to me that this is at least in part because he was still working it out when he wrote *Leviathan*, and regrettably, he seems to have stopped without bringing the strands of his thought into a unified whole. I shall therefore try to bring the strands together and show how the right of nature may be limited. The argument has three parts: obligation and the right to property, the reply to the fool, and the authorization of the sovereign and the right to punish.

If the life of persons in the natural condition of war is "solitary, poor, nasty, brutish, and short" (L.76, 13.9), then reason tells us "*that every man ought to endeavour peace as far as he has hope of obtaining it,*" to which Hobbes adds "*and when he cannot obtain it, that he may seek and use all helps and advantages of war.*" (L.80, 14.4) This latter part Hobbes identifies as the "sum of the right of nature," which remains the default option in normative space, but it is now qualified by the first part, which is the dictate of the primary law of nature, or theorem of reason directing persons who seek to escape the condition of war. And what must persons do to escape war? If holding an unlimited right to do as one likes gives rise to war, then one must limit this right. And so the second law or theorem requires each person to be willing "*when others are so too, . . . to lay down this right to all things and be contented with so much liberty against other men, as he would allow other men against himself.*" (L.80, 14.5)

The right of nature can be exercised. It, or some part of it, can also be given up—"laid down" in Hobbes's terminology. One may simply waive a right, such as the right to possess some book; one is no longer free to interfere with the attempts of others to possess it. Or one may transfer, as it were, one's right to possess some book to some other person. I say "as it were" because as Hobbes makes clear, no right is actually transferred. Since each person's right is unlimited, it cannot be augmented by transfer. Rather, one renounces one's liberty to impede some determinate person or persons in their exercise of their right to possess the book. He or they gain, not a new right, but the removal of an impediment to their exercise of their existing right.

Obligation is lack of right. The right to all things is the absence of any obligation; in the natural condition of mankind, then, obligation has no place. But in giving up right, one assumes an obligation—an obligation not to seek to exercise the abandoned right. The contours of normative space are changed—the impermissible is introduced and avoidance of it is obligatory.

Of course Hobbes does not suppose that we want to be under obligation. And he does not suppose that we put ourselves under obligation unilaterally. If you will not give up any portion of your natural right to do to me as you please, then I have no reason to give up a portion of my natural right to do to you as I please. When we reciprocally put ourselves under obligation in a way that will require at least one of us to trust the other, we are said to have made a covenant, and the idea of covenant occupies center stage in Hobbes's account.

Hobbes now has the conceptual resources to introduce a right to property as distinct from the mere right to possession. Property involves exclusive possession, but the connection between them is not direct. The permissive right to possess, say, a book is already a right to possess it exclusively. If I alone have physical possession of the book, then I possess the book exclusively. And this of course I have the natural right to do. But we should not identify the right of possession with the right of exclusive possession. If we share the possession of a book, then each of us successfully exercises his right of possession, but not of exclusive possession.

The right of exclusive possession leads us nowhere. What does lead to the right of property is the *exclusive right* of possession. To say that I have an exclusive right to a book is to deny that any other person has a permissive right to possess it. But how may we deny this? For if the right of nature is unlimited in its scope, and held by all persons, then all persons have a permissive right to possess the book. And if I have an exclusive right to possess the book, then all people have such a right—which is self-contradictory. To avoid the contradiction, we must, it seems, deny that there are exclusive rights. And so for Hobbes it would seem that there can be no right of property.

But this argument ignores Hobbes's insistence that some part of the right of nature may be given up by each person, and indeed must be given up if men are to live peacefully together. Suppose that I hold my natural right to possess the book, but that each other person gives up her right to possess it. Then my right is an exclusive right. The right of possession, together with the obligation on the part of others not to seek possession, gives me the exclusive right—and this is the right of property. My property is that to which I alone have retained my natural right of possession.

Thus Hobbes requires no different sense of "right" to pass from the permissive right to possession to the exclusive right to property. As long as we can accommodate both the exercise and the waiving of rights, we can show how to make this transition. We should note that a consequence of Hobbes's account is that all obligation, or lack of right, is self-imposed. Hobbes explicitly recognizes this when he insists that "there [is] no obligation on any man which ariseth not from some act of his own." (L.141, 21.10)

We have found what appears to be a simple, widely applicable procedure for passing from any natural permissive right to an exclusive right. All that is required is that others relinquish their corresponding permissive right. Of course they must have reason to relinquish their right, and this reason is found if the procedure is reciprocal, so that each comes to have a set of exclusive rights that the others are obliged to uphold. The reciprocal procedure creates a covenant between or among those whose rights are affected.

Since, as Hobbes has argued, we remain in the natural condition of universal war so long as we exercise our unlimited right of nature, we have good reason to make covenants with our fellows, and so transform at least some of our permissive rights into exclusive rights. The only way to adjudicate conflicts in a world of permissive rights is by force. In a world of exclusive rights there is less occasion for quarrel, since what is mine is determined not by whatever I can get but by the terms of the covenants I have made, and adjudication, without recourse to force, can apply these terms to the actual situation. Passing from permissive rights to exclusive ones is at the heart of our escape from war to the peace that Hobbes holds that every person ought to endeavor to achieve.

It may be objected that from a practical point of view, property and other exclusive rights could never be established because they would require what amounts to the known consent of everyone. Each person would be so preoccupied with negotiating all of the reciprocal agreements or covenants that no one would have time for anything else—a novel, but hardly feasible, way to bring about the end of the war of all against all. I shall return to this problem after introducing the sovereign.

III. THE FOOL'S CHALLENGE

But first a word about Hobbes's fool, who threatens to derail the Hobbesian enterprise. This is not the occasion to examine the fool in depth, but I want to identify what I believe to be the core issue between him and Hobbes. The fool is interested, not in whether we make covenants, but whether we should keep them—act within the bounds of the rights and obligations that we have accepted by covenant. Hobbes has introduced a further dictate of reason—"*that men perform their covenants made,*" (L.89,15.1) and the fool says—maybe yes, maybe no. It all depends on what is to your benefit. You can call breach of covenant injustice if you please, but then injustice may "stand with that reason that dictateth to every man his own good." (L.90,15.4) End of argument.

Hobbes will have none of it. "This specious reasoning is nevertheless false." He focuses on covenants "where one of the parties has performed already, or where there is a power to make him perform," is it "against reason, that is, against the benefit of the other, to perform or not?" (L.91, 15.4-5) The case that interests us is the first—the rationality of second performance. The second performer has gained what he wanted from the covenant; his performance would be a pure cost to himself. Absent such irrelevancies as repeated play or reputation effects, most economists and rational choice theorists would line up with the fool. It is not rational to adhere to one's covenant if adherence is not to one's benefit.

Hobbes's reply cuts to the heart of the matter. "[H]e that breaketh his covenant, and consequently declareth that he thinks he may with reason do so, cannot be received into any society that unite themselves for peace and defence, but by the error of them that receive him . . ." (L.92, 15.5) The fool thinks a rational person will always reason in terms of his own benefit. Hobbes replies that always to reason in terms of one's own benefit is not to one's own benefit. The covenant breaker has reasoned that breaking his covenant will be to his benefit; the Hobbesian replies that the covenant breaker's mode of reasoning will lead to his being cast out of society. Provided, of course, that his mode of reasoning is known or suspected by his fellows—but we cannot pursue this argument further.

IV. THE AUTHORIZATION OF THE SOVEREIGN

Rather, we want to know if Hobbes's technique for transforming permissive rights into exclusive rights will be successful in all cases in which we seek the transformation. In particular, can some part of the right of nature be transformed into the right to punish?

The right to punish is one of the essential attributes of sovereignty. However true it may be that it is irrational to follow the fool, he does not want for advocates (the economists and the theorists of rational choice prominent among them). Something more than mere words is needed to bring persons out of their natural condition. They must be tied "by fear of punishment to the performance of their covenants." (L.106, 17.1) Hobbes asserts this in the very first paragraph of the second part of *Leviathan,* in which he sets out the end of "Commonwealth," which for him is a term for any independent political body. Punishment requires a punisher; this is the sovereign, who is the essential element of any commonwealth. Who is he and how does he come to hold the right to punish—manifestly an exclusive right?

We can exercise a right, or we can renounce a right. There is a third possibility. We can *authorize* another person to exercise the right, to act in our name. Hobbes calls the person who authorizes the use of his right, the author. The person authorized is the actor. The author is responsible for what the actor does in his (the author's) name, just as if he had done it himself.

There are complications about authorization that we may bypass. The idea is simple and commonplace. Typically, authorization is limited in scope and duration. I authorize my accountant to prepare and submit my tax return. But Hobbes's principal interest in authorization envisages it as unlimited and permanent. "*I authorize, or take upon me, all his actions.*" (L.142, 21.14)) And this unlimited authorization is the basis of sovereignty. The sovereign is, as it were, the universal actor, all his actions being performed in the name of his subjects, so that each is author of all that the sovereign does.

It may be worth noting that the unlimited authorization that gives rise to sovereignty is possible because the potential subjects possess the universal permissive right of nature. Since everything is permissible, they are not constrained in the extent of their authorization. If the right of nature were constrained in some way, so that some actions were naturally forbidden or required, then such acts would remain forbidden to or required of the sovereign.

But this is speculation. For Hobbes unfortunately does not integrate his account of authorization with the framework of rights and obligations that I have sketched. No explanation is offered in the chapter, concluding part one of *Leviathan,* of what connection there might be between the discussion of persons and authors, and the account of the laws of nature. In part two Hobbes simply helps himself to the ideas of covenant and authorization in showing how sovereign right is instituted. He supposes a covenant, of all with all, to confer their rights on one person (or group of persons), so that whatsoever the designated person does, in exercising all of their rights, is done in the name and as the act of them all. (How this person or persons is selected—the fundamental coordination problem that must be solved—is fortunately not here our problem. We suppose it done.) All persons are then obligated, each to all of the others, to stand to their authorization, recognizing the acts of the person authorized as their acts, and so are bound to obedience to him, as to their own decisions—except of course that they cannot revoke his commands as they might reconsider their own decisions. He is the sovereign, and in exercising the rights of all of his subjects, he exercises sovereign right.

Hobbes has said that rights are not literally transferred when given up, since one's right of nature cannot be augmented. And he could, it seems, say that rights are not transferred in giving the use of them to the sovereign. But in acquiring the use of all of his subjects' rights of nature, is not the sovereign's right augmented? Hobbes need not accept this. The sovereign, strictly speaking, is not the natural person or persons in whom he is embodied. This person, like all the rest, confers the use of his right upon the person specified in the covenant. But the person specified, although embodied in a particular man (or, as Hobbes allows, assembly), should be thought of as an artificial person (defined by Hobbes as one whose words and deeds are to be taken for the words and deeds of some other person), created by the acts of authorization. His right is just the natural right of each of those who are his subjects, transformed by being exercised not separately or independently, but collectively. The natural conflict between persons each exercising his own right of nature is replaced by the (artificial?) harmony of persons all directed by the sovereign, to the end of peace among themselves, and protection from those who are subject to other sovereigns (for Hobbes does not envisage a single world government).

V. THE RIGHT TO PUNISH AND ITS ORIGIN

> A PUNISHMENT *is an evil inflicted by public authority on him that hath done or omitted that which is judged by the same authority to be a transgression of the law, to the end that the will of men may thereby the better be disposed to obedience.* (L.203, 28.1)

This is Hobbes's official definition of punishment. By "public authority" we are to understand the sovereign, or some person or persons delegated by the sovereign to inflict such evils, and "the law" is the commands of the sovereign addressed to those obliged to obey him, that is, his subjects. Hobbes needs to show how the sovereign right to punish is grounded in the right of nature, and the obligations arising from covenant.

Some ten chapters before he proposed this definition, Hobbes said that "if he that attempteth to depose the sovereign be . . . punished by him for such attempt, he is author of his own punishment, as being, by the institution, author of all his sovereign shall do," and claims "it is injustice for a man to do anything for which he may be punished by his own authority." (L.111, 18.3) This clearly treats punishment as evil visited by the sovereign upon those who, having authorized him to exercise their right of nature, now act contrary to that exercise, and so have authorized their own punishment. But when he develops his theory of punishment, Hobbes denies that the sovereign has been authorized by his subjects to punish them. For "no man is supposed bound by covenant not to resist violence, and consequently, it cannot be intended that he gave any right to another to lay violent hands upon his person." So the authorization of the sovereign, although it gives him the use of every man's right, does not give him the use of the right to inflict harm on any man. Hobbes has said that "the sum of the right of nature . . . is *by all means we can, to defend ourselves.*" (L.80, 14.4) We can give the sovereign the use of our right to defend ourselves, but we have neither right nor obligation to let someone inflict evil upon us. Not every grammatical phrase of the form "a right to x" can specify a possible right; a "right" to let someone inflict evil on me is no part of our normative space, which is bounded by what we can have reason to do or allow.

I shall shortly present a counterargument to Hobbes's insistence that the sovereign right to punish, unlike other sovereign rights, cannot arise from authorization. But we should give Hobbes the opportunity to state his case more fully. He allows that every person "obligeth himself to assist him that hath the sovereignty in the punishing of another, but of himself not. But to covenant to assist the sovereign in doing hurt to another, unless he that so covenanteth have a right to do it himself, is not to give him a right to punish." (L.204, 28.2) The sovereign must have the right to punish, if others are to be obliged to assist him in exercising that right. But no one gives a right to punish himself to the sovereign. "It is manifest therefore that the right which the commonwealth . . . hath to punish is not grounded on any concession or gift [or, we should add, authorization] of the subjects." (L.204, 28.2)

How then is the sovereign right to punish established? Hobbes argues that "before the institution of commonwealth, every man had a right to everything, and to do whatsoever he thought necessary to his own preservation, subduing, hurting, or killing any man in order thereunto. And this is the foundation of [the] right of punishing. . . . For the subjects do not give the sovereign that right, but only (in laying down theirs) strengthened him to use his own as he should see fit, for the preservation of them all; so that it was not given, but left to him, and to him only, and (excepting the limits set him by natural law) as entire as in the condition of mere nature, and of war of every one against his neighbour." (L.204, 28.2)

But the right of everyone in the state of nature is not a right to punish. It is a right to harm, but Hobbes is normally careful to distinguish the infliction of harm from punishment. The right to harm does not carry the implication of any wrongdoing on the part of the person being harmed; punishment does carry such an implication. One is punished for transgressing the law; in the natural condition of mankind there is no law to transgress. I have the natural right to inflict an evil upon you in order to better my prospects of survival; this has nothing to do with transgression. Punishment is also a public act. One cannot create public authority merely by restricting private authority. Persons would not be punished by their own authority, or authors of their own punishments, if the right to punish were simply the natural right to inflict harm, left to only one person. Sovereign right is founded on authorization; Hobbes seems here to have forgotten the core of his political theory.

The right to property is the right to exclusive possession. The right to punish is not the right to exclusive harming. The right to property can be understood in terms of the right of nature and the possibility of renouncing it. The right to punish can be understood only with the additional term of authorization. Hobbes's explication of the right to punish denies this. It will not do.

We may seem to be at an impasse. But why should we suppose that a person cannot authorize the sovereign to take such measures as are needed to enforce compliance with his edicts, since this is most conducive to one's preservation? Hobbes distinguishes between saying "kill me, or my fellow, if you please," and "I will kill myself, or my fellow." No one can be expected to kill himself, since this would be directly inimical to his preservation; but I may authorize the sovereign to enforce his edicts even at the expense of my life, if the expected benefit ex ante, of the authorization is sufficient to outweigh the cost to me of my being killed, discounted by its expected likelihood, which may well be low. To be sure, if the sovereign condemns a person to death he will resist, to the extent that he can, being killed. Hobbes considers self-preservation a natural necessity. But there is no reason I cannot authorize the sovereign to enforce his edicts by inflicting some evil on those who violate the edicts, and so on me if I am a violator. That I will resist the actual infliction of evil on me is compatible with my authorizing the sovereign to inflict it, since each has the same rationale—my preservation, which may motivate different behavior in different circumstances.

This would seem a convincing argument, if we were to suppose the issue to be whether I can authorize some evil short of death to be inflicted upon those who violate the sovereign's edicts, and so on me if I am a violator. But death—capital punishment—may be more recalcitrant. Since in some situations I cannot reduce the risk of death to zero whatever I do, it may seem that I should minimize the risk, and so may authorize the sovereign to kill me if by so authorizing him I reduce the overall likelihood of my death coming about, whether at the hands of the sovereign or in some other way. I accept the possibility of my authorized death, to reduce the overall probability of my death, authorized or not. Hobbes's actual defense of the right to punish is, I have argued, inadequate; whether a coherent defense is available to him depends, I think, on whether he could accept this argument.

My hesitation here in asserting that he could arises from my view of rational intention. I argue in "Assure and Threaten" that a person can intend to perform an action, not itself to his benefit, provided it is part of a course of actions that is to his benefit, *and provided* performance of the action would not leave him worse off than he would expect to have been had he not adopted the course of action in the first place. The analogue to this view would be that a person can authorize an act of the sovereign not itself to the person's benefit, provided it is part of an overall authorization to his (expected) benefit, *and provided* the sovereign's act does not leave him worse off than had he not authorized the sovereign. An agent may then authorize himself to be subjected to noncapital punishment, when it is part of a system of enforcement that benefits him in comparison with the natural condition of war, but it may plausibly be maintained that if he finds himself facing capital punishment, he would consider himself worse off than had he remained in the natural condition of war. I propose therefore to set capital punishment aside.

Let us then suppose that the case for the right to punish, at least in noncapital cases, is made by the argument just sketched, or in some other way. Then we could amend Hobbes's definition of punishment to reflect our insistence that it must be a part of sovereign right, stemming from authorization from his subjects, by adding (inelegantly) the capitalized words: "A Punishment is an evil inflicted by public authority on him that, HAVING AUTHORIZED THAT AUTHORITY, hath done or omitted that which is judged by the same authority to be a transgression of the law IT HAS COMMANDED, to the end that the will of men may thereby the better be disposed to obedience." I shall call this the Neo-Hobbesian definition of punishment. This definition is compatible with Hobbes's treatment of people as authors of their own punishment, and with the fundamental idea that authorization is the device used to transform the natural right to inflict harm into the sovereign right to punish. It is incompatible with Hobbes's account of how the right to punish is established, but much of what Hobbes says about punishment is equally incompatible with that account.

But before examining some of the detail of Hobbes's account, we might briefly consider the implications of the introduction of authorization for the right of property. In our earlier discussion of this right we showed it arising from a process similar to that which Hobbes mistakenly employs for the right to punish. Each person possesses a natural right, in this case the right of possession; all but one give up their right, so he alone is left with the right of possession, which now is exclusive. In practice, of course, it would be infeasible for this to be carried out. Authorization offers some refinements to this account. The first is to relocate the need for unanimity in the acts to authorize the sovereign. Instead of requiring unanimous consent to establish each particular property right, we need only unanimous consent to establish the sovereign—and this consent Hobbes is willing to assume, since once a potential bearer of sovereignty is identified, it behooves every person to join in authorizing him or it.

The sovereign is authorized to exercise his subjects' rights of possession. He may then create a framework of rules providing for persons to hold rights to possession that exclude their fellows, on such terms and conditions (such as the payment of an annual tax, or the acceptance of zoning that constrains the use to be made of the possession) as the sovereign deems appropriate. The particular detail of rights to property can be accommodated within the framework of authorization, since it may be introduced in the sovereign's edicts.

It should be evident that bringing authorization into the picture gives us a much more plausible framework for introducing property rights than does our initial account, which relies solely on covenant.

Although the neo-Hobbesian definition of punishment given above is incompatible with Hobbes's official account of how the right to punish is established, it is compatible with most of what Hobbes says about punishment. What does he say?

Punishment is an evil inflicted by public authority. But not every such evil constitutes punishment. Hobbes insists that if pain is inflicted "without precedent public condemnation," it is not punishment but "an hostile act, because the fact for which a man is punished ought first to be judged by public authority to be a transgression of the law." (L.204. 28.5) Furthermore, "all evil which is inflicted without intention or possibility of disposing the delinquent (or, by his example, other men) to obey the laws is not punishment but an act of hostility" (L.204, 28.7). Hobbes is quite strict in his insistence that the end of punishment be beneficial to the members of society, and not an expression of their rage or their desire for revenge.

Because "no man is supposed before he be judicially heard and declared guilty, any harm done to him before trial must be limited to what is required to "assure his custody."(L.207, 28.20) Thus Hobbes allows that a man accused may be deprived of his liberty, as may a man condemned, but the former only if and as necessary to prevent him from escaping trial. To inflict greater restraint or pain on a man accused but not condemned "is against the law of nature." (L.207, 28.20) As with inflicting harm on the accused before trial, inflicting harm on the innocent is "against the law of nature" (L.208, 28.22). But what is this? At the outset I claimed that Hobbes had one normative primitive—the right of nature. I have treated both Hobbes's account of punishment and the neo-Hobbesian alternative as requiring only the right of nature as the basis of normativity. Other normative conceptions, such as authorization and obligation, are derived from it. What then is the status of the law of nature?

There is no easy answer to this question. But in "Hobbes: The Laws of Nature" I argue, on the basis of an analysis of all that Hobbes says in his later writings about the laws of nature, that they are primarily "dictates of reason . . . conclusions or theorems concerning what conduceth to the conservation and defence" of persons. (L.100, 15. 41) And as theorems, they do not constitute a second normative primitive. We might then say, as Hobbes does, that "there can arrive no good to the commonwealth" by inflicting evil on the innocent subject, (L.208, 28.22) and, we might add, on the accused prior to his being found guilty. The authorization by which a commonwealth is instituted, has as end, that the citizens "live peacefully amongst themselves and be protected against other men."(L.110, 18.21) Inflicting harm on the innocent does not promote this end.

Hobbes holds, as we should expect, that "evil inflicted by usurped power, and judges without authority from, the sovereign, is not punishment, but an act of hostility." The reason he offers should however give us pause; he says "because the acts of power usurped have not for author the person condemned, and therefore are not acts of public authority." (L.204, 28.6) Four (longish) sentences previously, Hobbes insisted that "the subjects did not give the sovereign that right [i.e. to punish], but only (in laying(down theirs) strengthened him to use his own as he should think fit." (L.204, 28.2) But if this is so then the acts of punishment "have not for author the person condemned, and therefore are not acts of public authority." A clearer example of the contradiction we have found in Hobbes's theory of punishment would be hard to imagine.

All that the sovereign does, he does in the name of his subjects. Therefore all that the sovereign does, he must be authorized to do by his subjects. And this is to be given the right to do all that he does by his subjects. In denying this, in asserting instead that the sovereign has the right to punish in virtue of being the sole person to retain the natural right to inflict evil, Hobbes rules out the possibility of punishment as he understands it. In affirming that the sovereign punishes in the name of his subjects, and all that is thereby entailed, the neo-Hobbesian alternative removes the contradiction. But can the subjects authorize their own deaths at the hand of the sovereign? The neo-Hobbesian may find himself committed to the abolition of capital punishment.

I have taken authorization to be the key idea in Hobbes's account of sovereign right, which necessarily includes the right to punish. Unfortunately, Hobbes has not adequately integrated his account of authorization into his account of how the right of nature is transformed into sovereign right. He does not discuss giving the use of one's right to another, as distinct from giving up one's right in favor of another. The former, but not the latter, makes one author of the other's actions. He treats the institution of sovereignty as the outcome of a universal covenant, of every man with every man, to authorize all of the actions of some one man or group. Each man thus has an obligation to his fellows to own all that is done by the authorized man or group. But Hobbes does not carry through the implications of this account consistently, falling back on giving up right instead of giving the use of right, as our discussion of the right to punish makes evident.

But the several features of punishment that Hobbes notes—that it is a public act, beneficial to society, respecting due process, requiring proof of guilt—are equally parts of the neo-Hobbesian alternative and indeed are surely parts of any account that would be acceptable in a liberal democracy. Hobbes and liberal democracy may seem strange bedfellows, and no doubt in many respects they are. But not in respect to punishment. Hobbes's rejection of retroactive punishment, where the offense is prior to the law forbidding it, and of punishment in excess of what the law provides, are also parts of the neo-Hobbesian alternative that liberal democrats would endorse. But there is more to be said about what is or is not punishment in Hobbes's account, and this more will not fit so comfortably with liberal thought. It concerns "enemies"—those who have not authorized, or have repudiated their authorization of, the sovereign.

VI. PUNISHMENT AND THE SCOPE OF SOVEREIGN RIGHT

"(T)he punishments set down in the law are to subjects, not to enemies." (L.206, 28.13). Subjects have authorized the sovereign, and therefore are authors of all that he does, including punishment for violating his edicts. Enemies, those who have not authorized the sovereign, are of course not authors of what he does. "(T)hey were either never subject to the law, and therefore cannot transgress it, or having been subject to it and professing to be no longer so, by consequence deny they can transgress it, all the harms that can be done them must be taken as acts of hostility." (L.205)

But these harms, unlike those that we have been considering, are not wrongful. If an innocent person or one accused but not tried, is treated as if he were guilty, or if a subject is condemned by a usurper, or if harm is inflicted without regard to any social benefit, then the person inflicting the harm acts wrongfully. We shall have to explain this difference, since its basis may not be immediately evident.

"(H)arm inflicted upon one that is a declared enemy falls not under the name of punishment.... But in declared hostility all infliction of evil is lawful. From whence it followeth, that if a subject shall, by fact or word, wittingly and deliberately deny the authority of the representative of the commonwealth [i.e., the sovereign] he may lawfully be made to suffer whatsoever the representative will." (L.205–6) The sovereign may have fixed some penalty for the offense, but "in denying subjection" the subject "denies such punishment as by the law hath been ordained." (L.206) His relation to the sovereign remains that between two persons in the state of nature. And so the sovereign may exercise his full right of nature, by which all acts. Including the unlimited infliction of ill, are permissible.

I noted with approval Hobbes's rejection of punishment of the innocent. We might naturally suppose that he would equally reject imposing any harm on innocent persons. Not so. "But the infliction of what evil soever on an innocent man that is not a subject, if it be for the benefit of the commonwealth, and without violation of any former contract, is no breach of the law of nature. For all men that are not subjects are either enemies or else they have ceased from being so by some precedent covenant. But against enemies, whom the commonwealth judgeth capable to do them hurt, it is lawful by the original right of nature to make war, wherein the sword judgeth not, nor doth the victor make distinction of nocent and innocent as to the time past, nor has other respect of mercy than as it conduceth to the good of his own people." (L.208, 28.23)

Hobbes implicitly recognizes two fundamental normative relationships—between parties to a covenant, and between author and actor. Both are explicated in terms of the right of nature. Outside these relationships, persons act as they can and will. Hobbes's response to, say, Scanlon's idea of "what we owe to each other" is very simple—nothing, until the devices of covenant and authorization are in place. The default condition is enmity, and there are no rules for enmity. There is no basis, then, for condemning the treatment of persons who are not subjects. Hurtful it may be, but wrongful, not.

But what are the grounds for taking the infliction of evil on an innocent subject, or one accused but not tried, etc. to be wrongful? They are not forms of punishment, given either Hobbes's own definition or the neo-Hobbesian alternative definition, but why does this matter? Of course we are convinced that it does matter, but does Hobbes have the resources to show this? Since the subjects are all of them authors of all that the sovereign does and since as Hobbes insists "he that doth anything by authority from another doth therein no injury to him by whose authority he acteth ... to do injury to one's self ls impossible ... they that have sovereign power may commit iniquity, but not injustice or injury ..." (L.112–13, 18.6) Sovereigns cannot be unjust to enemies, because nothing is unjust in the state of nature, and they cannot be unjust to subjects, because the sovereign's acts are owned by the subjects as their own acts, and Hobbes consistently holds that no person can do injustice to himself.

The scope of sovereign right is determined by the extent of his authorization. Hobbes supposes the subject to say "*I authorize, or take upon me, all his actions.*" (L.142, 21.14, cf. L.110., 18.1) If the subject authorizes everything that the sovereign does, then nothing the sovereign does can be unjust to the subject. Hobbes, we should recall, is obsessed with the need for security. This obsession leads him to reject any proposal that would attempt to confer less than absolute power on the sovereign, as seeking to reduce his power to protect his subjects, from one another, and from other persons. Hobbes was traumatized by the English Civil War, and his reaction was similar to that of all too many persons, Americans but not only Americans, to the events of 9/11. To increase security becomes the overriding objective, and in Hobbes's thought this manifests itself in the demand that the sovereign's power be maximized. Hence his subjects must authorize *all* his actions.

Hobbes also lacks our understanding of the role of social institutions and political constitutions in making limited government effective within its limits. Of course, we should not expect Hobbes to have anticipated the knowledge we have acquired, through both theory and practice, of how institutions work. The neo-Hobbesian can take advantage of this knowledge, and can put aside Hobbes's obsession with security. The result will be an account of sovereign right that appeals to authorization, but that assumes limits to the authorization. The neo-Hobbesian will defend limited rather than absolute sovereignty. Some may question the appropriateness of the label "neo-Hobbesian," but if we take authorization, and not absolutism, to be Hobbes's most significant contribution to political thought, then surely the label is merited.

So suppose that we endorse limited authorization, contoured so that the features of punishment that Hobbes discusses distinguish justifiable from unjustifiable ways in which the sovereign may inflict evil or harm on his subjects. Since the infliction of harm upon his enemies does not require any authorization from his subjects, it may seem that no more need be said. The harm the sovereign inflicts on enemies or non-subjects needs no justification; it is simply an exercise of the right of nature.

But surely there is more to say, if we want to endorse a neo-Hobbesian position from the standpoint of liberal democracy. Hobbes can have no objection to inflicting pain on non-subjects without public condemnation, and without any attempt to establish guilt. He can have no objection if the sovereign imprisons non-subjects for the remainder of their lives, or puts them to death. Since drones provide a way of killing non-subjects without risk to the killers, we should expect a contemporary Hobbesian sovereign to embrace their use, and very probably to employ them to remove his enemies, in preference to taking them prisoner, or executing them in more conventional ways. If someone were to object to these measures on the ground that they offer no protection against mistaken identity, we have already encountered part of Hobbes's reply: the sword makes no distinction between the innocent and the "nocent," so that in inflicting harms on non-subjects, it is enough if the sovereign considers only the good of the commonwealth. While this will usually be best achieved by eliminating only those actually actively hostile to the sovereign, it may in some situations be better if the sovereign casts his net widely, so that some persons wrongly suspected of performing hostile acts, and some mistakenly identified with persons who have performed hostile acts, are caught in its meshes.

If the sovereign is to treat subjects and non-subjects in very different ways, then there needs to be a clear distinction between the two. For the most part this is no problem. But there are those who "having been subject to it [the law] and professing to be no longer so, by consequence deny they can transgress it." (L.205, 28.13) Hobbes says that "all the harms that can be done them must be taken as acts of hostility. But in declared hostility all infliction of evil is lawful." (L.205, 28.13) If someone openly proclaims that he repudiates his authorization of the sovereign, then he declares himself an enemy, and one might suppose that should settle the matter.[3] (And what if he does not openly proclaim his repudiation? How far must a person depart from obedience to the sovereign for him to be rightly judged an outlaw, and so not entitled to the protection afforded by the sovereign to all subjects, even those who have violated some of the laws and therefore are rightly subject to punishment? What would be the dividing line, in actual practice, between the commonwealth's delinquent members of society and its undeclared enemies?

These are, of course, not merely speculative questions. If, as I believe, Hobbes is on the right conceptual track when he treats the sovereign's right to rule as founded on the authorization of his subjects, so that the neo-Hobbesian definition of punishment is plausible, then the idea that each person is the author of his or her punishment makes excellent sense. But if, contrary to Hobbes, we hold that the sovereign does not enjoy carte blanche in his dealings with those not subject to him, we shall need a more fine-grained account of the relation between the sovereign and persons who are not his subjects—or better, from our standpoint, between the sovereign right of the commonwealth and the rights of persons who are not citizens of that commonwealth. The right of nature, which I have taken to be Hobbes's only normative primitive, may be sufficient to permit the introduction of both obligation and authorization, but it has nothing to say about persons who interact outside the bounds that it can accommodate. And this is a problem that reaches to the foundations of Hobbes's political theory.

VII. CONCLUSION: FROM THE RIGHT OF NATURE TO LAWS OF NATURE

There are passages in *Leviathan* that hint at an alternative account of normativity, with two primitives. Hobbes says "it is a precept, or general rule, of reason, *that every man ought to endeavour peace, as far as he has hope of obtaining it, and when he cannot obtain it, that he may seek and use all helps and advantages of war.* The first

3. But what if the Internal Revenue Service, as it will, refuses to recognize his act of repudiation? Who has the final word on a person's status vis-à-vis society?

branch of which rule containeth the first and fundamental law of nature, which is *to seek peace and follow it.* The second, the sum of the right of nature, which is *by all means we can, to defend ourselves.*" (L.80, 14.4) On this account, the natural condition of mankind is characterized by a permissive right, not unlimited in scope but rather restricted to situations in which a person is faced with a real threat to his life or well-being. In these circumstances, he may do whatever conduces to his defense; in this sense his right is to everything but it does not exhaust normative space. Coordinate with this right of nature is the law of nature, requiring of each person that he seek and follow peace, whenever his life or well-being is not directly threatened. The natural condition of mankind is one of war; the law of nature directs each man to exit this natural condition, if others are similarly willing.

From the standpoint of the sovereign, the world consists of subjects, enemies, and neutral parties, who have neither declared their hostility to the sovereign nor authorized him to act in their name. The sovereign does not possess carte blanche to deal with neutral parties as he pleases, but rather is constrained by the requirement that he seek peace with them, whether by accepting them as subjects, or recognizing them as constituting a distinct society, with whom he is obliged by the law of nature to seek peaceful relations.

I cannot here pursue this alternative further. To treat the law of nature as creating obligations coordinate with the right of nature would raise many problems, not the least of which would be what grounding it would require. If we take the right of nature as the sole normative primitive, we are in effect endorsing the idea that human life is at bottom competitive. Taking the law of nature as also primitive endorses rather the idea that human life is at bottom both competitive and cooperative. With these thoughts we would enter realms unexplored by Hobbes.

2

Sovereignty as a Right and as a Duty

Kant's Theory of the State

JACOB WEINRIB*

The modern concept of sovereignty stems from two watershed moments in the history of legal and political practice.[1] The first was the Peace of Westphalia in 1648, which recognized a plurality of sovereign states, each possessing the right to rule within its territory. The second was the aftermath of the Second World War, in which public law (both domestic and international) began to shift increasingly toward the idea that the sovereign's right to rule must be directed to the fulfillment of the human rights of the ruled.[2] This idea forms the bedrock of a range of postwar constitutions and the Universal Declaration of Human Rights. Each of these moments reflects a different aspect of sovereignty. The former acknowledges the sovereign's right to exercise authority over the ruled, while the latter recognizes the sovereign's duty to the ruled. So conceived, sovereignty encompasses a right that no private person holds (the right to exercise public authority) and a duty that

* I am deeply grateful to Ryan Liss, Ela Naegele, Sandy Steel, and Ariel Zylberman for insightful comments on a prior draft. I am also grateful to the participants at the Kant, Rights, and the State Conference at Merton College, Oxford University, including Ralf Bader, Philipp-Alexander Hirsch, Louis-Phillippe Hodgson, Alice Pinheiro Walla, Andrea Sangiovanni, Thomas Sinclair, and Luke Davies.

1. Daniel Philpott "Sovereignty," *The Stanford Encyclopedia of Philosophy* (Summer 2016 Edition), Edward N. Zalta (ed), forthcoming URL = <http://plato.stanford.edu/archives/sum2016/entries/sovereignty/>.

2. See, for example, Mauro Cappelletti, "Repudiating Montesquieu? The Expansion and Legitimacy of 'Constitutional Justice'" (1986) 35 Cath. U. L. Rev. 1, 28; Louis Henkin, "Human Rights and State 'Sovereignty'" (1996) 25 Ga. J. Int'l. & Comp. L. 31, 33–4; Anne Peters, "Humanity as the A and Ω of Sovereignty" (2009) 20 EJIL 513.

Sovereignty and the New Executive Authority. Claire O. Finkelstein and Michael Skerker.

no private person owes (the duty to govern in conformity with rights). The office of sovereignty is comprised of public right and public duty.

Such an understanding of sovereignty raises two basic issues. If sovereignty involves the right to rule, then any theory of sovereignty must explain how someone could have the right to change the normative situation of others by imposing and enforcing obligations that they would not otherwise have.[3] Whereas the first issue surrounds the very *possibility* of sovereignty, the second concerns its *purpose*. If the right of the sovereign to rule is accompanied by a duty to fulfill the rights of the ruled, then any theory of sovereignty must explain what this duty demands and why this duty attends sovereignty as opposed to human conduct in general. A philosophic exposition of the modern concept of sovereignty calls for a theory capable of jointly illuminating sovereignty's possibility and purpose.

Theoretical debates about sovereignty often oscillate between two extremes. On one side lie those that seek to justify the sovereign's right to rule but offer no resources for expounding the sovereign's duty to the ruled. Critics denounce this approach as dangerous because it empowers the state with one hand, and withdraws all constraints on how that power is exercised with the other. Persons are thereby subjected to the unlimited power of an absolute ruler. To protect persons from this threat, an alternate approach swings to the opposite extreme by denying "the existence of sovereignty altogether, asserting that it has no place whatever in the modern theory of the state."[4] This approach thus seeks to capture what a state is without acknowledging its most distinctive feature, the right to rule. Thus, these approaches offer a dichotomy between quietist accounts, which deny that a sovereign can do wrong, and anarchist ones, which reject the very notion of sovereignty.

The purpose of this chapter is to present a theory of sovereignty that steers a middle course between the anarchism and quietism of competing theories. The key to this approach lies in an integrated justification of the sovereign's right to rule and duty to the ruled. By articulating a standpoint from which the possibility and purpose of sovereignty may each be given their due, a theory of the modern concept of sovereignty comes into view.

In what follows, I turn to the legal and political philosophy of Immanuel Kant to formulate such a theory.[5] For many, Kant's thought might seem an unsuitable basis for elucidating the modern concept of sovereignty. While Kant lived in the post-Westphalian world, he had no knowledge of how the events of the twentieth century would culminate in a commitment to rights protection that would transform governance. Nevertheless, his legal and political philosophy offers a systematic exposition of the significance of sovereignty from the standpoint of a basic human right to equal freedom. The result is a theory that illuminates how equal

3. Stephen Perry, "Political Authority and Political Obligation" in Leslie Green and Brian Leiter (eds), *Oxford Studies in Philosophy of Law*, vol 2 (OUP 2013) 26.

4. Baron S A Korff, "The Problem of Sovereignty" (1923) 17 Am. Pol. Sc. Rev. 404, 404.

5. For references to Kant's legal and political writings, see Immanuel Kant, *The Cambridge Edition of the Works of Immanuel Kant: Practical Philosophy* (Mary Gregor tr, 1996). All citations to Kant's works refer to the pagination of the Prussian Academy.

freedom both justifies and regulates sovereign power. By articulating the right of the sovereign to exercise public authority and the duty that attends this right, Kant offers nothing less than an exposition of the modern concept of sovereignty.

Such an account makes a fundamental departure from the fragmentary tendencies of competing theories. Kant departs from theories that confine themselves to the question of how sovereignty is possible by demonstrating that the way in which authority is justified sets the moral parameters for its rightful exercise. For the same reason, Kant also departs from theories that take the possibility of sovereignty for granted and then confine themselves to the question of the purpose that the sovereign's powers should serve. The justification of public authority indicates its end. In this way, Kant offers an integrated exposition of the concept of sovereignty rather than an isolated account of one of its aspects. The rights and duty of sovereignty flow from a conceptually sequenced exploration of a single unifying idea, the right of each person to interact with others on terms of equal freedom.

I unpack Kant's theory of sovereignty in three Sections. The first presents the justification of the sovereign's right to exercise public authority over the ruled. The second explains why this justification imposes a duty on the sovereign to fulfill the rights of the ruled. The third shows that Kant's account of sovereignty steers a middle path between the pitfalls of anarchist and quietist approaches.

Three clarifications are in order from the outset. First, my aim is neither to provide an exhaustive account of Kant's justification of public authority nor his theory of justice. Instead, I will simply say enough about each of these components and their interrelationship to bring the distinctiveness of Kant's theory of sovereignty to light. Second, I focus on Kant's understanding of *internal* sovereignty, that is, the relationship between rulers and ruled within a state, as opposed to *external* sovereignty, which concerns the relationship between states. Third, my aim is to articulate the nature of sovereignty in a state *as such*, as opposed to states distinguished by some particular practice, for example, liberal constitutional norms. I take up the ramifications of Kant's framework for questions of constitutional design and doctrine elsewhere.[6]

I. KANT'S PRINCIPLE OF AUTHORITY: THE POSSIBILITY OF SOVEREIGNTY

In his recent book *Sovereignty: The Origin and Future of a Political and Legal Concept*, the German jurist Dieter Grimm rejects the view that the meanings attributed to the concept of sovereignty are so variable that the concept must be a label concealing arbitrariness. While acknowledging that the concept of sovereignty "is certainly open to interpretation,"[7] and that interpretations have responded to "great changes in the development of political rule" spanning centuries,[8] Grimm

6. Jacob Weinrib, *Dimensions of Dignity: The Theory and Practice of Modern Constitutional Law* (CUP 2016).

7. Dieter Grimm, *Sovereignty: The Origin and Future of a Political Concept* (Belinda Cooper tr, Columbia University Press, New York 2015) 103.

8. Ibid 3.

maintains that the concept nevertheless has a core meaning that has persisted through these variations:

> What was always unique to [the concept of sovereignty], even in its use before Bodin, was its quality as highest and ultimate authority regarding the right to make decisions and give orders that are binding on others. Sovereignty in its legal usage has a connection to rule, in the sense that it involves the *right* to rule, in which the holder of this right, as far as it extends, is controlled by no one else. Bodin's contribution was to separate the concept of sovereignty from individual prerogatives or powers and to consolidate them into public power per se, including the right to make law, as well as the concentration of this power in one holder, thereby eliminating the numerous, mutually independent holders. . . . The coexistence of various highest authorities with a claim to exclusivity was made possible by the territorial limitation of sovereignty.[9]

For Grimm, the core meaning of sovereignty emerges at the intersection of three components: (1) the right to rule, (2) the state as the holder of this right, and (3) the territory on which this right extends.[10]

Each of these components raises a basic question about the nature of sovereignty. The first, the right to rule, is commonly understood to refer to the capacity to change the normative situation of others, whether by conferring rights or by imposing coercible obligations. The right to rule raises the basic question of political authority: How could one person have the authority to establish rights and duties that persons would not otherwise have? A further question emerges from the second component: Why is the right to rule vested in the state as opposed to some private entity? In other words, why is the state sovereign? Finally, the third component generates the question: What entitles a particular state to rule a particular territory? In what follows, I sketch how Kant's theory of sovereignty responds to each of these questions.

Sovereignty divides persons into rulers and ruled. Within this relationship, rulers possess the authority to confer rights or impose duties by enacting positive law. Before asking what purpose positive law should serve, Kant raises the more basic question of how anyone could have the authority to issue it. He notes that unlike natural law, positive law consists in norms that "do not bind without actual external lawgiving," that is, unless they are promulgated by a lawgiver.[11] But if positive law is binding because it is promulgated, then the claim that positive law imposes obligations presupposes an account of "the authority of the lawgiver

9. Ibid 103–4.

10. See also Philpott (n 1): "Sovereignty, though its meanings have varied across history, also has a core meaning, *supreme authority within a territory*"; and Hans Morgenthau, "The Problem of Sovereignty Reconsidered" (1948) 48 Colum. L. Rev. 341, 341.

11. Immanuel Kant, *The Metaphysics of Morals* in *The Cambridge Edition of the Works of Immanuel Kant: Practical Philosophy* (first published 1797, 1996) 6:224 and 6:237.

(i.e., his authorization to bind others by his mere *choice*)."[12] Thus, Kant sets out to determine whether sovereignty is possible by taking up the question of whether persons can stand in a relationship of rulers and ruled.

For Kant, the reason that authority is problematic indicates the basis on which it must be justified. The very notion of the right to rule—regardless of who holds this right or how it is exercised—clashes with a basic conviction. Kant presents this conviction in terms of the *innate right* of persons to freedom: "*Freedom* (independence from being constrained by another's choice), insofar as it can coexist with the freedom of every other in accordance with a universal law, is the only original right belonging to every man by virtue of his humanity."[13] The innate right is an irreducibly relational idea.[14] When persons interact with one another, each has the right to determine and pursue his or her own purposes and the corresponding duty to respect the right of all others to the same. This duty is violated by persons who impose their ends on you or who use your means in pursuit of their ends. Because the innate right requires persons to interact on the basis of reciprocal limits on freedom, it is a right to *equal* freedom. In describing this right as "original," Kant indicates that no act is needed to acquire it. The right to interact with other persons on terms of equal freedom is a human right.

The innate right of each person to freedom forms the backbone of Kant's legal and political philosophy. The position that he defends is not that any question about rights can be answered by looking directly to the innate right, but that every right is either innate or acquired through the performance of some act.[15] The striking feature of Kant's approach is his insistence that freedom forms the one and only original right. This means that all other rights must be acquired, and that the possibility of their acquisition turns on their consistency with the innate right to freedom. Thus, in developing a theory of private right, Kant seeks to demonstrate how innate right justifies acquired property, contract, and familial rights. Likewise, in developing a theory of public right, Kant explains how the innate right to freedom (and the private rights that it underwrites) both justifies and constrains state authority. Thus, every passage of Kant's legal and political project is informed by the same idea: freedom must answer to nothing other than its own systematic requirements. No one may be rightfully coerced for the sake of some

12. Ibid 6:224.

13. Ibid 6:237.

14. On this point, see Arthur Ripstein, *Force and Freedom* (Harvard University Press, Cambridge, MA 2009) 15: "Kantian independence is not a feature of the individual person considered in isolation, but of relations between persons. Independence contrasts with dependence on another person, being subject to that person's choice. It is relational, and so cannot be predicated of a particular person considered in isolation . . ." For critical discussion of Ripstein's account of innate right, see Katrin Flikschuh, "A Regime of Equal Private Freedom? Individual Rights and Public Law in Ripstein's *Force and Freedom*" in Sari Kisilevsky and Martin J Stone (eds), *Freedom and Force: Essays on Kant's Legal Philosophy* (Hart Publishing, Oxford 2017) and Ripstein, "Replies" in the same volume.

15. Kant, *Metaphysics of Morals* (n 11) 6:237.

consideration extrinsic to equal freedom, whether the importance of another's ends or the advancement of one's own perfection or happiness.[16]

Kant's justification of the sovereign's right to rule takes the following form. Private persons must interact with one another on terms of equal freedom. Such interaction is possible only in the presence of a legislative institution possessing the authority to establish common standards of conduct, an adjudicative institution possessing the authority to provide uniform interpretations of those standards, and an executive institution possessing the authority to implement and enforce these standards. Thus, every private person must submit his- or herself to these public authorities. The relationship between these authorities and the persons subject to them forms a state. Kant's claim, then, is not that the state is a particularly effective instrument for the promotion of rightful interaction; rather, the state is necessary insofar as rightful interaction is impossible apart from it.[17]

To interact on terms of equal freedom, persons must be subject to a common set of norms that differentiate prohibited, permitted, and required conduct. In the absence of a public legislative institution capable of establishing a common set of norms binding on all, private persons might formulate their own detailed proposals about what interaction on terms of equal freedom entails. Such proposals are problematic from the standpoint of a commitment to equal freedom, even if individuals offer them in good faith. Insofar as each person is free, each person may advance his or her own understanding of what interaction on terms of equal freedom entails. Insofar as each person is equal, no person possesses the authority to bind others by issuing a unilateral assertion. In a juridical world populated solely by private persons, the problem is irresolvable: each private person must interact with every other on the basis of common standards of conduct, but no private person has standing to impose standards on anyone else. For Kant, the solution to this problem is institutional. Private persons must submit themselves to a public legislative institution possessing the right to bind private persons to a set of common standards of conduct.

The introduction of a legislative institution addresses one problem but raises another. A legislative institution addresses the problem of unilateral lawgiving by subjecting private persons to common standards of conduct. But if these rules are to govern conduct, they must be more general than the contingent instances to which they apply. Accordingly, disputes may arise about how a general rule is to be applied to a particular. We may disagree about the rights that we have—about whether I have acquired this piece of property, or about whether we have entered into a contract with one another. Or we may disagree about the implications of these rights—about where my property ends or what our contract requires. The problem is not that rights are invariably disputed, but that they may be disputed. And in the event of a dispute, each person is, by virtue of her freedom, entitled to assert her own view and, by virtue of her equality, entitled to reject the competing view of any other private person. Such disputes raise a challenge for rightful

16. Louis-Phillipe Hodgson, "Kant on the Right to Freedom: A Defense" (2010) 120 Ethics 791.

17. For an elaboration of the justification that follows, see Ripstein (n 14) 145–81.

interaction because persons do not interact on the basis of common standards of conduct if different people interpret those standards in conflicting ways. This problem of unilateral judgment calls for an institutional resolution that no private person can offer.[18] Disputes are to be resolved by the public authority of a judicial institution, an impartial forum that issues authoritative judgments regarding the concrete meaning of general rules.

A further problem remains. Even if one interacts with others in accordance with general norms, as promulgated by a legislature and applied to particulars by courts, in the absence of an executive institution there is no assurance that others will do the same.[19] The problem is not that others will necessarily interfere with my rights. Rather the problem is that how others conduct themselves toward me depends not on my rights, but on their purposes. An executive body resolves this problem by ensuring that legislation is enforced and that judicial verdicts are implemented. In a legal system, rights are secured through public coercion rather than subject to private force or forbearance.

For Kant, a *rightful condition* "is that relation of human beings among one another that contains the conditions under which alone everyone is able to *enjoy* his rights."[20] In such a condition, the enjoyment of private rights depends not upon unilateral assertions, interpretations, or modes of enforcement but upon public legislative, adjudicative, and executive institutions. Each of these institutions resolves a problem of lawless interaction by introducing a right that no private person can possess. The legislature enables a plurality of persons to interact on terms of equal freedom by subjecting each to a set of common standards of conduct and by empowering public officials to implement legislation and to resolve disputes. The judiciary ensures that when the concrete meaning of these common standards is disputed, private persons are subject to a uniform interpretation. Finally, the executive ensures that legislated norms and judicial decisions are elevated from a mere normative constraint on conduct into a coercible standard so

18. William O'Brian's contribution to this volume, "Sovereignty, Political Obligation and Fairness," criticizes philosophic justifications of the state for "simply [assuming] that the functions that are currently provided by states can only be provided by states." Applying this objection to Kant, he suggests that "disputes over rights violations" can be resolved in the absence of a sovereign by a private "neutral decisionmaker." The objection poses no threat to Kant's justification of a public judicial institution. Kant characterizes private persons as free and equal. As free, each private person may assert her own view about the rights and duties that structure interaction. As equal, each may refuse to subordinate herself to another's view about what rightful conduct entails. Thus, when disputes arise, each person is entitled to refuse to capitulate to the other's opposing claim. The difficulty that private dispute resolution raises is that even if there are private persons who are not party to the dispute, their view of the dispute reproduces the problem of the disputing parties: no private person has standing to issue a binding decision about the rights or duties of another. In contrast, a public judicial institution does not raise this problem insofar as it resolves disputes without subjecting any private person to the unilateral judgment of another.

19. Kant, *Metaphysics of Morals* (n 11) 6:256; 6:307.

20. Ibid 6:305–6.

that no one's rights depend on the force that she can muster or the goodwill that another happens to extend. These three public authorities—the legislature, the judiciary, and the executive—form a *sovereign*.[21] For Kant, sovereignty matters because private persons cannot interact rightfully with one another in its absence.

Kant formulates the duty of private persons to submit to a sovereign's rule in what he terms the *postulate of public right*. If private persons find themselves in a lawless condition, the postulate enjoins them to "leave the state of nature and proceed with [all others] into a rightful condition."[22] If private persons find themselves in a rightful condition, the postulate enjoins them to act in accordance with public legislation, adjudication, and enforcement.[23] Persons violate the postulate by perpetuating the lawless interaction of the state of nature or by seeking to supplant the sovereign's public authority with their own private power.

Kant characterizes violations of the postulate of public right as "wrong in the highest degree."[24] Such wrongs are worse than violations of the rights of particular persons because violations of private rights can be remedied by public institutions, whereas violations of the postulate are inconsistent with the very possibility of public institutions. As Kant puts the point, resistance to the public authority is prohibited because it "would take place in conformity with a maxim that, made universal, would annihilate any civil constitution and eradicate the condition in which alone people can be in possession of rights generally."[25] Kant's claim is conceptual, not empirical. His claim would be empirical if it proceeded, as some interpreters have suggested, from an "assumption about human behavior, namely that widespread acceptance of a right to disobey unjust laws would inevitably lead to chaos."[26] Such a claim requires "empirical support," which Kant does

21. Ibid 6:338. In this passage, Kant uses the term "der Souverän" to refer to the three powers or authorities of a state. Earlier, Kant used the same term with reference to the legislator. See 6:313 and 6:317. In this chapter, I provide an exposition of Kant's account of sovereignty in the broader sense in order to bring his thought into contact with contemporary debates about sovereignty.

22. Ibid 6:307.

23. Ibid 6:316.

24. Ibid 6:307–8. See also "On the Common Saying: That May Be Correct in Theory, But It Is of No Use in Practice" in *The Cambridge Edition of the Works of Immanuel Kant: Practical Philosophy* (first published 1793, 1996) 8:301 ["Theory and Practice"]. On wrongs in the highest degree, see Jacob Weinrib, "The Juridical Significance of Kant's Supposed Right to Lie" (2008) 13 Kantian Rev. 141.

25. Kant, "Theory and Practice" (n 24) 8:299.

26. Allen D Rosen, *Kant's Theory of Justice* (Cornell University Press, Ithaca 1993) 159. Indeed, this appears to be a version of the empirical argument that David Hume defends in "Of the Original Contract" in E F Miller (ed), *Essays, Moral, Political, Literary* (first published 1748, Liberty Classics, Indianapolis 1985) 480: "A small degree of experience and observation suffices to teach us, that society cannot possibly be maintained without the authority of magistrates, and that this authority must soon fall into contempt where exact obedience is not paid to it." Hume's empirical argument for obedience can be refuted by pointing to legal systems that persist without exact obedience.

not provide, and could be refuted by pointing to any situation in which legal order co-exists with a general acceptance of a right to disobey. However, Kant's argument focusses not on the consequences of disobedience or the attitudes that support it, but on the "maxim" that underlies it.[27] A rightful condition enables persons to enjoy their rights in relation to one another. Such enjoyment is possible only if persons are bound by common norms of conduct that are enacted, interpreted, and enforced by public institutions. As Kant puts the point, resistance to public lawgiving is impermissible because no person may assert a right that is "*diametrically* opposed" to the very condition in which rights can be enjoyed.[28]

Kant is notorious for the claim that the duty of private persons to obey public authority is "*unconditional.*"[29] However, this does not mean—as his critics sometimes claim—that Kant endorses the thesis that the decrees of the most egregious regimes must be obeyed by their unfortunate inhabitants.[30] While Kant accepts that whatever is publicly authoritative demands obedience, he rejects the view that any regime or norm could be publicly authoritative. For Kant, public authority is not a descriptive term referring to the attitudes of (supposed) officials toward the norms that they promulgate,[31] but the solution to a moral problem concerning the interaction of bearers of rights. Public authority consists in the conditions under which persons can interact with one another in accordance with their private rights. It follows that any regime or decree that is incompatible with the enjoyment of private rights cannot be publicly authoritative.[32] Kant characterizes arrangements in which the exercise of force is at odds with the security of private rights as *barbarous.*[33] Further, Kant indicates that barbarism may characterize a

27. Kant, "Theory and Practice" (n 24) 8:299; and 8:302 ("nevertheless the people did wrong in the highest degree by seeking their rights in this way; for this way of doing it (adopted as a *maxim*) would make every rightful constitution insecure and introduce a condition of complete lawlessness . . . in which all rights cease, at least, to have effect") (emphasis added).

28. Kant, *Metaphysics of Morals* (n 11) 6:320.

29. Kant, "Theory and Practice" (n 24) 8:299.

30. See, for example, Robert Alexy, *The Argument from Injustice: A Reply to Legal Positivism* (OUP 2002) 118; John Finnis, "Natural Law Theories," *The Stanford Encyclopedia of Philosophy (Fall 2008 Edition)*, Edward N. Zalta (ed), URL = <http://plato.stanford.edu/archives/fall2008/entries/natural-law-theories/>.)

31. H L A Hart, *The Concept of Law* (OUP 1994).

32. On the dismantling of private law by the Nazi regime, see, for example, Karl Loewenstein, "Law in the Third Reich" (1936) 45 Yale L.J. 779, 807; and Michael Stolleis, *The Law under the Swastika: Studies on Legal History in Nazi Germany* (Thomas Dunlap tr, University of Chicago Press, Chicago 1998) 51.

33. For Kant's discussions of barbarism, see *Anthropology from a Pragmatic Point of View* (Robert B. Louden ed, first published 1798, CUP 2006) 7:330–31; Kant, *The Metaphysics of Morals* (n 11) 6:337, 6:351; Kant, "Toward Perpetual Peace" in *The Cambridge Edition of the Works of Immanuel Kant: Practical Philosophy* (first published 1975, 1996) 8:354–55, 8:357, 8:359, and 8:376.

particular regime[34] or a particular norm within an otherwise rightful condition.[35] When barbarism obtains, the postulate of public right persists and requires private persons (and supposed officials) to submit themselves to the public authority of a rightful condition.[36] I contrast barbarism with injustice below.

We began this Section with three questions about the concept of sovereignty. First, insofar as sovereignty involves the right to rule, how could someone have the authority to rule another? Second, why is the state (as opposed to some private entity) sovereign? Third, why does a particular state have a right to rule a particular territory?

Kant's response to each of these questions emerges from his guiding idea that each person has an innate right to freedom. With respect to the first question, private persons must submit themselves to the authority of a sovereign power because they cannot interact rightfully with one another in its absence. With respect to the second, the sovereign must be a state because persons with an equal right to freedom could not have a duty to submit themselves to the authority of another private person. As for the third question, I cannot provide a full response here, but I will say this: Kant's approach to territoriality makes a decisive departure from competing approaches. On the one hand, Kant rejects the Lockean story, in which individuals acquire land by laboring on it and then subsequently transfer it to the state. [37] On the other, he rejects the nationalist story, in which a people defined by shared culture, language, and traditions have a right to particular territory that is then ceded to a particular state.[38] The common thread uniting both of these views is that they make determinations regarding a state's entitlement to govern its territory dependent on some set of historical facts.[39] Kant's concern is not the empirical problem that the relevant facts might be lost in the mists of time, with the result that even a perfectly just state would be incapable of establishing a right to its supposed territory. The problem is that these views make the state's authority over its territory—and with it the ongoing rightful interaction between persons—dependent on facts about the state's origin. In contrast, Kant

34. Kant, *Anthropology from a Pragmatic Point of View* (n 33) 7:330–31.

35. Kant, *Metaphysics of Morals* (n 11) 6:371.

36. For discussions of the distinction between law and barbarism, see Julius Ebbinghaus, "The Law of Humanity and the Limits of State Power" (1953) 3 Phil. Q. 14; Jan Joerden, "From Anarchy to Republic: Kant's History of State Constitutions" in Hoke Robinson (ed), *Proceedings of the Eighth International Kant Congress*, vol 1 (Marquette University Press, Milwaukee 1995) 139; Ripstein (n 14) 325–52; and Weinrib (n 6) 76–107.

37. For a defense of the Lockean approach, see A John Simmons, "On the Territorial Rights of States" (2001) 11 Phil. Issues 300. For criticism, see Anna Stilz, "Why Do States Have Territorial Rights?" (2009) 1 Int'l Theory 185, 188–94.

38. For critical discussions, see Chaim Gans, *The Limits of Nationalism* (CUP 2003) 97–123 and Anna Stilz, "Nations, States, and Territory" (2011) 121 Ethics 572, 575–78.

39. Kant would also reject the presupposition common to both the Lockean and nationalist views, namely that private persons could have a conclusive right to (real) property prior to the existence of a state. I cannot discuss this issue here.

holds that a rightful condition has authority within its territory simply by being a rightful condition—that is, by establishing, interpreting, and enforcing common standards of conduct. No fact about the origins of a rightful condition could serve as a justification for depriving the state of territory that it governs or for depriving the inhabitants of this territory of governance.[40] Of course, this is not to claim that current borders must persist in perpetuity,[41] but to insist that no one may extract territory from a rightful condition simply by pointing to some historical fact. The alteration of borders must proceed through law.[42]

II. KANT'S PRINCIPLE OF JUSTICE: THE PURPOSE OF SOVEREIGNTY

The postulate of public right establishes the possibility of sovereignty, an arrangement in which public institutions possessing the right to rule enable private persons to interact with one another rightfully. Kant's theory of sovereignty seeks to demonstrate that the possibility and purpose of sovereignty stand in a relation of mutual implication: the justification of the sovereign's right to wield public authority indicates how it must be exercised. This Section explicates the duty incumbent on the sovereign by exploring what Kant terms the *idea of the original contract*.

By the time Kant invoked the notion of an "original contract," the term had come under heavy fire. Jeremy Bentham held that the idea of an original contract "had been effectually demolished by Mr Hume" and observed that "we hear not so much of it now as formerly."[43] The core of Hume's attack is the claim that consent does not justify the obligation that subjects owe their sovereigns. Combining philosophical and historical analysis, Hume argues that consent does not ground the authority of existing states, which were founded "either on usurpation or conquest, or both, without any presence of a fair consent or voluntary subjection of the people."[44] However, even if history had been different and the original generation of subjects had in the distant past given their consent, they could not thereby bind the generations that followed.[45] As for democratic governance,

40. Kant, *Metaphysics of Morals* (n 11) 6:318; 6:339–40.

41. For criticism of accounts that build in a "conservative bias" in favor of existing borders, see Simmons (n 37) 300, 310–12.

42. See, for example, the decision of the Canadian Supreme Court in *Reference re Secession of Quebec*, [1998] 2 S.C.R. 217.

43. Jeremy Bentham, *A Fragment on Government* (first published 1776, CUP 2001) 51–52.

44. Hume (n 26) 471.

45. Ibid 470–1: "If the agreement, by which savage men first associated and conjoined their force, be here meant, this is acknowledged to be real; but being so ancient, and being obliterated by a thousand changes of government and princes, it cannot now be supposed to retain any authority." Hume raises additional arguments against contractarian thought that I cannot take up here. For discussion see Dario Castiglione, "History, Reason and Experience: Hume's Arguments against Contractarian Theories" in David Boucher and Paul Kelly (eds), *The Social Contract from Hobbes to Rawls* (Routledge, New York 1994) 95.

Hume notes, on the one hand, that the number of citizens canvassed for consent is invariably outnumbered by the number of persons subject to law's authority and, on the other, that citizens are not typically afforded the opportunity to vote on every issue. Thus, Hume dismisses the very notion of an original contract as an anarchical idea by which subjects reserve the "power of resisting their sovereign, whenever they find themselves aggrieved by that authority, which they have, for certain purposes, voluntarily entrusted him."[46] However, Hume is careful not to issue a conclusion that outstrips his arguments. His claim is that "in fact and reality" consent is incapable of grounding the authority of existing sovereigns. But Hume acknowledges that where consent is given and periodically renewed, it forms "the best and most sacred of any" foundation of governmental authority.[47]

Kant's response to Hume's challenge is twofold. As a historical matter, Kant accepts Hume's empirical claim that existing legal systems were founded on force rather than consent.[48] As a philosophical matter, Kant is more skeptical about consent than Hume. For Hume, consent is a *possible* basis of political obligation, but, given the contingent origins of existing states, consent is not its *actual* basis. In contrast, Kant holds that consent has no bearing on determinations about whether particular persons are bound by a particular state. As we saw in the prior Section, Kant holds that private persons must submit themselves to the governance of public institutions because they cannot interact with one another on terms of equal freedom in its absence. If it were true that private persons in some time and place had in fact consented to the sovereign's rule, consent would be irrelevant because the obligation obtains on other grounds. Likewise, the refusal to consent is irrelevant, for refusal would matter only if it was permissible. But no one could have a right to reject a lawful order (in which all can interact on terms of equal freedom) in favor of a lawless one (in which none can). Thus, Kant remarks that persons are not wronged by being compelled to submit to the public authority of a rightful condition.[49]

The idea of the original contract plays a distinctive role within Kant's theory of sovereignty. Whereas Hume criticizes theories that invoke consent to ground an account of political obligation, Kant introduces the idea of the original contract

46. Hume (n 26) 466. For a parallel passage, see Kant, "Theory and Practice (n 24) 8:302: "where there is to be found no instrument of an actual contract submitted to the commonwealth, accepted by its head, and sanctioned by both, they take the idea of an original contract, which is always present in reason as the basis [of a commonwealth] as something that must actually have taken place, and so think they can always save for the people authorization to withdraw from the contract as it sees fit, though by its own appraisal, the contract has been grossly violated."

47. Hume (n 26) 474. The full passage reads: "My intention here is not to exclude the consent of the people from being one just foundation of government where it has place. It is surely the best and most sacred of any. I only pretend, that it has very seldom had place in any degree, and never almost in its full extent; and that, therefore, some other foundation of government must also be admitted."

48. Kant, *Metaphysics of Morals* (n 11) 6:339.

49. Ibid 6:312.

only after his account of political obligation has been fleshed out. The idea concerns not the basis of the sovereign's right to exercise public authority but the duty of public justice that attends it.

The idea of the original contract is a compound of three technical terms. For Kant, a *contract* is a right to another's performance.[50] For contracts between private parties to be consistent with the freedom of each, the rights and duties that flow from the contract must be the product of an act evincing mutual consent.[51] However, in characterizing the contract between the state and the people subject to it as *original*, Kant signals that the people hold a right "directly on the basis of principle (*lege*), that is, without any special act being required to establish this right."[52] This original right "bind[s] every legislator to give his laws in such a way that they *could* have arisen from the united will of a whole people."[53] The final term in the compound is "idea," which Kant defines as a "concept of reason whose object can be met with nowhere in experience."[54] By referring to the original contract as an idea, Kant emphasizes that even though existing states do not fully conform to this principle, it nevertheless forms the relevant standard for "appraising any public rightful constitution."[55]

Kant's exposition of the idea of the original contract is obscure, even by his own formidable standards. While he frequently invokes the principle, he does not explicitly articulate its basis. In the Preface to Kant's most systematic work of legal and political philosophy, he explains that "[t]oward the end of the book I have worked less thoroughly over certain sections" because "they can be easily inferred from the earlier ones and partly too, because the later sections (dealing with public right) are currently subject to so much discussion, and still so important, that they can well justify postponing a decisive judgment for some time."[56] In what follows, I will explain how the idea of the original contract can be inferred from the justification of the postulate of public right.

For Kant, public authority solves one problem and raises another. In the absence of public institutions, every legal entity is a private person, and all juridical relationships have private persons as their parties. As we have seen, these relations generate a set of moral problems. The public institutions that comprise a legal system address these problems by supplanting unilateral lawgiving,

50. Ibid 6:271.

51. Ibid: "A right against a person can never be acquired originally and on one's own initiative."

52. Ibid 6:280; cf. 6:262.

53. Kant, "Theory and Practice" (n 24) 8:297.

54. Immanuel Kant, *Lectures on Logic* (J Michael Young ed, CUP 1992) 1:90; cf Kant, *Metaphysics of Morals* (n 11) 6:371: "Every actual deed (fact) is an object in *appearance* (to the senses). On the other hand, what can be represented only by pure reason and must be counted among *ideas*, to which no object given in experience can be adequate—and a perfectly *rightful constitution* among human beings is of this sort—is the thing in itself."

55. "Theory and Practice" (n 24) 8:302; Kant, *Metaphysics of Morals* (n 11) 6:372.

56. Kant, *Metaphysics of Morals* (n 11) 6:209.

interpretation, and force with public legislation, adjudication, and enforcement. While these institutions resolve a set of problems that are inescapable in the absence of legal order, these institutions also raise a problem that can arise only within a legal order, a problem that concerns the juridical relationship between rulers and ruled. Even if public institutions secure freedom between private persons, these institutions might themselves impose arbitrary constraints on the ruled, that is, constraints that legal order does not itself require.

The idea of the original contract is a principle holding that public authority must be arranged and exercised in a manner that adheres to its own justificatory logic. Since public authority is justified on the basis of the right of persons to equal freedom, Kant holds that internal to the justification of public authority is the moral standard for assessing its adequacy and directing its reform. A legal system conforms to the terms of its justification to the extent it "makes *freedom* the principle and indeed the condition for any exercise of coercion."[57] In turn, an exercise of public authority adheres to the terms of its justification to the extent that it is directed toward bringing the existing legal order into the deepest possible conformity with its own internal moral standard. Insofar as the right to rule presupposes the right of each person subject to it to freedom, government cannot deny the right of persons to freedom without thereby undermining the justificatory basis of its own authority. As Kant compactly puts the point, "apart from [the idea of the original contract] no right over a people can be thought."[58]

The idea of the original contract has procedural and substantive ramifications, which taken together demand the lawful transition to liberal democracy.[59]

For Kant, the relevance of democratic procedures turns on the standpoint from which they are considered. As a matter of the postulate of public right, whether the people are the authors of the law or merely subjected to them is a matter of indifference. Private persons must interact on the basis of common standards of conduct. Because no private person has standing to establish standards that bind others, a legislative authority is required. Such an authority can be arranged "in three different ways: either that one in the state has command over all; or that *several*, equal among themselves, are united in command over all the others; or that *all* together have command over each and so over themselves as well. In other words, the *form of a state* is either *autocratic, aristocratic,* or *democratic.*"[60] Each of these arrangements satisfies the postulate of public right by subjecting a plurality of private persons to a legislative authority. But from the standpoint of the idea of the original contract, democracy alone is adequate.[61] The three forms of a

57. Ibid 6:340.

58. Kant, "Toward Perpetual Peace" (n 33) 8:344.

59. Kant, *Metaphysics of Morals* (n 11) 6:341.

60. Ibid 6:338.

61. Here I depart from Simone Chambers, "Discourse and Democratic Practices" in Stephen K. White (ed), *The Cambridge Companion to Habermas* (CUP 1995) 236: "Kant, as we know, was no democrat in our modern sense. The sovereign's mandate to rule could be explained through the idea of a contract and therefore through consent, but there was no question of actual, universal,

state can be distinguished by the disposition of the people toward the legislative authority. In an autocracy, one person determines the laws by which all others are bound. In an aristocracy, legislative authority is exercised by an elite few. In a democracy, legislative authority is held by a self-governing people. Autocracy and aristocracy are problematic for the same reason. Both of these forms of lawgiving deny those who are subject to the law of the right to contribute to its enactment. Such a denial violates the idea of the original contract by imposing a constraint on freedom that legal order does not itself require. These forms of government therefore represent a gratuitous infringement of the freedom of persons subject to them. Of the three forms of state, democracy alone conforms to the idea of the original contract because the citizens subject to the law are also sovereign insofar as they exercise legislative authority over themselves.[62]

and renewable consent." My claim is that the idea of the original contract imposes a duty on the sovereign to create, maintain, and refine a democratic form of lawgiving. Hypothetical consent requires actual consent.

62. In holding that the idea of the original contract requires the adoption of a democratic mode of lawgiving, I offer an alternative interpretation to B Sharon Byrd and Joachim Hruschka, *Kant's Doctrine of Right: A Commentary* (CUP 2010) 186. Byrd and Hruschka rightly recognize that Kant's republican ideal is a democratic form of state rather than an autocratic or aristocratic form, but they also claim that the sovereign "may not change" the form of state. Their interpretation stems from a cryptic passage in which Kant issues seemingly incompatible claims. On the one hand, Kant holds that "if the existing constitution cannot well be reconciled with the idea of the original contract" then it must be possible, for the sovereign to change it." On the other, Kant continues that "this change cannot consist in a state's reorganizing itself from one of the three forms into another, as, for example, aristocrats agreeing to submit to autocracy or deciding to merge into a democracy, or the reverse, as if it rested on the sovereign's free choice and discretion which kind of constitution it would subject the people to. For even if the sovereign decided to transform itself into a democracy, it could still do the people a wrong, since the people itself could abhor such a constitution and find one of the other forms more to its advantage." Kant, *Metaphysics of Morals* (n 11) 6:340. Byrd and Hruschka emphasize the second quotation, and so deem the duty to reform articulated in the first as excluding the form of state. This interpretation is puzzling because it violates Kant's central tenet that right must never bend its knee before expediency by elevating considerations of advantage over the democratic order, which the idea of the original contract demands as a matter of right. I believe another interpretation is available that neither subordinates the idea of the original contract to considerations of expediency nor requires the sovereign to institute all required reforms at once. In "Toward Perpetual Peace" Kant acknowledges that a ruler is permitted to temporarily delay implementing requirements of right "lest implementing the law prematurely counteract its very purpose." Kant (n 33) 8:347. Perhaps the situation in which Kant describes fits this structure. For if the disposition of the people toward democracy means that the transition to such a form of lawgiving would imperil the state itself or undercut its approximation of the idea of the original contract, then perhaps the permissive law justifies the temporary delay of instituting the democratic processes that the idea of the original contract ultimately require. For an elaboration of what Kant calls permissible laws of public right, see Jacob Weinrib, "Permissive Laws and the Dynamism of Kantian Justice" (2014) 33 Law & Phil. 105. For the opposing view that permissive laws play no role in Kant's theory of public right, see Joachim Hruschka, "The Permissive Law of Practical Reason in Kant's *Metaphysics of Morals*" (2004) 23 Law & Phil. 45.

If we turn from the procedure in which legislative authority is exercised to the substance of the laws, we see that sovereigns have an overarching duty to transform the existing legal order from an aggregate of inherited customs and traditions into a system of equal freedom. This duty is incumbent on whoever exercises public authority, whether an autocrat, an aristocracy, or the citizens of a democracy. The sovereign must give laws to which each subject could, in keeping with the innate right to freedom, consent. Kant argues that this principle requires the sovereign to, *inter alia*, supplant the hereditary privileges of the nobility with equality of opportunity,[63] dismantle the supposedly perpetual estates of churches and knightly orders,[64] and introduce public provisions for the poor.[65] Kant's examples have an undeniably eighteenth century flavor, but his broader aim is to formulate the principle for distinguishing between arrangements that "may have crept into the machinery of government from older times" and those that reconcile public authority with the freedom of the private persons subject to it.[66]

The procedural and substantive branches of the idea of the original contract form a commitment to liberal democracy, in which the citizens act through democratic procedures to give themselves positive laws adequate to the innate right of each of its members. As Kant formulates his republican ideal: "Any true republic is and can only be a *system representing* the people, in order to protect its rights in its name, by all the citizens united and acting through their delegates (deputies)."[67]

The postulate of public right and the idea of the original contract form the principles of Kant's theory of sovereignty. These principles can be distinguished by (1) the aspect of sovereignty that they capture, (2) the parties to which they impart rights and duties, (3) the conditions under which these rights and duties are satisfied, (4) the condition under which each principle is applicable, and (5) the pathology that follows from their violation. Because the most prominent objections to Kant's theory of sovereignty reflect a failure to distinguish these principles, I take up each of these grounds in turn.

First, the postulate of public right and the idea of the original contract capture different aspects of sovereignty's nature. The postulate of public right is the *constitutive* principle of sovereignty because it enables instances of sovereignty to be identified. Sovereignty consists in the system of publicly authoritative institutions that enable private persons to interact with one another rightfully.

63. Kant, *Metaphysics of Morals* (n 11) 6:326–29; 6:369–70. For discussion, see Ripstein (n 14) 287–95.

64. Kant, *Metaphysics of Morals* (n 11) 6:324–25; 6:369–70.

65. Kant, *Metaphysics of Morals* (n 11) 6:326–27. For discussion, see Ripstein (n 14) 267–87; Ernest J. Weinrib, *Corrective Justice* (OUP 2013) 263–96.

66. Kant, *Metaphysics of Morals* (n 11) 6:329; cf. 340.

67. Ibid 6:341. For Kant's view on representative democracy, see "On a Supposed Right to Lie from Philanthropy" in *The Cambridge Edition of the Works of Immanuel Kant: Practical Philosophy* (first published 1977, 1996) 8:429.

The question of whether sovereignty is present in a particular place and time is answered by looking to the postulate. In contrast, the idea of the original contract forms the *regulative* principle of sovereignty. This principle sets out sovereignty's internal standard for assessing the moral adequacy of its instances and directing their reform.

Second, the postulate of public right and the idea of the original contract delineate the rights and duties of sovereign and subject. The postulate integrates the right of the sovereign to enact authoritative rules and the corresponding duty of private persons to interact in accordance with their strictures. The idea of the original contract recognizes that given the terms on which public authority is justified, subjects have a (non-coercive) right and the sovereign a corresponding duty to govern in a manner that reconciles the authority of the sovereignty with the freedom of subjects. Thus, subjects find themselves in different juridical situations than their sovereign. Whereas private persons have a right to a legal order in which they can direct their own means toward the lawful pursuit of their own self-chosen ends,[68] the sovereign's means come with their own end. All public authority must be directed toward the "final end of all public right,"[69] a legal order in which authority leaves the freedom of each person subject to it "undiminished."[70]

Third, these principles are satisfied by different kinds of arrangements. The postulate of public right is satisfied when private persons subject themselves to the governance of public institutions. The postulate calls for legal order without qualification or condition. In contrast, the idea of the original contract calls for legal order characterized by the reconciliation of the sovereign's authority and the subjects' freedom. A legal order is adequate to the extent that it conforms to this standard. Public authority is exercised adequately to the extent that it is directed toward bringing the legal order into the deepest possible conformity to its own internal standard of adequacy. No matter how defective a legal system might be, the duty that the idea of the original contract imposes on the sovereign remains the same.

Fourth, the principles of sovereignty have different conditions of application. The postulate of public right applies whenever private persons interact with one another regardless of whether they find themselves in a lawless condition or a rightful one. In the former, private persons must submit themselves to the publicly authoritative institutions that comprise a sovereign. In the latter, private persons must act in accordance with valid lawgiving. In contrast, because the idea of the original contract concerns the adequacy of the relationship between sovereign

68. Ibid 6:316.

69. Ibid 6:341.

70. Ibid 6:316. For an illuminating interpretation of this passage on non-instrumental grounds, see Ariel Zylberman, "The Public Form of Law: Kant on the Second-Personal Constitution of Freedom" (2016) 21 Kantian Rev. 101, 117.

and subject, the principle lacks its condition of application in circumstances where the parties to this relationship are not present.[71]

Although John Rawls's theory of justice is known for its Kantian inspiration,[72] his methodology departs fundamentally from Kant's. In developing justice as fairness, Rawls begins by looking to the special case of a liberal democracy committed to certain fundamental ideas, including that citizens are free and equal and that society is a fair system of social cooperation. He then draws on these commitments to formulate principles of justice that are appropriate for instances of the special case. Thus, his argument is structured as a conditional: if this society is an instance of the special case, then justice as fairness applies to it.[73] As for societies that are not instances of the special case, justice as fairness—as a theory of domestic justice—lack its condition of application.[74] In contrast, Kant's theory

71. The distinction between the constitutive the regulative aspects of sovereignty resolves a tension articulated by Elisabeth Ellis, *Kant's Politics: Provisional Theory for an Uncertain World* (Yale University Press, New Haven, CT 2005) 126–27: "Kant's view . . . of the relationship between the state of nature and the civil condition is obscure because he makes two different arguments simultaneously. In the first place, Kant argues for the requirement to exit the state of nature. . . . In the second place, Kant argues for a transition not merely to an orderly state but to republican governance, including not only common authority but also respect for human rights. . . . The two stories of the exit from the state of nature—one account of the duty to submit to some common authority, and one more purely Kantian account of the ideal republic—do not fit together very well." On the interpretation that I offer, the two stories fit together perfectly. Private persons have a duty to interact within a legal system. The question of what constitutes a legal system is answered by looking to sovereignty's constitutive principle, the postulate of public right. In contrast, those who exercise public authority have a duty to bring the existing legal order into the deepest possible conformity with the ideal of a true republic, as specified by sovereignty's regulative principle, the idea of the original contract. Insofar as these duties bind different parties, no contradiction arises from uniting them in a common scheme.

72. Dworkin, *Justice in Robes* (Harvard University Press, Cambridge, MA 2006) 261: "The work of philosophical icons is rich enough to allow appropriation through interpretation. Each of us has his or her own Immanuel Kant, and from now on we will struggle, each of us, for the benediction of John Rawls."

73. See, for example, John Rawls, *Justice as Fairness: A Restatement* (Harvard University Press, Cambridge, MA 2001), 39: "[J]ustice as fairness is framed for a democratic society. Its principles are meant to answer the question once we view a democratic society as a fair system of social cooperation between citizens regarded as free and equal, what principles are most appropriate to it. Alternatively: which principles are most appropriate for a democratic society that not only professes but wants to take seriously the idea that citizens are free and equal, and tries to realize that idea in its main institutions."

74. My claim that Rawls's theory of domestic justice applies only to societies that are instances of the special case is consistent with his discussion of decent hierarchical societies in the *Law of Peoples* (Harvard University Press, Cambridge, MA 1999). After all, the issue in that discussion is how liberal peoples should treat other (non-liberal) peoples, not how those non-liberal should treat their own members. Ibid 82. Rawls makes this point in different ways. In one passage, he notes that political liberalism's principles of justice are "for the basic structure of a liberal democratic society" and are not "fully general principles. They do not apply to all subjects: not to churches or universities, or even to "the basic structure of all societies." Ibid 85. In another

of justice has a broader reach. It applies to legal systems *as such* because it emerges from an account of what a legal system is. It is only once the justification of public authority comes into view that Kant presents the idea of the original contract as the "rational principle for appraising any public rightful constitution."[75] On this approach, the right of persons to just governance stems not from some contingent feature of a particular legal system, whether the commitments its people happen to endorse or the words that appear in a constitutional text. Rather, the right is implied by the justification of the public institutions that constitute a legal system. Every legal system must therefore adopt democratic modes of lawgiving and enact a system of positive law adequate to its free and equal inhabitants. Whereas Rawls's aim is to set out how a liberal democracy must govern itself, Kant also seeks to explain why any legal system must become a liberal democracy.

Fifth, the violation of the principles of sovereignty result in two distinct pathologies, barbarism and injustice. A barbarous arrangement violates sovereignty's constitutive principle by denying the capacity of some private persons to limit the conduct of others by virtue of their freedom.[76] This is the principle of sovereignty that was violated by the Spartans when they engaged in the wholesale slaughter of the Helots.[77] The same principle was violated by the Nazis even before they turned to exterminating their perceived enemies. For Nazism was rooted in the idea that certain persons lacked the capacity for rights and thus could neither impose duties on others nor be wronged by them. Accordingly, the rights of these persons—whether the innate right to one's own bodily integrity or acquired rights to property, contractual performance, or familial relations, could be violated with impunity.[78] As one Kantian observer of Nazi power remarked, those whom the Nazis target are "condemned to death unconditionally; for they are deprived, in principle, of any power at all to restrict the liberty of others in such a way that they could live among them."[79] Since public authority is that which secures the freedom of each private person in relation to every other, barbarous arrangements cannot be publicly authoritative. Whereas barbarism indicates the

passage Rawls emphasizes that "an original position argument for domestic justice is a liberal idea, and it does not apply to the domestic justice of a decent hierarchical regime." Ibid 70. As a decent hierarchical society is not an instance of the special case, the domestic theory of justice that Rawls develops is inapplicable to it. For a defense of the conditional character of Rawls's theory of domestic justice, see Burton Dreben, "On Rawls and Political Liberalism" in Samuel Freedom (ed), *The Cambridge Companion to Rawls* (CUP 2003) 328–29.

75. Kant, "Theory and Practice" (n 24) 8:302.

76. Ebbinghaus (n 36).

77. I am grateful to Ernest Weinrib for this example. On the slaughter of the Helots, see Victor Duruy, *History of Greece, and of the Greek People from the Earliest Times to the Roman Conquest* (Estes and Lauriat, Boston 1892) 449–50. *F3,*

78. On the Nazi disregard for private law, and withdrawal of private law protections, see, for example, Karl Loewenstein, "Law in the Third Reich" (1936) 45 Yale L.J. 779 and Stolleis (n 32) 51.

79. Ebbinghaus (n 36) 21.

absence of public authority, injustice presupposes that public authority is present. Injustice violates sovereignty's regulative principle by constraining the freedom of subjects in a manner that legal order does not itself require, that is, in a manner that cannot be justified with reference to securing the freedom of a plurality of persons under law. As we saw above, injustice might concern the process through which laws are given or the substance of those laws. An undemocratic procedure constrains the freedom of subjects by denying them the freedom to enact the laws by which they are bound. In turn, a law that "compels [subjects] to salute the governor's hat, or forbids them to sniff the perfume of violets' offends the same principle by imposing a constraint on freedom that is extraneous to legal order as such. Such arrangements are wrongful but they are not barbarous: they do "not annul anyone's capacity to limit other people's freedom by his own."[80] Because each pathology concerns the violation of a different principle, the pathologies are different in kind rather than merely extent.[81] As distinct pathologies, barbarism and injustice demand different remedies. Barbarism calls for public authority to supplant private violence. Injustice calls for an existing public authority to be reformed.

These pathologies cannot be combined. After all, what is barbarous cannot be publicly authoritative. And where public authority is absent, the idea of the original contract lacks its condition of application. For the idea of the original contract binds the sovereign in the exercise of public authority, but a barbarous condition is characterized by the absence of public authority and so too a sovereign. The same point can be put in terms of the principles of sovereignty: if the idea of the original contract is the regulative principle of sovereignty, then where sovereignty has not been constituted, the idea of the original contract is inapplicable. A barbarous regime might *differ* from the republic envisioned by the idea of the original contract, but a barbarous regime is not *deficient* in relation to that ideal.[82]

One might object that Kant's theory of justice is too abstract to engage with the concrete circumstances of existing legal systems. Versions of this objection arise in legal, political, and constitutional theory. Gustav Radbruch rejected the schools of natural law for failing to connect formal ideals of legality to the historical and sociological circumstances of existing societies.[83] Ronald Dworkin renounced

80. Ibid 20.

81. For the dominant view, that the difference between justice and barbarism is one of degree rather than kind, see Lon L Fuller, *The Morality of Law* (Yale University Press, New Haven, CT 1969) 122; Gustav Radbruch, "Statutory Lawlessness and Supra-statutory Law (1946)" (2006) 26 O.J.L.S. 1, 7: "The conflict between justice and legal certainty may well be resolved in this way: The positive law, secured by legislation and power takes precedence even when its content is unjust and fails to benefit the people, unless the conflict between statute and justice reaches such an intolerable degree that the statute, as 'flawed law,' must yield to justice."

82. For an opposing view, in which barbarism is conceived of as a violation of the postulate of public right *and* the idea of the original contract, see Ripstein (n 14) 339–40.

83. Gustav Radbruch, *Legal Philosophy* in Kurt Wilk (ed), *The Legal Philosophies of Lask, Radbruch, and Dabin* (Harvard University Press, Cambridge, MA 1950) 121.

the idea of an imagined people "writing social contracts on blank slates" because it failed to engage with the political contexts in which actual people strive for justice.[84] The same objection appears in Bruce Ackerman's constitutional theory:

> The modern [American] Constitution does not express a timeless philosophy of right revealed in the Declaration of Independence or some Herculean labor of philosophical reflection. It is the product of ongoing political struggle—generation after generation mobilizing itself to critique and reconstruct large chunks of the received constitutional understanding. The guiding image should be Neurath's Boat, not Kant's Critique. In the aftermath of Civil War, Americans ripped gaping holes in the traditional structure, replacing them with new planks that didn't fit the old design. The question was whether the ship would keep sailing during such a shattering reconstruction, not whether its overall design would survive a philosophy seminar . . .[85]

Ackerman's point is that a constitutional order that has evolved in response to a series of contingent episodes and crises cannot be elucidated through a timeless philosophic theory.[86] Thus, he envisions a dichotomy between broad theories that are incapable of engaging with particular constitutional orders and narrow theories that illuminate the contingencies of a particular constitutional order but that lack broader application. Ackerman's constitutional theory of the United States is an instance of the latter. But it shares a point of agreement with the more general projects of Radbruch and Dworkin: a theory that admits no particularity is incapable of illuminating anything particular.

Kant's framework is not vulnerable to this objection because it does not exclude particularity. On his view, sovereignty pivots on two principles, the postulate of public right and the idea of the original contract. Instead of introducing particularity, the idea of the original contract presupposes that particularity is already present. The idea provides the internal moral standard for critically assessing the totality of publicly authoritative arrangements, including constitutional norms, institutional structures, ordinary laws, and judicial doctrines. In contrast, the postulate of public right establishes that such arrangements can be

84. Ronald Dworkin, *Law's Empire* (Harvard University Press, Cambridge, MA 1986) 164.

85. Bruce Ackerman, "Rooted Cosmopolitanism" (1994) 104 Ethics 516, 520.

86. For elaboration see, Bruce Ackerman, *We the People* (Harvard University Press, Cambridge, MA 1991) 3: "[T]he study of the American Constitution is dominated by categories that owe more to European than to American experience. The result has been a peculiarly ahistorical kind of understanding. Because dominant theories have not been designed with American constitutional history in mind, they do not reveal its most distinctive features. Many of the most remarkable parts of the story are entirely ignored—since they would only embarrass European notions never designed to take them into account. To discover the Constitution, we must approach it without the assistance of guides imported from another time and place. Neither Aristotle nor Cicero, Montesquieu nor Locke, Harrington nor Hume, Kant nor Weber will provide the key."

publicly authoritative. By justifying the public authority of existing legal systems, the postulate introduces particularity that must be scrutinized in terms of its conformity to the idea of the original contract. The point of departure for the pursuit of a just society is not a blank slate but the contingent contours of a given society.

III. ANARCHISM AND QUIETISM

Debates about sovereignty often lurch between two poles. Those who uphold the idea of sovereignty appear to their critics as quietists eager to affirm the justice of whatever arrangements happen to issue from the sovereign's command. If the features of an existing legal system form the standard for assessing its moral adequacy, then no legal system can fail to be fully adequate. Alternately, those who reject the idea of sovereignty appear to their critics as anarchists who make conformity to morality the condition for the valid exercise of public authority. The result is that any arrangement tainted by injustice is incapable of imposing obligations.

In dismissing sovereignty as an "intrinsically" objectionable concept, the Catholic philosopher Jacques Maritain takes the latter approach.[87] For Maritain, the concept is dangerous because it elevates the ruler into a mortal god who serves as the arbiter of an individual's obligations, the "master of good and evil as well as life and death."[88] If the concept is accepted, then individuals might mistakenly perceive themselves to be bound by the ruler's demands, regardless of whether they conform to the unyielding dictates of morality. The problem that lies at the heart of sovereignty is the claim that law need not be moral to impose obligations.[89] Maritain's solution is to discard the concept of sovereignty by, on the one hand, denying that those who rule are insulated from the demands of morality and, on the other, maintaining that some decrees are too wicked to be obeyed. Although Maritain conceives of morality in terms of natural law, the same objection to sovereignty continues to be raised today under the guise of "universal values"[90] and "human rights."[91]

Maritain seems "serenely unaware" of the anarchic implications of his position.[92] By making the ruler's authority to enact legal obligations contingent on the conformity of those obligations to morality, Maritain renders the right to rule either

87. Jacques Maritain, "The Concept of Sovereignty" (1950) 44 Am. Pol. Sc. Rev. 343, 343 ("political philosophy must eliminate Sovereignty both as a word and as a concept").

88. Ibid 354.

89. Ibid.

90. Grimm (n 7) 123: "Human rights movements frequently view sovereignty as morally unacceptable because it places national interests above universal values."

91. W. Michael Reisman, "Sovereignty and Human Rights in Contemporary International Law" (1990) 84 AJIL 866, 876.

92. Gregory Vlastos, "Of Sovereignty in Church and State" (1953) 62 Phil. Rev. 561, 573 [reviewing Jacques Maritain, *Man and the State* (University of Chicago Press 1951)]. I offer a different exposition of Maritain's anarchism than Vlastos.

redundant or irrelevant. If conformity to morality is a condition of law's authority, then the right to rule is confined to echoing existing obligations and is therefore redundant. Alternately, if the ruler enacts a law that conflicts with morality, then that law fails to constrain conduct and is therefore irrelevant. The result in either case is that persons are bound not by common standards of conduct enacted by public institutions, but by the shifting vagaries of their own perceptions of morality. What Maritain offers is not a legal order guided by morality, but "the recipe for anarchy."[93]

Maritain offers a stark choice between the quietist theories of sovereignty that he rejects and the anarchist view that he advances. Each of these positions is problematic for both conceptual and contextual reasons. As a *conceptual* matter, each view does violence to one of the concepts that it touches. Quietism dissolves the concept of morality by bending it to fit the contours of the existing legal order. The result is that no legal system can fail to be a perfect expression of morality. Anarchism dissolves the concept of authority by confining its application to the domain of morality. The result is that no legal system can impose obligations on individuals that they would not otherwise have. As a *contextual* matter each of these views eschews one of the moments encompassed by the modern concept of sovereignty. In denying the right of states to rule, the anarchist rejects the structure of the post-Westphalian world. In denying that the right to rule might be exercised unjustly, the quietist rejects the postwar recognition of human rights as imposing obligations on public authorities. An adequate exposition of the modern concept of sovereignty must steer a middle course between the quietism that Maritain rightly rejects and the anarchism that his approach exhibits.

If critics of Kant's legal and political philosophy agree about one thing, it is that his theory of sovereignty collapses into one of these extremes. For example, the legal positivist Hans Kelsen described Kant as a quietist who held "that the positive law is simply the emanation of a natural or divine order or of a system of reason—the emanation of an absolutely 'right', just order."[94] If positive law is regarded as the instantiation of justice, then positive law cannot be criticized from that standpoint. More recently, this interpretation has been revived by the nonpositivist Robert Alexy[95] and, in turn, adopted by the natural lawyer

93. Michael Oakeshott, *On History and Other Essays* (Basil Blackwell, Oxford 1983) 160 (criticizing natural law theories that make conformity to *jus* the condition of the authority of *lex*).

94. Hans Kelsen, *An Introduction to the Problems of Legal Theory* (OUP 1997) 18; Kelsen, "The Natural-Law Doctrine before the Tribunal of Science" (1949) 2 W. Pol. Sci. Q. 481, 493.

95. Robert Alexy (n 30) 118: "One might think that [Kant's] argument for the necessity of positive law leads to the conclusion that the natural rights that are supposed to be secured by positive law are somehow incorporated into the basic norm. But that is not the case. Kant's basic norm is exclusively oriented to legal certainty and civic peace. While it confers validity on the positive law, the content of that law is of no more consequence to Kant's basic norm than to Kelsen's." Alexy supports his interpretation claim by drawing on Kant's rejection of the right to revolution and his description of the role of jurists. Neither of these discussions support Alexy's interpretation.

John Finnis.[96] Others have adopted the opposing view by describing Kant as an anarchist whose philosophy involves "an unacknowledged competition between morally grounded *human rights* and the *principle of sovereignty*."[97] On Jürgen Habermas's interpretation, Kant denies the sovereign's authority whenever its exercise conflicts with the demands of morality, as determined by the idea of the original contract.[98] The chasm that divides these interpretations is so vast that one wonders how they could stem from the same texts. But taken together they suggest that Kant's theory of sovereignty offers nothing more than "either the utter condemnation or unquestioning endorsement of existing legal and political relations."[99]

This chapter explains why Kant's theory of sovereignty is neither anarchist nor quietist. The rejection of these one-sided positions follows from the interrelationship between the principles that constitute and regulate a legal system.

Anarchism is the view that what is unjust cannot impose legal obligations. Kant's theory of sovereignty cannot be anarchist because the idea of the original contract forms the moral standard for assessing the adequacy of authoritative arrangements validated by the postulate of public right. Thus, in assessing the moral adequacy of such arrangements, their authoritative character is presupposed. Far from repeating

For Kant, the content of a legal norm is relevant in two senses. First, as I noted in Section I, Kant does not accept Kelsen's thesis that the legal norms may have any content whatsoever. Since public authority is that which secures the rights of private persons, norms that are incompatible with such security cannot be lawful. On this point, see note 33 and the discussion of barbarism in the accompanying text. Second, as I argued in Section II, the idea of the original contract forms the internal moral standard of all public authority. Kant can therefore say what Kelsen and other legal positivists cannot: a law or legal system might be defective on its own internal standard of moral adequacy.

Alexy's interpretation also relies on Kant's deflationary comments about jurists. Alexy quotes from passages in which Kant describes jurists as those who are familiar with the laws that have been institutionally enacted, the obligation that these laws impose on private persons, and the way in which these laws are to be applied to cases that arise in experience. Thus, Alexy concludes that Kant's theory concerns merely the validity of law rather than its justice. What Alexy overlooks is that Kant holds up the jurist not as a description of his own approach but as the label for an inadequate methodology. As Kant indicates in the *Metaphysics of Morals*, the jurist's approach is inadequate because it illuminates neither the authority to give law nor the universal criterion against which the adequacy of law may be assessed—the two central issues that Kant's principles of sovereignty address. Kant, *Metaphysics of Morals* (n 11) 6:229–30. For instances in which Kant heaps additional criticism upon the methodological shortcomings of mere jurists, see 6:236, 6:335, 6:345, 6:357; Kant, *The Conflict of the Faculties* (first published 1798, Mary Gregor tr, University of Nebraska Press, Lincoln 1992) 7:24–25; and "On a Supposed Right to Lie from Philanthropy" (n 67) 8:426.

96. Finnis (n 30).

97. Jürgen Habermas, *Between Facts and Norms: Contributions to a Discourse Theory of Law and Democracy* (MIT Press, Cambridge, MA 1999) 94.

98. Ibid 120–1.

99. Kimberly Hutchings, *Kant, Critique and Politics* (Routledge, New York 1996) 55.

the anarchist's claim that conformity to justice is the condition of the law's authority, Kant holds that the presence of public authority is the condition for assessing its justice. When persons look to the idea of the original contract to criticize existing laws and legal systems, what is at issue is not their authority but their adequacy.

The same principles that indicate why Kant's theory of sovereignty is not anarchist also indicate why it is not quietist. Quietism is the view that what imposes legal obligations cannot be unjust. Kant's theory cannot be quietist because the justification of the ruler's right to exercise public authority implicates a moral standard for its assessment. In Kant's terms, the idea of the original contract forms the standpoint for assessing the moral adequacy of any legal system, that is, of any arrangement that satisfies the postulate of public right. All public authority must be directed toward bringing the existing legal order into the deepest conformity with the idea of the original contract. As I argued in Section II, this duty stems not from some contingent feature of legal systems in a particular time or place, but is implied by the justification of a legal system's constitutive feature, the right of the sovereign to exercise public authority. Thus, Kant's theory offers a moral standpoint for criticizing existing legal systems and directing their reform.

Anarchism and quietism are the opposing products of a common error: the failure to distinguish between the constitutive and regulative principles of a legal system. Section I of this essay presented the constitutive principle of a legal system, the postulate of public right. A legal system consists in the set of publicly authoritative institutions that create the conditions under which private persons can interact with one another rightfully. Section II presented the idea of the original contract as the regulative principle of a legal system. This idea forms the standard for assessing whether a legal system is adequate on its own internal moral standard. The common confusion at the root of both anarchist and quietist theories consists in reducing a legal system to either its constitutive or its regulative principle. For the anarchist, the regulative principle swallows up the constitutive one: the standard for determining a law or legal system's adequacy is also the standard for determining its authority. The result is that wherever injustice enters, authority retreats. In turn, the quietist takes the constitutive principle of a legal system to also form its regulative principle. If the existing legal order is elevated into a standard for assessing its moral adequacy, then no authoritative arrangement can fail to be fully adequate. Public authority is thereby immunized from moral criticism. And as Bentham observed, "if nothing is ever to be found fault with, nothing will ever be mended."[100] Kant does not follow the anarchist and quietist method of collapsing the distinction between the constitutive and regulative principles of legal order. Instead, his theory of public right consists in a systematic exposition of the nature of and the relationship between these distinct principles.

The distinction between the constitutive and regulative principles of a legal system enables Kant to confront a problem that is invisible to both anarchists and quietists, that laws and legal systems may be authoritative even though they are unjust. This possibility reflects the dichotomy at the core of Kant's account of

100. Bentham (n 43) 10.

sovereignty. On the one hand, because arrangements that satisfy the postulate of public right are authoritative, no private person can refuse obedience to a law or to a legal system on the grounds that it deviates from its relevant regulative standard. As Kant maintains, even a constitution "afflicted with great defects and gross faults" and that stands in need of "important improvements" may not be resisted.[101] On the other, because the exercise of public authority is accompanied by a duty to bring the existing legal order into conformity with the idea of the original contract, arrangements that depart from this standard stand in need of reform:

> A moral politician will make it his principle that, once defects that could not have been prevented are found within the constitution of a state . . . it is a duty, especially for heads of state, to be concerned about how they can be improved as soon as possible and brought into conformity with natural right, which stands before us as a model in the idea of reason, even at the cost of sacrifices to their self-seeking inclinations.[102]

Neither an anarchist nor a quietist could write this passage. For an anarchist, that which is defective is not publicly authoritative and so could not form a part of a state's constitution. For a quietist, that which is publicly authoritative is not defective and therefore might be altered but cannot be reformed (or as Kant puts it, "improved"). By holding that the sovereign must bring the existing legal system into the deepest possible conformity with its own internal standard of moral adequacy, Kant's theory of sovereignty jointly departs from its anarchist and quietist counterparts.

IV. CONCLUSION

Kant's legal and political philosophy offers an integrated response to two questions about the nature of sovereignty: How is sovereignty possible? What is its purpose? In responding to each of these questions, Kant formulates a theory of sovereignty unified by the idea that each person has an innate right to freedom, which answers to nothing but its own systematic requirements. The result is a conception of sovereignty that offers two related advantages over its fragmented counterparts. First, in expounding both the possibility and purpose of sovereignty, Kant escapes the anarchism of those who conceive of justice as excluding sovereignty's possibility and the quietism of those who conceive of sovereignty as precluding considerations of justice. Second, by elucidating the public right and the public duty that comprise the office of sovereignty, Kant offers a conception that illuminates the components of sovereignty that animate contemporary legal and political practice.

101. Kant, *Metaphysics of Morals* (n 11) 6:372.

102. Kant, "Toward Perpetual Peace" (n 33) 8:372.

3

Sovereignty, Political Obligation, and Fairness

WILLIAM E. O'BRIAN JR.

In this chapter I propose to re-evaluate arguments for political obligation to the sovereign based on the Principle of Fairness. The predominant view among political theorists seems to reject the idea that citizens have obligations to obey the laws of their governments,[1] although there is a significant body of contrary opinion. I have long been sympathetic to the majority view, but have recently concluded that that this view is mistaken, at least as to most citizens of modern Western democracies. However, I conclude that those of us, among whom I number myself, of an essentially libertarian or anarchist persuasion have no such obligations. Along the way, I will also address the recent resurgence in Kantian arguments for political obligation, which I believe raise closely related issues and lead to similar results—political obligations for those who are broadly content with the status quo but not for those who prefer very different arrangements.

In his book *Force and Freedom,*[2] Arthur Ripstein has attempted both an exposition and a defense of Kant's approach to political philosophy, including his approach to political obligation. I will take Ripstein's account of the Kantian position as authoritative for my purposes, recognizing that there are undoubtedly places where other Kant scholars may have different readings; as my purpose is to arrive at a correct theory, not an exegesis of Kant.[3]

1. Classic accounts include A. J. Simmons, *Moral Principles and Political Obligations* (Princeton: Princeton University Press 1981), Leslie Green, *The Authority of the State* (Oxford: Clarendon Press 1990), and Joseph Raz, *The Authority of Law* (Oxford: Oxford University Press 2d ed. 2009). For a good summary of the arguments each way, see Christopher Heath Wellman and A. John Simmons, *Is There a Duty to Obey the Law?* (Cambridge: Cambridge University Press 2005).

2. Arthur Ripstein, *Force and Freedom* (Cambridge, Masachusetts: Harvard University Press 2009).

3. For one such account, see Jacob Weinrib, "Kant on the Right and Duty of Sovereignty," this volume.

Sovereignty and the New Executive Authority. Claire O. Finkelstein and Michael Skerker.

The central problem for Kant is this: How can one person's freedom (in the sense of independence from the constraint of the will of others) coexist with the similar freedom of others? For Kant the sovereign is the answer to this question: by subjecting us all to an omnilateral will (a will that speaks on behalf of all of us), it solves three problems that would otherwise not be solvable: the indeterminateness of each of our particular rights (in property at least), the lack of assurance that you will respect my rights if I respect yours, and the general impermissibility of my imposing duties on you unilaterally.

For Kant, the answer to the problem of political obligation flows directly from his account of what the sovereign does. Essentially, it is only in a state where my actions are governed by law that I can rightfully assert property and other rights that go beyond my basic right to bodily integrity. For Kant this is a conceptual matter, not a factual one; I cannot rightfully call an external object mine if there is no legal system that separates what is mine from yours. Because assertions of rights necessarily involve the possibility of coercion against those who do not accept them voluntarily, Kant argues that they are inconsistent with each person's right to be independent of coercion by others unless these rights are authorized by an omnilateral will.

This argument of Kant viewed in this way seems to be seriously overstated. For one thing, it entirely overlooks the possibility that property rights could be established and maintained by convention, along the lines of accounts by Hume, David Lewis,[4] and others. Animals seem to use similar conventions in their tendency to respect (within limits) each others' territories, and there are good evolutionary game theory explanations for why a tendency to do so might evolve and persist.[5] It is likely that even in the absence of a sovereign, most humans would observe a similar convention because it is overwhelmingly in their interests to do so.[6] Compliance with a convention that is in our mutual interests is not an objectionable imposition on the freedom of one person on another.

Of course in the absence of a sovereign, compliance with the rights of others is likely to be less than perfect, but it is also likely to be less than perfect even where states exist; at most the difference is likely to be one of degree, not of kind.[7] Assurance problems, of which Kant's argument is an example, do not provide us with a conceptual or categorical reason to think that we must agree to a state; at most they provide a relevant consideration, one that is subject to being outweighed by countervailing considerations. One obvious countervailing consideration is the familiar question of *quis custodiet ipsos custodes*: Is not the danger

4. David Lewis, *Convention: A Philosophical Study* (Oxford: Blackwell 1969). For a recent recasting of this argument, see Andrei Marmor, *Social Conventions* (Princeton, NJ: Princeton University Press 2009).

5. John Maynard Smith, *Evolution and the Theory of Games* (Cambridge: Cambridge University Press 1982).

6. See Robert Sugden, *The Economics of Rights, Cooperation and Welfare* (New York: Palgrave-MacMillan 2d ed. 2004).

7. See Victor Tadros, "Independence Without Interests?" (2011) 31 OJLS 193–213, 210–12.

that the sovereign itself will fail to protect our property, and will even confiscate it, enough to outweigh any marginal increase in the extent to which property rights are respected under the sovereign?

Similar considerations weigh against the remaining argument for the sovereign given by Kant, that it renders property rights that would otherwise be indeterminate more determinate. But again this is only a matter of degree, not of kind; it is quite likely that people could come by a conventional process to a reasonably determinate understanding of their rights, and also come to conventional methods of resolving disputes as to the exact scope of those rights peacefully when they arose. Kant's argument hardly shows that we cannot intelligibly speak of rights outside the state or that we must support a sovereign on pain of contradiction; at most they point to considerations that might favor a sovereign in some circumstances.

Kant's arguments do suggest, however, one difficulty for the familiar Lockean theory, sometimes relied on by philosophical anarchists,[8] that in a state of nature anyone may enforce the "law of nature" (a law we may assume is conventional for the benefit of those, like myself, who are deeply suspicious of concepts of "natural law" that are based on anything more). The difficulty is that unilateral enforcement by A against B of B's obligations amounts to a unilateral imposition of A's will on B if B disputes the existence of the obligation or its violation. In a recent paper[9] Ripstein hints at an argument that justifies the sovereign on this basis.

The difficulty is that this argument at most justifies a requirement of a neutral decision-maker to decide disputed issues of fact and possibly law, not necessarily the sovereign. Although one core function that states traditionally provide is that of adjudicating disputes over rights violations, there is no reason such a service cannot be provided privately.[10] Indeed this is a common shortcoming of most arguments that proponents of the state proffer: they simply assume that functions that are currently provided by states can only be provided by states, when in fact in many cases states have displaced private provision that worked better than the state provision that replaced it.[11]

These arguments are, I believe, decisive against any claim that the sovereign is categorically or conceptually necessary to making the use of coercion rightful. Of course by themselves they do not demonstrate that states are illegitimate either: even if states are not the only way something can be done, they could turn out to be better at what they do than the alternatives. Establishing this would however require a detailed examination of the costs and benefits of state provision

8. E.g., John Simmons, see Wellman & Simmons, note 1 above 192.

9. Arthur Ripstein, "Beyond the Harm Principle," (2006) 34 Phil. & Pub. Affairs 215–45.

10. See, e.g., Bruce Benson, *The Enterprise of Law: Justice without the State* (San Francisco: Pacific Research Institute 1990).

11. For a strong argument that this is true in the United Kingdom with respect to the welfare state, see James Bartholomew, *The Welfare State We're In* (London: Politico's 2004). For a similar argument with respect to the United States, see Daniel Shapiro, *Is the Welfare State Justified?* (Cambridge: Cambridge University Press 2007).

compared to the alternatives, something most theorists shy away from because it requires us to venture beyond our armchairs.

This defect is also characteristic of many non-categorical arguments for the duty to obey the law, such as those based on the Principle of Fairness. They argue that the sovereign provides important or even vital benefits that no reasonable person could not value, and from this conclude that we must therefore obey the laws of the state we happen to live in, usually with some qualifications along the lines of "the reasonably just laws of a reasonably just state." There are two clear problems with this strategy. First, it overlooks the very significant costs that come with states, costs that go well beyond taxes to include wars, prisons, police brutality, and inefficient or even disastrous regulation. Second, it largely ignores the existence of nonstate alternatives, alternatives that of course are not perfect either but that in many cases may be better than the sovereign.[12]

For example, most of us would no doubt agree that having a sovereign that prohibits murder is a good thing. Although we give up the "right" to commit murder, we gain far more from having other people prevented or deterred from killing us. This is true even though the law will invariably make mistakes and occasionally imprison people for murders they did not commit; the only way to avoid this would be to make it so difficult to obtain convictions that the law would be practically unenforceable and lose its deterrent value. But if we consider that a state that can prohibit murder may also enact things such as drug laws, which in the view of many, myself included, are both unjust and cause massively more suffering than they prevent,[13] it becomes far more debatable whether the costs exceed the benefits. Arguments that discuss only the benefits of government without adequately addressing the costs, as almost all arguments by political philosophers do, are massively deficient.

Or consider another example. Virtually everyone concedes that is very difficult to argue that there could be non-market provision of national defense,[14] and that therefore state provision of at least this good may be necessary. A principled pacifist (that is, one who opposes everyone using force in defense, as opposed to those

12. See generally Michael Huemer, *The Problem of Political Authority* (New York: Palgrave-MacMillan 2013); A. John Simmons, *On the Edge of Anarchy* (Princeton, NJ: Princeton University Press 1993); Alan Carter, "Presumptive Benefits and Political Obligation," (2001) J. Applied Phil. 229–43.

13. See, e.g. Peter MacWilliams, *Ain't Nobody's Business If You Do: The Absurdity of Consensual Crimes in a Free Society* (Los Angeles: Prelude Press 2003); Douglas Husak, *Legalize This! The Case for Decriminalising Drugs* (London: Verso 2002). On the general extent to which the criminal law has been massively overextended in the United States, see Harvey Silverglate, *Three Felonies a Day: How the Feds Target the Innocent* (New York: Encounter Books 2009) and Douglas Husak, *Overcriminalization* (Oxford: Oxford University Press 2008).

14. The individualist anarchist David Friedman refers to national defense as "the hard problem." See David Friedman, *The Machinery of Freedom: Guide to a Radical Capitalism* (Chicago: Open Court 2d ed. 1989) 135. He concludes that it might be impossible to abolish this function just yet, and that in that case a government providing national defense "would be like a gang of bandits who, while occasionally robbing the villages in their territory, served to keep off other and more rapacious gangs." Ibid. 143. This might give rise to obligations to the state for a limited time: if the choice is between being governed by Churchill or being governed by Hitler, as it was during

who simply prefer not to fight themselves)[15] might not even accept this, but let's set this possibility aside; it is arguable that such pacifists are in truth free riders on the willingness of others to confront wrongdoers with force, who would give up their beliefs (or be wiped out) if actually confronted with their very probable consequences. As George Orwell put it, "Those who 'abjure' violence can only do so because others are committing violence on their behalf."[16] It also seems difficult to dispute that the anarchist's typical methods of providing defense (roughly, a citizens' militia) would be less potent as a defensive force than a standing army with sophisticated weapons that might not be procurable without taxes. But once we remember that a state empowered to defend the country can also do things such as invade Iraq without cause, the outcome of the test might not be so obvious. Republicans, American founding fathers, and other theorists wrestled mightily for centuries with the issue of whether standing armies carried more risks than benefits. It seems clear to me that reasonable people could differ on this question.

More generally, very few anarchists oppose the state because they believe that the benefits provided by states are valueless; rather it is because they believe that the costs of states are very high, and that the alternatives are not as bad as is usually thought. Even if refusing to recognize the benefits provided by the sovereign would be by itself irrational, it is far from irrational to conclude that the costs outweigh the benefits. There is a large anarchist literature that does just this.[17]

Similar problems are presented by a recent attempt at justifying the state by Massimo Renzo.[18] He argues that those refusing to support the state undermine its ability to provide the coordination functions and similar functions relied on by Kant, and that this actually harms those who support the state. The analogy he draws is to passengers on a boat refusing to row to shore where their refusal means the remainder cannot reach the shore in time; this, he contends, constitutes harming the others, at least where the presence of the dissenters in the boat causes their failure to be able to reach shore with only some rowing. He might well be right in his hypothetical example, at least if one accepts his stipulation that those who want to require rowing are right that it is necessary. In a real case, the problem is that we will not know if the rowers are right at the time we have to decide.

World War II, we should of course choose to be governed by Churchill. But perhaps when the emergency is over we should return like Cincinnatus to our ploughs and abolish the sovereign.

15. Someone who objects to fighting in a war, but not to paying taxes to fund someone fighting in one's stead, is to my mind morally self-indulgent and inconsistent. If it is wrong to do something, it is every bit as wrong to pay someone else to do it. The theorist who saw this most clearly was Henry David Thoreau—see his "On the Duty of Civil Disobedience" in Henry David Thoreau, *Walden and Civil Disobedience* (New York: Harper & Row 1965) 257.

16. George Orwell, "Notes on Nationalism" in idem., *England Your England and Other Essays* (London: Sacker and Warburg 1953).

17. See the sources collected in notes 12 and 14 above and 41 below for recent examples. There is of course a large earlier anarchist literature as well.

18. Massimo Renzo, "State Legitimacy and Self Defence" (2011) 30 Law & Philosophy 575–601.

The difficulty with transferring Renzo's hypothetical boat example to the issue of duties to obey the law is the assumption that states are on balance beneficial, something most anarchists will deny. Although they might concede all the benefits that Renzo, like Kant, ascribes to state enforcement of a common set of rules, they would argue that these benefits are outweighed by the massive harms states inflict when they overstep the bounds[19] of these functions, as they inevitably do. One can of course stipulate that the anarchists are wrong about this, as Renzo seems to do, but then the argument simply begs the important questions.

The other problem this creates is that once we recognize that the argument for the state is a matter of balancing costs and benefits, rather than a conceptual or categorical matter, it is not only no longer a matter suitable for armchair theorizing, but it is also no longer reasonable to assume that the cost-benefit calculation will come out the same for everyone. Perhaps the state is justified for those who are conformists, or who are middle income, or whose desire to control the behavior of others is strong, but not for those who are rich (they could secure adequate protection for less than their likely share of the taxes) or poor (they are more likely to be the subject of an erroneous charge or conviction, or to lose their breadwinners to incarceration, or to have their crimes punished severely),[20] or nonconformist (they are more likely to have their deviant but harmless behavior criminalized). And if is justified for some of us but not all, by what right do those who are net beneficiaries of the state impose it on those who are not?[21]

Finally of course there is the possibility that alternative states to the one you happen to live in would be better than the state you are in. For example, even if the state as it exists, with its drug laws and other monstrosities, is narrowly better than any nonstate alternative, another state, one that did not have these defects, might be still better. Why am I obligated to support this state rather than a viable alternative that fares much better on a cost-benefit test? Must I (as a U.S. citizen) support the United States, with its defense budget equal to that of the next

19. Renzo concedes that his argument only justifies a minimal state. Ibid. 580.

20. See Jeffrey Reiman, *The Rich Get Richer and the Poor Get Prison: Ideology, Class and Criminal Justice* (Boston: Pearson 7th ed. 2004).

21. In a number of articles and books Christopher Wellman argues that we may have Samaritan duties to support the state even if it fails a cost-benefit test narrowly for us, due to the benefits it provides others. See Wellman and Simmons, note 1 above; C. Wellman, "Liberalism, Political Legitimacy and Samaritanism," (1996) 25 Phil. & Pub. Affairs 211–37 and "Toward a Liberal Theory of Political Obligation," (2001) 111 Ethics 735–59. Apart from the fact that I deny we have enforceable Samaritan duties, it is far from clear that these arguments would work if, as I suspect, those for whom the state fails a cost-benefit test tend to be worse off than most of those for whom it passes such a test, or if the state fails for some of us by a wide margin, since even under Wellman's theory we are not obligated to make large sacrifices for the benefit of others. The latter idea is the main point of George Klosko's criticism of Wellman—see G. Klosko, "Samaritanism and Political Obligation: A Response to Christopher Wellman's 'Liberal Theory of Political Obligation,'" (2003) 113 Ethics 835–40. But Wellman is right that for most of us, a cost-benefit test will not just consider the effects that states have on us personally, but also on those about whom we care, including in many cases strangers.

eight countries in the world combined,[22] and with troops in over 150 countries around the world,[23] if I would prefer to live in a state that provided defense in a manner similar to Switzerland? An argument that we must obey the state because it provides important benefits simply ignores these possibilities.

The final difficulty with Kant's theory as it stands relates to his idea of an omnilateral will. It seems to derive from Rousseau's idea of the general will, and his notion that in obeying the general will we are simply obeying ourselves and therefore lose none of our freedom.[24] The difficulties with this idea are familiar; in many, probably most, contexts people have dramatically different interests and values, and only a hopeless romantic could think that by subjecting ourselves to rule by a majority we remain as free as we were before.

Yet perhaps this last conclusion is too quick. All existing states provide services that in modern parlance at least purport to constitute "public goods," in addition to adjudicating disputes and promulgating rules necessary to make determinate and compossible our respective rights to independence from each other's wills. Kant's theory does not provide for public goods, and in many places he suggests that a legitimate government can only act to preserve freedom. This would seem to preclude government from acting to provide public goods, at least beyond those needed to preserve freedom.[25]

If this is correct, it serves to reduce and perhaps even eliminate the main source of conflict in interests and values that serve to undermine the possibility of a truly omnilateral will. This is because virtually all "public goods" do not benefit everyone, at least if the costs of providing them are considered. Rather, such goods generally benefit some and harm others; the most we can hope for is that the benefits outweigh the harms. To use the language of welfare economics, they are at best Kaldor-Hicks efficient, not Pareto efficient. Any goods that are truly Pareto efficient (i.e., benefit everyone more than they cost them) are presumably not a problem, since they will not generate a conflict of interest.

For some however this cure will be thought worse than the disease. It effectively limits the state to very minimal functions (although not as minimal as those espoused by libertarians such as Robert Nozick,[26] since at least according to Kant his theory does require the state to provide some support for those unable to meet

22. According to President Obama in his 2016 State of the Union address.

23. See https://en.wikipedia.org/wiki/United_States_military_deployments (visited October 6, 2016). This source will suffice for our purposes since the precise number is not important to the argument.

24. Jean-Jacques Rousseau, *The Social Contract* (Maurice Cranston, trans.) (Harmondsworth, UK: Penguin 1968) 60 (book I, chapter 6).

25. In *Force and Freedom*, note 2 above, 232–66, Ripstein discusses roads as an example of something that states provide that might be thought to be public goods but can also be rationalized on the basis of preserving freedom. I doubt that a very extensive system of roads can be justified in this way, but cannot discuss that issue in depth here.

26. Robert Nozick, *Anarchy, State and Utopia* (New York: Basic Books 1974).

their basic needs).[27] This is likely also true of other leading candidates at justifying duties to obey the state, however: Wellman admits that his theory can only justify a "night watchman" state,[28] and Klosko strains to use his theory to justify much beyond law enforcement, national defense, and possibly sufficient infrastructure such as roads to permit these functions to be carried out.[29] The truth is that states that go beyond minimal states are indeed very difficult to defend. Below I discuss whether and in what circumstances states can justifiably provide public goods.

One final difficulty with most existing theories of political obligation is their status quo bias. In his recent book *Political Obligations* George Klosko makes this explicit when he says that anarchist arguments are unacceptable if they would require us to make large changes from current ways of living,[30] but this requirement is implicit in much recent argument in the area. But of course this argument will not move those of an anarchist bent, who for the most part are not particularly happy with current arrangements and will not see their preservation as a sine qua non of an acceptable theory. It should come as no surprise that the state can be justified to those who are more or less happy with their country as it is; what is needed is a justification that can made good against those who would prefer to live under radically different arrangements.

I. THE PRINCIPLE OF FAIRNESS

The Principle of Fairness plays a key role in most current arguments for political obligation. For example it is the cornerstone of Klosko's theory, although he has recently admitted that it requires supplementation to yield anything remotely approaching states of the size and scope of present states. And Wellman's theory, which begins with a duty of Samaritanism, is also supplemented by the Principle of Fairness. It is thus important to see what work this Principle can and cannot do.

Although early versions of the Principle of Fairness required that one do one's part in any scheme in which others had sacrificed their own freedom of action, this proposal was subject to a devastating objection from Nozick,[31] as it would require us to participate in schemes from which we derive little or no benefit when compared to their costs, and would permit others to thrust obligations on

27. Ripstein, note 2 above, 270–86. I would dispute this conclusion, but cannot discuss it here. For my view of the distributive implications of Kant's theory, see William O'Brian, "Distributive Justice and the Sovereignty Principle." (2011) 31 OJLS 1–21.

28. Wellman (2001), note 21 above 758.

29. See George Klosko, *The Principle of Fairness and Political Obligation* (Savage, MD: Rowman & Littlefield 2d ed. 2004). In his later book *Political Obligations* (Oxford: Oxford University Press 2005), Klosko argues that the Principle of Fairness supplemented with other principles will support the activities of most modern states. I discuss below why I believe we should reject this argument.

30. Ibid., *Political Obligations* at 19–20.

31. Nozick, note 26 above, 90–95.

us. There have been various attempts to avoid this problem, the most prominent of which are by Richard Arneson[32] and Klosko.[33] They differ in detail, but both require that one do one's share in cooperative schemes for which the benefits exceed the costs to the person whose obligations are at issue. This requirement is sufficient to avoid Nozick's objection, as a person will not be subjected to a requirement that he participate in cooperative schemes where he prefers the nonexistence of the scheme to its existence given the costs to him of participating.

This will be clearer if we examine Nozick's own example: a scheme in which each person must spend one day a year doing a broadcast on a loudspeaker for his neighbors in exchange for being able to listen to the broadcasts of others the rest of the year. Nozick objects to being required to participate in this scheme merely because one cannot avoid hearing the broadcasts, and his objection is well-taken if he would prefer no broadcasts to a scheme of broadcasts with the requirement that he perform one day a year. But the objection is much less cogent if he would actually prefer the existence of the scheme, with his required participation, to the nonexistence of the scheme. It is hard to see a principled objection to required participation in the latter case. Requiring that benefits exceed costs for each participant seems to cure the objection; it amounts to nothing more than a fairly narrow version of the first form of Kant's Categorical Imperative.[34]

Simmons handles this issue by requiring that each participant accept the benefits of the scheme knowing that this involves paying the costs.[35] I agree with a recent suggestion by Massimo Renzo,[36] however, that for these purposes acceptance is best viewed as of evidentiary significance rather than a requirement of principle. If one freely accepts the benefits of the scheme knowing the costs that are required, one can be taken to have benefited to a sufficient extent. But what matters is that one has benefited sufficiently; acceptance effectively estops one from denying this. It may well be that absent acceptance one cannot safely assume that a reluctant participant is sufficiently benefited to justify coercing him,[37] but this will not preclude us from saying that anyone who does sufficiently benefit is obligated to pay the required costs.

32. Richard Arneson, "The Principle of Fairness and Free Rider Problems" (1982) 92 Ethics 616–33.

33. Note 29 above.

34. It is narrow because it only applies to actually existing schemes; it does not require one to act as one would prefer others to act if they are not actually so acting. The Principle thus avoids one of the main objections to Kant's Principle as he actually formulated it.

35. A. John Simmons, *Justification and Legitimacy* (Cambridge: Cambridge University Press 2001) 18–26.

36. Massimo Renzo, "Fairness, Self-Deception and Political Obligation" (2014) 169 Philosophical Studies 467–88.

37. Indeed, the law of restitution in common law countries normally includes a requirement of free acceptance of benefits for exactly this reason. See generally Peter Birks, *Unjust Enrichment* (Oxford: Clarendon Press 2d ed. 2005) 53–58.

Arneson and Klosko also include a requirement that costs be fairly distributed. My own proposal is that we incorporate this into the costs side of the equation: the Principle of Fairness requires us to bear only our fair share of the costs of the scheme. This prevents us from avoiding paying our own fair share of the costs of a scheme simply by questioning the fairness of the distribution of costs to others.

II. A NUMERICAL ILLUSTRATION

I believe a numerical illustration will clarify some of the above discussion. In using this illustration I am not arguing that all of the costs and benefits of states are susceptible to the sort of quantification I am using here. Rather I think the numbers clarify the issues. In some cases we will have to deal with costs and benefits that resist such quantification, but we can analyze them more clearly if we first examine cases where such problems do not cloud the issues.

Consider a group consisting of ten similarly situated people, each of whom can contribute to a common good at a cost of 5 units to himself. His doing so provides 1 unit of benefit to each of the group, including himself, or 10 units of total benefit. Each of them is thus better off if all of the others contribute, but would be even better off if they contribute and he does not, as he derives 9 units of benefit, without incurring the costs. Classical economic theory would predict that no one would contribute in these circumstances, as the costs outweigh the benefits for each individual although the benefits if all contribute clearly outweigh the costs.

In public good experiments this generally takes the form of the experimenter doubling the contributions that individuals make; thus an individual contributes $5 and the experimenter doubles it and distributes the pot among all participants, whether or not they contributed. Of course most real world "public goods" are not like this, but rather are more akin to the experimenter stealing half the contributions.[38] We might instead view the example as one where parties agree not to engage in actions whose costs clearly exceed their benefits. For example theft is usually a very negative sum game, with the value of goods stolen generally being far less to the thief than to the victim. Thus everyone benefits from a general agreement not to steal, although each person would be still better off if he were free to steal while others were obligated not to steal.

My version of the Principle of Fairness requires that you contribute in these circumstances, rather than free ride on the contributions of others. In general, it would require contribution whenever the practice of others contributing benefits you more than the costs of your own contribution. In the example, you benefit by 9 from the contributions of others, and contributing only costs you net 4, so you should contribute. But this requirement is not satisfied unless others are also contributing. You would have no duty to contribute to this scheme if others were not doing so, since you would not be benefiting from their contributions.

38. See Friedman, note 14 above.

What if some are contributing and not others? How general does compliance need to be for the Principle to apply? The answer is that there has to be sufficient compliance for the practice to be beneficial to you net of the costs to you. In my example this is true if 5 others are contributing; then you derive a benefit from the practice of 6 (including your own contribution) at a cost of 5. Accordingly, the Principle of Fairness tells you that you should comply if at least 5 others are complying, and not otherwise. But this result follows from the numbers I have used in my example; had I chosen different numbers a much higher or lower rate of compliance would be needed to trigger your own obligation. Of course nothing precludes you from contributing if fewer than 5 are doing so. You might do so because you value the benefits your contribution provides to others, or because you want to set an example for others with a view to getting a mutually beneficial scheme going. But doing so is not required by the Principle of Fairness as I have formulated it.

In my example the costs and benefits were stated in common units, so it was indisputable whether you benefited from the scheme: if everyone contributes you gain 10 units at a cost of 5 units, and can thus not complain about being obligated to comply. This does not necessarily mean you would not have a complaint if you were coerced to comply, as we would need to consider the costs of the coercion itself. In many real life examples of course the costs and benefits may not be so clearly commensurable: if compliance costs me 5 apples but I benefit to the extent of 10 oranges from the compliance of others, whether or not I am obligated depends upon how much I value apples and oranges. Even if most people would prefer 10 oranges to 5 apples, if I would not then I am not benefited by the scheme and have no obligation to contribute to it.

My example also involved benefits that accrued to each member of the group equally, but of course many situations might involve unequal benefit. To change the example, imagine that compliance costs me 5 units and benefits the 5 males of my group (including myself) by 2 units each but does not benefit the 5 females. Then it seems to me that I am still obligated to contribute if the remaining males do, as I benefit by 10 at a cost of 5. It should not matter to me how the benefits to others are distributed.[39] But in this example, the females have no obligation to contribute since they are not benefited.

Of course, most of us actually do value benefits to at least some other people, and a full account would need to take account of this fact. In the modified example in the previous paragraph, suppose each of the males is married to one of the females, and that spouses value benefits to their spouses as equal to benefits to themselves. In that case the females are obligated to contribute, as the benefits to them of the scheme now outweigh the costs. We would of course want to avoid double counting in any analysis we might do, but subject to that qualification

39. It is of course imaginable that I might be outraged at the failure of the scheme to benefit the females, so that the cost of that outrage outweighs the benefits to me personally. I will ignore this possibility in what follows. If it helps, imagine that the failure of the scheme to benefit the females is unavoidable—for example it prevents a disease that only males suffer from.

I can be obligated as a result of benefits accruing to others to the extent I value those benefits.

As thus reformulated, the Principle of Fairness is hard to quarrel with. If I agree that the goods my particular state provides are valuable, are worth their costs, and cannot be provided voluntarily, it seems highly unreasonable for me to refuse to pay my fair share of these costs. No theorist of whom I am aware defends a right to "free ride" in these circumstances. Indeed, a vague version of the Principle of Fairness may well be innate in humans, as it seems to underlie much of the basic cooperativeness observed in virtually all human societies, although I take no position on that disputed issue here.[40]

III. APPLICATION TO POLITICAL OBLIGATION

The difficulty, as Klosko recognizes, is that the Principle of Fairness is unlikely to justify much beyond the minimal state, and for some people perhaps not even that. For a sizeable group of people, most activities of modern states are probably not cost justified, especially when we include in the costs not just the taxes but the harms done by states. Those of us who object to state provision of these services do not assert a right to free ride on the efforts of others. Rather we typically assert that the services in question are either not worth their costs or could be provided without coercion by voluntary schemes.

Klosko tries to handle some of this by a notion of "presumptive benefit," which applies to services that are necessary for minimally decent lives. For such services, Klosko believes, people with differing valuations can be forced to go along unless they carry an onerous burden of justifying their own preferences. But anarchists reject the entire premise of this argument; they do not believe that states provide the conditions for minimally decent lives; indeed in many cases they would argue that states are the main obstacle to minimally decent lives for most people. Anarchists are not free riders; they want everyone to reject the state, and believe that we will all lead better lives if we do.[41]

Klosko and others who defend the state make only vague and conclusory efforts to address the arguments of those who oppose state provision. For the most part they ignore the manifold harms that states cause and downplay the viability of

40. On this see generally Samuel Bowles and Herbert Gintis, *A Cooperative Species* (Princeton, NJ: Princeton University Press 2011).

41. See Huemer, note 12 above. For a good recent example of an argument along these lines, which is polemical rather than theoretical, see Gary Chartier, *The Conscience of an Anarchist* (Apple Valley, CA: Cobden Press 2011). For shorter and more theoretical version of aspects of the same author's position, see G. Chartier, "In Defence of the Anarchist," (2009) 29 OJLS 115–38, and G. Chartier, "Enforcing the Law and Being a State," (2012) 31 Law & Philosophy 99–123 and his *Anarchy and Legal Order* (Cambridge: Cambridge University Press 2012). For an interesting journalistic treatment, see Dominic Frisby, *Life after the State* (London: Unbound 2013). For a recent argument that anarchy works better than many people think, see Peter Leeson, *Anarchy Unbound: Why Self-Governance Works Better than You Think* (Cambridge: Cambridge University Press 2014).

non-coercive alternatives.[42] And they also tend to assert that any scheme that effectively did provide the services in question would be tantamount to a state. They at most show that they themselves, and perhaps the majority of current state residents, will likely prefer state provision to its alternatives; they do not come close to showing that those with different preferences are irrational.

In effect then we have this situation: a majority of residents in a given area might prefer a state that provides a given package of services, with a minority preferring either a smaller state or no state. The Principle of Fairness cannot justify forcing the later to give in to the former. Only if they agreed that the state was on balance a good thing, but still refused to pay their share of the costs, would their refusal violate the Principle of Fairness. The minority do not have to justify their own preferences any more than the majority do.[43]

Klosko also argues that once a justified state is established based on the Principle of Fairness, its functions can be extended based on a Principle of Public Good, which apparently requires people to pay for state activities that are overall beneficial even if the benefits do not exceed the costs for the particular individual. Klosko provides no argument for this principle, however, beyond his own intuitions. It is hard to see what can possibly justify this new principle: Why should Smith feel any obligation at all to support a program that is not on balance beneficial to him merely because it provides benefits to others? Of course a utilitarian will not shrink from endorsing such a duty, but most of us are not utilitarians and accept no duty to sacrifice our own interests to benefit others. Why should anyone who is not a utilitarian accept Klosko's Public Good Principle?

The idea that may underlie it is this: even if I do not benefit from a particular state activity, I may benefit overall from a system that permits states to do things that benefit fewer than all. The benefits from the resulting package of programs overall may outweigh the overall costs of the package, even if there are many items within the package that I would prefer to do without. This possibility is real, and a suitable theory needs to accommodate it.[44] But Klosko's suggested principle is too broad; it might well be that for many persons even the total package is a bad deal.

42. For detailed factual discussion of both the harms that states cause and the viability of non-state provision, see Edward Stringham, ed. *Anarchy and the Law: the Political Economy of Choice* (New Brunswick, NJ: Transaction Publishers 2007). See also his *Private Governance: Creating Order in Economic and Social Life* (Oxford: Oxford University Press 2015).

43. To the extent that any justification is given for this majority preference, it appears to be based on the idea that someone with differing preferences must be acting in bad faith, pretending to have preferences he doesn't in order to avoid paying his fair share of the costs. Although bad faith is a real concern, the supposition that anyone whose preferences differ from those of the majority must be acting in bad faith is wholly unwarranted.

44. For a discussion along acceptable lines, see James Buchanan and Gordon Tullock, *The Calculus of Consent* (Ann Arbor: University of Michigan Press 1962). What the authors require is unanimous consent to a constitution that permits subsequent decisions to be made on less than a unanimous basis. However, there is no supposition that subsequent decisions can be made by simple majority, and indeed good reason to think that much more than simple majority voting should be required before the government funds putative public goods.

If so, there is no reason they should be compelled to participate merely because others are benefited by the package, any more than they can be compelled to support a single state program merely because others benefit.

Reasonable people considering these problems in advance of an actual dispute[45] would probably reason as follows. Ideally we would never coerce anyone to contribute to a cooperative scheme where he disagreed in good faith that the scheme provided benefits worth its total costs. However, giving effect to this idea might in practice lead to people either falsifying their preferences to enable them to free ride, or perhaps even deluding themselves into so thinking (my own view is that sincere pacifists suffer from this sort of self-deception).[46] This would in turn lead to one of two results: either the dissenters are sufficiently numerous as to prevent the scheme from operating at all, in which case the majority lose the benefits of the scheme, or they are not, in which case the scheme is implemented but some unfairly avoid paying their share.

Now I think reasonable people would not be overly concerned about the second case: although it may be unfortunate that some get to benefit without paying the costs, it is hard to see how that outweighs the harm resulting from being forced to support a scheme that one rejects. Indeed by limiting their principles to presumptively beneficial goods, fairness theorists such as Klosko and Arneson implicitly accept this, since they don't think the existence of free riding on benefits such as attractive lawns justifies coercion. But even if a good is presumptively beneficial, if it is in fact provided then the fact that some get the good for free is morally inconsequential; indeed except for the amounts involved it is no different.

But the first case, where free riding prevents the good from being supplied at all, presents a serious challenge, since tolerating the dissenters precludes the majority from concluding a scheme that they sincerely believe is beneficial. A rational person, in considering the rules that should be applied to resolve disputes of this kind, would need to balance the costs of losing the benefits of justified (from his perspective)[47] schemes against the costs of being forced to contribute to unjustified (from his perspective) schemes. But if the primary legitimate concern

45. This idea bears a superficial resemblance to a Rawlsian "veil of ignorance," but the parallels should not be overemphasized. I am speaking of actual people who know their values and preferences as well as their talents and abilities, but who recognize that as they go through life they will encounter various occasions where they differ from their fellows on issues and need to derive reasonable ways of resolving such differences. This does not begin to justify imposing on them a requirement to behave as they would behind a much thicker Rawlsian "veil of ignorance"; I see no reason at all why people should pay any attention to what people in the latter situation would choose.

46. On self-deception as the best way to successfully deceive others, see Robert Trivers, *Deceit and Self-Deception: Fooling Yourself the Better to Fool Others* (London: Allen Lane 2011).

47. Nothing I say here is premised on any idea that there is a right answer to disputes of this sort. Indeed, as a value subjectivist I am inclined to doubt that there is any such thing as a right answer to disputes over whether a given public scheme is justified or not; it is likely to hinge on disagreements about value that are not reasonably resolvable. But nothing I say depends on that assumption either.

addressed by the Principle of Fairness is situations where free riding would prevent the good in question from being supplied at all, the rationale for using coercion is dramatically undercut by two facts.

To begin with, despite the economic arguments urged by Klosko and Arneson that people will not contribute to public goods where free riding is possible, empirical research shows that in fact people do contribute to public goods even where they cannot be forced to do so. The literature on this is large and growing.[48] One cannot therefore simply assert an argument that such goods will not be provided, invoking homo economicus type arguments, in the face of clear evidence that people do not in fact behave *like* homo economicus in such situations.

Second, to the extent the problem is that the goods will not be provided or will be provided in insufficient amounts, the problem is solvable by assurance contracts. Under this type of contract, people agree to contribute if enough others also do so, thus avoiding the problem of wasted contributions. If enough people are willing to support the good in question if others do so, an assurance scheme can provide the good without coercing those who do not want the good.[49]

Defenders of democracy are likely to point to majority rule as a suitable method, but Buchanan and Tullock's arguments refute such a simplistic approach. A rational person would instead weigh how often he is likely to be on either side of this issue and also the magnitude of the costs of being wrong in either direction. After all there are many wasteful, misguided, exploitative, and unfair cooperative schemes out there. There are arguments strongly suggesting that reasonable people would require something more than a majority, but less than unanimity, before allowing dissenters to be coerced to participate.

For example, suppose we had a rule that said "we will fund public goods if and only if 75 percent of people support the scheme." I might reason that in the long run I will gain more from the benefits of the schemes that are thus funded when I am in the majority than I will lose from those schemes where I am in the minority who prefer the nonexistence of the scheme. If so I should support the 75 percent rule, even though I know that it will occasionally work to my disadvantage.

The problem with an argument of this sort is that it only moves the disagreement back a stage. We may not only disagree about whether a particular scheme is justified, but we may also have widely differing views about the proper general balance of costs and benefits that might flow from differing views. My own position, for example, is informed by the public choice literature, which strongly suggests that most so-called public goods are really public bads and that therefore stringent barriers should be put in place before such schemes are implemented.[50]

48. A good summary is in Rachel Croson, "Public Goods Experiments" in Steven Durlauf and Lawrence Blume, eds, *Behavioural and Experimental Economics* (New York: Palgrave-MacMillan 2010). See also Bowles and Gintis, note 40 above.

49. On assurance contracts as a solution to public goods problems, see David Schmidtz, *The Limits of Government: An Essay on the Public Goods Argument* (Boulder, CO: Westview Press 1991).

50. For a short introduction to this literature see Gordon Tullock, Arthur Seldon, and Gordon Brady, *Government Failure: A Primer in Public Choice* (Washington, DC: Cato Institute 2002).

Others are much more sanguine about the public sector and much more troubled by the consequences of failure to implement alleged public benefits. We would undoubtedly want to draw the line at dramatically different points on the spectrum.

Of course, reasonable people recognize that there needs to be some give and take in such matters. If some for example would favor a cutoff of 75 percent while others would favor 80 percent, neither side is likely to want to come to blows over such a small difference.[51] But what if the majority want an agreement that funds public schemes supported by any majority, but I would prefer no public provision at all to the bloated public sector that such a mechanism is likely to create. Must I give way? I see no argument as to why I must.

The other argument that might be used to justify such a requirement is that if a majority benefit from a state that goes beyond the activities of a minimum state, the minority who would not benefit from the additional state functions cannot reasonably ask the majority to restrict their activities to accommodate their minority preference. But it is hard to see how this argument justifies compelling the minority to participate in functions that are not to their benefit. Why can't a minimal state be established that includes everyone, and a state consisting of less than everyone that provides more extensive benefits for those who think the latter are worth their costs?

For example, assume an island of 100 inhabitants, 40 of whom would prefer a minimal state that only resolved disputes and defended the islanders against external threats, and 60 of whom would prefer a more extensive state. Why must all 100 residents be part of the more extensive state? Why not one state to which all belong that performs the functions all agree to, and a "substate" whose membership is limited to those who want the additional benefits the minority reject? Klosko's argument only works if we tacitly assume that the minority are in bad faith: what they really want is the benefit of the larger state without the costs. But that is just wrong and arrogant too: those of us who want a smaller state really do think life would be much better without the added state functions. You can disagree with us because your preferences differ, but do not question our good faith.

Statists such as Klosko and Arneson also maintain that in some circumstances one could justify imposing the state on people who disagree with its existence on unreasonable grounds. The example Arneson uses is of someone who refuses to pay taxes because he believes the services do not cost anything but rather fall like manna from heaven.[52] That might be right as to persons whose opposition

For a more detailed treatment, see Randy Simmons, *Beyond Politics: The Roots of Government Failure* (Oakland, CA: Independent Institute 2011). For a good overview of public choice generally, see Dennis C. Mueller, *Public Choice III* (Cambridge: Cambridge University Press 2003).

51. This is very similar to Gerald Gaus's Justificatory Liberalism. For the most recent exposition of this, see Gerald Gaus, *The Order of Public Reason* (Cambridge: Cambridge University Press 2011); for a shorter version, see his "On Two Critics of Justificatory Liberalism," (2010) 9 Politics, Phil. & Econ. 177–212. The general idea is that if I agree that something must be decided by a group, I should agree to a reasonable procedure for arriving at such a group decision, but this does not apply if I do not agree that it is a matter for group decision at all.

52. Arneson, note 32 above 213.

to the state is based on straightforwardly false views about factual matters, as in Arneson's example. But the disagreements between anarchists and statists are rarely so straightforward. My own sense is that the disagreements are mainly about values, with anarchists placing a much higher value on freedom. But they are also about matters of counterfactuals: anarchists' views about how things would be factually in the absence of the state differ dramatically from the views of statists. I do not see how one side can legitimately be forced to give way on such a dispute.

For most people, who prefer the existence of the sovereign, with all of its costs and benefits, to its nonexistence, the Principle of Fairness obligates them to do their part in support, which includes at least a prima facie duty of obedience to the sovereign's law. The argument for this is straightforward—if I expect and demand that other people obey even those laws they disagree with, I therefore must do the same. If I gain more from other people acting in compliance with this principle than I lose by complying with it myself, the Principle of Fairness requires my obedience.[53] On this account, political obligations are essentially owed to other citizens, and not to the sovereign itself. But the obligations are, nonetheless, real.[54]

In short, the Principle of Fairness at most requires us to pay our fair share of the costs of schemes we support. It cannot begin to justify requiring us to support schemes we would prefer did not exist. It might be inconsistent with the positions of a few philosophical anarchists who, one senses, actually do prefer the existence of states that perform roughly the functions that most liberal states do, but want to deny that we owe duties of obedience to such states.[55] But it in no way threatens the position of genuine anarchists who would prefer the nonexistence of such states, or of those who would prefer much smaller states. Imposing Leviathan states on the latter is, quite simply, naked aggression and nothing more.

IV. CONCLUSION

While fairness arguments such as those of Klosko and Renzo arguably do show that the sovereign is justified for most people in modern liberal states, and arguably that they therefore have political obligations, they do not show that the sovereign is justified to those who sincerely believe that, as to them, the costs of

53. Although the Principle of Fairness does not require that I pay for or otherwise reciprocate every minor benefit someone bestows on me that I value at more than its cost, Klosko's arguments that the benefits of the sovereign are relevantly different because more important is hard to argue with if its factual predicate is sound. Klosko note 29 above. My argument is that for some, it is not sound, but this does not undermine his argument's validity for those for whom it is sound.

54. For a similar idea, see Gaus, note 51 above 460–70.

55. This seems to be the position of the leading modern exponent of philosophical anarchism, John Simmons—see his "Justification and Legitimacy" in his book of the same name, note 35 above. As the discussion above should make clear, I disagree with Simmons on this. It seems clear to me that if I prefer the existence of the sovereign to his nonexistence, then I am obligated to do my part to support the sovereign, and that a prima facie duty of obedience is part of that duty.

the sovereign outweigh the benefits. The next question is then, so what? Nothing I have said entails that the sovereign may not, therefore, coerce them. To show that, I would need to establish that the sovereign is precluded from coercing those who do not have political obligations, and I have not even tried to show that. Perhaps the answer is that as to such persons, their relationship is one of blameless freedom: the sovereign is free to coerce them, and they are free to resist if they can.

This last possibility is consistent with a number of "realist" approaches to political theory, the most plausible of which is the one argued by Bernard Williams in his mainly posthumous writings, for the most part collected in his *In the Beginning Was the Deed*.[56] Under this approach it may be enough that the sovereign is accepted by the large majority of citizens and the remainder are coerced, at least if the coercion is enough to induce reasonable levels of compliance.[57] Most anarchists are not bomb throwers, and many will frankly concede that although the sovereign is unjustified and not owed allegiance, actively working to overthrow it would do more harm than good.[58] This may be all we can hope for.

Nonetheless, those who, like myself, take seriously the obligation to respect the freedom of others, and indeed are inclined to affirm that everyone is entitled to his or her own personal sovereignty of the sort advocated by Mill in *On Liberty*,[59] will not be satisfied to stop there.[60] Discussing how to reconcile sovereign authority with individual freedom is the subject of a book I am working on, but is likely to involve a consent theory of political obligation that requires the sovereign to provide robust exit rights, including a territory, for opt-outs.[61] Only then can the sovereign live up to its claims to rightfully impose obligations on all of its citizens.

56. Bernard Williams, *In the Beginning Was the Deed: Realism and Moralism in Political Argument* (Princeton, NJ: Princeton University Press 2005). For an excellent recent summary of Williams's position, see Edward Hall, "Bernard Williams and the Basic Legitimation Demand: A Defence" (2015) 63 Political Studies 466–80.

57. See Mark Philip, "Realism without Illusions" (2012) 40 Political Theory 629–49 at 634.

58. See, e.g., Friedman, note 14 above, 149–51 ("Revolution *Is* the Hell of It").

59. John Stuart Mill, *On Liberty* (Arlington Heights, IL: Crofts Classics 1947).

60. For my own views, see my "Sovereignty and Freedom," unpublished paper available from the author, and O'Brian, note 27 above, where I defend what I call the Reciprocal Sovereignty Principle.

61. For a relatively undeveloped suggestion along these lines, see Harry Beran, *The Consent Theory of Political Obligation* (London: Croom Helm 1987).

PART TWO

Sovereignty in the Present Age

Modern Executive Authority in a Constitutional Democracy

4

Defining and Constraining the Sovereign

"The Most Difficult of All Tasks"

CHARLES FRIED*

> *Thus while man may try as he will, it is hard to see how he can obtain for public justice a supreme authority which would itself be just, whether he seeks this authority in a single person or in a group of many persons selected for this purpose. . . . [This] highest authority has to be just in itself and yet also a man. This is therefore the most difficult of all tasks, and a perfect solution is impossible. Nothing straight can be constructed from such warped wood as that which man is made of.*[1]

* This essay grows out of the inaugural lecture delivered in May 2017 at the Surrey Centre of Law and Philosophy at the University of Surrey Law School. I am grateful to the participants in the discussion following the lecture for their reactions, and particularly to Marie Newhouse, who organized the event and invited me to deliver the lecture. I also presented an early version at a faculty workshop at the Harvard Law School, where I received many useful suggestions. I am particularly grateful to Professor Richard Tuck of the Harvard Government Department, who allowed me to attend his course on Kant's political philosophy in the spring of 2017. I learned a great deal from him and from the students in the course. My knowledge of and thinking about the framing of the U.S. Constitution were immeasurably enriched by Michael Klarman's THE FRAMERS' COUP: THE MAKING OF THE UNITED STATES CONSTITUTION (Oxford University Press, 2016), of which I was invited to do an extensive review that appeared in the *Michigan Law Review* (April, 2018, vol. 116, 981). Thanks to my colleagues Richard Fallon, Michael Klarman, and John Goldberg who commented on early drafts. Samantha Miller of the Harvard Law School class 2019 provided invaluable research assistance.

1. Immanuel Kant, Political Writings, ed. Hans Reiss, second enlarged edition, transl. H.B. Nisbet (Cambridge University Press, 1991), 41.

Sovereignty and the New Executive Authority. Claire O. Finkelstein and Michael Skerker.

In the 1780s and 1790s, Immanuel Kant was struggling with the two most difficult problems of sovereignty: how to submit the person(s) who embody sovereignty to the rule of law, and how to assign the attributes of sovereignty in the government of large nation states. So were the framers of our constitution. Though the framers came up with, to use Kant's phrase, "no completely straight thing," they did a remarkably good job on both counts and came up with solutions that have endured and have instructed constitution builders from their time to ours.

I. NO COMPLETELY STRAIGHT THING

The Crooked Timber of Humanity is the title Isaiah Berlin chose for one of his collections of essays. This was a constant theme of his and it was intended to hint at the fact that idealism and utopian thought tend to come a cropper in surprising, unexpected ways. Although Berlin's message overall was brilliant and engaging—Berlin was a famously brilliant raconteur, one of the best in the country of raconteurs—it was pessimistic.[2]

Berlin had come on the phrase in a lecture at Oxford by the eminent historian R.G. Collingwood.[3] Collingwood in turn was quoting and translating from Immanuel Kant's 1784 *Idea of a Universal History with a Cosmopolitan Purpose.*[4] It is a short, lucid essay by that greatest of philosophers. In it Kant said the highest purpose of nature, which is the development of all the capacities that can be achieved by mankind, is attainable only in society, and more specifically in the society with the greatest freedom. And here I quote in full from a recent translation of the crucial passage:

> *This problem is both the most difficult and the last to be solved by the human race.* The difficulty (which the very idea of this problem clearly presents) is this:—if he lives amongst others of his own species, *man is an animal who needs a master.* For he certainly abuses his freedom in relation to others of his own kind. And even although, as a rational creature, he desires a law to impose limits on the freedom of all, he is still misled by his self-seeking

2. See generally JOSEPH MALI ET. AL., ISAIAH BERLIN'S COUNTER-ENLIGHTENMENT, ed. Joseph Mali and Robert Wokler (Transactions of the American Philosophical Society, 2003). The editors point out that Berlin's perspective might have been influenced by the times; during the Cold-War era Berlin and his readers "had come to mistrust the great metanarratives of modernity and to believe that both Eastern and Western utopian schemes of social regeneration had proven a sham." Id. at viii.

3. See Henry Hardy, Editor's Preface, in ISAIAH BERLIN, THE CROOKED TIMBER OF HUMANITY: CHAPTERS IN THE HISTORY OF IDEAS (Princeton: Princeton University Press, 2013), xxii–xxiii. Hardy writes that a similar phrase appears ("Out of the cross-grained timber of human nature nothing quite straight can be made") in Collingswood's unpublished papers, which seem to be notes from a lecture delivered in 1929. Hardy posits that "[i]t seems likely that Isaiah Berlin attended the lecture and was struck by this passage, which then matured in his memory." Id. at xxiii.

4. KANT, *supra* note 1, AT 41.

> animal inclinations into exempting himself from the law where he can. He thus requires a *master* to break his self-will and force him to obey a universally valid will under which everyone can be free. But where is he to find this master? Nowhere else but in the human species. But this master will also be an animal that needs a master. Thus while man may try as he will, it is hard to see how he can obtain for public justice a supreme authority which would itself be just, whether he seeks this authority in a single person or in a group of many persons selected for this purpose. . . . [This] highest authority has to be just *in itself* and yet also a *man*. This is therefore the most difficult of all tasks, and a perfect solution is impossible. Nothing straight can be constructed from such warped wood as that which man is made of. Nature only requires of us that we should approximate to this idea. . . .[5]

Now, you can see how Berlin's disposition might seize upon this as the motto of his whole work, a phrase of which he rendered "out of the crooked timber of humanity no straight thing can be made." Except Berlin mistranslated this phrase. The phrase in Kant's German original is:

> Aus so krummen Holz, als woraus der Mensch gemacht ist, kann kein ganz Gerades gezimmert werden.[6]

The literal translation of Kant's phrase is "for from such crooked timber as man is made nothing completely straight can be built."[7] And this is at the conclusion of Kant's account of the perennial problem of authority. *Sed quis custodiet ipsos custodes?* But who shall guard these guardians?[8]

No *completely* straight thing can be built out of the crooked timber of humanity. The emphasis is on the adverb, not on the adjective.

Justice and reason require that a free and rational person obey only such laws as he sets himself.[9] But such laws are those which all reasonable persons must acknowledge apply to, limit, and control their actions: human beings must have the greatest freedom compatible with a like freedom for all.[10] A just republic is one in which the laws accord with this overarching principle. But Kant recognized over and over again, persons are not perfect. They have perverse and evil inclinations, and force may be applied to them in order to assure that in their behavior to each other they comply with laws that embody this universal principle. But given

5. Id. at 46–47.

6. IDEE ZU EINER ALLGEMEINEN GESCHICHTE IN IN WELTBÜRGERLICHER ABSICHT—PROJEKT GUTENBERG-DE

7. The translation is mine.

8. See Juvenal, Satire VI, lines 347–348.

9. See KANT, METAPHYSICAL ELEMENTS OF JUSTICE, transl. John Ladd (Library of Liberal Arts, 1797, 1965), 76–81.

10. Id. at 35.

the crooked timber of humanity, this requires not only a lawgiver but an executive, a sovereign, who will use force as necessary to assure compliance with such constraining laws. And that is where the conundrum of the crooked timber comes in.

You can see that Kant was much troubled by this antinomy; who would not be? He did, at many places, reach for a solution. It was a solution not in terms of what we must do, but in terms of what we can hope. He writes in many places of the system of nature, and that nature has designed human beings so that in the end, maybe the very distant end, everything will come out all right.[11] Nature tends toward perfection. This is a hope I will come back to at the end of this essay.

Looking at existing regimes in some of which (perhaps that of his patron Frederick the Great[12]) he saw the possibility of a certain approximation to the principle of right: that human beings must have the greatest freedom compatible with a like freedom for all—approximation only, because out of such crooked timber no completely straight thing can be made. Indeed, he tended to make a virtue out of necessity. Speaking of man's unsociable sociability, he saw in the disposition to struggle, to contest, and even to violate the norms of reason a source of some value. Out of struggle come novelty, distinctness, and better ideas. In one sense one might see here an anticipation, a more benign anticipation, of Heidegger's concept of *Auseinandersetzung*,[13] the opposition of struggling nations and cultures out of whose differences the richness of human possibility emerges.

But this benign, somewhat whiggish, notion of perfectibility is at its most troublesome in the international arena. And it is international relations that Kant addressed in the essay *Idea of a Universal History with a Cosmopolitan Purpose*.[14] In that essay he seems to look forward to a regime of international harmony because indeed he viewed war as an abomination, a manifestation of our animal nature, and he is reluctant to admit an analysis that seems to make war final and inevitable.[15] Kant seems to suggest a tendency toward a superstate, a state like the ordinary states that we know, except consolidated into one state.[16] But it may be that the crooked timber analogy indicates that especially this is a much more remote, perhaps even unattainable goal, even under the benign guidance of nature.

11. See, e.g., Kant, *Perpetual Peace: A Philosophical Sketch*, in POLITICAL WRITINGS, *supra* note 1, at 130.

12. See id. at 101.

13. See GREGORY FRIED, HEIDEGGER'S POLEMOS: FROM BEING TO POLITICS (Yale University Press, 2000).

14. See KANT, *supra* note 1.

15. Id. at 47–48.

16. Id. at 50–51.

In a later essay, "On Perpetual Peace" (1795–1796),[17] Kant reaches for a more modest, but perhaps more complete, solution. In that essay, Kant firmly rejects the notion of a universal state.

> The idea of international right presupposes the separate existence of many independent adjoining states . . . [T]his . . . is still to be preferred to an amalgamation of the separate nations under a single power . . . For the laws progressively lose their impact as the government increases its range, and a soulless despotism, after crushing the germ of goodness, will finally lapse into anarchy.[18]

Rather, he sees something that is like the balance of powers that obtained in Europe after 1815: a system of rules of international law enforced by the great powers acting in their own best interest. It was to be a system of alliances and treaties, like the United Nations without the Security Council, or the WTO, where the final sanction for breaking the rules is the authorization of retaliation.

This progression of ideas and the sense of a particular antimony, harken back to Montesquieu and Rousseau who despaired of a true republic having any great scope: size as the enemy of civic virtue. Montesquieu, put it this way in 1748:

> It is natural for a republic to have only a small territory; otherwise it cannot long subsist. In an extensive republic there are men of large fortunes, and consequently of less moderation; there are trusts too considerable to be placed in any single subject; he has interests of his own; he soon begins to think that he may be happy and glorious, by oppressing his fellow-citizens; and that he may raise himself to grandeur on the ruins of his country.
>
> In an extensive republic the public good is sacrificed to a thousand private views; it is subordinate to exceptions, and depends on accidents. In a small one, the interest of the public is more obvious, better understood, and more within the reach of every citizen; abuses have less extent, and, of course, are less protected.[19]

And Rousseau elaborates on this theme, concluding that a republic, as soon as it became so large that it had to depend on a representative body standing for the general will, was ethically problematic:

> One of the greatest disadvantages of large states, the one which above all makes liberty most difficult to preserve in them, is that the legislative power

17. Kant, *Perpetual Peace: A Philosophical Sketch*, in Political Writings, *supra* note 1, at 93.

18. Id. at 113. See also Kant, *On the Common Saying "This May Be True in Theory But It Does Not Apply in Practice,"* in Political Writings, *supra* note 1, at 93 ("such a universal peace is in turn even more dangerous to freedom, for it may lead to the most fearful despotism (as has indeed occurred more than once with states which have grown too large)").

19. Montequieu, *The Spirit of Laws*, Volume 1, Chapter 8, Document 1, 1748. Trans. Thomas Nugent, 1750. Accessed at: http://presspubs.uchicago.edu/founders/documents/v1ch8s1.html.

> cannot manifest itself directly, and can act only by delegation . . . A legislature made up of the whole citizen body is impossible to corrupt, but easy to deceive. Representatives of the people are hard to deceive, but easy to corrupt; and it rarely happens that they are not so corrupted. You have before you the example of the English Parliament . . .[20]

Thus a republic of any great extent was doomed to failure, doomed to be unable successfully to translate the general will, the union of free wills of free persons, into a practical entity. On the international level, in an essay entitled "A Project of Perpetual Peace"[21] with which Kant was familiar, Rousseau proposed a confederation of smaller states as the model of an international order. And this brings me to a most remarkable coincidence, though perhaps given the intellectual history of the eighteenth century it was no coincidence at all.

II. *AUSEINANDERSETZUNG* AT THE FRAMING

Kant's struggles with the conception of a manageable republic and of a tolerable international order coincided with the struggle of the framers of the United States Constitution between 1787 and 1789 to arrive at a constitution for the United States, a constitution that in its essential features is very much as we enjoy it today.[22]

20. Rousseau, *Political Writings*, trans. F. Watkins, (Madison: University of Wisconsin, 1986). Considerations for the Government of Poland.

21. Transl. E. Nuttall 1761, 1927.

22. See Armin Mattes, *Democracy and the Pursuit of Peace: The Domestic and International Sovereignty of the Nation in James Madison's and Immanuel Kant's Essays on Perpetual Peace*, in Citizens of a Common Intellectual Homeland: The Transatlantic Origins of American Democracy and Nationhood (2015). Mattes calls attention to Madison's short essay, "Universal Peace," published in 1792 in *The National Gazette*. Less well known than Kant's "Perpetual Peace," this was one of several pieces explaining Madison's increasing divergence from the views and policies of his recent comrade in arms, Alexander Hamilton, and indeed from his own earlier views as expressed in the Philadelphia Convention and in the Federalist Papers. The collection as a whole explains Madison's (and his patron Jefferson's) disagreement with what he considered the monarchic, excessively consolidating and textually untethered interpretations of the Constitution, all in aid of Hamilton's assuring the new nation's financial, economic, and military strength in a dangerous time of European conflicts brought about by the French Revolution. Madison hoped the young nation's security in this dangerous neighborhood could best be assured by firm adherence to the Constitution's republican principles—he and Jefferson progressively aligning themselves with the revolutionaries in France, Hamilton with the British. Madison is realist enough to conclude that "a universal and perpetual peace . . . is in the catalogue of events, which will never exist but in the imaginations of visionary philosophers, or in the breasts of benevolent enthusiasts." He does, however, explicitly refer to Rousseau's work. Insofar as Rousseau imagined a confederation leading to perpetual peace "the project . . . was . . . as preposterous as it was impotent." On the other hand he thought, as did Kant, that a system of true republics, where the people themselves would determine whether or not to go to war, would be far more reluctant to go to war. It is striking that both Kant and Madison thought that to procure this beneficent tendency of true republics it was important that each generation would have to pay the cost of any war out of its own resources and not—through debt—pass the burden off on

In the above-quoted passage from "Perpetual Peace," following Rousseau, Kant concludes that a consolidated superstate is not only a practicable impossibility; it is something like a moral mistake. But the representatives of the states meeting in Philadelphia in 1787 for a constitutional convention were faced with a practical necessity. The national constitution then in force under the Articles of Confederation was essentially a system of treaties between sovereign states, with, as in the WTO, no superseding enforcement mechanism.[23] This presented a cornucopia of anomalies rendering the nation—newly emerged from a war of independence—virtually ungovernable when delegates from all the states but Rhode Island assembled in Philadelphia in 1787 to draft a proposal for a new constitution.[24] The reasonable expectation was that unless some solution to the existing, as one delegate put it, "Idiot System," was found, the work of the American Revolution would founder and disintegrate.[25] The different parts of the union would pull apart. There were so many divergent interests that any reasonable observer would conclude that in due course some states would seek to become independent or join with others in separate confederations. Others might seek to reunite with Great Britain.[26] And the great experiment of the first

to future generations. Kant too in "Perpetual Peace" concludes that states governed directly or indirectly by the people are less likely to go to war, and would be even less likely to do so if debt financing—"the ingenious invention of a commercial people in the present century" is limited to financing public works but never for the financing of war. Preliminary Article 4.

I know of no evidence that Madison or any of the other framers were familiar with Kant's writings, nor is there any reason to believe that Kant was aware of the work of the framers. The timeline of his writing mapped against the events in America also makes that unlikely. But Kant was interested in a general way in developments in North America. First of all, he roundly deplored the action of the Europeans, who settled in America as if it were uninhabited territory, as they did in Africa and parts of Asia. Europeans at most had the right, if invited, to be treated as guests, but no more. See Kant, *Perpetual Peace* in POLITICAL WRITINGS, *supra* note 1, at 106. In his *Metaphysics of Morals*, Kant does mention that the United States confederation was different from that which he envisaged because the association of "the American states . . . is based on a political constitution and is therefore indissoluble." See Kant, *The Metaphysics of Morals, § 61* in POLITICAL WRITINGS, *supra* note 1, at 171. Published in 1798, this could refer either to the Articles of Confederation or to the Constitution of 1789. Kant's enthusiasm for the French Revolution, as from 1789 it seemed to move France in the direction of a republican monarchy, and in 1792 with the abolition of the monarchy, to a full-fledged republic, is well known and expressed in many of his writings. So is his sharp condemnation of the regicide. His sympathy for the colonists' resistance to British rule and for the American Revolution as far as I know is found only in records of his conversations. See MANFRED KUEHN, KANT: A BIOGRAPHY (Cambridge University Press, 2001) 155, 400. See also Hans Reiss, *Postscript*, in POLITICAL WRITINGS, *supra* note 1, at 261.

23. See MICHAEL J. KLARMAN, THE FRAMERS' COUP: THE MAKING OF THE UNITED STATES CONSTITUTION (Oxford University Press, 2016), 14.

24. See KLARMAN, id. at 117–22.

25. See id. at 126.

26. See PAULINE MAIER, RATIFICATION: THE PEOPLE DEBATE THE CONSTITUTION, 1787–1788 (2010), 16.

major democratic republic on the face of the earth would soon dissipate in chaos. This was the expectation of practical politicians, not only in America but also in Europe.[27]

It was to save the union—and to save the idea of a republic—that the framers managed to wring from the confederation congress an authorization to draft a new document. And the framers' vision was radical indeed. Madison proposed, and seven of the twelve states (Rhode Island didn't make the scene) in an early straw vote agreed, that the national government would have the authority to veto any and all state legislation—a radical proposal, a radical form of consolidation, more radical than exists even today.[28] The framers had other radically consolidating proposals. The national government could regulate both interstate and international commerce.[29] A central government would have the power not only to lay taxes directly on the population but to collect them—an abomination to the backwoodsmen in what would become the new states of Kentucky and Tennessee.[30] It was a conception at least as radical and complete as that against which certain states' rights proponents even today vehemently inveigh.

Finally, there would be a very strong, unitary executive—that is, not an executive committee[31]—serving perhaps for as much as a seven-year term, and in some proposals for life.[32] And both the executive and the legislature would be chosen by means that were likely to assure that the elites, particularly the commercial elites of the Atlantic coast, would retain control and would not cede to the more popular demands of the rural population, which in those days exceeded the urban populations. Indeed the only body that directly represented the people would be the House of Representatives, in which each member represented a very large body of persons. And that was for the reason, closely argued by James Madison in *Federalist 10*, that having each representative represent a variety of interests, no individual faction would be able to gain control or in fact voice.[33]

So the American republic instituted in 1789, the first true large republic, was far from Rousseau's conception of a republic built on the general will, far from the

27. For an intriguing recent exercise in imaginative alternative history, see Adam Gopnick, *We Could Have Been Canada: Was the American Revolution Such a Good Idea?*, The New Yorker, May 15, 2017, http://www.newyorker.com/magazine/2017/05/15/we-could-have-been-canada. In fact, during this period there were rumors that Vermont was negotiating with the British Governor of Canada about joining that British colony. See Maier, *supra* note 26.

28. See Klarman, *supra* note 23, at 156.

29. Id. at 152.

30. Id. at 148.

31. This notion of a unitary executive is most definitely not that advanced during the George W. Bush administration, as at times above the law, but rather an executive the powers of which—though subject to law—were not divided up among several persons or bodies.

32. Klarman, *supra* note 23, at 228–29.

33. See Publius, Federalist No. 10. This was very similar to an argument in Rousseau's *Social Contract* (Book II, chapter 3).

kind of republic that Kant imagined, and much closer to the consolidated state to which he objected on both practical and moral grounds.

III. INTELLIGENCE, SKILL, AND LUCK

What had happened was truly remarkable. In the 1787 Philadelphia Convention there were strong objectors to the Federalists' project for the national government. And their objections, by those who came to be known as the anti-Federalists, echoed in many ways Rousseau's objection to large states in general[34] and Kant's objections to a consolidated world state.[35] The anti-Federalists believed that such a consolidated state would not represent the people, would be elitist, and would eradicate the cultural, historical, and political differences among the different entities comprising the new republic—it would be "a soulless despotism," the kind of malign *Gleichschaltung* Kant decried.[36]

But the Federalist vision mostly prevailed and the anti-Federalist position largely failed. As my colleague, Michael Klarman, in his recent magisterial and definitive work, *The Framers' Coup: The Making of the United States Constitution*, has demonstrated, the Federalist program was not the program of the nation. The population, in terms similar to Kant's (of whom they surely knew nothing), was against consolidated government, against long-serving officials, in favor of rotation in office, and in favor of representatives who represented much smaller groups of individuals.[37] They were indeed what would be called strong populists. And they were the majority of the nation. Nevertheless, the Federalists prevailed almost entirely.

How did the framers accomplish their coup? It was an accomplishment made up of equal parts remarkable powers of mind, and remarkable powers of explanation and persuasion; one might call it rhetoric—but the rhetoric was cool, intelligent, and reasoning. But it was also brought about by good luck and shrewd political maneuver.

The great centrifugal force was not at all the moral issue of slavery, but the divergent interests of the smaller states (New Hampshire, Rhode Island, Connecticut, New Jersey, Delaware, and Maryland) and those of the larger states (Massachusetts, New York, Pennsylvania, and Virginia).[38] It is the smaller states that most credibly threatened to walk out of the convention.[39] If that had happened, the country would have had a geographical fissure in the mid-Atlantic, and the smaller states credibly threatened to form alliances, and perhaps in the

34. See Rousseau, *supra* note 20.

35. See Kant, *Perpetual Peace*, in POLITICAL WRITINGS, *supra* note 1, at 113.

36. See id.

37. See id. at 7–8.

38. See id. at 395.

39. See id. at 192–94.

end reunite, with Great Britain.[40] Madison, Hamilton, and Washington, who were adamant on many scores and willing to face down credible anti-Federalist threats in many directions, were quite convinced that the smaller states' threat was real and would bring down the whole project.[41]

And so there was a compromise, known as the Connecticut Compromise or the Great Compromise, and it shaped the government that citizens of the United States live with today.[42] Its main feature was that in one of the two houses of the Congress—the Senate—two senators would represent each state, regardless of its size and population.[43] The disparities were dramatic: a senator from Virginia represented many times the number of persons as did a senator from Delaware or Rhode Island.[44] Second, even in the House of Representatives, where the Federalists had succeeded in limiting the total number of representatives so that each representative would represent a large variety of persons and interests, each state was guaranteed at least one representative.[45] And finally, this system of radically unequal representation was to some extent reproduced in the Electoral College, which chose the president.[46]

Once the concerns of the smaller states were satisfied, everything else fell into place. The disputes between southern and northern states about shipping and the control of trade were satisfied. The southerners were convinced that they would have relatively free access to foreign shipping or to northern ships at competitive rates, for the sale of their exports.[47] The northern states felt that they in turn would have protection against foreign manufactures so that their infant industries could flourish.[48] On the subject of slavery, the southern states were quite ready to agree to a strong central government, including a centrally directed military, because the new constitution contained a provision that guaranteed each state "on the application of [its] legislature" protection against invasion or "domestic violence."[49] The southern states particularly feared Indian depredations and slave revolts.[50] To pay for this assurance that the military would protect against such domestic

40. See Maier, *supra* note 26.

41. See Klarman, *supra* note 23, at 127.

42. See id. at 190–96.

43. Id.

44. The disparities persist and have become more acute: today the ratio between California and Wyoming is more than 1:65. See id. at 626–27.

45. Id. at 356.

46. See id. at 369.

47. Id. at 281–82.

48. Id.

49. See id. at 291–94. See also U.S. Const., art. IV, sec. 4 ("Fugitive Slave Clause").

50. See Klarman, *supra* note 23, at 426.

violence they were willing to agree to give Congress the power, if it chose, to put an end to the slave trade in twenty years.

If the Philadelphia Convention was in large part an elite cabal, the state ratification conventions were another matter. They were an entirely extraconstitutional, purpose-invented set of entities.[51] The existing arrangement, the Articles of Confederation, provided for changes to the Articles only on the unanimous vote of the states through their legislatures.[52] That is understandable because the Articles were in fact a web a multilateral treaties—of just the sort Kant imagined in *Perpetual Peace*.

The Philadelphia Convention of 1787 proposed changes in the arrangement, which, first of all, did not depend on unanimous approval by the states. Those changes were to go into effect if at least nine out of the thirteen states agreed—though only among those so agreeing.[53] And the other radical departure from what one might call "constitutional" or Kelsenian legality was that the ratification was not to be effected through the ordinary organs of each of the states' government—that is to say its legislature—but by conventions within the states. These conventions were nonexistent entities.[54] They were called into being by the Philadelphia convention's proposals altogether. So this was really, as it says on our dollar bill today, *novus ordo seclorum*. It was a constitutional break with the past. And intended to be.

The ratification conventions were a far harder test for the Federalists than was the Philadelphia Convention with its mostly well-educated, upper-class members drawn from the Atlantic coast cities. The state ratifying conventions were made up of some two thousand delegates from all over the participating states, and they in turn had been elected by an electorate often broader than that qualified to vote in their own state elections.[55] Yet the Federalists were able to bring it off. They attained unanimity (with the usual comedic last hold-out of Rhode Island, which was finally brought into line by threats of annexation by neighboring states and secession by the Federalist-leaning cities of Newport and Providence) by an extraordinary combination of substantive persuasion, strategy, and good luck.[56] If any of these had failed, the United States would not be what it is today.

In many respects it had been a close thing. Madison, Hamilton, and Washington were particularly concerned that the state ratifying conventions might demand[57] a second convention in which might come to the fore and prevail some of the

51. See id. at 112.

52. See id. at 9, 11.

53. Id. at 413–14, 540.

54. Id. at 416.

55. For example, the New York legislature did away with its property qualifications for voting before selecting their ratifying convention delegates; all free males over twenty-once could participate in the election. See KLARMAN, *supra* note 23, at 485.

56. See id. at 540.

57. See id. at 531–33.

anti-Federalist concerns about too concentrated a government, the number of particular powers granted to the national government, and the elitist nature of both the legislative and the executive branches.[58]

Another threat to be warded off was the demand of anti-Federalists that ratification be accompanied by a Bill of Rights. This was both a stalling tactic and a heartfelt appeal to tradition. In the Philadelphia Convention, Madison and others of the Federalists had opposed a Bill of Rights as a condition of ratification.[59] They feared that the Bill of Rights would include many provisions that would undo the centralizing and elitist elements of the Philadelphia draft.[60] But the draw of the Bill of Rights notion was too difficult to resist. In addition to the appeal of the example of the British Bill of Rights of 1689, there was the fact that many of the state constitutions had Bills of Rights. So solemn assurances were given that once the constitution had been ratified and put into effect, the first Congress would indeed adopt a Bill of Rights.[61] And that is what happened. The Bill of Rights was adopted in 1791 in the form in which we now know it today.[62] This Bill of Rights must have seemed at the time a relatively anodyne document: it undid none of the crucial work of the Federalists in the Philadelphia Convention.[63] The power of the central government to regulate trade and to tax the people directly were untouched.[64] The one exception and, of course it came to be a crucial exception, was the First Amendment. I shall come to that monumental provision shortly, as it relates to my general theme, the crooked timber of humanity. The other amendments had to do with details mainly of criminal and to some extent civil procedure that were hardly controversial then and are hardly controversial now.[65]

What Americans ended up with was a remarkable structure of government quite unfamiliar in the rest of the world. Recall that Kant, in opposing the notion of a consolidated world state and indeed in embracing Montesquieu's and Rousseau's idea that large republics are unstable and unlikely sites for republican institutions, argued that the safeguarding of peace among nations presented an insoluble puzzle and that the appropriate and only possible solution was one of a system of contractual alliances with no Hobbesian sovereign to oversee, adjudicate, and enforce them. Following Rousseau,[66] Kant indeed argued that a

58. Id.

59. Id. at 549.

60. Id. at 554–55.

61. Id. at 591, 593.

62. Id. at 590.

63. Id. at 594.

64. Id. at 593.

65. For a different view of the significance of the Bill of Rights, see generally Akhil Reed Amar, The Bill of Rights (New Haven: Yale University Press, 1998).

66. "The Social Contract" ch. II, "Sovereignty Is Indivisible" (1762).

universal sovereign was a kind of a political solecism: given that each of the constituent states are sovereign and must be sovereign, how could there be a sovereign above them?[67] There could be no *imperium in imperio*, a perplexity that U.S. Supreme Court Justice Anthony Kennedy claimed the framers resolved when they "split the atom of sovereignty."[68]

IV. THE CUNNING OF REASON

In his *Idea for a Universal History with a Cosmopolitan Purpose* of 1784 (which I have already quoted, but to another purpose), Kant addresses a different conundrum, one that today troubles legal and particularly constitutional scholars. The traditional constitutional scholar works with doctrine and its development. And doctrine consists of reasons given for outcomes. One might say it consists of maxims that later judges and scholars and jurists seek to universalize. This is in a way a version of the traditional Kantian method. It is the method of reason: an argument is propelled by the force of its logic. This is the work of free and rational beings. This is Kantian pragmatics.

Yet, in recent decades, many scholars—constitutional scholars particularly—have grown weary of this traditional exercise and pursue a different method: a method that looks to social science. Judges and their work are tabulated in accordance with who appointed them and what their inferred political valences might be. These are then carefully charted, collected, and, in the way of that kind of research, published.[69] This stinks in the nostrils of us traditional doctrinal constitutional scholars, because it implicitly and sometimes explicitly denies that the driving force of each decision is the propulsion of reason, but rather is driven by inclination. Or, what Kant describes as "nature."

It is hard to deny that the social science idea of research in fact delivers explanations, maps trajectories, and perhaps even anticipates the future. At the very outset of his 1784 essay, Kant notes and struggles with this conundrum:

> Whatever concept one may hold, from a metaphysical point of view, concerning the freedom of the will, certainly its appearances, which are human actions, like every other natural event are determined by universal laws. However obscure their causes, history, which is concerned with narrating these appearances, permits us to hope that if we attend to the play of freedom of the human will in the large, we may be able to discern a regular movement in it, and that what seems complex and chaotic in the single individual

67. Kant, *The Metaphysics of Morals § 46*, in Political Writings, *supra* note 1, at 141–42.

68. See United States Term Limits v. Thornton, 514 U.S. 779 (1995) (Kennedy, J., concurring).

69. See, e.g., Jeffrey A. Segal & Harold A. Spaeth, The Supreme Court and the Attitudinal Model (New York: Cambridge University Press, 1993) and The Supreme Court and the Attitudinal Model Revisited (New York: Cambridge University Press, 2002); Theodore W. Ruger, *The Supreme Court Forecasting Project: Legal and Political Science Approaches to Predicting Supreme Court Decisionmaking*, 104 Colum. L. Rev. 1150 (2004).

> may be seen from the standpoint of the human race as a whole to be a steady and progressive though slow evolution of its original endowment. Since the free will of man has obvious influence upon marriages, births, and deaths, they seem to be subject to no rule by which the number of them could be reckoned in advance. Yet the annual tables of them in the major countries prove that they occur according to laws as stable as [those of] the unstable weather, which we likewise cannot determine in advance, but which, in the large, maintain the growth of plants the flow of rivers, and other natural events in an unbroken uniform course. Individuals and even whole peoples think little on this. Each, according to his own inclination, follows his own purpose, often in opposition to others; yet each individual and people, as if following some guiding thread, go toward a natural but to each of them unknown goal; all work toward furthering it, even if they would set little store by it if they did know it.[70]

Apply this thought now to the tale of the U.S. Constitution. As I have said, it is scarcely possible to read the statements of men of genius such as Madison and Hamilton without attaining the conviction that it was the force of their reasoning that moved events to their conclusion, a conclusion that in many ways determines our present. And yet as the story I have told demonstrates, though reason played a large maybe even the largest part in its unfolding, the way in which we got here was a wandering way, of inclination, of interest, and of forces often far removed from the power of reason.

It is a wonder, then, that the work of so many men of genius operating in an environment of interest, conflict, passion, and often malignity should have delivered the result that we have—a result that has created a lasting, true republic and an early inspiration and a model for republics all over the globe. It invented a form of government, dual sovereignty, which for a long time was distinctive to America and was, as I said, deemed by both Kant and the anti-Federalists as a solecism.[71]

And finally they gave us an institution, judicial review, which is an improbable and, as many scholars have pointed out,[72] a democratic anomaly. And yet it is judicial review (which was anticipated during the Philadelphia Convention, though very little invoked and then principally as a means of policing the boundary between state and federal authority[73]), which has in fact resolved—imperfectly to be sure—the conflict between democratic sovereignty and the human dignity of free and reasoning individual citizens. It is a resolution that Kant anticipated in his making in the right of argumentation and of free speech an exception to the citizens' general duty to obey the sovereign. Kant in his political writings

70. Kant, *Universal History*, in POLITICAL WRITINGS, *supra* note 1, at 41–42.

71. See generally JACKSON TURNER MAIN, THE ANTIFEDERALISTS: CRITICS OF THE CONSTITUTION (Chapel Hill: The University of North Carolina Press, 1961).

72. For a forceful recent statement, see JEREMY WALDRON, POLITICAL POLITICAL THEORY: ESSAYS ON INSTITUTIONS (2016).

73. See KLARMAN, *supra* note 23, at 160–61.

consistently inveighs against the right of revolution, the right to resist the sovereign. So in 1789 he writes:

> An alteration in a (defective) constitution of a state, which may sometimes be required, can be undertaken only by the sovereign himself through reform, and not by the people through a revolution. . . .
>
> . . .
>
> Moreover, if a revolution has succeeded and a new constitution has been established, the illegitimacy of its beginning and of its success cannot free the subjects from being bound to accept the new order of things as good citizens, and they cannot refuse to honor and obey the suzerain (*Obrigkeit*) who now possesses the authority.[74]

As strong as this language is (the spirit of Leviathan hovers over it), he did seem to make one exception, and that in regard to freedom of speech, in an earlier essay of 1784, "*What Is Enlightenment*"?:

> Enlightenment is man's emergence from his self-incurred immaturity. . . .
>
> For enlightenment of this kind, all that is needed is freedom . . . the freedom to make public use of one's reason in all matters. But I hear on all sides, "Do not argue!" The officer says, "Do not argue, get on parade!" The tax collector, "Do not argue but pay!" The cleric, "Do not argue but believe!" Only one prince in the world, [Kant's Hohenzollern sovereign Frederick the Great] says, "Argue as much as you will, and about what you will, but obey!" . . . The public use of one's reason must always be free, and it alone can bring about enlightenment among men . . . The citizen cannot refuse to pay the taxes imposed on him. Nonetheless, the same citizen does not contravene his civil obligations, when, as a scholar, he publicly expresses his thoughts on the inappropriateness or even the injustices of such fiscal measures. . . .
>
> A contract, concluded with a view to preventing all further enlightenment, is absolutely null and void even if ratified by the supreme power, by parliaments, and by the most solemn peace treaties. . . . That would be a crime against human nature. . . . Finally, it affects the principles of government, which find that they can themselves profit treating man, who is more than a machine, in a manner appropriate to his dignity. . . .[75]

74. *Rechtslehre* paragraphs 321–323 (Metaphysical Elements of Justice).

75. Kant, *What Is Enlightenment?*, in POLITICAL WRITINGS, *supra* note 1, at 54–60.

To the same effect: "The freedom of the pen is the only safeguard of the rights of the people, although it must not transcend the bounds of respect and devotion towards the existing constitution, which should itself create liberal state of mind among the subjects." See Kant, *On the Common Saying: "This May Be True in Theory, But It Does Not Apply in Practice,"* in POLITICAL WRITINGS, *supra* note 1, at 85.

Kant did not resolve what he would have regarded as a contradiction inherent in these two assertions about the powers of government. But we did—in the anomalous and imperfect institution of judicial review. For it has become one of the most distinctive features of our imperfect democracy, that increasingly this anomalous third branch of government (recall how much more modestly Locke conceived its role) has regularly adjudicated and enforced the freedom of speech, invoking our First Amendment rights of argumentation and free speech, against the sovereign at all its levels and guises—whether petty local officials, the chief executive of a state, a state or national legislature, or the president.

But recall how we came to this signal resolution. Madison, the principal author of the First Amendment,[76] was initially a strong opponent of appending a Bill of Rights to the Constitution or even making its passage an implicit condition of its ratification.[77] On grounds of logic and constitutional principle, he thought it inappropriate and unnecessary, but more pointedly he and the Federalists resisted it as an entering wedge that would be used to undo the really critical work of the Convention, which concentrated power in a national government led by the intellectual and economic elite of the new nation.[78] And yet the body of the Constitution in its implicit endorsement of judicial review (itself a compromise between state sovereignty and the Federalists original proposal of a national veto on all state legislation[79]), and its inclusion of the First Amendment, whose time did not come until the aftermath of the First World War, was indeed a resolution of the antinomy in a format that Kant did not imagine.

The constitutional resolutions, both of the dual sovereignty problem and of the relation between individuals and the state, best illustrate what Kant referred to as the "crooked timber of humanity out of which no completely straight thing could be built." Surely, our regime of human rights, of individual liberty, and of democratic participation is imperfect. It is not completely straight. And yet, *pace* Berlin, it is built. Those of us who work in doctrine—either as judges, as advocates, or as scholars—are acutely aware of the "crooked timber of humanity," but also of the fact that out of that crooked timber, though the structure is not completely straight, it does stand up. After all, it is these imperfections that keep us busy—out of which we make our living.

V. WHAT MAY WE HOPE?

There are two ways of looking at this antinomy of the free exercise of reason by individual moral beings nonetheless tracing a trajectory that outside, objective observers (social scientists) can discern. Kant viewed it as a trajectory tending to the perfection of the human condition. His was a remarkably optimistic

76. See KLARMAN, *supra* note 23, at 560.

77. See id. at 530.

78. See id. at 549, 554–55.

79. Id. at 140, 607.

long-range outlook. He had as a premise not something that he purported to be able to prove: nature (that is the term he used over and over again) tended through the opposition of forces to advance the human condition. He could not prove it. But it was one of the three things he asked at the end of the *First Critique: What can I know? What should I do? What may I hope?*[80]

Is this a reasonable hope? Is it a hope that may sustain us in our work as jurists? What, after all, is the alternative? There is an alternative. It is one that Kant noted and that was well known. He attributed it to Democritus and Lucretius. Its most engaging statement has recently been offered by the Shakespearian scholar, Stephen Greenblatt, about the discovery in the fifteenth century of the lost manuscript of Lucretius' *de Rerum Natura.*[81] In that system, all was chance. The regular movement of atoms through space is disturbed from time to time in unaccountable and random ways from their regular course. These swerves, what Lucretius called *clinamina,* caused the agglomeration of particles that led to their further agglomeration into material objects and ultimately life, consciousness. Indeed, Lucretius's conception is a remarkably prescient statement of the reigning conception of cosmology and of modern science.

In 2012 in a surprising and (to some) scandalous book, the eminent philosopher Thomas Nagel raised a doubt about this Lucretian model. The title of that book gives the gist: *Mind and Cosmos: Why the Materialistic Neo-Darwinian Conception of Nature Is Almost Certainly False.*[82] How, he asks, could a phenomenon as remarkable as human consciousness be the random outcome of random events? An atheist, Nagel does not propose here an intelligent design account of cosmology, much less of evolution, but rather suggests that a different concept of causality, a different concept of cosmological as well as biological, evolution should be contemplated—one that has a more teleological bent and therefore suggests that consciousness is not simply the deliverance of random swerves but of a disposition in the materials from the beginning. I must admit that I am intrigued by this suggestion, but unconvinced. Thirteen point eight billion years and the whole universe are quite long enough and the universe quite large enough to accommodate the occurrence of all things probable and improbable, including the remarkable phenomena of human consciousness, human reasoning, and morality, as outcomes of entirely random processes. Nor to my mind does this detract in the slightest from the authority of reason. If there is a different, teleological kind of causality, not that of the social scientists, it is the causality of reason. However consciousness and, following consciousness, reason came into the world, reason has an empire and a mechanism of its own. Arguments have premises that lead to conclusions, ideas have not only consequences but entailments,

80. Immanuel Kant, Critique of Pure Reason, trans. Paul Guyer and Allen Wood (1998) A804f/B833f.

81. The Swerve: How the World Became Modern (2011).

82. Thomas Nagel, Mind & Cosmos: Why the Materialist Neo-Darwinian Conception of Nature Is Almost Certainly False (Oxford University Press, 2012).

and those entailments are perhaps not at first anticipated by those who embrace the premises.[83]

I am suggesting that the interplay of the forces, the reasons and the forces, launched in 1787 by Hamilton and Madison, pushing up against opposition, compromising with much less pure, more self-interested, ungeneralizeable forces, combined to produce a unique, persistent, and remarkable product—one that in one way or another, whether in contemporary America or in Europe or in systems throughout the democratic world—is a way of reconciling the forces of politics, of democracy, of passion, and those of dignity and reason. It is not that out of the crooked timber of humanity no straight thing can be made, but rather that no *completely* straight thing can be made.

Kant is very much in Nagel's camp, more so than am I. The term Kant uses is "nature," and in the passage from the 1784 *Idea for a Universal History* with which I began and to which he returns throughout his work, it is nature that takes these uncaused events, the deliverance of reason, of free human action of the free will, and consolidates them into an ever-approaching state of perfection. To be sure, Kant unlike Nagel, invokes behind this process of what he calls "nature," a postulate of God and immortality. Perhaps he thought that, unlike Nagel, nature all by itself could not produce so magnificent or benign a result.

Kant returns to this point again in one of his last writings, *The Contest of Faculties* of 1798:

> Only nature and freedom, combined within mankind in accordance with principles of right, have enabled us to forecast [that the human race will achieve an ideal state of right and virtue]; but the precise time at which it will occur must remain indefinite and dependent upon chance.[84]

I end—because how could I not—by a brief meditation on our present state of affairs in America and perhaps in Britain and in Europe. I allow myself to say that recent developments are far from edifying elaborations of the great themes of the Constitution and of constitutional order. But with Kant, I allow myself to hope. I think that what we are seeing today may very well be an example of the fact that the "crooked timber of humanity" has not built a completely straight thing, and yet I think we may hope and we surely must work to straighten the structure after all.

83. See Charles Fried, *Moral Causation*, 77 Harv. L. Rev. 1258 (1964).

84. Kant, *The Contest of Faculties*, in Political Writings, *supra* note 1, at 184–85.

5

Sovereignty and Executive Power

CHRISTOPHER W. MORRIS

"[W]hen the president does it that means that it is not illegal." Richard Nixon's oft-quoted remark provides a focus for some of the recent debates about the power of the president in the American system. The context of Nixon's claim suggests that it may be less radical a challenge to the rule of law than it is often thought to be.[1] He is often thought of as a president who believed the chief executive officer of the United States is sometimes "above the law," and this interpretation may be uncharitable. There are, however, many modern thinkers who have thought that the sovereign is above the law, that is, not bound by the law. And, we may add, many political actors have claimed to answer only to the Deity (or to History). They may also be thought to deny the old principle, *nemo est supra legem*. So we use the famous quotation to introduce our topic.

Early modern conceptions of sovereignty would place the sovereign above the law; indeed, they would endow sovereigns with quite extraordinary powers. Speaking of the monarch-in-Parliament, William Blackstone wrote that

> It hath sovereign and uncontrollable authority in making, enlarging, restraining, abrogating, repealing, reviving and expounding of laws, concerning matters of all possible denominations, ecclesiastical, or temporal, civil, military, maritime or criminal; this being the place where that absolute despotic power, which must in all governments reside somewhere, is entrusted by the constitution of these kingdoms. All mischiefs and grievances, operations and remedies, that transcend the ordinary course of the laws, are within the reach of this extraordinary tribunal. It can regulate or new model the succession of the crown.... It can alter the established

1. Quoting Nixon out of context is misleading, so I have reproduced the short section of the interview in an appendix.

Sovereignty and the New Executive Authority. Claire O. Finkelstein and Michael Skerker.

> religion of the land. . . . It can change and create afresh even the constitution of the kingdom and of parliaments themselves . . . It can, in short, do every thing that is not naturally impossible. . . .[2]

Blackstone also thought, as have many theorists, that in every form of government there *must* be a sovereign. Interestingly this thesis may have been influential amongst the founders of the American system. Gordon Wood writes that "By the early 1770's, particularly with the introduction of Blackstone's *Commentaries* into the colonies, the doctrine that there must be in every form of government 'a supreme, irresistible, absolute, uncontrolled authority, in which the *jura summi imperii*, or rights of sovereignty, reside,' had gained such overwhelming currency that its 'truth,' many Americans were compelled to admit, could no longer 'be contested.'"[3] I mention this for two reasons. The first is that the idea that every state must have a sovereign is not dead today, and it often influences debates about sovereignty. The second is that the powers of the executive have long been a concern to many. Many of the American founders and the anti-Federalists were quite worried about the possibility that the new framework of government would permit the executive to acquire the powers of a monarch: in the words of George Mason, "if strong and extensive Powers are vested in the Executive, and that Executive consists only of one Person, the Government will of course degenerate, (for I will call it degeneracy) into a Monarchy."[4]

Today in the context of debates about executive powers and privilege, the concept of sovereignty has been invoked in defense of allowing the executive branch of government more power.[5] There are reasons it might be good to endow the executive branch of government in systems such as that of the United States with more power, and there are reasons it might not be good to do so. I will not take a stance on this debate. Rather I propose to ask first whether traditional modern doctrines of sovereignty lend support to either side of this debate about strong and relatively unconstrained executives. I shall argue they do not. In fact, they may support constraints on the executive. I shall conclude by arguing that it is a mistake to frame contemporary debates about executive power in terms of the notion of sovereignty. Instead I shall suggest that these debates concern difficult questions about institutional design as well as the rule of law.

The first part of this essay will offer an analysis of the classical conception of sovereignty, as well as more attractive conceptions of limited sovereignty. I consider

2. William Blackstone, *The Sovereignty of the Law*, in *Selections from Blackstone's Commentaries on the Laws of England*, G. Jones (ed), (University of Toronto Press, 1973) 36, 71.

3. Gordon Wood, *The Creation of the American Republic, 1776–1787* (Norton, 1969) 350; see also 345.

4. *The Founders' Constitution*, Philip B. Kurland & Ralph Lerner (eds), (University of Chicago Press, 1987), vol 4, George Mason on Article 2, Section 2, Clause 1, http://press-pubs.uchicago.edu/founders/documents/a2_2_1s1.html.

5. See the description of the Conference on Sovereignty and the Rule of Law held at the Center for Ethics and the Rule of Law of the University of Pennsylvania School of Law, April 19–20, 2013: https://www.law.upenn.edu/institutes/cerl/conferences/sovereignty/.

the question of who, if anyone, might be sovereign, that is, possess the powers of sovereignty. The second part of the essay focuses on the question of the possible connections between notions of sovereignty and debates about executive power.

The concept of sovereignty has played an important role in modern politics and political thought. The origins of the notion are ancient, in Roman times, but it comes to life and acquires its shape in modern times, in seventeenth and eighteenth century Europe. It continues to play a role in contemporary politics, but its importance today is primarily in international affairs and law. It is a complex notion, and it is not clear how best to understand it. A commonplace distinction is often made between "internal" (or "vertical") and "external" (or "horizontal") sovereignty, the first pertaining to the governance of a state, the second to a state's independence from other states. These two kinds of sovereignty were once connected. It is said that states are or ought to be the ultimate authorities in their territories while being independent of the authority of other states. The notion of external sovereignty figures centrally in international relations and associated areas of government and law. But today the relation between the two and indeed the concept unifying them are not always clear. Many questions in politics and law turn on how we understand the concept. The rights of states or international agents to intervene in the "internal" affairs of another state may depend on how we conceptualize the central notion of sovereign authority. The autonomy of peoples, such as American Indian tribes, or the powers of branches of government may also be affected by our understanding of the notion. Perhaps our understanding of the powers of the executive branch of government will as well.

I propose an analysis of the concept. Basically, something has sovereignty insofar as it is the ultimate source of authority within a realm. I explicate this understanding and show how the internal and external conceptions are related. Elsewhere I discuss what is problematic about the concept and how it is not easy to determine who or what might possess it; I have argued that it is not clear that anything is in fact sovereign or whether anything has all of the authority that makes up sovereignty.[6] But I won't emphasize my skepticism here. Our focus will be on sovereignty and the power of the executive branch of government in systems such as that of the United States. I propose now to ask whether traditional modern doctrines of sovereignty lend support to partisans of a strong and relatively unconstrained executive, and I shall argue they do not.

Our interest here in sovereignty is primarily in the idea of a ruler or government that is not itself legally constrained. This is a feature of what I shall call classical sovereignty. By contrast, the kinds of sovereignty that tend to appeal to us today are all forms of *limited* sovereignty. These do not claim that the sovereign is legally unconstrained. They do, however, claim that the legal limits on sovereign power are to be ascertained by the sovereign itself, and so these conceptions of sovereignty raise some of the same concerns as the classical conception. I shall first lay out an account of sovereignty.[7]

6. I have defended this skeptical thesis in my *Essay on the Modern State* (Cambridge University Press, 1998).

7. See *An Essay on the Modern State* ch. 7.

What is sovereignty? It is a mistake to think that modern sovereignty is merely a restatement of ancient ideas about power and authority. Some elements may be present in different forms, especially in Roman law and of course in certain theological accounts of the Deity's power. But the conception of political power attached to a new type of political order is novel: "at the beginning, the idea of sovereignty was the idea that there is a final and absolute political authority in the political community . . . and no final and absolute authority exists elsewhere."[8] The concept of the modern state in fact develops along with that of sovereignty, as is evident in the work of the master theorist of the modern state, where "Soveraignty is an Artificiall *Soul*" of "that great LEVIATHAN called a COMMON-WEALTH, or STATE, (in latine CIVITAS)."[9]

States not only claim ultimate power within their realms, they also claim independence of one another ("external sovereignty"). In rejecting the authority of popes and emperors, sovereigns asserted the state's autonomy from other states. Not only is the state the author of its own laws—the etymological meaning of *autonomos*—the laws of others have no claim on it. With the advent of the sovereign state, relations between states or "international relations" become possible. Prior to this, there were no "foreign affairs" or distinction between internal and external, and the modern conception of the nature of world politics as a "anarchical" or unregulated was not yet possible. Once the sovereignty of states is recognized, their relations are thought to constitute a *state of nature*, one which, for many early modern theorists, was beyond law, a thesis defended now by some "realists". For some, to such a state (of nature), "this also is consequent; that nothing can be Unjust. The notions of Right and Wrong, Justice and Injustice have there no place. Where there is no common Power, there is no Law: where no Law, no Injustice."[10]

In the early modern quarrel between monarchs and lords on the one side and popes on the other, the kings for the most part won, and they claimed what we now call sovereignty for themselves or their estates: *they* were to be the ultimate source of political authority within a realm.[11] Their realm (or kingdom) was theirs, and unlike in medieval times, their authority over it was to be shared with no one. In the writings of early modern thinkers such as Bodin, Hobbes, and Rousseau, what we now think of as internal and external sovereignty are tightly connected. These thinkers thought sovereignty to have three important properties. It is *absolute* (legally unconstrained or unlimited), *indivisible* (unique and undivided), and *inalienable* (cannot be delegated or "represented"). It is the first that is of concern

8. "If we are to appreciate the significance of the idea we must also add to this thought. With the notion of sovereignty, a new or at least an altered meaning has been acquired by every element in this statement—by 'political authority', by 'political community', by 'final and absolute'." F.H. Hinsley, *Sovereignty*, 2nd ed (Cambridge University Press, 1966) 25–26.

9. Thomas Hobbes, *Leviathan,* Richard Tuck (ed), (Cambridge University Press, 1991 [1651]), "Introduction," 9.

10. Hobbes, *Leviathan*, ch. XIII, 90.

11. In the UK of course, the monarchs reached a settlement with the nobles that eventually led to attributing sovereignty to the monarch-in-Parliament.

here. If absolute sovereignty is attributed to states, then their authority cannot be constrained by international law or possibly even by the rights of individuals. Conceiving of sovereignty as absolute thus requires granting states considerable autonomy or liberty in their "international relations": nothing is forbidden.

The core idea of sovereignty, that of the ultimate source of political authority within a realm, requires unpacking. Sovereignty is associated with modern kingdoms and states; the "realms" in question are the well-defined territories of such states. The relevant notion of political authority is more controversial. Something is an authority, in the sense relevant here, only if its directives are (and are intended to be) action-guiding. The law forbids us from doing certain things, and it intends these prohibitions to guide our behavior; specifically, these prohibitions obligate and are (meant to be) reason-providing. Authorities, then, mean to guide behavior by providing reasons for action to their subjects. On this view, political authority is not to be understood simply as justified coercion or force; sanctions or force may frequently be necessary as a means to make effective this authority, but the two are not to be conflated.[12]

Sovereignty is a kind of *authority*. The key to the notion is the idea of *ultimate* authority. What is it for a source of authority to be ultimate? An authority may be ultimate if it is *the highest* in a hierarchy of authorities. Such an authority may also be *final*: there is no further appeal after it has spoken (it has "the last word"). Lastly, an ultimate authority may be one that is *supreme* in a particular sense: it has authority over all other authorities in its realm. The state's authority is thought to be sovereign in this sense; it takes precedence over competing authorities (e.g., corporate, syndicate, church, conscience). Summarizing, then, *sovereignty is the highest, final, and supreme political authority within a modern territorial realm.*

States claim sovereignty and also demand considerable loyalty from their subjects and citizens. Their power is considerable, and they frequently appear to resort to the use of force in securing their will. Presumably this is the source for the common characterization of states in terms of their concentrated power and their control over the use of force, and specifically, the source of the appeal of misleading Weberian characterizations (monopolies of legitimate force).[13] The social order or, rather, orders from which the modern state emerged were ones in which governance was decentralized, fragmented, varied, overlapping and nonexclusive, mediated, and personal. These social orders were also part of Christendom, which constrained them, though its power and practical unity should not be exaggerated. Governance in the modern state is, by contrast, relatively centralized, unified, uniform, hierarchical and exclusive, non-mediated or direct, penetrating, impersonal and territorial. This is the home for the modern concept of sovereignty.[14]

12. Here and elsewhere I move quickly over very large topics and controversies, familiar to contemporary political and legal philosophers. See Morris, "State Coercion and Force," [2012] *Social Philosophy & Policy* 28–49, and the references therein.

13. Morris, *An Essay*, 43–44 and "How (Not) to Define the State" (unpublished).

14. Even if elements of the notion of sovereignty are ancient, the concept as I analyze it is modern.

Why endow anything with sovereignty? Why entrust humans or human institutions with that power? The answer to this question will help us see how the notion might figure in debates about executive power. A common view is that while humans form large societies because of the benefits made possible by size, large societies are also threatened by conflicts (interests, values, culture, identities, religions). In addition, even in many shared projects that have considerable support, there may be significant incentives to "free ride" on the contributions of others. So a sovereign is needed to settle conflicts and to force free riders to support beneficial collective projects. Both require an authority whose directives (e.g., laws) can settle conflicts and deter behavior that would undermine the common good. Many political thinkers have offered reasons of this kind for the establishments of modern states, and thinkers such as Hobbes and Rousseau have argued that sovereignty is needed for these purposes.[15] We shall return to this general conception of state activity later.

Concerns about endowing humans or human institutions with such power are ancient. Among Hobbes's contemporaries there were many who were not persuaded that it was wise to give rulers this power or that human rulers could have such authority. Leibniz argued that "Hobbesian empires ... [are] neither possible nor desirable, unless those who must have supreme power are gifted with angelic virtues.... Hobbes' demonstrations have a place only in that state whose king is God, whom alone one can trust in all things."[16] No contemporary takes seriously the prospect of attributing to mere mortals the classical sovereignty that Hobbes and others defended; our partisans of sovereignty all think that sovereignty is limited, not absolute in the sense characterized above. But, as I noted earlier, our states recognize that their powers are limited, but also claim that these limits are set by law and that the state ascertains what these are. Some of the concerns we have about absolute sovereignty carry over to more attractive notions of limited sovereignty.

Let us now turn to the question as to who or what might possess sovereignty. This question is important for the larger topic about the powers of executives. The original claimant was of course *the Sovereign* , that is *the ruler* who achieved dominance in his or her realm over lords, emperors, and popes. As no serious thinker advocates a single ruler today, we shall put this candidate to the side for now. In British history sovereignty is attributed to the trinitarian being, *the monarch-in-Parliament*. Given the important role of the judiciary in the American system, the president-and-Congress has never been thought to have sovereignty, but we are merely canvassing the historical candidates for this role. *The state* is perhaps the most common candidate for possession of sovereignty. The notion that states are sovereign is widely accepted today, though this is not to say that everyone adopts my characterization of the concept.

15. See Morris, *An Essay*, ch. 7.

16. Georg Wilhem Leibniz, *Caesarinus Fürstenerius (De Suprematu Principum Germaniae)* [1677], in *Political Writings*, P. Riley (ed), 2nd ed. (Cambridge University Press, 1988) 120.

The next candidate appears in the opening words of the Preamble to the U.S. Constitution, "We the People". *The People* here are the set of members of a political society (e.g., a state). In the American and French political traditions, the People are often said to have a foundational role: ultimate political power rests with them, and they create or authorize the state. The doctrine is usually dubbed that of popular sovereignty. The French Declaration of the Rights of Man and of Citizen expresses a similar view in Article III: "*Le principe de toute Souveraineté réside essentiellement dans la Nation. Nul corps, nul individu ne peut exercer d'autorité qui n'en émane expressément.*"[17] The term "nation" is ambiguous, then as now. We might take it to refer to the state or *nation-state,* and it might refer to the People in the sense above. We can't resolve these questions of textual interpretation here. Instead I wish merely to read this famous sentence in a nationalist spirit: sovereignty resides with the nation, that is, with the people in the sense of a national group. To make this idea clearer, let us distinguish *the People* from *a people.* The first notion is a political one: the People is the set of members of a state (whom we may think of as citizens). The other notion, that of a people (indefinite article, small "p"), is that of a set of individuals with common histories, cultures, language, and the like, who recognize one another by virtue of these shared characteristics.[18] Our last view, then, is "nationalist"; it attributes sovereignty to national peoples. It is a nineteenth and twentieth century view, but an early statement is found in the less-cited opening paragraph of the American Declaration of Independence: "When in the Course of human events, it becomes necessary for one people to dissolve the political bands which have connected them with another, and to assume among the powers of the earth, the separate and equal station to which the Laws of Nature and of Nature's God entitle them . . ." On Jefferson's view, separate peoples are entitled by natural law to separate and equal stations.[19]

Who might possess sovereignty? We have several candidates then; these are:

(1) the ruler (e.g., the monarch),
(2) the monarch-in-Parliament, or the executive + legislature,
(3) the state,
(4) the nation or the national people, or
(5) the People (popular sovereignty).

I assume that most readers of this piece will be unsympathetic to alternatives 1 and 4. Alternative 2 is ill-suited to the American constitutional system as it would involve rejecting the distinctive role the judiciary has had at least since *Marbury*

17. "The principle of any sovereignty resides essentially in the Nation. No body, no individual can exert authority which does not emanate expressly from it."

18. See Morris, *An Essay,* 230–54.

19. See Morris, "Peoples, Nations, and the Unity of Societies," in *Cultural Identity and the Nation-State,* Carol C. Gould and Pasquale Pasquino (eds) (Lanham, MD: Rowman & Littlefield, 2001), 19–29.

v. Madison. Our interest lies in determining the significance of traditional understandings of sovereignty for contemporary debates about executive power. Supporters of expanded executive powers certainly don't endorse the first option (or 2 or 4). Consider then alternative 5, the sovereignty of the People. Suppose we endorse that view; what are the implications for the power of the executive? It's not clear how this view could help the proponent of unconstrained or relatively unconstrained executive power. Surely the executive would then be constrained by the will of the People (i.e., the general will). We note that Rousseau, one of the greatest theorists of popular sovereignty, conceived of the People's power as essentially legislative; for him executive power does not belong to the sovereign.[20] We need not explore the details of Rousseau's view here, and it seems quite clear that the view that the executive branch of government should be unconstrained or relatively unconstrained gains no support from attributions of sovereignty to the People.[21]

The last view is that the state is sovereign. As is probably already clear, state here is not to be identified with government. The distinction between the two is commonplace in European settings, especially in countries with parliamentary systems; in the United States, government and state are not always clearly distinguished.[22] In any case, it is hard to see how attributing sovereignty to the state or to the American federal government would help partisans of an unconstrained or less constrained executive. Why would the other branches of government wish to abandon their role in the sovereign body? Legislation, the making of law, is an essential power of sovereignty; it's hard to conceive a sovereign who would lack it. We have said nothing about the traditional inalienability of sovereignty. Classical thinkers such as Hobbes and Rousseau claim that sovereignty can be destroyed but not alienated. It's not obvious we need to endorse the inalienability of sovereignty, but if we do, then the constitutive members of the sovereign body cannot give up their power—that is, they lack the (Hohfeldian) power to do so.

20. "Nous avons vu que la puissance législative appartient au peuple, & ne peut appartenir qu'à lui. Il est aisé de voir au contraire, par les principes ci-devant établis, que la puissance exécutive ne peut appartenir à la généralité comme législatrice ou souveraine, parce que cette puissance ne consiste qu'en des actes particuliers qui ne sont point du ressort de la loi, ni par conséquent de celui du Souverain, dont tous les actes ne peuvent être que des loix." ("We have seen that the legislative power belongs to the people and can only belong to it. On the contrary, it is easy to see, by the principles established above, that the executive power cannot belong to the whole as legislator or sovereign, since this power consists solely of particular acts that are not in any way proper to law, nor consequent of that of the Sovereign, all of whose acts can only be laws.") Jean-Jacques Rousseau, *Du Contrat social, Oeuvres completes,* vol 3, Bernard Gagnebin and Marcel Raymond (eds) (Bibliothèque de la Pléiade 1964), vol III, ch. I.

21. See Morris, "The Very Idea of Popular Sovereignty: 'We the People' Reconsidered," [2000] Social Philosophy & Policy 1–26.

22. One of the reasons is that the original American political societies were "states" or "commonwealths" and thus the term "state" is now used for the subunits of the American federal system. For further discussion of the distinction, see Morris, *An Essay,* 20–23.

None of these attributions of sovereignty, aside from the first, offer support to lessening the constraints on executive power in a system such as ours. Ours are systems of mixed government, with different branches sharing state power. There may be good reasons for relaxing some of the constraints on the executive in the American system or for giving this branch of government more power, but traditional doctrines of sovereignty don't seem to have any clear implications for these matters. Classical sovereignty would have the sovereign be unconstrained by human-made law, but absolute sovereignty is widely rejected today and was already controversial in early modern Europe. There is reason to want executives to have considerable discretion as well as certain powers in times of emergency. A famous model of an arrangement of this kind is Roman dictatorship. Appointed *magister populi* for a limited time to address a particular task, the office of dictator was fashioned for different kinds of emergency situations. But these offices were constrained and limited, in extent and in duration.

I should mention a way of thinking about sovereignty, popular at different times in different circles, which some might expect would lend some support to partisans of unconstrained sovereigns. John Austin, influenced by Bentham's views about law and sovereignty, was puzzled by federal systems such as the American one as it was hard to locate the sovereign. Federal states were composite polities where "the several united governments of the several united societies, together with a government common to those several societies, are jointly sovereign in each of those several societies, and also in the larger society arising from the federal union." But "the common or general government is not sovereign or supreme." Sovereignty "resides in the united governments as *forming one aggregate body.*" Given the multiple governments in the United States and the different ways of amending the Constitution, the sovereign turns out to be a peculiar and somewhat haphazard group of persons.[23] This kind of view leads to the identification of the sovereign with the members who happen at any time to make up the set of persons and bodies of persons with the power to make law (including the power to change the Constitution). It is an odd view, and it certainly gives no support to partisans of an unconstrained or less constrained executive.

Another unusual view is Carl Schmitt's muscular account of sovereignty that attributes it to whoever decides in exceptional circumstances: "*Souverän ist, wer über den Ausnahmezustand entschneidet.*"[24] Sovereigns act by intervening occasionally. They can be confidently identified only after the fact, after they have assembled and asserted their power, and sometimes they can be identified counterfactually as in the case of a very powerful military that intervenes when there is disorder or political uncertainty. If partisans of an unconstrained

23. John Austin, *The Province of Jurisprudence Determined,* Wilfrid E. Rumble (ed) (Cambridge University Press, 1995 [1885]) 206–11. John Dewey thought that Austin's view represents "a confusion of sovereignty with the organs of its exercise . . . " See John Dewey, "Austin's Theory of Sovereignty," [1894] *Political Science Quarterly* 31–52.

24. Carl Schmitt, *Politische Theologie: Vier Kapitel zur Lehre von der Souveränität* (Duncker & Humblot, 1996 [1922]) 13.

executive were to adopt Schmitt's view, they could say that "the executive" is who or what decides in exceptional circumstances. But it's not clear this would pick out the designated executive. There are also just too many exceptional circumstances and too many people deciding when these circumstances occur. But the important point is a view such as this merely becomes a version of the first attribution of sovereignty. When the executive "decides" in exceptional circumstances, it has become a sovereign ruler. This is hardly an attractive view or one that would appeal to partisans of executive power.

There may be several reasons that we might want to expand the powers of the executive in the American system. But sovereignty traditionally understood seems to play no part in making the case for expanding the power of the executive. The legislative power is an essential element of sovereignty, and we have seen that no one attributes sovereignty to the executive alone. We have to now considered the concept of sovereignty abstractly and its classical form. Let us now consider whether the notion could be adapted in some way to bolster the case for expanded executive powers.

We might start by asking why might expanded executive powers be desirable and justified? In many contexts, there are reasons to fear an executive with expanded powers, and the American tradition in particular was founded on a fear of strong executives. Let us step back for a minute and ask quite generally: Why have governments and law in the first place? Historically an important reason for government was the need of the few to control the many, an urgent need when the many were conquered and unhappy about this. But our interest is in normative and not mere explanatory reasons for government, so we shall focus on just governments. An influential tradition, already referred to in this essay, would think of one of the main tasks of government and law as being "conflict resolution," as it were. There is much conflict amongst humans, and much of it can lead to serious losses to many. This may be an antiseptic way of referring to homicide and war and related ills of the human condition. But addressing conflicts affecting a population, including external threats, is usually the primary explanatory and normative reason for government. Governments are protective.[25] The first task of a government is protecting its subjects, securing persons and possessions. The "resolution" of important conflicts can benefit most members of a population, especially in the case of what we now think of as national defense. This first task of government consists in the provision of a good to a group of people, one that is difficult for individuals to provide for themselves. The first task of government is thus the provision of an important collective or public good, to invoke the technical concept of political economy.[26] Why have governments and law in the

25. See James Buchanan on the notion of the "protective state" in *The Limits of Liberty* (University of Chicago Press, 1975).

26. Collective or public goods are defined by *indivisibility* (or *jointness of supply*) and *nonexcludability*. Once produced, a collective or public good is available to everyone at no additional cost (indivisibility), and it is not feasible or efficient to exclude individuals from the benefits of the good (nonexcludability).

first place, we ask; a familiar and influential answer is the provision of important public goods.[27]

We have talked quite generally about government and law. Now let us ask: Why have an *executive* branch of government? For much of human history our familiar distinctions among legislative, judicial, and executive powers were not drawn, and all these powers were in effect attributed to the same individuals. The main purpose of the executive came to be recognized to be the enforcement of law. Why have an executive branch of government? Enforcement. Contemporary debates about lessening the constraints on the executive might then be said to be about enforcement broadly understood. But I think it more useful to think of them as about certain features of the different parts of government. The decisions of legislatures and judicial bodies are often compromises and thus not always as "decisive" as we might wish. More importantly, they are not always *swift*. In certain contexts, we may want government to act decisively and swiftly. The executive may so act, especially if its head is a single individual as it often is. In classical and contemporary writings, the acts of great leaders and sometimes tyrants are praised for their decisiveness and swiftness, at least as compared to their legislative and judicial rivals. When *action*, especially decisive and swift action, is needed, less restrained executive powers may be desirable. And such action may secure an important collective or public good and consequently be justified.

It is not surprising that the powers of executives are often much less constrained in emergency settings, for instance, insurrection and war. The "emergency powers" of executives are traditionally the most expansive. It is clear how emergencies often call for swift and decisive action, and that this may require lessening restraints on those who are tasked with addressing them.[28] Similarly, negotiating with foreign powers is often facilitated by giving individuals powers that normally might be reserved for legislatures.

We can all appreciate how a case can be made for lessening the constraints on executives in certain settings. My objective, however, is not to adjudicate the debate about executive power, but to see how the concept of sovereignty might be enlisted in support of those who seek to lessen the constraints. The first point to make concerns the irrelevance here of the classical notion of sovereignty. This notion would have the sovereign unconstrained by law and, on some reading of the classical thinkers, unconstrained by justice. This understanding of sovereignty leaves no room for international law and makes familiar understandings of constitutions impossible. As I mentioned earlier, the notions of sovereignty

27. A rival view is often thought to be that which posits justice as the first or most important task of government. This view is also very influential today, and a discussion of it here would distract from our main topic. But I should say that justice must be a *constraint* on governments and states, and that where the provision of justice is itself a collective or public good, it may and usually should be provided by government.

28. And, it should be noticed, that many ethical norms are widely thought to be suspended or less binding. Fire fighters may invade and damage dwellings because of the urgency of their job. And of course everyday norms governing the taking of human life are suspended in time of war.

espoused today are all "limited." The sovereign is not unconstrained by law (and justice), *nemo est supra legem.*

We should also recall that sovereignty today is never attributed to the executive branch of government. Even in the British system, said to be a constitutional monarchy, the sovereign is not the monarch but the trinity of the "monarch-in-Parliament." Further, the executive is constituted by law or tradition as one of several branches of government and is thereby authorized to act in various ways, and this authorization is legally constituted and typically constrains. A paradigmatic example of the legal constitution of a powerful executive is Roman dictatorship, and it was highly constrained.

It is very hard to see how the notion of sovereignty helps support a case for lessened constraints on the executive. We may appreciate the reasons for wanting executives to face fewer constraints in certain settings. But it is also easy to understand the reasons for concern. Executive powers are entrusted to humans, and these creatures are fallible in multiple and familiar ways. The judgment of executives may often be poor, and their powers may often be abused. The concerns that many had about classical sovereignty—Leibniz: "Hobbes' demonstrations have a place only in that state whose king is God, whom alone one can trust in all things"—spill over to limited sovereigns and to relatively unconstrained executives. Strong leaders, even if constrained, may be a source of concern.

An appreciation of the reasons we might want to lessen the constraints on executive power in some settings, coupled with an appreciation of the dangers of so doing, point to familiar and difficult problems with institutional design. We want our institutions to do many things and to strike a balance between different capacities, to be not too hot and not too cold. In some contexts we need an executive that can act decisively and swiftly, but we also worry about abuse and excess. The right balance, here and elsewhere, is often hard to achieve. Trade-offs between multiple institutional elements is as difficult a problem as that between competing ends or values, perhaps more difficult. Institutions also change and are often transformed and subverted.

There may also be some tensions here between the need for decisive and swift executive action and the rule of law. Executives may exceed their powers, sometimes clearly violating the law. As David Frost said to President Nixon, "where the president can decide that it's in the best interests of the nation or something, and do something illegal." The latter's reply was that "Well, when the president does it that means that it is not illegal." We think neither that the sovereign is above the law (i.e., not subject to the law) nor that the president is sovereign. We might believe that the president is permitted to act illegally in some circumstances, or that if the president were to so act, he or she would be immune from prosecution. But that would be determined by the law. *Nemo est supra legem*—no one and *no office* need be above the law.[29]

29. Sharon Lloyd's insightful chapter in this volume, "Locating Sovereignty in Systems of Divided and Limited Government," takes up a number of questions about sovereignty parallel or similar to those considered in this essay. I am grateful to her for showing me a draft of this essay.

APPENDIX: NIXON (FROST INTERVIEWS)

FROST: So what in a sense, you're saying is that there are certain situations, and the Huston Plan or that part of it was one of them, where the president can decide that it's in the best interests of the nation or something, and do something illegal.

NIXON: Well, when the president does it that means that it is not illegal.

FROST: By definition.

NIXON: Exactly. Exactly. If the president, for example, approves something because of the national security, or in this case because of a threat to internal peace and order of significant magnitude, then the president's decision in that instance is one that enables those who carry it out, to carry it out without violating a law. Otherwise they're in an impossible position.

http://landmarkcases.org/en/Page/722/Nixons_Views_on_Presidential_Power_Excerpts_from_a_1977_Interview_with_David_Frost.

6

Locating Sovereignty in Systems of Divided and Limited Government

S.A. LLOYD

To characterize a political entity such as a nation or state as sovereign is usually to assert that it is entitled to govern itself independently of the will of any superior earthly body. Sovereign polities are regarded as agents who act on the basis of their own decisions and are properly assigned full responsibility for their actions. A state's sovereignty is exercised through the actions of its internal sovereign, usually its government.[1] When that government takes a simple form, absolute monarchy for instance, there is little difficulty in locating the agent who exercises that state's sovereignty. In that case, the state's sovereign will is expressed by the public will (the will in matters of state) of the monarch.

A puzzle arises though, as to where sovereignty is located in governments characterized by the division of rights to exercise powers essential for governance. Sovereignty involves possession of the characteristics required to be an agent, to be entitled to govern, and to be able to do so effectively. This trilogy of characteristics includes the personal *capacities* to deliberate, to judge and to will; the *authority* to impose its judgments and will on its subjects or citizens; and the *power* to effect its will. Multiple, potentially competing, branches of government and / or levels of government, as well as constraining instruments such as constitutions or moral or religious codes, threaten to undermine not just effective sovereign power, but the most basic conditions for sovereign *agency*. The seventeenth

1. Conceptions of internal sovereignty are historically specific and differ widely among theorists in both the attributes of sovereignty (e.g., as absolute, indivisible, or limited) and its location (e.g., in the legislature, the government as a whole, the people, the nation, local communities or states.) A classic survey of Western conceptions from Bodin to 1900 can be found in Merriam Jr., *History of the Theory of Sovereignty Since Rousseau* (1900) and a survey reflecting more recent research in Raia Prokhovnik, *Sovereignty: History and Theory* (2008).

Sovereignty and the New Executive Authority. Claire O. Finkelstein and Michael Skerker.

century English philosopher Thomas Hobbes, a renowned systematic theorist of sovereignty, developed an early and elaborate articulation of this puzzle, and a profoundly influential argument that sovereignty is strictly incompatible with separation of governmental powers. Further, he purported to demonstrate that governmental sovereignty cannot be legally limited.

After presenting and examining Hobbes's arguments that any attempt to divide or limit sovereignty undermines the agency requirement for sovereignty, and noting some allied arguments from Rousseau and Kant, I argue that a complex system of divided and limited government comprised of a specific sort of rule-governed procedure would in fact allow for sovereign agency of the sort Hobbes insisted is needed. I explain how locating sovereignty within such systems depends crucially on considerations of temporality. However, the problem Hobbes flags of ensuring that the coercive power needed to govern effectively is reliably attached to the locus of agency in a complex system remains important, and requires another solution that Hobbes did not consider, and which I outline. I conclude by identifying the particular difficulty of locating moral responsibility for the state's actions that attends a system of the mixed sort described, even when that state can function as a sovereign agent.

I. A SOVEREIGN IS AN ARTIFICIAL PERSON

In his masterwork *Leviathan*, Hobbes grounds sovereignty in the web of obligations that unifies a group of individuals into a commonwealth. Hobbes defines a commonwealth as "one person" authorized by each of many individuals to use their physical and economic resources at its own discretion in pursuit of peace and common defense.[2] The commonwealth is a man-made, or artificial person.[3] The individual or assembly of individuals that "carries" the person of the commonwealth is called the sovereign,[4] and "*sovereignty* is an artificial soul, as giving life and motion to the whole body."[5] A person, Hobbes explains, is he whose words or actions represent himself or another human or being or thing, such as a corporation or university. When one's actions are considered as being one's own (that is, when one is acting or speaking on behalf of oneself), one is termed a natural person. When one's words and actions represent the words and actions of others, one is termed an artificial person.[6] (A single individual can be both a natural person and an artificial person.) Commonwealths, and the sovereigns who carry or animate them are thus artificial persons, representing each of the individuals

2. XVII.13. References to *Leviathan* (1651) are by chapter and paragraph number. References to the Latin *Leviathan* (1668) are to chapter and paragraph number preceded by OL.

3. Introduction.1

4. XVII.14.

5. Introduction.1

6. XVI.2.

who have authorized them. A multitude becomes a unity only by having a unified representative, Hobbes insists:

> A multitude of men are made one person, when they are by one man, or one person, represented so that it be done with the consent of every one of that multitude in particular. For it is the unity of the representer, not the unity of the represented, that maketh the person one. And it is the representer that beareth the person, and but one person, and unity cannot otherwise be understood in a multitude.[7]

So the sovereign that bears the person of the commonwealth is a unitary artificial person, whether that person is comprised by a single individual who is also a natural person (say a monarch) or rather by an assembly composed of multiple individuals (all as in a democratic assembly, or more than one but fewer than all, as in an aristocratic assembly).[8] This artificial person is thought of as the result of an imagined or actual process in which all

> confer all their power and strength upon one man, or upon one assembly of men, that may reduce all their wills, by plurality of voices, unto one will, which is as much as to say, to appoint one man or assembly of men to bear their person, and every one to own and acknowledge himself to be author of whatsoever he that so beareth their person shall act, or cause to be acted, in those things which concern the common peace and safety, and therein to submit their wills, every one to his will, and their judgments, to his judgment.[9]

In acknowledging themselves to be the authors of the sovereign's actions and judgments, subjects undertake the *moral obligation* to subordinate their several private judgments and wills to the public judgment and will that the sovereign expresses. This obligation to defer to the sovereign's public judgment—to act on it rather than on one's own private judgment—is understood to be owed to one's fellow subjects in the case of sovereignty by institution. Hobbes imagines that sovereignty by institution of a new commonwealth involves a procedure in which each person agrees with every other to grant sovereign authority to represent oneself to whichever individual or assembly the votes of the majority of persons select. Here the sovereign has no part in the sovereign-making agreement. In the case of sovereignty by acquisition, the conquered have agreed with the conqueror

7. XVI.13.

8. Notice that for Hobbes there is a limited, technical sense in which all commonwealths are democratic: they represent every single subject/citizen, even if the sovereign that animates the commonwealth takes the form of a monarch or an aristocratic assembly, and even if subjects/citizens do not decide which individuals occupy the office of sovereign. Individuals who are not properly deemed to own and authorize all the sovereign's actions as representing their will on public matters are not members of the commonwealth.

9. XVII.13.

to grant it authority to represent themselves on condition that they be allowed life and corporal liberty. People who are subsequently born into an ongoing commonwealth established by either mode or who join it by immigration are thought of as likewise owning and authorizing the sovereign's actions as representing their own will on public matters.[10] In every case, the obligation to give priority to the public will over one's own private will in cases of conflict is underwritten by the natural duty under the law of nature to hold oneself to the same standards of behavior one demands from one's fellow subjects.[11]

Absent these ties of obligation, the group of individuals attempting to unify themselves would remain a mere concourse of like-minded people, what Hobbes terms an *irregular system*. In an irregular system such as a group of soccer club enthusiasts or members of the Republican party, individuals' private wills may happen to converge on some course of action, but there is no *obligation* to take some single will as representing the will of them all. Such individuals may by chance find themselves "ensuing or eschewing the same things," which condition Hobbes terms "consent" or co-assenting; but this sort of *agreeing that* does not create any obligation in the way that *making an agreement* may sometimes do.[12] If irregular systems can act as agents at all, it is only because of a contingent or accidental convergence of the private judgments of all the individuals in them. Commonwealths, by contrast, are absolute and independent *regular systems*, whose members are duty-bound to make their representative's (the sovereign's) will the guide of their actions in public matters. The obligation of their members to act on the will of their representative makes regular systems capable agents. So the first requirement of sovereignty, namely that sovereigns be agents capable of exercising will, is met only by regular systems whose members are represented by one and the same representative, where representation is understood to entail an obligation to act as the representative wills on behalf of the represented.

10. On the account of political obligation Hobbes develops, an individual may have an obligation to obey the commands of the sovereign under whose protection she lives even though she was not a party to the institution of the commonwealth ruled by that sovereign, or conquered by that sovereign, nor gave her actual consent to be governed by that sovereign when joining the commonwealth upon immigration or upon reaching what Locke called the age of reason. Anyone who wants others to lay down their right of private judgment in favor of a public authority—as all of us must want because we must want to live in an environment conducive to our own agency—is required by the basic moral law of reciprocity to lay down his or her own right of private judgment. For the details of Hobbes's moral but non-contractual argument for political obligation, see S.A. Lloyd, *Morality in the Philosophy of Thomas Hobbes: Cases in the Law of Nature* (Cambridge University Press 2009) chapter 5.

11. That is, by what *Leviathan* numbers the tenth law against arrogance and also, in case the subject has been called upon to promise allegiance, the 3rd requiring that covenants be performed. The second law of nature requires that upon entrance into conditions of peace, no one reserve to himself any right he would not be content to have all others reserve to themselves as well. What Hobbes calls the "sum" of the laws of nature, and sometimes refers to as the law of nature itself, is the reciprocity requirement that we do unto others all that we require from them.

12. *De Cive* V.4. Such mere "conspiring of many wills to the same end" is too unstable to be counted on as the foundation of social peace. DC V.5.

II. THE PUZZLE OF THE SOVEREIGN ASSEMBLY

We noted earlier that Hobbes allows that the artificial person bearing sovereignty may be an assembly rather than an individual natural person. Any sovereign, qua artificial person, must be able to perform the personal actions of deliberating, deciding, and willing. Hobbes analyzes the process of deliberation as entertaining alternating appetites and aversions, with the will being the last appetite or aversion immediately adhering to the action done or to its omission.[13] But while it is easy to understand how sentient creatures such as individual humans can have appetites and aversions, and so, on Hobbes's account can will, it is not obvious how a *collectivity* can have appetites, aversions, or a will. Analogously, according to Hobbes, the judgment is the last opinion in a string of alternating opinions of the truth or falsity of some proposition being entertained, and although no particular mystery attends how individuals may have opinions and so arrive at judgments, how an abstract entity such as a *set* of individuals could have and do such things is obscure. The underlying point is that although natural persons can easily be understood to desire, opine, will, and judge, as can an artificial person constituted by a single natural person, how a collection or aggregation or bunch of people could be an artificial person capable of such actions is not so easily understood.

A further difficulty for locating sovereignty in an assembly is that Hobbes holds that a multitude can become a unity only if they authorize a *single* representative. How then, is an assembly picked out as a unitary person, if not by having its own members each represented by the same individual? It would seem that for a sovereign assembly to be a person, it would have to be represented by an individual; but this would defeat Hobbes's claim that an assembly rather than an individual can be sovereign, for then the subjects would be represented by the individual who represents the assembly that represents themselves.[14]

The natural solution to this problem is to admit as the unifying element of the assembly a will-determining *procedure it uses* instead of a personal *judgment it privileges*. Majority vote is the procedure Hobbes suggests for determining a "voice," or expressed will or judgment, across members of a group. Such a procedure uses the personal opinions and appetites of the natural persons who are members of the assembly as inputs. He writes

> If the representative consist of many men, the voice of the greater number must be considered as the voice of them all. For if the lesser number pronounce (for example) in the affirmative, and the greater in the negative, there will be negatives more than enough to destroy the affirmatives; and thereby the excess of negatives, standing uncontradicted, are the only voice the representative hath.[15]

13. VI.53

14. This problem, and a procedural solution to it of the sort I develop below, is discussed in Douglas Wadle, "The Problem of the (Representative) Assembly in Hobbes's *Leviathan*," *Hobbes Studies* 30(2) 2017, pp. 178–201.

15. XVI.15.

The suggestion here is not that partisans literally fight it out to determine who wins, for in such a case any victory of the majority would be contingent on the relative strength of individuals and not just sheer numbers. Rather, Hobbes is thinking of pro and con votes as like units of positive and negative number that cancel each other out, leaving a remainder.[16] In the Latin *Leviathan* he explains that "the negative voices exceeding the affirmative, as [the excess] is not contradicted by [the affirmative], it is the voice of the person, i.e., of all. For otherwise the person would be mute, which is contrary to nature."[17]

It is important that a sovereign assembly not be mute, for subjects, who are ultimately the instruments through which the sovereign's agency is effected, cannot be expected to obey commands they cannot hear.[18] But what is crucial is that the representative of a group be a person, in Hobbes's specified sense of something that is able to exercise the personal actions of judging and willing. A majoritarian voting procedure will, in an assembly of uneven number in which each member has a single vote, enable the assembly to act as a person.[19] Such an assembly cannot find itself in the paralyzed position of simultaneously willing equally strongly both to do and not to do an action.

The capacity for agency requisite to personhood imposes further constraints on acceptable procedures for the deliberations of sovereign assemblies. Although it is consistent with sovereign agency that one member of the assembly possesses a veto, it is not possible for all or even for more than one to possess a veto. A majority vote to Phi yields a determinate decision to Phi; and such a vote with an added unique power of veto exercised yields a determinate decision not to Phi. But when a decision to Phi is vetoed by one member of the assembly, and the contradictory decision not to Phi is vetoed by another member of the assembly, the voice of the assembly must be either self-contradictory (deciding both and neither to Phi and not to Phi) or, as Hobbes says, silent. In such a case, there is no con decision by default, as there would be if a pro decision required a supermajority but fell short of it. There is simply no decision, because the body is incapable of exercising agency. It is not a person (or is in this case a radically disabled, or comatose person.) But nothing that is not a person or cannot function as a person can represent anyone, and so no such procedure can serve as the sovereign of a commonwealth. This intuitively plausible claim will play a major role in Hobbes's argument against systems of divided sovereignty.

16. Rousseau embraces a similar account of how what he terms the general will might be identified through a voting procedure in which although every person votes her particular will (rather than, as she should, her opinion on whether some proposed general measure does or does not comport with the common interest), the differences cancel out each other with what remains being the general will. See *Of the Social Contract* Book II chapter 3.

17. OL XVI.15 (note 10 in Curley).

18. And, Hobbes insists, positive laws must be promulgated if they are to be enforceable through punishment under the law of nature.

19. In an assembly of even number, a supermajoritarian procedure would be needed to ensure that it could act as a person.

III. HOBBES'S ARGUMENT AGAINST DIVIDED SOVEREIGNTY

Hobbes held that all simple forms of government—such as monarchy, aristocracy, and democracy— can function adequately to maintain social peace, so long as their authority is not limited and they possess all of what he termed the essential rights of sovereignty. He saw some practical reasons to prefer monarchy, including its more limited scope for the exercise of personal corruption because if we assume that it is human nature to seek to advantage oneself and one's friends, the larger the ruling group, the greater the number who will feed at the public trough; and further, democratic assemblies invite demagoguery and partisan bickering. However, monarchy has its own weaknesses, so which form of government to prefer is open to reasonable debate. The crucial point, Hobbes insists, is that it is always more prudent to maintain an effective simple government—one that secures the safety and general good of its people—when it exists, regardless of its form, than to risk the perils that attend efforts to alter the form of government, particularly by acts of disobedience. Populations will divide on questions of how to reform and on who should rule, and entrenched regimes will resist reforms, so that potentially destabilizing conflict is bound to ensue.[20] But unlike simple forms of government, "mixed" forms, in which the essential rights of sovereignty are divided amongst multiple bodies, cannot reliably exercise sovereignty.[21] The essential rights of sovereignty, among which Hobbes included rights of legislation, adjudication, enforcement, taxation, and use of armed forces, are interconnected in such a way that the exercise of one will not produce its intended effect without the cooperative exercise of others.[22] When partial sets of these essential rights are held by different bodies and those bodies refuse to cooperate in exercising them, the government as a whole becomes incapable of acting. Unenforced laws will not reliably regulate behavior; raising an army without granting funds to support it

20. Hobbes maintains that "they that go about by disobedience to do no more than reform the commonwealth shall find they do thereby destroy it, like the foolish daughters of Peleus (in the fable) which, desiring to renew the youth of their decrepit father, did by the counsel of Medea cut him in pieces and boil him, together with strange herbs, but made not of him a new man. This desire of change is like the breach of the first of God's commandments . . . " XXX.7

21. Hobbes derisively termed such systems "mixarchy." In his history of the English Civil War, Hobbes wrote that many of the lords in Parliament and the English gentry aimed to "bring the government to a mixed monarchy, as they called it; wherein the absolute sovereignty should be divided between the King, the House of Lords, and the House of Commons." "But how," asks his interlocutor in this dialogue, "if they cannot agree?" "I think they never thought of that" replies Hobbes's mouthpiece. *Behemoth* (Chicago, 1990) p. 33. Among agitators in the civil war, lawyers and gentlemen "were in love with *mixarchy* which they used to praise by the name of mixed monarchy, though it were indeed nothing else but pure anarchy." Pp. 116–17.

22. Hobbes also included among the essential rights of sovereignty the right to regulate doctrine, including religious doctrine, through active education and also censorship, "for the actions of men proceed from their opinions, and in the well-governing of opinions consisteth the well-governing of men's actions, in order to their peace and concord. And though in matter of doctrine nothing ought to be regarded but the truth, yet this is not repugnant to regulating of the same by peace." XVIII.16

will not enable prosecution of war. The way to ensure that the essential rights will be exercised cooperatively is to vest all of them in the same individual or assembly. Hobbes writes that if the sovereign

> (t)ransfer the Militia, he retains the judicature in vain, for want of execution of the laws; or if he grant away the power of raising money, the militia is in vain; or if he give away the government of doctrines, men will be frighted into rebellion with the fear of spirits. And so if we consider any one of the said rights, we shall presently see that the holding of all the rest will produce no effect in the conservation of peace and justice, the end for which all commonwealths are instituted.[23]

Here Hobbes is describing the potential for paralysis of effective government when the essential rights are divided. A government in which powers are separated and cooperation is lacking may simply be unable to function.[24] If its paralysis is widespread and of long duration, the government may find itself unable to secure domestic peace and foreign defense.

Another way of understanding what happens in such cases is that the government as a whole cannot act as a person. It cannot judge or will because its component elements jointly affirm contradictory judgments and volitions. When the legislature wills that taxes be collected and the executive wills that taxes not be collected, the government becomes, in Hobbes's language, mute. Separating essential rights is tantamount to issuing veto rights to multiple parties. Because no exercise of an essential right can achieve its intended effect without the cooperation of other rights-holders, every holder of an essential right holds a power of veto. As we saw earlier, for a group to be able reliably to exercise agency, it must operate according to some decision procedure that yields a determinate result; but if more than one of its members possesses the power of veto, there can be cases in which no determinate result can be reached; the group will neither will

23. XVIII.16. "These are the rights which make the essence of sovereignty, and which are the marks whereby a man may discern in what man, or assembly of men, the sovereign power is placed and resideth. For these are incommunicable and inseparable."

24. Recent U.S. history provides multiple instances of government shutdowns (depriving the government of the funds to pay its employees, and pensions to retirees and veterans, and to provide services to citizens) caused by the failure of the House, Senate, and president to reach agreement on a funding bill. In 2018, there were two brief government shutdowns despite the fact that Republicans held the Presidency, House and Senate. In 2013, the government shut down for sixteen days when the Senate refused to act on a funding bill in which the House had reinstated a provision to defund or delay Obama's Patient Protection and Affordable Care Act that the Senate had previously removed from the House bill. There were two periods of government shutdown during the Clinton administration, including twenty-one days when the Republican-controlled Congress and the president could not agree on which budget office's numbers to use. There were eight instances of brief government shutdowns during the Reagan administration as a consequence of stalemate between the president and the Democrat-controlled House, and one during the G.H.W. Bush administration when the president vetoed a continuing resolution passed by the Democrat-controlled Congress whose veto the House failed to override.

nor not will, or both will and not will. Hobbes's argument against the separation of powers comes down to the claim that governments with this feature cannot be artificial persons. This is an argument of considerable theoretical power.[25]

The necessity of possessing all of the essential rights of sovereignty has not been lost on those who have possessed partial sets of those rights. Typically, says Hobbes, they attempt to grab the other rights they need in order to make those they possess effective, resulting in multiple overlapping sovereigns. When multiple powers claim sovereign authority over the same group of subjects "the commonwealth cannot but be in great danger of civil war and dissolution."[26]

IV. HOBBES'S ARGUMENT AGAINST LIMITED SOVEREIGNTY

Hobbes is notorious for having argued that sovereignty must be absolute and unlimited. Understanding the reasoning underlying that position will prove useful in answering our main question concerning the location of sovereignty in complex systems. Hobbes noted that if a limit to sovereign authority is imposed, the question will arise in particular cases of whether that limit has or has not been overstepped. Of course there may well be an objectively correct answer to that question, which may or may not be difficult to discover, but Hobbes calls attention to the more immediate problem of who is authorized to decide the question. The sovereign was, *ex hypothesis,* the authoritative adjudicator of all disputes, subjects being understood as morally obligated to subordinate their private judgments and wills to its public judgment and will. Supposing then it is the sovereign who rightly decides whether the sovereign has or has not overstepped the limits of its legitimate authority, there is no practical problem. The sovereign's powers of agency remain intact. But those advocating limits on sovereign power will object that for the sovereign to decide whether the limits are being respected is like permitting the fox to decide whether the henhouse is safe.

If limited sovereignty means then, that someone other than the sovereign is authorized to decide whether or not the sovereign is doing its job correctly, the

25. Hobbes writes that where there is a division of the essential rights of taxation, enforcement, and legislation, the result is "not one independent commonwealth, but three independent factions, nor one representative person, but three. . . . To what disease in the natural body of man I may exactly compare this irregularity of a commonwealth, I know not. But I have seen a man that had another man growing out of his side, with an head, arms, breast, and stomach of his own; if he had had another man growing out of his other side, the comparison might then have been exact." XXIX.16 The problems for effective agency of conjoined triplets of the sort Hobbes describes are not hard to imagine.

26. XXIX.15. This complete multiplication of sovereignties often happens when temporal (civil) and spiritual (ecclesiastical) sovereigns compete, but it can also happen within the civil realm when, for example, Parliament and Crown assert overlapping sovereignty, as Hobbes explains they did during the English Civil War. Hobbes likens a body politic subjected to multiple overlapping sovereigns to an epileptic individual, whose mind cannot control its bodily motions. This analogy assumes that only one of the competing sovereigns has genuine authority (and diagnoses epilepsy as unreasoned movement of the limbs by an unnatural obstruction of the nerves that would normally convey movement from "the soul in the brain".

question becomes who, exactly, is authorized to decide this? On Hobbes's understanding, it is strictly conceptually incoherent that each individual subject should be entitled to decide this, for that would be for each simultaneously to retain the right to privilege his own private judgment while authorizing a sovereign public judgment to which all including himself must rightfully defer. The state of nature is a condition in which all have a right to act on their own private judgment in all matters, including how to govern themselves and others. The state of being a subject/citizen in a commonwealth is a condition in which members are morally bound to defer to a public judgment, that is, to the sovereign's judgment of how they are to be governed. These moral conditions cannot obtain for the same person at the same time, so it cannot be that sovereignty is limited by the private judgments of individual subjects.[27] If public judgment trumps, we have a commonwealth and sovereignty; if private judgment trumps we have a state of nature.

Apart from this conceptual incoherence, to suppose sovereign authority is limited is to think of sovereignty as having been granted conditionally, or as Hobbes says, by way of "precedent covenant" of the sovereign to the subjects. On that supposition, Hobbes writes of subjects that

> If any one, or more of them, pretend a breach of the covenant made by the sovereign at his institution; and others or one other of his subjects, or himself alone, pretend there was no such breach, there is in this case, no judge to decide the controversy: it therefore returns to the sword again . . . contrary to the design they had in the institution. It is therefore in vain to grant sovereignty by way of precedent covenant.[28]

Actions are "in vain" when they do not achieve our intended ends. As a practical matter, if every subject retains the right to judge in every case whether the government is ruling correctly and to resist or defend it accordingly, diverse private judgments are apt to undermine the government's effectiveness at every turn, and may easily result in armed conflict in continuous attempts to resettle different governments.[29] So to the extent political stability is desirable, limiting government's authority and letting individuals judge its conformity with the limits is not. But these practical considerations distract from Hobbes's conceptual

27. Recall that the sovereign carries the commonwealth, which is defined as one "person" (assembly or individual) authorized to use their strength and means *as it shall think fit* for their peace and common defense. To retain the right to act on one's private judgment of how the peace and common defense are to be conducted is to remain in a state of nature.

28. XVIII.4.

29. In *Behemoth* Hobbes describes the multiple political upheavals between the rules of Charles I and Charles II as in part a natural consequence of the view, widespread among religious and political factions, that individuals may rightly resist government they judge to be acting beyond its limits. In *Leviathan* Hobbes cites the belief that it is permissible for people to privilege their private judgment as disposing people "to debate with themselves, and dispute the commands of the commonwealth, and afterwards to obey or disobey them, as in their private judgments they shall think fit. Whereby the commonwealth is distracted and weakened." XXIX.6

point: a sovereign is a unified public judgment, so when numerous diverging private judgments rule, no sovereign exists.

Who else could decide whether the government has exceeded the limits of its authority, if not each and every citizen? We might envision some sort of reviewing agency to serve as the meta-authority; perhaps a supreme court that decides whether constitutional limits have been overstepped by the sovereign. Hobbes responds to this suggestion by saying that if a reviewing agency has that power it is in fact properly described as sovereign, and the government it reviews is in fact exercising only delegated or ministerial functions. In this case, we would merely have mislocated sovereignty, not shown that it is limited. If the reviewing agency has ultimate authority (its own actions not being subject to further review) then it is sovereign, and its sovereignty is unlimited.

It may seem though, that something has gone wrong in the argument Hobbes offers against limiting sovereignty when he claims that an agency with the authority to limit the sovereign must itself be sovereign. It is not in general true that having authority to judge another's performance confers on the judge the authority to exercise those very same powers. If, for example, an Olympic Games judge's authority to disqualify a competitor in an event does not entail her authority to compete in that event herself, why should a reviewing agency's authority to void the decisions of the governing sovereign entail its own authority to govern? Why think its authority to release subjects from their obligation to obey their sovereign confers the right to be obeyed on itself?

The difference between ordinary judges like those of Olympic competitions and supreme judges in political systems is that while the former cannot make use of the athlete's powers themselves to compete, a supreme judge or court can make use of the government's powers itself to rule. Such a court's authority to invalidate a law may not in theory give it the authority to legislate a new rule out of whole cloth, but in practice it can invalidate the law in such a way as to attach the government's own lawmaking authority to the content it chooses. And because it is subject to no superior who can review its actions, its "interpretations" will be law no matter how dubious, outrageous, or absurd they may be. Between the selective validation and invalidation of governmental actions, and reinterpretation of the requirements they impose on citizens, a body with the authority to oversee the government can in fact govern. If this is correct, the ultimate judge of questions of correct governance will in fact be sovereign.[30]

A second possibility Hobbes considers is that the reviewing agency does not have ultimate authority, and it remains an open question who decides whether the sovereign has overstepped its limits when the sovereign and that reviewing

30. It is worth noting that Hobbes does think of sovereign authority as a right to be the ultimate judge. Many political philosophers, including Locke, Rousseau, and Kant, locate sovereignty in the power of legislation whereas Hobbes locates it in the authority to judge (decide). Sovereigns decide whether statute law is required or unwritten natural law suffices, what behaviors natural law demands or forbids, who shall do the legislating and whether it has been done correctly, what legislation means, whether it applies, whether to enforce it, etc. Judgement is the alpha authority according to Hobbes.

agency disagree. Each claims ultimate authority. In such a case, the question of proper governance remains unresolved; we have a stalemate and a paralysis of effective agency of the sort experienced by a deadlocked assembly or a system of multiple overlapping sovereignties. In such a case subjects are thrown back on their own private judgments to decide which if either claimant to follow. Hobbes thinks we can expect individuals' private judgments to diverge on this as on most other questions, raising the specter of taking up arms to force some resolution of the conflict. Whichever the result—paralysis of effective government or civil war to resolve the dispute—a system in this condition is not a commonwealth but rather an incomplete removal from the state of nature, because subjects must, and so may permissibly, resort to use of their own private judgment.[31]

A third possibility Hobbes considers would be to posit a meta-meta-authority to decide the dispute between the sovereign and the reviewing agency. Again, if this body has ultimate authority, then it is actually sovereign over both those lesser powers whose dispute it adjudicates, and its authority is unlimited. If not, the dispute remains unresolved or else we must posit some further, meta-meta-meta authority empowered decisively to settle the dispute, inviting an infinite regress of limited authorities and unresolved conflicts. Hobbes concludes that if sovereignty exists at all, it is unlimited.

Although Kant did not work through as carefully as did Hobbes the question whether sovereignty can be limited, he draws on Hobbes's conceptual points that commonwealths are inconsistent with the retention of private judgment and that attempts to limit sovereignty invite a vicious regress to argue that subjects can have no right of resistance against their government, even if its laws and policies violate the moral law. Morality requires that all submit to a public authority that can turn possession into rightful property and secure the independence of each under law. To reserve a right to rebel against the public authority when we privately judge it to act wrongly is to assert a private authority inconsistent with the existence of public authority. Kant writes, following Hobbes, that

> the power of the state to put the law into effect is also irresistible. . . . for such resistance would be dictated by a maxim which, if it became general, would destroy the whole civil constitution and put an end to the . . . commonwealth, for it destroys its very foundation. This prohibition [on resistance to the supreme authority] is *absolute*. And even if [the sovereign has] in the eyes of the subject, forfeited the right to legislate, the subject is still not entitled to offer counter-resistance. The reason for this is that the people, under an existing civil constitution, has no longer any right to judge how the constitution should be administered. For if we suppose that it does have

31. When a commonwealth cannot protect subjects "in their loyalty," that is subjects who are willing to obey legitimate authority, subjects are released from their moral obligation to obey, and are free to exercise their own private judgment in seeking protection where they can find it. This inability to protect subjects may be the result of its subjects being in the power of an enemy (say captured on the battlefield, see XXIX.23), but it can also occur either because the government is paralyzed or because its factions are at war with each other.

> this right to judge and that it disagrees with the judgment of the actual head of state, who is to decide which side is right? Neither can act as judge of his own cause. Thus there would have to be another head above the head of state to mediate between the latter and the people, which is self-contradictory. . . . [To judge whether the social contract were violated] there would then have to be a *publicly constituted* opposing power, hence a second head of state to protect the rights of the people against the first ruler, and then yet a third to decide which of the other two had right on his side.[32]

On Hobbes's conception, where argument comes to an end, the final court of appeal, or where "the buck stops" is where sovereignty lies. Once we understand a sovereign as the ultimate arbiter of *all* disputes, including under "*all* disputes" disputes concerning its own performance as the ultimate arbiter of all disputes, sovereignty cannot, conceptually, be limited. Unless its authority is unlimited, it is not a sovereign. To appreciate the appeal of this argument, it is helpful to think again of Hobbes's idea of a sovereign as an (artificial) *person*. A person whose actions are properly determined by an alien will or judgment rather than her own is not sovereign over herself, because she is not independent and self-governing.

V. SOVEREIGNTY IN COMPLEX SYSTEMS

It may seem that real-world political practice belies Hobbes's pristine theoretical arguments that sovereignty cannot be divided or limited. Of course, Hobbes intends his analysis to be prescriptive not descriptive:

> An argument from the practice of men that have not sifted to the bottom, and with exact reason weighed the causes and nature of commonwealths, and suffer daily those miseries that proceed from the ignorance thereof, is invalid. For though in all places of the world men should lay the foundation of their houses on sand, it could not thence be inferred that so it ought to be.[33]

Hobbes aimed to discover rules for the construction of a perpetually internally stable commonwealth, one that would not be destroyed "but by foreign war." His experience of the English Civil War conditioned his view that social stability is a

32. *Theory and Practice*, II. Conclusion. (Kant 1970) Kant misunderstands Hobbes as having claimed that a sovereign does no wrong in acting unjustly toward subjects and so "may act toward them as he pleases." But, Kant says, "this proposition would be perfectly correct if injustice were taken to mean any injury which gave the injured party a *coercive right* against the one who has done him injustice." Here Kant has endorsed Hobbes's actual position without realizing it, perhaps because he has attended to neither Hobbes's insistence that subjects retain certain "true liberties" nor his distinction between iniquity (moral wrongdoing) and injustice (violating a valid covenant). Sovereigns who act iniquitously toward subjects (in violation of the laws of nature) act wrongly, and are subject to divine punishment, even though subjects may not permissibly punish them.

33. XX.19

prerequisite for being able to achieve our many ends. The possession of property and a sphere of liberty free from the interference of others, both needed to make our agency effective, depend upon enjoying some degree of personal security, which is the raison d'etre of the commonwealth. But unlike bees and ants and other naturally "sociable creatures," humans are not hardwired to converge in their private judgments thereby cooperating seamlessly, and so need to construct a public judgment that can coordinate their activities. And

> Though nothing can be immortal which mortals make, yet if men had the reason they pretend to, their commonwealths might be secured at least from perishing from internal diseases. . . . [But men] cannot, without the help of a very able architect, be compiled into any other than a crazy building, such as, hardly lasting out their own time, must assuredly fall upon the heads of their posterity.[34]

Were the architects of the United States of America able architects? At first look, the complex system they designed appears to break all Hobbes's rules. It contains horizontal separation of the essential rights of legislation, adjudication, and enforcement conferred on separate bodies; it contains vertical multiplication of sovereignty at the federal and state levels; it purports to limit its own authority by a written constitution. There are two Hobbesian responses available to answer the charge that the American system proves Hobbes wrong about the best constitution of a sovereign state. First, as Hobbes notes

> The greatest objection is that of the practice, when men ask where and when such [unlimited and undivided] power has by subjects been acknowledged. But I ask them in turn where and when there has been a commonwealth free of sedition and civil war, where the power was not absolute.[35]

The United States did not last even one hundred years before it descended into a devastating civil war. It can serve as no counterexample to Hobbes's claim about the proper design of a maximally stable system.

Second, and more relevant to our purpose, is the perhaps surprising response that the political system of the United States, despite its surface appearance, is not in fact a case of divided or limited sovereignty. Hobbes argued that in order for a commonwealth to function reliably to fulfill its ends of securing peace and common defense, its sovereign, the entity that "carries its person" or represents it, must be able to judge, will, and act. Does this mean that a sovereign commonwealth must locate internal sovereignty entirely in a single individual or assembly? It may seem that Hobbes thought it does, as when he writes that in commonwealths

> Because the sovereignty is either in one man, or in an assembly of more than one; and into that assembly either every man hath right to enter, or not every

34. XXIX.1

35. OL XX.19 (Latin variant).

> one . . . it is manifest, there can be but three kinds of commonwealth. For the representative must needs be one man, or more: and if more, then it is the assembly of all, or of but a part. . . . Other kind of commonwealth there can be none, for either One, or More, or All must have the Sovereign Power (which I have shown to be indivisible) entire.[36]

Some commentators have thought on the basis of such remarks that Hobbes thought that in order for a state to have sovereign status in the international realm, some element within that state must have the same kind of sovereign status. One describes the position he attributes to Hobbes as a fallacy, and explains

> The fallacy is contained in holding that the necessary characteristics of an independent system of authority must be possessed by some identifiable part of the system. It is as simple an error as holding that because clocks tell time, the power of telling the time must be a characteristic possessed by some identifiable part of a clock.[37]

The suggestion is that just as the power of a clock to tell time is a function of the organization of its various parts, so too the power to govern could be a function of some rule-governed organization of numerous elements of the commonwealth rather than necessarily being a characteristic possessed in full by one unique entity in the commonwealth. This is of course true, and it is nothing Hobbes need deny. Strictly speaking, the analogy is inaccurate because although the power to tell time cannot belong to a single sub-element of a clock—a spring or a gear or a battery, etc.—sovereignty can belong to a single element such as a monarch or democratic assembly in a commonwealth. But the underlying idea that sovereignty could be located in a procedurally ordered system is one we saw Hobbes embrace in his analysis of sovereign assemblies as collections of individuals duty-bound to employ a determinate decision procedure to direct their judgments, wills, and actions. In such a case, the assembly is a type of rule-governed complex system whose parts individually possess no sovereignty, but which itself can exercise sovereignty. Hobbes thus explicitly affirms the possibility of locating sovereignty in a determinately rule-governed complex system composed of multiple elements.

Divided political systems, "mixarchies," and limited political systems fail to ensure the personal capacities needed to exercise sovereignty because they potentially allow crucial questions of how to act to go undecided. They allow for the government to be "mute," or to suffer conflicting wills (like the conjoined triplets Hobbes imagined) to the point of paralysis, and so to invite internecine warfare to force some determinate conclusion. But a *fully determinately rule-governed* system would suffer no such disabilities. Such a system might allocate a

36. XIX.1.

37. M.M. Goldsmith, "Hobbes's 'Mortall God': Is There a Fallacy in Hobbes's Theory of Sovereignty?," *The Social Contract Theorists,* Christopher Morris ed. (Maryland 1999), p. 30.

complementary partial set of essential rights to multiple entities provided that all entities were duty-bound to adhere to a shared set of rules about how they are to exercise those rights that fully determined their cooperation on a unique course of action in any given case.[38]

In the passage quoted earlier alleging only three possible forms of government, Hobbes does seem to have assumed that the decision must always be made by the same entity—that in order for there to be any place where "the buck stops" it must always stop in the same place. That assumption would be correct if decisions did not have a temporal coordinate, that is, if all decisions were made at the same time. Then in order for the buck to stop, all decisions would have to be made by one and the same entity, as a matter of logical necessity. But, of course, political decisions occur in time; and there is nothing inconsistent about a decision-making system that locates authority to give the final word at T1 to one specific entity and at T2 to an entirely different entity, so long as the determination of which entity determines the judgment at any given time is fully settled by the rules. A system could seat final authority at different times in diverse entities by for example, treating *as a binding norm* a statute passed by Congress and signed by the president at T1, the overturning or vacating of that statute by the Supreme Court at T2, and the reinstituting of that statute pursuant to a constitutional amendment at T3. The same measure can be not law at T1 when passed by Congress but vetoed by the president; law at T2 when Congress overrides the president's veto; not law at T3 when a district court invalidates it; law at T4 when an appellate court validates it; not law at T5 when the Supreme Court invalidates it as unconstitutional; law at T6 when a differently constituted Supreme Court overturns its prior decision, and not law again at T7 when a differently constituted Supreme Court reinstates the decision of T6; law at T8 when the Constitution is amended to allow for such a law and a law is passed by Congress and signed by the president, etc. At each moment there is an authoritative answer to the question whether the norm is legally binding, and which authority settles that answer differs across moments.

Although there is no logical inconsistency in a determinately rule-governed system of division of powers ordered temporally, problems of principle arise.[39] When segments of time are differentiated not by the clock but by steps in a procedure, how are disagreements about whether one step has been exhausted and

38. As Garrath Williams observes in his entry on Hobbes in the *International Encyclopedia of Philosophy*, Hobbes's "greatest insight, still little recognized by many moral philosophers, is that any right or entitlement is only practically meaningful when combined with a concrete judgment as to what it dictates in some given case."

39. Instability of policy is one. For instance U.S. presidents can act not only without Congress but against its will through agency rules, executive actions, and decisions about how vigorously (or whether) to enforce laws. In the words of Senator Elizabeth Warren, "personnel is policy"; whether laws or rules are enforced depends on who runs an executive agency. (Opinion, *New York Times*, January 29, 2016) An extreme form of this view was voiced by President Richard Nixon in his May 19, 1977, interview with David Frost when he declared the principle that "when the President does it, that means that it is not illegal." His remark was made in the context of national

the next step instituted to be resolved?[40] Further, new situations may arise for which the procedure gives no instruction. Whereas a natural person or sovereign assembly can fashion a creative response to unanticipated or unimagined situations, fixed procedures cannot. In addition, questions concerning whether the procedure has or has not been correctly carried out, or about what, precisely, the procedure requires, will generate disputes that cannot be resolved by the procedure itself. Notice that these problems of principle may arise even among people of goodwill all of whom are committed to carrying out their obligation to adhere to the procedure, and who are acting conscientiously.[41]

It is impossible to say in advance how seriously destabilizing these sorts of principled problems for even the best-designed complex procedural systems of sovereignty will be. It cannot be known whether such disagreements or new situations will arise, or how often, nor how disabling they will be to a system that cannot resolve them. If they are infrequent and over only minor matters, disputes stemming from these principled problems may not pose any significant problem for the functioning of the political system. It is certainly not Hobbes's view, nor should it be ours, that all systems containing any indeterminacy at all must necessarily collapse. In fact, even the most poorly designed procedure might function tolerably in the lucky event that it confronts no new challenges and its elements happen to be like-minded.

security policy; perhaps he did not intend it as a general claim about executive authority under the U.S. system.

40. In February 2016, during the second month of the last year of the second term of Barak Obama's presidency, a conservative justice of the Supreme Court died, leaving that court with only eight members whose political ideological tendencies were evenly divided, with half of those eight tending conservative, and the other half tending liberal. The Republican-controlled Congress declared that it would not fulfill its constitutionally mandated role to give advice and consent on any nominee to the Court put forward by the president (pursuant to his official duty of nominating Supreme Court justices). Republican congressional leaders asserted the principle that the choice of Supreme Court justice "ought to be left to the people" in voting for president in the next election, presumably because they hoped the next president would be of their own party and would nominate a more conservative justice (which is in fact what happened). This example of disagreement among holders of partial sets of essential rights over whether *at this particular time* their right to exercise their limited function is determinative demonstrates the problem Hobbes sees as endemic to such systems. Who decides what time it is? Why, by the same justificatory principle, should a Congress not "leave it to the people" to decide by voting for the next president rather than the one in office when he belongs to the opposition party, to fill every court vacancy in *every year* of that president's term? If the authority to exercise the necessary power of sovereignty to judge cases is left to one branch that declines to act unless except when it can secure its preferred substantive outcome, the temporally sensitive system of rule-governed sovereignty is thwarted. What that means practically, is that the judgment of various courts at the appellate level stand as final, even if they are mutually contradictory, and so make actions both legal and illegal, until some new functional Supreme Court is constituted by a Congress that decides to consider and confirm some or other presidential nominee to it.

41. John Rawls offers a seminal discussion of what he calls "the burdens of judgment" in Rawls, *Political Liberalism* (1993) and Rawls, *Justice as Fairness: A Restatement* (2001).

As a practical matter, there can be a great deal of disagreement even among conscientious officeholders under ordinary circumstances; and disagreement increases exponentially when they do not behave conscientiously, as all too often they do not. Entities may not properly fulfill their procedural roles because they are corrupt, or seeking personal advantage, or because they are ideologues who prioritize others of their values over fidelity to the procedure. Or they may be motivated by malice to stymie their adversaries by refusing to cooperate in their procedural role, or they may "payback" earlier instances of perceived noncooperation by other officeholders.[42]

These principled and practical problems for a rule-governed complex system of sovereignty, even for a well-designed one, may perhaps be illustrated by the American case. For instance, political actors have disagreed about nullification, the legal theory that a state has the right to invalidate any federal law that the state has deemed unconstitutional. Supporters claim that nullification is one of the rights reserved to the states under the Tenth Amendment to the Constitution. Jefferson and Madison set forth this theory in the Kentucky and Virginia resolutions of 1798. One supporting theory is that as creators by compact of the federal government, states are the final interpreters of the extent of the federal government's powers. Opponents of nullification cite the supremacy clause of

42. The refusal to perform their constitutional role of advice and consent to a Democratic president's nominee to the Supreme Court was justified by some Republican members of the House of Representatives in 2016 on the ground that House and Senate Democrats had used equally wrong obstructionist tactics in earlier nomination fights, and that turnabout was fair play. They argued that their own duty to perform their constitutional role conscientiously was contingent on others having also performed (in their opinion) conscientiously. By this logic, no one who believes anyone else has acted corruptly in office has himself any obligation not to act equally corruptly in office. This sort of reasoning defeats the functioning of any procedure. The Republican senator from South Carolina, Lindsey Graham, acknowledged in the 2016 refusal to consider Obama's nominee that "We're setting a precedent here today—Republicans are—that in the last year [of a presidential term] ... you are not going to fill a vacancy of the Supreme Court.... That's going to be the new rule." (reported in the *New York Times,* March 11, 2016) He went along with his party's decision despite acknowledging that "the President of the United States deserves the right to pick judges of their philosophy and that goes with winning the White House." But the indeterminacy of the Constitution's appointment clause allows one legal commentator to argue that "it is altogether proper to view a decision by the Senate not to act as a waiver of its right to provide advice and consent" because the Supreme Court has ruled that a right may be forfeited "by the failure to make timely assertion of the right before the tribunal having jurisdiction to determine it." The commentator notes that such action would engender a "dispute between the president and the Senate about the meaning of the Constitution," but opines that a Supreme Court decision on this matter "could restore a sensible system of government" because "the threat that the president could proceed with an appointment if the Senate failed to do so would force the Senate to do its job—providing its advice and consent on a timely basis so that our government can function." Gregory L. Diskant, "Obama Can Appoint Merrick Garland to the Supreme Court if the Senate Does Nothing," *The Washington Post,* April 8, 2016. Graham and Diskant understand their shared Constitution to settle diametrically opposed outcomes: senatorial non-consent defeats a nomination (Graham) or it confirms a nomination (Diskant).

Article VI and Article III of the Constitution, and the Supreme Court's decision in *Ableman v. Booth* rejecting Wisconsin's attempt to nullify the Fugitive Slave Act.

Arguably, the constitutional question that split the Union was of who held the power of decision with respect to slavery in the territories.[43] The indeterminacy, or malleability of the rule-governed system of sovereignty of the Constitution in the contested election of 1860 allowed four competing answers. Henry Clay's Constitutional Union Party (conservatives) held that the customary balancing of a new slave area for every area prohibiting slavery should be written into an irrepealable constitutional amendment. Lincoln's Republican Party agreed that Congress had the authority to decide the question of slavery for the territories, but affirmed the Wilmot proviso prohibiting all slavery in the new territories, based on its understanding that the due process clause of the Fifth Amendment prohibited establishing slavery "by positive legislation." Stephen A Douglas's Northern Democrats held that the principle of self-government underlies the Constitution, and has precedence so that members of new states should decide the slavery question for themselves. Southern Democrats, represented by Jefferson Davis, theorized that state sovereignty gave slave states the authority to promote slavery's expansion because their state laws must be given extraterritorial effect wherever their citizens were; this right was to be enforced by the federal government acting as an agent for the sovereign states, its principals. One sees vividly in this case how vast the chasm among interpretations of the rules of a system can be. Only civil war could resolve that particular interpretive dispute.

Hobbes does not insist that constitutional crises are inevitable when a sovereign system has internal divisions that authorize multiple centers of judgment, but only that crisis becomes more likely. An insightful analysis of what occasions constitutional crisis is provided by Levinson and Balkin.[44] Crises occur when (1) actors publicly violate the constitution (and other stakeholders refuse to go along with the violation), (2) when following the constitutional forms leads to disaster, and (3) when constitutional disagreements lead to (mass) use of force to prevail. To this analysis our study of Hobbes provides a fourth possibility, (4) that crises occur when constitutional forms result in polity paralysis, disabling effective governmental agency. This last is the danger Hobbes sees in even well-designed, rule-governed complex systems of government.

VI. ENFORCEMENT POWER MUST FOLLOW THE LOCATION OF DECISION AUTHORITY

According to Hobbes, it is men and arms, rather than laws, that rule. Hobbes notes that the raw material of laws, absent their enforcement by people, is merely words on paper. Laws are inert; they cannot *do* anything; they cannot *make us do*

43. The following account is drawn from the classic one given by Arthur Bestor, "The American Civil War as a Constitutional Crisis," *The American Historical Review* vol. 6992) 1964, pp. 327–352.

44. "Constitutional Crises," *University of Pennsylvania Law Review*, Vol. 157 No. 3, February 2009.

anything. Legal injunctions would operate as mere counsel or advice or wish if the power to compel compliance did not stand behind them. It is true that people may sometimes conform to the requirements of some laws out of a sense of duty, or out of habit, rather than for fear of punishment if they do not. But for laws that require behavior contrary to people's impulses or conceptions of their narrow self-interest, and particularly behavior contrary to their ideals, motivation to conform to those laws will depend on their being backed up by force. Hobbes thinks not just of laws, but also of the general covenant to be ruled by the sovereign's laws, as requiring enforcement if it is to be efficacious. He writes

> Covenants being but words, and breath, have no force to oblige, contain, constrain, or protect any man, but what it has from the public sword; that is, from the untied hands of that man, or assembly of men that hath the sovereignty, and whose actions are avouched by them all, and performed by the strength of them all, in him united.[45]

The simple point, which does seem correct, is that the power to enforce decisions is essential to the effective functioning of any rule-governed system. If rightful authority cannot enforce its decisions, it cannot govern; whereas even a wrongful pretender to authority can in fact govern if it deploys sufficient force to have its will carried out.[46] In U.S. history we find illustrations of this basic point. When in 1957 local authorities in Little Rock Arkansas decided to defy federal court orders to admit Negro students to its Central High School, President Eisenhower sent federal troops to the scene, activating 10,000 members of the Arkansas National Guard and 1,000 members of the 101st Airborne Division, to effect the physical movement of those students into their classrooms, and to compel the people of Arkansas (and the South generally) "to preserve and respect the law even when they disagree with it." "The very basis of our individual rights and freedoms," President Eisenhower asserted, "is the certainty that the President and the Executive Branch of Government will support and insure the carrying out of the decisions of the Federal Courts, even, when necessary with all the means at the President's command." Eisenhower's reason for committing Federal troops to enforce judicial decisions was a Hobbesian appeal to the need

45. XVIII.4.

46. In *Behemoth* Hobbes writes that of the "power of pressing and ordering soldiers," that is, of the ability to deploy coercive force, "which power whosoever has, has also, without doubt, the whole sovereignty." Ibid. p. 79. "For he that hath the power of levying and commanding the soldiers, has all other rights of sovereignty which he shall please to claim." P. 80. Hobbes recounts the effort of the House of Commons to wrest sovereignty from the king in January 1641 as presented in the form of a petition prayer that "his Majesty would be pleased to put forthwith, first, the Tower of London, secondly, all other forts, thirdly, the whole militia of the kingdom, into the hands of such persons as should be recommended to him by both the Houses of Parliament. . . . It is also worth observing, that this petition began with these words, "Most gracious Sovereign": so stupid they were as not to know, that he that is master of the militia, is master of the kingdom, and consequently is in possession of a most absolute sovereignty." P. 98.

to avoid anarchy: "Mob rule cannot be allowed to override the decisions of the courts. . . . There would be no security for any except that which each one of us could provide for himself."[47]

The difficulty is that when coercive power does not follow the correct temporal seat of sovereign decision-making, or when disputes arise as to whether or not it has, the legitimacy of the system is called into question along with its capacity to function as intended. In the period leading up to the American Civil War, the legislature of South Carolina called a convention of southern states, which voted unanimously to secede on the ground that the northern states were not fulfilling their federal obligations under the Constitution to enforce slaveholders' rights. The outgoing president James Buchanan thought that although the southern states were not justified in leaving the union, "the power by force of arms to compel a State to remain in the union" was not among the "enumerated powers granted to Congress,"[48] but Lincoln thought the Constitution ruled out their secession as "legally void."[49]

This implies that in a complex system of rule-governed separation of powers, where sovereignty rests at different temporal moments with different agents, the actual power to exercise coercive force must follow, or attach to, the locus of sovereignty if that system is to function. If at a time the final decision rests with a court, but the power to order the armed forces (police, national guard, or military, as the case may be) to implement its decision does not rest with the court, the court's decision will be but "words and paper, of no use." Coercive power—the police or national guard or military—certainly cannot be allowed to decide for itself how to act, "for they that keep an army, and cannot master it, must be subject to it as much as he that keeps a lion in his house."[50] That is a recipe for military coup, and martial rule. As a practical matter, "He that is master of the militia, is master of the kingdom, and consequently is in possession of a most absolute sovereignty,"[51] and "He that hath the power of levying and commanding the soldiers, hath all the other rights of sovereignty which he shall please to claim."[52] This is one of those ugly truths that led Rousseau to say of Hobbes "It is not so much what is false and terrible in his political philosophy, but what is just and true, that has drawn hatred upon it."[53] Might does not make right. But for right to function effectively, it

47. "President Sends Troops to Little Rock, Federalizes Arkansas National Guard; Tell Nation He Acted to Avoid an Anarchy," *New York Times*, September 25, 1957.

48. James Buchanan, "Fourth Annual Message to Congress on the State of the Union," December 3, 1860.

49. Abraham Lincoln, "First Inaugural Address," March 4, 1861.

50. *Behemoth*, p. 193.

51. Ibid. p. 98.

52. Ibid. p. 80.

53. *Social Contract*, IV.8. This quote refers specifically to Hobbes's view that secular and religious sovereignties must be united in order to maximize the prospects for social stability, but it

must command might.[54] So any sovereign system operating on a set of rules governing the uses of the powers of its various parts at various times will need also to have enforcement powers that travel in real time along with the changing locus of sovereignty.

VII. WHO BEARS MORAL RESPONSIBILITY FOR THE SOVEREIGN'S ACTIONS?

In complex sovereign systems, a serious question arises as to whom to hold responsible when the system behaves immorally. When such a state conducts an unjust war, or punishes an innocent person, who should be held responsible? It seems wrong to hold the last governmental agent in the temporal chain fully responsible because it is, in a very real sense, just bad luck that that agent held the power of decision at the moment in time that the wrong decision was made by the system. Its decision may have been conditioned or even dictated by decisions by other agencies prior in time and according to the rules. On the other hand, we cannot allow the system to deflect responsibility on the ground that no element within it bears responsibility. Perhaps then, we should hold everyone who participates in the system responsible, including the voters and those who in their apathy fail to vote or fail to reign in the actions of their government? Are all citizens of complex democratic sovereignties responsible for everything their state does? This effort to apportion responsibility may seem an abstract exercise until we recognize that having a correct understanding of who bears responsibility in complex sovereign systems affects such basic questions as whether terrorists do wrong in targeting the civilian populations of a democratic society. [55]

epitomizes Rousseau's general attitude toward Hobbes. See for instance his recognition in his *Second Discourse* that Hobbes's state of nature does in fact correctly describe human nature as it is now, even if it might have been better under different social conditions. Much antipathy toward Hobbes is more a matter of shooting the messenger than of rejecting the message.

54. Hobbes opines on the folly of the Long Parliament that "he that would set up a democracy with an army should have an army to maintain it; but these men did it, when those men had the army that were resolved to pull it down." Force must follow sovereignty. *Behemoth,* 155.

55. For discussion of this question see S.A. Lloyd ed., *Hobbes Today* (Cambridge University Press, 2013), Chapter 14, especially pp. 296–303.

7

The Publian President in the Twenty-First Century

SANFORD LEVINSON

No one conversant with "American constitutional development" could fail to recognize that the very term requires taking cognizance of significant changes over the roughly 225 years that the Constitution has structured basic aspects of American politics. One could not possibly understand the actual powers of Congress today concerning vast domains of American life by reference to what was thought, or expected, by those designing the Constitution in Philadelphia or ratifying it thereafter in Williamsburg, Boston, or the other sites of the state ratifying conventions. Similarly, it is difficult to comprehend the powers of modern presidents—the "chief executive" and "commander-in-chief," among other "hats" they are described as wearing[1]—without taking into account shifting realities since 1789, when George Washington was inaugurated as our first president. Stephen Griffin, for example, has written an especially fine book about the post–World War II presidency and the remarkably enhanced "war powers" widely thought to be held by presidents in the aftermath of that war.[2]

These enhanced powers in part follow from the decision of the United States firmly to reject Washington's caution about refraining from entangling alliances and the widespread prewar opposition to any foreign involvements more generally, embraced under the term "isolationism." The new reality included NATO and the ostensible duty of each of its members to come to the aid of any militarily threatened ally, not to mention the United Nations and its similar commitment to collective

1. See especially Clinton Rossiter, THE AMERICAN PRESIDENCY (Baltimore, MD: Johns Hopkins Press, 1956), for the influential "hats" metaphor.

2. Stephen M. Griffin, LONG WARS AND THE CONSTITUTION (Cambridge, MA: Harvard University Press, 2014).

Sovereignty and the New Executive Authority. Claire O. Finkelstein and Michael Skerker.

self-defense. It was, of course, the United Nations Charter that served as the basis of President Truman's unilateral decision to send American forces, almost literally overnight, to defend South Korea (to whom we had no formal treaty obligations) against North Korean aggression. And, of course, the last seventy years have also featured the development of modern weaponry and awareness of the concomitant dangers posed by what have come to be called "weapons of mass destruction." Deterrence theory, for example, did not rest on the old-fashioned mobilization of armies, which could, after all, both take time and be thought to require congressional approval. Instead, the basic structure of MAD (mutually-assured destruction) was the ability of the United States to send missiles basically immediately to the Soviet Union even upon the perception (and then, most certainly, the reality) of military threat (including such attacks on our NATO allies). Perhaps the most important single episode of presidential autonomy, even more so than Truman's actions in Korea, was the Cuban Missile Crisis, where John F. Kennedy created an extraconstitutional "Executive Committee," none of whom were members of Congress; they were basically charged with advising Kennedy on whether to risk World War III by attacking Cuba or their Soviet suppliers, or instead, as ultimately happened, to take more restrained, but still highly dangerous, action.

An important part of Griffin's argument, though, is that we scarcely have a worked-out doctrinal justification for this new constitutional order; Supreme Court decisions, of which there are relatively few, are, as a whole, more confusing than helpful, not least because they tend to involve basic matters of national security and to elicit professions of judicial restraint. In any event, contemporary presidents from both parties do not hesitate to defend a variety of actions that seem to raise the specter of unlimited, even "dictatorial," power. Those who oppose the particular actions do not hesitate in turn to accuse them of behaving in "bad faith" regarding their duty faithfully to honor the Constitution and the limits it places on raw presidential power.[3] And, of course, underlying many of the legalistic arguments about presidential power are deep worries, as with the Cuban Missile Crisis, of the most dire of consequences should unilateral decisions turn out to be wrong. In our present polarized polity, such exertions of what might be called "muscular presidentialism" have tended simply to reinforce the bitterness of the debate and the denunciations of a president not from one's own political party. Looking only at the twenty-first century, if one is a Democrat, it is easy to point to a variety of actions by George W. Bush vis-à-vis the Iraq war, ranging from the circumstances of its initiation to the authorization of what was by any plausible analysis "torture," whatever the claims made in John Yoo's memorandum defending the conduct of American officials.[4] If one is a Republican,

3. See, e.g., the valuable comments in David Pozen's extremely suggestive essay *Constitutional Bad Faith*, 129 Harv. L. Rev. 885 (2016).

4. See, e.g., id., ft. 192, citing Jack Goldsmith, THE TERROR PRESIDENCY (New York: W. W. Norton & Co., 2007), pp. 144–167 (2007) and its description of Yoo's memorandum as so "legally flawed, tendentious in substance and tone, and overbroad" that it required repudiation and withdrawal.

one can just as easily express concern about President Obama's unilateral decision to bomb Libya and then to proffer the view that it did not involve the kind of "hostilities" that would trigger any duties under the War Powers Act,[5] not to mention the widespread resistance to his threat to bomb Syria without congressional authorization (and his subsequent backing down). It must be noted, of course, that there were some Republicans who were appalled by the Bush administration and Democrats who rejected Obama's claims. Still, in both—and many other—cases, there are accusations that presidents are embracing the illegitimate role of "sovereign" rather than accepting a far more limited role as simple "caretakers" of the laws entrusted to their enforcement.

Almost inevitably, given the particularities—and what many would regard as the peculiarities—of American constitutional culture, the debates even in the twenty-first century often involve appeals to the presumptive rules established during the founding era. Although those references to the past are often interesting in themselves for what they reveal about assumptions made in the eighteenth century, that is not why they are sometimes thought to have purchase on the present. Instead, a significant strand of contemporary constitutional analysis involves the purported duty to adhere to "originalist" views of constitutional meaning. But one should recognize as well that a significant aspect of "American exceptionalism" is the near-obsession, throughout our history, with demonstrating a connection between views and actions at any given time and the wishes, hopes, and, indeed, legal commands of those we have been taught to revere as "the Founders." There is nothing ordained about this kind of obsession. Indeed, in an interesting recent book,[6] historian David Sehat demonstrates that there have been valiant attempts by significant leaders, including John Quincy Adams and Ulysses S. Grant, to liberate us from the cult of the Founders, but they have been altogether unsuccessful. It is simply taken as a matter of course, whatever the degree of one's formal commitment to "originalism" as a method of constitutional interpretation, that the Founders established a legacy that we ignore at our peril. One could not understand the popularity of books by David McCullough or Joseph Ellis, among many others, without placing them within this wider cultural context.

It is certainly not the point of this essay to rehash the now-extensive debates about the "original meanings" of presidential authority within our constitutional order. What I do want to do, however, is to look at the implications of the arguments made in one particular eighteenth century source that many Americans continue to privilege as a fount of constitutional wisdom. For better and, quite possibly, for worse, even today we find special emphasis on the arguments presented by James Madison, John Jay, and Alexander Hamilton—writing under the name "Publius"—in *The Federalist*. Indeed, there is every reason to believe that these essays are given far greater weight today, most certainly by the Supreme Court,

5. See id., 923–34.

6. David Sehat, THE JEFFERSON RULE: WHY WE THINK THE FOUNDING FATHERS HAVE ALL THE ANSWERS (New York: Simon and Schuster, 2015).

than they were at the time of their writing. Often, and this is obviously true with regard to citation by the Court, *The Federalist* is turned to in the context of debates about "constitutional interpretation," that is, the best way to give meaning to disputed passages of the U.S. Constitution. Or one might simply regard the concrete figures hiding behind the Publian drapes as unusually wise and worth attending to even two centuries later. After all, Alexander Hamilton has given his name to what is widely regarded as the most truly important piece of American musical theater in several decades! One of the few things that might unite contemporary Americans is the belief that even in the twenty-first century *The Federalist* is an apt source to turn to for guidance.

I have recently published a book, *An Argument Open to All: Reading the Federalist in the 21st Century*,[7] that in effect has as its central question whether Publius in fact still speaks to us as twenty-first century readers and what, if so, his lessons might be. My concerns in the book have almost literally nothing to do with "constitutional interpretation" as defined above. I think it can be demonstrated that relatively few of the eighty-five essays that comprise *The Federalist* are truly interested in, or, therefore, relevant to, the enterprise of "constitutional interpretation." And, for what it is worth, it can be shown both that decision-makers in 1789 and then John Marshall in 1819 felt entirely free to reject quite specific assurances in *The Federalist*. Thus Congress in 1789 simply ignored what Publius had declared in *Federalist* 77 and instead acquiesced in presidential power to dismiss members of his cabinet without seeking the same degree of approval from Congress that was (and is) necessary to legitimate an initial appointment.[8] And in 1819, Marshall was similarly indifferent to what Publius said in *Federalist* 33 about the concurrent power of states to tax whatever or however they wished, subject only to the few specific limitations set out in the Constitution's text.[9]

As already suggested, though, I am not at all interested in mining *The Federalist* for guidance as to resolving specific cases and controversies involving constitutional meaning. Rather, I have been struck—and thus chose to write my book—by the extent to which the general political dilemmas discussed by Publius continue to haunt our world today and by the implications of the proffered Publian advice. *The Federalist* was not written for lawyers or, even more so, judges. It was directed to Publius's fellow citizens, who were, at least in terms of the rhetoric adopted in the very first of the papers, trusted to engage in "reflection and choice" about how best to govern themselves—and, therefore, in the absence of radical change, ourselves today. So the central question is what Publius might have to tell us about presidents and their powers, and to what extent we should accept

7. New Haven: Yale University Press, 2015.

8. See Federalist No. 77 and the "Decision of 1789" to allow unilateral removal (a decision reached when Vice President John Adams broke a tie in the Senate in favor of presidential authority).

9. See Federalist No. 33, blithely rejected by Chief Justice Marshall in *McCulloch v. Maryland*, 17 U.S. (4 Wheat.) 316, 433–34 (1819) on the basis that the "texture" of the Constitution (rather than the text) invalidated the ability of Maryland to tax the Bank of the United States.

or reject his message, *not* on the basis of some dubious theory of "constitutional interpretation," but, instead and altogether more importantly, because our own capacity for "reflection and choice" leads us in the twenty-first century to agree or disagree as to the wisdom of the arguments he is putting forth. One further important point: the "us" in the twenty-first century may well include an international audience, many of whom, for example, might be the recipients of copies of *The Federalist,* distributed by the United States or the American Bar Association (ABA) to those charged with designing constitutions in the contemporary world. It might be interesting to compare what the United States. or ABA thinks or hopes contemporary readers might learn with the reality of the lessons actually taught. These lessons are the central topic of this essay, and, as shall be amply seen, some of them might be quite discomforting.

Federalist 1 features not only a paean to the capacity for "reflection and choice" on the part of its readers. It also literally begins with a reference to our "unequivocal experience of the inefficiency of the subsisting federal government." Perhaps a twenty-first century reader would appreciate more the sharp language of *Federalist 15,* which referred to the "imbecility" of the purported government established by the Articles of Confederation. Many of the first quarter or so of the eighty-five essays are devoted to one or another particular "imbecility." But the dominant one surely appears to be the inability of the government established by the Articles, with its extraordinarily weak government—and, among other things, lack of a standing army—to protect the new nation from the inevitable clear and present dangers posed by other countries (including Indian tribes) in the international system that the United States had entered into by virtue of its successful secession from the British Empire.

The immediately ensuing essays all warn against the quite likely possibility that the alternative to ratifying the new Constitution would be disintegration into two or even three separate countries along the western coast of the Atlantic Ocean. (One might imagine New England, Atlantica, and Dixie.) In vivid prose and muscular argument, Publius argues that such a state of affairs would provide only a basis for endless war. "A man must be far gone in Utopian speculations," he warns in *Federalist 6,* "who can seriously doubt that, if these States should either be wholly disunited, or only united in partial confederacies, the subdivisions into which they might be thrown would have frequent and violent contests with each other." To deny this is "to forget that men are ambitious, vindictive, and rapacious." It therefore takes a willful ignorance of "the uniform course of human events" and "the accumulated experience of ages" to expect "harmony between a number of independent, unconnected sovereignties in the same neighborhood." Thus the importance of unity. Although, as we shall see, a key Publian argument, in terms of constitutional design, is the creation of a strong national government, with potentially "unlimited" powers sufficient to meet the challenges, the brunt of the early *Federalist* essays has little to do with constitutional design per se and everything to do with recognizing the baleful consequences of fragmentation.

Here the key essay is *Federalist 8,* in which Publius continues to insist that a truly *United* States offers far better prospects for maintaining security and liberty than does adherence to the Confederation and the likelihood of ultimate dissolution into separate countries along the Atlantic coast. He posits that "[s]afety from external danger is the most powerful director of national conduct," which is little more than an extension of the central insights of both Hobbes and Locke: people are motivated to live under organized government because it offers them security against threats by ill-motivated others. To provide adequate security against "external danger" requires establishing "standing armies" of military personnel always ready to defend the country against invasion. One of the most controversial features of the 1787 Constitution was its legitimation of such an army, as opposed to sole reliance on militias composed of sturdy yeomen who could be mustered when dangers presented themselves. Publius, like George Washington, had little faith in such militias, whatever their place in American myth. Both understood the virtues of a well-trained professional military, not to mention having the help of allies, such as the French, with their own professional militaries.

Yet Publius, who is certainly politically sagacious enough to know that many of his readers will be wary of a standing army, offers as a central advantage of the new Constitution, and the attendant unity of the constituent states, the fact that the threat of foreign invasion would be so remote that a *large* standing army would be basically unnecessary. Thus he reassures his readers that the highly advantageous geographical position of the United States, separated from Europe by an ocean, renders unnecessary "to our security" what he calls "[e]xtensive military establishments." But "if we should be disunited, and the integral parts should either remain separated, or, which is most probable, should be thrown together into two or three confederacies, we should be, in a short course of time, in the predicament of the continental powers of Europe—our liberties would be a prey to the means of defending ourselves against the ambition and jealousy of each other." Such fragmentation would generate, "in a little time," the establishment "in every part of this country the same engines of despotism which have been the scourge of the Old World." So, at least so long as we remain free of what Washington would call "entangling alliances" linking us to the Old World, we could take advantage of the existence of what some designated "the pond" that separates the United States from potential European adversaries and then later, the similar utility of the Pacific with regard to threats from what we would come to call the Far East.

But, of course, ponds are not what they used to be, and the post–World War II world, with its combination of entangling alliances and modern weaponry, is the context for any contemporary discussion of the limits, if any, on a government (or president) charged with safeguarding what the Preamble terms the "common Defence." To be sure, the phrase comes after the aspirations of "a more perfect Union, establish[ing] Justice, [and] insur[ing] domestic Tranquility," but there can be little doubt that the "common Defence" may well take priority as the central goal of the new country. After all, if unity were not seen as essential to protecting the collectivity against enemies, then there would have been no need to make shameful compromises with slaveowners in order to create a single Union.

For all of the talk of whether Publius and other members of the Founding generation were more influenced by Locke, Montesquieu, or Hume, it seems impossible to deny the presence of Thomas Hobbes in the bleak national-security-oriented vision enunciated above. The "international state of nature" is not for the faint of heart, and one must respond accordingly. We are well aware of where that line of argument took Hobbes! So do a fast forward, relatively speaking, to *Federalists 40* and *41*, both of which, incidentally, were written by Madison, whereas Nos. 1 and 6 were penned by Hamilton. But it is almost certainly a mistake to assume a gulf between the two, whatever their later differences, with regard to the most fundamental realities of "constitutional politics." *Federalist 40* is endlessly fascinating for its defense of the Philadelphia Convention's ruthlessly first setting aside the rather limited mandate given them by Congress—to suggest "revisions" to the Articles rather than in effect to tear them up and start all over again—and then, even more dramatically, the clear and unequivocal rule set out in Article XIII of the Articles of Confederation as to how the terms of ostensible "perpetual Union" could be amended. The answer is by the unanimous consent of the legislatures of all thirteen states. This clearly enumerated textual veto power is what empowered Rhode Island to make the disastrous decision, from their ex post perspective, to refuse even to send anyone to Philadelphia to participate in what they correctly perceived would be what we today might term a "runaway" convention. They thought, altogether mistakenly, that they could count on Article XIII to protect them. They were wrong. Instead, from one perspective, the most audacious feature of the new Constitution was Article VII, which decreed that the new Constitution would spring into juridical life upon ratification by *nine conventions* elected by the residents of the respective states.

So the heart of the matter is this: What do we expect from political leaders, whether those in Philadelphia or, more to the point, those in contemporary Washington, when confronted with ostensible crises? Publius offers a quite simple maxim in *Federalist 40*: "[I]n all great changes of established governments, forms ought to give way to substance." He condemns "a rigid adherence" to "forms," inasmuch as that "would render nominal and nugatory the transcendent and precious right of the people to 'abolish or alter their governments as to them shall seem most likely to effect their safety and happiness.'" He is obviously evoking the Declaration of Independence, which gives consent of the governed priority over the "forms" of "established governments." How are such revolutionary transformations achieved? Here, too, Publius supplies an answer: because "it is impossible for the people spontaneously and universally to move in concert towards their object; . . . it is therefore essential that such changes be instituted by some INFORMAL AND UNAUTHORIZED PROPOSITION made by some patriotic and respectable citizen or number of citizens" (capitalization in the original). There should be no doubt that his means rejecting legal form in favor of doing what the situation demands. Publius praises those who brought about the American Revolution for having "no little ill-timed scruples, no zeal for adhering to ordinary forms." If there is a time for legal fidelity, there is also a time for placing the law to one side and doing what is necessary to overcome a crisis. The delegates are saved from condemnation not only by goodness of their motives but by the fact that their proposals were "to be submitted TO THE PEOPLE THEMSELVES"—or, more accurately, to conventions elected by a relatively wide (for the time) franchise of the people. Should "the people" themselves approve the new Constitution, this would "blot out antecedent errors and irregularities."

Publius concludes *Federalist 40* by stating that even if the delegates "had violated both their powers and their obligations, in proposing a Constitution, this ought nevertheless to be embraced, if it be calculated to accomplish the views and happiness of the people of America." The message appears to be that the United States, at least in its origin, should be viewed less as a "rule of law" regime than as one in which the people, under presumptively patriotic leaders, are always free to determine that the law must be bent and subordinated when this is necessary to achieve great national purposes, including, perhaps most obviously, national defense and preservation. It is easy enough to see the origins of Ackerman's "constitutional moments," including the willingness of political leaders to play fast and loose with settled forms, in Publius's arguments.

Consider in this context the recurrent debate over the degree to which one could possibly view Abraham Lincoln as a model of legal fidelity in addition to giving him credit for having saved the Union (and freed the slaves). The New York diarist George Templeton Strong had almost no patience for those, such as former Supreme Court justice Benjamin Curtis, who criticized Lincoln for going beyond his constitutional authority. "To save the country," Strong wrote, was a purpose that amply served "to justify a little unconstitutionality." Should those Strong sarcastically described as "learned counsel" demonstrate "by word-splitting that he saved the country unconstitutionally, I shall honor his memory even more reverently than I do now."[10] Spoken, perhaps, like a true Publian.

The question, as with all of *The Federalist* essays sounding the same theme, is whether we can restrict this message to the particular crises or "exigencies" of 1787–1788, when the essays were written and published, or whether Publius's denunciation of "ill-timed scruples" and the need to accept the leadership of "patriotic" leaders has purchase in the twenty-first century. It takes little effort to think of post-Lincolnian presidents, all of them undoubtedly patriotic and devoted to their notions of the public weal, which often involved defending the nation from perceived dangers, who pushed various envelopes of legal constraints. Some have literally been memorialized on our currency or atop plinths in Washington; two others were impeached by the House of Representatives, though acquitted in the Senate, while a third resigned when threatened with almost certain impeachment and, more to the point, conviction.

The United States is always faced with adversaries, both internal and external, who themselves are less than paragons of legal fidelity. Is the Constitution ultimately to be dismissed as the mere "parchment" about which Publius often raised the most severe doubts; "parchment barriers," he repeatedly stated, could be easily ignored whenever such adversaries generate a crisis that must be met. Is the "constitutional order" different from a single aspect of that order, the written Constitution? And if there is a conflict, is not Publius justifying the subordination of the latter to the former?

10. Quoted in Sanford Levinson, CONSTITUTIONAL FAITH 142 (Princeton, NJ: Princeton University Press, 2nd ed. 2011).

This bring us, then, to *Federalist 41*, which elaborates on the ineluctable tension between fidelity to law and higher duties generated by exigencies and emergencies. One may well regard the following sentences as the most ominous found in the entire body of essays. "The means of security," Publius writes, "can only be regulated by the means and the danger of attack. They will, in fact, be ever determined by these rules, and by no others. *It is in vain to oppose Constitutional barriers to the impulse of self-preservation. It is worse than in vain; because it plants in the Constitution itself necessary usurpations of power, every precedent of which is a germ of unnecessary and multiplied repetitions*" (emphasis added). Thus even "the most pacific nations" will be obliged to "maintain[] constantly a disciplined army, ready for the service of ambition or revenge" when it faces an armed enemy.

It is worth parsing these sentences very closely. Perhaps they refer only to the collective (and de facto unlimited) powers of the national government as a whole, with the assumption that Congress will necessarily play a dominant role in declarations of war and other actualities of "national self-preservation." In *Federalist 23*, for example, Publius makes no bones about the necessity for such unlimited power:

> These powers ought to exist without limitation, BECAUSE IT IS IMPOSSIBLE TO FORESEE OR DEFINE THE EXTENT AND VARIETY OF NATIONAL EXIGENCIES, OR THE CORRESPONDENT EXTENT AND VARIETY OF THE MEANS WHICH MAY BE NECESSARY TO SATISFY THEM. The circumstances that endanger the safety of nations are infinite, and for this reason no constitutional shackles can wisely be imposed on the power to which the care of it is committed. . . .
>
> This is one of those truths which, to a correct and unprejudiced mind, carries its own evidence along with it; and may be obscured, but cannot be made plainer by argument or reasoning. It rests upon axioms as simple as they are universal; the MEANS ought to be proportioned to the END; the persons, from whose agency the attainment of any END is expected, ought to possess the MEANS by which it is to be attained. (All capitalizations in original.)

These statements can scarcely bring comfort to the devotees of "limited government," for, in good Hobbesian fashion, Publius seems to be arguing that that vision is basically chimerical within the "rapacious" international order. But one might take refuge in the belief that *Congress* must play the essential role when moving toward exertions of basically sovereign authority, even if this necessarily means, as is argued in No. 41, that any constraints on congressional authority will properly be ignored given the overriding value of preserving the nation itself. But, inevitably, we can easily wonder today about the potential for *presidential* action when, perhaps, Congress is unavailable or, more likely, is so mired in partisan gridlock that essential actions necessary to vindicate core American interests will simply be impossible. So for many people today the real question involves the degree to which one person, that is, the president, should instantiate this basically unlimited power that Publius seems to endorse. There are obviously

Schmittian overtones to this aspect of the Publian argument, which, for equally obvious reasons, we may be reluctant to acknowledge. Who, precisely, does the Constitution authorize to declare the existence of "exigencies"—or Schmittian "exceptions"—legitimizing the deviation from ordinary norms seemingly endorsed by Publius? Does—or should—the Constitution contain within it the seeds of de facto "dictatorial" authority to confront dire threats to the United States? Perhaps an equivalent question is whether we would—or should—expect a president to "rise to the occasion," as it were, and simply respond to the imperatives seemingly attached to the occasion and ignore the question of legality. The remaining possibility, of course, is that we would—and should—expect a president to proclaim that although we are confronted by dire threats, he has, alas, no legal authority to confront them, whatever the cost to the nation. The only thing one can say with confidence is that our 1787 Constitution does not respond to such questions with any clarity. We are basically on our own in giving meaning to the Constitution.

One should be clear that constitutional fidelity as such is not the equivalent of saying "Let justice be done though the heavens fall." That perhaps makes a certain amount of sense even if there are few people indeed who really adopt such a rigorous maxim when the heavens do seem to be falling. Still, one can make sense of an argument that gives priority above all to honoring the demands of "justice," whatever the costs. (That is, obviously, just what it means to reject any form of utilitarianism.) But can we really make similar sense of, and honor, the maxim "Let an unwise constitutional limit be followed though the heavens fall"? Is that not precisely the kind of legalistic "zeal" for hollow "form" that Publius castigates in *Federalist 40* and then again in the following essay? What else could he mean by referring to "necessary usurpation"? Is that a reference "merely" to presumptive overreaching, at least from a legalistic perspective, by Congress, or does it refer to, and thus anticipatorily legitimate, the kind of overreaching of which Lincoln, and then many of his successors, was accused? There is also a question of "constitutional design" about which I have written elsewhere: that is, if one recognizes the necessity for occasional "constitutional dictatorships," whether or not denominated as such, does the United States Constitution present a desirable model, especially if we take Publius seriously with regard to the ubiquitous presence of political "ambition" attached to the evocation of institutional power? Perhaps there are other models available, beginning with that of ancient Rome and moving toward the present day in a number of post–World War II (or Cold War) constitutions that reflect acute awareness of both the prospects and dangers of "emergencies" that might require deviation from ordinary constitutional norms.

Before moving on more directly to the consideration explicitly of *presidential* power in Publius's vision, it is worth noting the fact that the word "sovereignty" rarely if ever appears in the entire corpus of *The Federalist*. Both the Declaration of Independence and the Constitution might proclaim a commitment to the conceptual popular sovereignty of "one people" and then of "We the People," respectively, but, especially in the Constitution, it is a decidedly desiccated embrace of actual popular power. There is not a scintilla of any kind of "direct democracy"—of actual decision-making by the people themselves—in the document. There is, instead, an exclusive reliance on *representative* democracy, with the practical entailment that all decisions will be made by individuals who can claim, with whatever degree of plausibility, to be authorized to make them. Publius makes this especially clear in *Federalist 63*: The "true distinction" of the proposed constitutional order lies "IN THE TOTAL EXCLUSION OF THE PEOPLE IN THEIR COLLECTIVE CAPACITY from any share" in actual policymaking, except insofar as representatives are contingently attentive to public opinion. Inasmuch as Publius frequently expresses his suspicions about the capacity of ordinary Americans actually to think truly cogently about politics, it is clear that his vision of "representation" is quite close to that of Edmund Burke's. He would, one suspects, be appalled by a contemporary devotee of almost mindless mirroring of whatever preferences one's constituency (or "base") might possess or even a proponent of mass decision-making who privileges the "wisdom of crowds" over unilateral decision-making of a wise executive.[11] Publius not only had high confidence in those likely to be chosen as chief executives; he was also unaware or unafraid of the phenomonen of what would be called "groupthink" within a tightly cloistered executive office.[12]

Why is there such a conspicuous absence of sovereignty language? One might speculate that the central partisans of "sovereignty" were likely to be devotees of *state* sovereignty, suspicious of the claims of the national government. Defenders of an enhanced national government would scarcely be well advised to admit that indeed the new constitutional order is meant to limit, if not to outright negate, the notion of protected state sovereignty. It is no coincidence that the most zealous champions of "sovereignty" on the contemporary Supreme Court, for example, are the justices most protective of "state's rights" and almost contemptuous at times of the claims of overriding national interests.

Indeed, the first great constitutional debate about "sovereignty" had come in the 1793 case *Chisholm v. Georgia,* dealing with the ability of an ordinary citizen, in this case a South Carolinian, to sue a state.[13] Although the Court, by a 4-1 vote that included two ringing defenses of popular sovereignty by Chief Justice Jay and Justice Wilson, dismissed Georgia's claim to possess "sovereign immunity," the Eleventh Amendment overrode *Chisholm* in relatively short order. Moreover, the Court has greatly—and some would say grotesquely—expanded the scope of that Amendment to give states a far greater immunity from suits by wronged citizens than is warranted by a close reading of the Amendment's text.[14]

11. See, e.g., Helene Landemore, DEMOCRATIC REASON: POLITICS, COLLECTIVE INTELLIGENCE, AND THE RULE OF THE MANY (Princeton, NJ: Princeton University Press, 2013).

12. See Irving Janis, VICTIMES OF GROUPTHINK: PSYCHOLOGICAL STUDIES OF POLICY DECISIONS AND FIASCOES (Boston: Houghton Mifflin, 1972).

13. 2 U.S. (2 Dall.) 419 (1793).

14. See, e.g., John F. Manning, *The Eleventh Amendment and the Reading of Precise Constitutional Texts*, 113 Yale L.J. 1663 (2004).

Consider in this context the response, for example, of Justice Antonin Scalia in a June 2012 case addressing the duty of Arizona to submit to national law regarding unauthorized immigrants.[15] The United States, defending the proposition that the national law "preempted" Arizona's legislation, gave as one of the supporting arguments that immigration involves delicate questions of foreign policy; Arizona's measures, by antagonizing the Mexican government, made our relationship with Mexico more difficult. The majority agreed that "foreign countries['] concern[s] about the status, safety, and security of their nationals in the United States" were relevant in deciding how much autonomy the "sovereign State" (as Scalia repeatedly called it) of Arizona could have in pursuing its own policy. Scalia totally disagreed. "[T]he fundamental sovereign powers of the States," he thundered, cannot be "abridged to accommodate foreign countries' views. Even in its international relations, the Federal Government must live with the inconvenient fact that it is a Union of independent States, who have their own sovereign powers," even if the exercise of those powers turns out in effect to be "a nuisance and a bother in the conduct of foreign policy." Scalia altogether accurately reminds his readers (and his colleagues) that the Court in 2008 refused President George W. Bush's request that it "interfere" with the operation of Texas criminal courts in a case where those courts had sentenced a Mexican national to death without notifying the Mexican embassy of his arrest, as required by international treaty.[16] Scalia interpreted that decision to mean that "Though it may upset foreign powers—and even when the Federal Government desperately wants to avoid upsetting foreign powers—the States" retain significant autonomy, including "the right to protect their borders against foreign nationals, just as they have the right to execute foreign nationals for murder" in circumstances where international law has been violated.

Perhaps the most fundamental theoretical issue posed by federalism was *imperio in imperium,* that is, how is that two "sovereigns" could genuinely share power inasmuch as "sovereignty" for almost all theorists entails a singular supremacy over all potential competitors. The American answer was "popular sovereignty," whereby "We the People" in effect created by state and national governments with their own particularized powers, with neither of them being "sovereign." Yet, as already indicated, "the people" were systematically deprived of what might described as an "active voice" in their government—no initiatives and referenda or recalls, thank you, at least at the national level of governance. Partisans of state authority always felt free to continue to use the language of sovereignty; the most dramatic use involves claims to be able to secede, though more common in our history has been the assertion of a state's right to "nullify" objectionable national laws or judicial decisions by declaring them "unconstitutional," whatever might be the view of national authorities, including the Supreme

15. Arizona v. United States, 567 U.S. 387 (2012).

16. Medellin v. United States, 552 U.S. 491 (2008).

Court.[17] Though secession does not currently appear to be a live threat in the United States, it remains true that defenders of state power feel free to invoke the magic terms "sovereignty" and even "nullification."[18] Devotees of national power, on the other hand, are reduced to pointing out the practical consequences of such state assertions, including, in cases such as *Arizona* and *Medellin*, alienation of foreign countries and concomitant costs to an effective foreign policy, but they do not proclaim the "sovereignty" of the national government, a notion that indeed has no warrant in conventional American political or constitutional thought. At least at the rhetorical level, defenders of a strong national government must fight with one hand behind their back; it is almost *always* a foul to cry "sovereign power" against defenders of "states rights."

Still, it is obvious that Publius is saturated in the operational reality of what might be called "sovereigntist" arguments even if he is hesitant to use the magic word. His view of the Philadelphia Convention and then the subsequent ratifying conventions can easily be compared with the invocation of the *pouvoir constituant*, the power of the sovereign people to transform their government at will and, along the way, to ignore any existing legal constraints that seemingly stand in that power's way. And even if we are speaking of something less than total transformation, what Carl Schmitt notably called "sovereign dictatorship," there is still the possibility of what he labeled the "commissarial dictatorship," in which the fearless leader exercises dictatorial power in order to maintain the overall constitutional order even at the price of violating particular norms within that order. It is not without interest that Schmitt admired Abraham Lincoln and cited him as an almost perfect representative of this latter form of dictatorship, perhaps as evidenced by Lincoln's own famous question, "Are all the laws, but one, to go unexecuted, and the government itself go to pieces, lest that one law be violated?" In any case, Schmitt quoted Lincoln's "House Divided" speech in defending the Nazi takeover of the dissident Prussian government in 1932.[19] It's not even certain that Schmitt believed that German law was necessarily being violated, given the overarching importance of maintaining national unity at all costs.

So, whatever the high theory of sovereignty, it is clear that the underlying foundation of Publius's argument is that national (and nationalist) political leaders should realize that one of their responsibilities, at least in times of "exigencies," is to rise to the occasion and do basically whatever is necessary, in terms of means, to achieve the all-important end of preserving the nation itself. One should note, of course, that "preserving the nation" is not necessarily synonymous with

17. See the essays that comprise Sanford Levinson, ed. NULLIFICATION AND SECESSION IN MODERN CONSTITUTIONAL THOUGHT (Lawrence: University Press of Kansas, 2016).

18. See, e.g., the introduction to id., Sanford Levinson, *Introduction: Zombie (or Dinosaur Constitutionalism? The Revival of Nullification and Secession.*

19. Peter Caldwell, POPULAR SOVEREIGNTY AND THE CRISIS OF GERMAN CONSTITUTIONALISM: THE THEORY AND PRACTICE OF WEIMAR CONSTITUTIONALISM 172 (Durham, NC: Duke University Press, 1997).

preserving a particular constitutional order that may serve to define the nation at a particular moment. So it is appropriate to move on to consider the particular role of the Publian president with regard to the ultimate responsibilities of office.

It is worth noting that the discussion of executive power comes quite late in the overall structure of *The Federalist*. The first essay on that topic, No. 67, was published only on March 11, 1788. By that date, six of the constitutionally required nine states had already ratified the Constitution. This only underscores the difficulty presented by attempting to use *The Federalist* as evidence of "original meaning," since, obviously, a majority of the ratifying states had deliberated and voted without the very possibility of considering Publius's arguments; with regard to the remaining states, there is relatively little evidence that *The Federalist* was widely read at the time. But the point of *this* essay is that it truly does not matter to what extent Publius accurately captured the sense of the time or influenced others at the time to change their views in accordance with his own. Instead, it is to reflect on the degree to which the Publian argument offers insights, either helpful or cautionary, in coming to terms with executive (and, beyond that, governmental) power in the twenty-first century.

New York was a notably close call, the final vote being 30-27. It is obvious why Hamilton/Publius, as a wily politician, might be hesitant to be completely candid about the extent to which the Constitution, correctly understood, did indeed create the "consolidated," potentially all-power government of the anti-Federalist nightmares. Fortunately, the New York delegates were unaware of Hamilton's remarkable speech of June 18, 1787, at the Philadelphia Convention; he took full advantage of the pledge of secrecy on the part of all of delegates to declare that "he had no scruple in declaring, supported as he was by the opinions of so many of the wise & good, that the British Govt. was the best in the world: and that he doubted much whether any thing short of it would do in America."[20] We should not, as a nation, be forced to rely on Congress to secure the great ends of the new Constitution. The reason is quite simple. Even "members most tenacious of republicanism," he observed, "were as loud as any in declaiming agst. the vices of democracy." That is, it was all too likely that Congress would be too responsive to an almost inherently unreliable public opinion, what he refers to later in his speech as "the amazing violence & turbulence of the democratic spirit," with the consequence that "[w]hen a great object of Govt. is pursued, which seizes the popular passions, they spread like wild fire, and become irresistable." Thus the need for establishing an executive that can truly balance—perhaps the better term is "outweigh"—the

20. See http://founders.archives.gov/?q=Ancestor%3AARHN-01-04-02-0098&s=1511311111&r=3 This extremely valuable site explains that there are no fewer than five sources for Hamilton's speech, http://founders.archives.gov/?q=Ancestor%3AARHN-01-04-02-0098&s=1511311111&r=1; not surprisingly, they differ in some aspects. Hamilton's own notes, for example, are really little more than an outline. I have thus chosen the version from Madison's notes, though, as Mary Bilder has recently demonstrated, no one should treat those notes as exhibiting anything close to stenographic reliability. See Mary Sarah Bilder, MADISON'S HAND: REVISITING THE CONSTITUTIONAL CONVENTION (Cambridge, MA: Harvard University Press, 2015).

more democratic branches. Then the shocker, at least to those who viewed the American Revolution as an unequivocal repudiation of the English system root and branch: "The English model was the only good one on this subject. The Hereditary interest of the King was so interwoven with that of the Nation, and his personal emoluments so great, that he was placed above the danger of being corrupted from abroad—and at the same time was both sufficiently independent and sufficiently controuled, to answer the purpose of the institution at home."

Indeed, Eric Nelson has recently argued that Hamilton was one of many American revolutionaries who turned against George III only quite late, around 1775, when it had become clear that he was in fact, from their perspective, a lamentably weak king who was unwilling to exercise what they believed was his power—and duty—to veto oppressive laws passed by the English Parliament.[21] Nelson argues that many Americans, including Hamilton, were the last Stuarts, wholly unaccepting of the radical transformation produced by the Act of Settlement and other implications of the Glorious Revolution of 1688, among them the de facto elimination of the veto power and acceptance of the supremacy of Parliament. In any event, Hamilton begged his colleagues to give full heed to the strengths of the English system. It was one thing, altogether acceptable, to reject the hereditary principle of the English monarchy or the particular ineptitude of George III. As to the former, especially, one can do no better than quote a somewhat acerbic author of a letter to the *New York Times* on the occasion of the June 2014 abdication of the Spanish king Juan Carlos in favor of his son, Felipe. "I found it amusing," wrote the author, "to read that Felipe, the current prince, 'has solid credentials' to replace his father. The only real 'credential' that matters is Felipe's bloodline."[22] So one altogether facile response to any charge of "monarchy" directed at the American president is to point out that succession in office is not established by bloodline.

But rejection of blood succession does not require one also to reject the attractions of other important attributes of the monarchical principle; Hamilton found the latter altogether severable from the hereditary basis of selection and succession.[23] "Let the Executive also be for life," Hamilton suggested. One reason, ironically or not, is that executives serving shorter terms will be tempted to generate the kinds of emergencies, including those involving national security that might lead to proposals that they remain in office. "An Executive for life," however,

21. Eric Nelson, THE ROYALIST REVOLUTION: MONARCHY AND THE AMERICAN FOUNDING (Cambridge, MA: Harvard University Press, 2014).

22. Quoted in Sanford Levinson, AN ARGUMENT OPEN TO ALL: READING THE FEDERALIST IN THE 21st CENTURY 255 (New Haven, CT, Yale University Press, 2015).

23. See Nelson, *supra* n. 21, CH, 5, "All Know that a Single Magistrate is Not a King: Royalism and the Constitution of 1787, for an especially good discussion of the differences between those such as Thomas Paine, who identified monarchy with prerogative and thus wished a limited executive, and others who argued that monarchy meant only hereditary succession, leaving open the possibility, as argued by Hamilton, of a "republican monarch," chosen in a convoluted fashion by the people, but possessing both the life tenancy and prerogatives of power linked with kingship.

"has not this motive for forgetting his fidelity, and will therefore be a safer depository of power." As is true throughout *The Federalist,* there is a decidedly unsentimental view of human nature and the character structure of those who will fill America's highest offices. To those who will object "that such an Executive will be an *elective Monarch,*" his answer in effect seems to be a version of "so what?" In his recent book *Imperial from the Beginning,* Sai Prakash notes the frequency with which the American president envisioned by the Constitution was described as an "elective monarch."[24] Sometimes this was used as a term of opprobrium, but for many the real point was that it would be best for the country to create a version of what Bolinbroke labeled "the Patriot King," empowered to stand throughout his lifetime above the all too likely tumult of democratic politics to impose what the "public interest" truly demanded.

It is, then, easy enough to explain why Hamilton might be reluctant to convey the full extent of what he called his "private" views to the readership of *The Federalist,* especially those undecided delegates who might be persuaded to swallow their doubts and vote to ratify if assured that their worst fears were baseless. Thus the essays as actually written. Still, as already suggested, even the "suitable for mass distribution" version of Publius's argument has implications enough for us today when wrestling with questions of executive authority.

Twenty-first century political discourse is rife with often acrimonious debates about how to describe certain exertions of purported presidential authority. It is one thing to say that George W. Bush or Barack Obama was wrong on the merits of some decision; it is quite another to describe either as behaving like a monarch or, more commonly in twenty-first-century rhetoric, like a "dictator." I certainly was not immune from using such language with regard to President Bush, particularly with regard to arguments about the propriety of engaging in torture as part of what the Bush administration labeled the "Global War on Terror." His successor has certainly not escaped similar epithets, even if the examples are quite different. Indeed, President Obama can be said to have contributed to some of the outrage generated by some of his actions. After all, with regard to his assertion of executive power regarding the treatment of unauthorized aliens, he had rebuffed earlier calls by political liberals to act by reminding them that he was not a "king" or an "emperor." Perhaps what happened in the aftermath is that the president's lawyers persuaded him that statutes passed by Congress in fact delegated to him sufficient power to make some of the changes set out in his post-election November 2014 proclamations. But, of course, many of Obama's opponents—and even some liberal observers as well—dismiss these lawyers as mere agents of the president willing to rubber-stamp whatever he wishes to do. Monarchs, after all, are able to appoint all sorts of courtiers who offer flattering assessments of their desires. This is certainly one of the central themes of Hillary Mantel's remarkable books on the rise (and then fall) of Thomas Cromwell within the kingship of Henry VIII.

24. Saikrishna Bangalore Prakash, IMPERIAL FROM THE BEGINNING: THE CONSTITUTION OF THE ORIGINAL EXECUTIVE 15–28 (New Haven, CT: Yale University Press, 2015).

Publius in 1788 was concerned to compare the presumptive powers of the American president with the actual powers of kings at the time, though, as a matter of fact, he might well have exaggerated even then the degree of these powers on the part of the English monarch. After all, he mistakenly believed that the king continued to possess an absolute veto power. But for us, such historical comparisons are really beside the point. We are interested in twenty-first century realities, not the esoterica of eighteenth century political regimes. In the present day, one may be more inclined to describe the president's war powers, whether or not intended or foreseen at the time,[25] as at least quasi-monarchical. The powers of the modern-day president are especially impressive, of course, if we compare them with actual contemporary monarchs such as Queen Elizabeth II or the sitting kings and queens of Denmark, Sweden, Spain, or Belgium.

Although the United States has not "declared" war since 1942 (against Romania and Bulgaria), Harry Truman notably went to war in Korea in June 1950 without seeking any congressional authorization at all. Instead he based his claim of unilateral authority on his duties as president to enforce the new constitutional order ostensibly created by the United Nations Charter, ratified by the United States by an 89-2 vote on July 28, 1945, even before the formal end of World War II. Subsequent "big" wars—Vietnam, the two wars in Iraq, and the war in Afghanistan—were authorized by congressional resolutions that served, in effect, to hand the president a blank check to decide whether and when to initiate hostilities and how to carry them out. Moreover, in several smaller wars, in Granada, Panama, and Serbia, Presidents Reagan, George H. W. Bush, and Clinton acted unilaterally without even the pretense of explicit congressional authorization. And President George H. W. Bush argued that he had no duty to get Congress's authority to invade Iraq in 1991 after its seizure of Kuwait; it was, he insisted, a courtesy that served to bolster the war's political legitimacy. President Obama notably intervened in Libya in 2011 without authorization; he also threatened unilateral intervention in Syria in 2013, though he backed down. However, the American bombing campaign against the "Islamic State" seeking to establish a new caliphate in the territory now belonging to Syria and Iraq began and continued without explicit authorization. Perhaps most bizarre, from one perspective, was the process by which the so-called "Iran Deal" of 2015 was adopted. One might believe that anything that important should have the approval of Congress, whether or not one regards it as a "treaty" demanding ratification by a full two-thirds of the Senate. Instead, it was structured in such a way that the president basically had the unilateral authority, granted by earlier statutes, to proceed as he wished, in relevant respects, unless his opponents were able to muster a two-thirds vote in each House of Congress sufficient to override his veto of legislation forbidding the deal. As a matter of fact, that turned out not to be necessary because the contemporary Senate operated, as it now does most of the time, under a procedural rule by which the support of sixty senators is necessary even to bring

25. Prakash, argues that the assignment of the war power was intended and was taken to limit considerably unilateral presidential power.

a bill or resolution to a vote on the floor of the Senate, and that proved impossible. No one could possibly look at the actions of President Obama with regard to Iran or, earlier, Cuba, without being impressed with the power that is now placed in the hands of the American president.

President Obama, moreover, made far more use of drones than did his predecessor, including attacking even American citizens located physically in countries with which we are not at war. Or recall the major political controversy that was generated in 2014 when he traded five Taliban prisoners confined at the Guantanamo Bay prison camp for an American soldier held as a prisoner of war in Afghanistan. The problem was that a statute passed by Congress and signed by the president required him to notify Congress thirty days in advance of any movement of a prisoner detained at Guantanamo. Obama clearly and unequivocally violated the statutory command. Law professors and others subsequently debated the statute, suggesting that it placed constitutionally illegitimate fetters on the Commander-in-Chief's authority to make tactical decisions as to when exchanges of prisoners, quite common during times of war, were merited. But that, of course, is to beg the question, whether the Commander-in-Chief in effect enjoys sovereign power over congressional attempts to limit his power. The point is not to determine whether these arguments were correct but to note the conflict between two visions of presidential authority, one of which can fairly be described as more "monarchical" in its origin and implications than the other.

But when we look at the British or any of the other constitutional monarchs in the West, we must acknowledge that they are all hollow shells of what the monarchy once represented, even as the president of the United States has become ever more powerful. Even if we plausibly argue that the monarchical power formerly possessed by English kings and queens has passed on, in substantial form, to British prime ministers, so that Tony Blair, for example, felt no duty to seek parliamentary authorization before joining President Bush's venture in Iraq, it is at least true that Blair was accountable to a parliamentary majority that could have deposed him at any time through a vote of no confidence. Indeed, even if old-fashioned votes of general no-confidence have become rare, it is certainly possible, as happened most dramatically with Margaret Thatcher and in some ways to Tony Blair, that internal party revolts would play the same role. Neither, of course, is possible within the United States. It just does not matter if overwhelming majorities, including substantial parts of the president's own party, lose confidence in his judgment on matters of war and peace, life and death. Unless the president is also a criminal who can be successfully impeached, there is guaranteed tenure in office until the next Inauguration Day.

So let us return to the specific terms used by Publius when presenting the president as the model executive. The key essay is *Federalist 70*, which presents a canonical defense of a conception of the presidency that is alive and well in the twenty-first century. "Energy in the executive," Publius writes, "is a leading character in the definition of good government." One might read the Constitution as creating a reasonably passive president whose primary contribution would be to "take care" that the laws passed by Congress will be "faithfully executed."

From this perspective, energy is more something we look for in those "policy entrepreneurs" (a decidedly un-Publian term) whom we call legislators. This, to put it mildly, is definitely not Publius's view, nor is it the view of more than a handful of analysts in the twenty-first century. "Energy in the executive" has become valorized, especially, of course, in matters touching on national security. As noted earlier, perhaps the most telling example, with regard to our own era, is the glorification of President Kennedy, particularly concerning the Cuban Missile Crisis. *That* provides the underpinning for the notorious ad by then-senator Clinton in 2008 suggesting that the key attribute we want in a president is the ability to act at 3 a.m. upon being awakened with the news that an emergency has arisen demanding immediate action.

What is quite stunning is Publius's overt reference to, even if not rhetorical support of, the Roman dictatorship, by which that noble "republic was obliged to take refuge in the absolute power of a single man" to protect liberty, either by resisting a foreign invasion or by cracking down "against the intrigues of ambitious individuals, who aspired to the tyranny, and the seditions of whole classes of the community, whose conduct threatened the existence of all government." As I have explored elsewhere,[26] Machiavelli was a strong proponent of the Republican dictatorship; more to the point, perhaps, Clinton Rossiter, a leading mid-twentieth century political scientist, argued in his stunning and still underappreciated book *Constitutional Dictatorship* that the United States Constitution was decidedly inferior to that of ancient Rome inasmuch as the framers simply had not thought through the kinds of procedures appropriate to emergency governance. Quite literally the last thing one might have imagined Publius doing is arguing that the Constitution left us with a too-weak president and, therefore, open to potential dangers attached to limited power in times of emergency. Instead we are assured in effect that the president will be up to the job in part because the Constitution provides him (or, in the future her) with the requisite powers.

"The ingredients which constitute energy in the Executive," Publius tells us, "are, first, unity; secondly, duration; and thirdly, adequate provision for its support; fourthly, competent powers." What provides us with suitable "safety in the republican sense," in turn "are, first, a due dependence on the people, secondly, a due responsibility." The rest of *Federalist 70* is devoted to defending this proposition. We have a direct interest today in engaging in suitable "reflection and choice" as to whether the Publian vision of the presidency created in Philadelphia calms us or frightens us. A great deal of work is being done by the word "due" in the quoted sentence. As already suggested, the inability to fire an incumbent, non-criminal president may make us wonder if there is indeed a "due dependence on the people" (or, at least, Congress). Similarly, "due responsibility" allows us to go in several different directions. Is he implying, or do we infer, responsibility to be faithful to the Constitution, including observing limits on presidential power,

26. See Sanford Levinson, FRAMED: AMERICA'S 51 CONSTITUIONS AND THE CRISIS OF GOVERNANCE 359–360 (New York: Oxford University Press, 2012).

or responsibility instead to safeguarding vital national interests, including "preservation" of the nation itself?

Most observers would consider it naive to talk about "the president" rather than "the presidency." The latter connotes a complex institution, presided over by someone we call "the president" but not single-handedly operated by that person. Presidents often complain about their *lack* of power. Richard Neustadt's famous book *Presidential Power* reduced the operative power of the president mainly to the ability, at best, to persuade or cajole people, whether in his own administration or in Congress, to adopt his policies, rather than to command them. Publius offers a far more romantic, "Great Man" evocation of the president, a noble colossus stepping in to serve (and sometimes save) the republic. And before one agrees too much with Neustadt's picture of the president as a glorified "clerk," we must remember as well, for good or ill, a host of presidents who happily accepted the term made famous by George W. Bush: "I'm the decider, and I decide what's best." Whether or not he had ever read a page of Thomas Hobbes, this certainly has overtones of sovereign authority. He was referring to his ability to decide who stays and goes in his cabinet, but it is not difficult to think of a host of other decisions, ranging from the invasion of Iraq in 2003 to his veto, in 2006, of a bill that would have allowed research on stem cells and cell lines taken from aborted embryos. And of course it was President Obama who decided, without the participation of anyone from Congress, to violate Pakistan's sovereignty—formally an act of war—in order to kill Osama bin Laden. Publius unabashedly declares that "[d]ecision, activity, secrecy, and despatch will generally charcterize the proceedings of one man." As the number of decision-making officials increase, "these qualities will be diminished." Too many cooks spoil the broth. But is one master chef the answer?

How much decision-making authority *do* we really want to place in the hands of a single individual, even if that person conveys Publian "energy" and "unity" (and quite likely is surrounded by "advisers" and admirers who will tend to reinforce both)? This latter question takes on special import during what Publius calls "the most critical emergencies of the state." To be sure, the United States will often need to respond to such emergencies with dispatch, but we should still ask ourselves if there is not some danger in overemphasizing the need to do so unilaterally. Interestingly, Publius also commends the "differences of opinion" common to legislatures; "though they may sometimes obstruct salutary plans," they "often promote deliberation and circumspection, and serve to check excesses in the majority." But, he insists, "no favorable circumstances palliate or atone for the disadvantages of dissention in the executive department." It is surely anachronistic to accuse Publius of advocating what Irving Janis, analyzing the Vietnam debacle, labeled "groupthink," but a twenty-first-century reader may well believe that the "lessons of... experience" that Publius recurrently suggests that we should attend to might make us skeptical of his enthusiasm for a conception of the unitary executive that seems antagonistic to adequate debate and promotes a notion of quasi-sovereign authority that may frighten at least as much as it reassures.

In any event, it should be obvious that Publius is scarcely reducible to an anachronistic voice from the past. The style of the prose—and the examples—may be drawn from the eighteenth century, but the issues that he presents for our "reflection and choice" are scarcely absent today. Indeed, with regard to presidential power itself, it is surely the case that they are, practically speaking, *more* present today than at the time he was writing. To a remarkable degree, we continue to live within the structures of the institutional forms created and ratified in 1787–1788. Whether that should comfort or frighten us is the key question.

Certain paragraphs would obviously be rewritten to take account of the remarkable presidency of Donald Trump and his own testing of the nature of the realities of the American constitutional order. Unlike Barack Obama, for example, who backed off from his threat to bomb Syria, Trump has twice done so, each time without the slightest pretense of congressional authorization. By unilaterally withdrawing from the Paris climate agreements and issuing veiled threats even of a possible withdrawal of American membership in NATO, not to mention his unilateral declaration of a trade war and imposition of heightened tariffs against almost all of our trading partners, he highlights the extent to which the United States, at least in the realm of foreign and military policy, can be said to illustrate a particular form of what Clinton Rossiter called a "constitutional dictatorship."

But perhaps the most ominous issue surrounding the Trump presidency is whether we can genuinely assume, as set out in the text above, that he is a genuine "patriot" devoted to protecting American interests, as even their most hostile critics might concede was true with regard, say, to George W. Bush and Richard Cheney. There is not enough space remaining to quote even conservative critics of Trump who view him as a dangerously narcissistic and, perhaps by definition, entirely self-absorbed and self-serving, compulsively lying, demagogue either incapable of ascertaining, or recklessly indifferent to, what constitute genuine American interests. The Constitution was drafted by perhaps deluded Framers who believed that their complicated machinery would protect us against such flawed persons. Hamilton had offered a full-throated, now altogether irrelevant, defense of the Electoral College in Federalist 68 as a guarantee against election of an unfit president. And Madison, in an important debate in the first Congress involving presidential authority to remove federal officials without the consent of Congress, also suggested that we were well protected against the possibility that "an unworthy man will receive that mark of the public confidence which is required to designate the President of the United States." It turns out that both Hamilton and Madison were unreliable narrators with regard to the long-term future of American politics, and we wrestle today with the consequences.[27]

27. Quoted in Ray Raphael, MR. PRESIDENT: HOW AND WHY THE FOUNDERS CREATED A CHIEF EXECUTIVE 162 (New York: Alfred A. Knopf, 2012).

PART THREE

Vertical Sovereignty

Presidential Powers and National Security

8

The Imperial Presidency and the Rule of Law

CLAIRE O. FINKELSTEIN

I. INTRODUCTION

Throughout his campaign and presidency to date, Donald Trump has challenged numerous practices and institutions that have served as anchors of American democratic governance. These include journalists and the media, the intelligence services, the State Department, Congress, as well as international partners in democratic governance, such as the United Nations, NATO, and the heads of state of the most democratic nations of Western Europe and North America.[1] He has also challenged basic liberal commitments to the rule of law in numerous ways, such as openly firing or threatening those who are investigating his misdeeds, suggesting he would be entitled to pardon himself or any members of his family for federal crimes, ignoring traditional lines of authority within the executive branch relied upon to assure objectivity and impartiality, ignoring divisions of labor and dismissing within his own administration, and flouting basic norms of honesty, transparency, and an avoidance of self-dealing.

Some of the more structural threats are overshadowed in the mind of the public by the extreme focus on race and religion-based reform measures, which the president has used as a lever on public opinion. He has rallied anti-Muslim and anti-immigrant sentiment time and again, thus giving encouragement to white supremacist groups who are biased against Muslims. He continues to press for building a wall between the United States and Mexico, and he repeatedly challenges core liberal values of tolerance and diversity that have prevailed since the civil rights movement of the 1960s and 1970s. Often the administration

1. Trump has consistently attacked the chancellor of Germany, Angela Merkel, and the president of France, Emmanuel Macron, the prime minister of Canada, Justin Trudeau, and the former president of Mexico, Enrique Pena Nieto.

Sovereignty and the New Executive Authority. Claire O. Finkelstein and Michael Skerker.

undertakes such measures in the name of national security: protecting the country from an influx of immigrants from predominantly Muslim countries is presented as necessary for our protection from terrorism, building a wall along the Mexican border is seen as necessary to protect Americans from illegal voting, limiting access of the press to the administration is necessary to protect against "fake news," denying reports of the intelligence community helps to protect the public against distorted, agenda-driven information, and so it goes. But the linkage between the stoking of racial and religious hatred and the external threats to U.S. national security have not been made clear.

The administration's rationales for its anti-progressive positions have not in general served to convince the American people that the public would be safer under its proposals. This is at least in part because the rationales are not credible, given the contradictions inherent in their implementation: the administration calls for a wall between the United States and Mexico or a ban on immigrants from countries such as Syria, at the same time that it places no additional restrictions on those seeking to emigrate from countries that have typically produced the most terrorists, such as Saudi Arabia. The racial and xenophobic overtones of the administration's national-security-oriented initiatives have served only to breed mistrust; they have not convinced the public that the government is truly driven by national security concerns or threats to core U.S. security interests. As a result, deep divisions in the United States have been exposed that tear at the fabric of social cohesion to an unprecedented degree.

In the midst of all the outcry and controversy around race and gender, there has been only minimal attention paid to the deeper structural changes that are occurring under the Trump administration, changes that affect the robustness and resilience of democratic governance in the face of a profound breakdown in the common values that might otherwise sustain it. The values in question are nonpartisan in nature, representing a commitment to living in a society governed by law, and as well as shared ethical and moral sensibilities. While disagreement may be robust, these nonpartisan values have historically made agreement on the most basic, foundational aspects of democratic governance possible. Without them, we are left to political power struggles without the constraining effect of a shared commitment to the values that will sustain our system. We thus experience an erosion of democratic norms, one that has come to seem normal, and that exacerbates the profound disagreements that have torn the United States apart of late. It is easy to maintain democracy against the background of shared perspectives and interests; it is possible to maintain it in the face of disagreement, if there are shared common values. It is difficult to maintain democracy in the face of both divergent interests and profound disagreement about norms and values. The result is that the foundations of democratic governance, and with it the rule of law, have come under greater threat than at any time in U.S. history since the Civil War, and these changes to our basic governance will not easily be reversed any time soon.

While Donald Trump and the Trump administration appear to be pressing the boundaries of executive authority in a way that poses an unprecedented threat to the rule of law, it is critical to keep matters in perspective by observing that the progressive weakening of democratic values did not begin on January

20, 2017. These changes have, in fact, been long in the making. In 1973, Arthur M. Schlesinger Jr. published a provocative book entitled *The Imperial Presidency*, a work inspired by the Nixon administration's rejection of constraints on presidential power and its autocratic approach to the conflict in Vietnam,[2] and concerns about expanding executive authority have been heard by constitutional scholars for many years.[3] After 9/11, however, the pace of the expansion of the "imperial presidency" quickened, as concerns about national security have grown. This is typically how it goes—in times of national emergency, constraint by ethics and law seems a "luxury" that our nation can ill afford. From Lincoln's suspension of the right of habeas corpus during the civil war, to Roosevelt's interning of Japanese Americans during the Second World War and the Supreme Court's acquiescence in that practice, to Truman's seizing of the steel mills during that same war, we have known the felt need to suspend the more quotidian legal rules that guarantee our rights to liberty and property for the sake of securing our nation against external threat.

Yet there is something unusual and unexpected in the present day that sets our current situation apart from earlier emergency exercises of presidential power: the current emergency, unlike other instances in our history, does not have an end in sight. In the words of a recent author's take, we are now in a "permanent state of emergency."[4] This means that the perceived justification for suspending ordinary domestic rights and guarantees continues unabated. Given the pervasiveness of war, as the last several executive branches have conceived our antiterror operations, the president now acts permanently in his capacity as *Commander-in-Chief*, rather than reverting to that power in times of rare, unanticipated national emergencies.[5] Thus what is striking and new about the current expansion of executive powers is that it is combined with a greatly expanded conception of war, one that essentially inserts national security interests into every aspect of domestic life. The traditional separation between the executive branch's protection of the homeland against external threats, on the one hand, and its governance of domestic affairs, on the other, has consequently been eroded. The presidency can now been seen as a permanent institution whose powers are defined and justified by the ever-present defense posture in which we believe ourselves to be relative to outside military threats.

With our current president, the expansive nature of the Commander-in-Chief power fits particularly well with Trump's temperamental unwillingness to accept the legitimacy of anything that presents a limit to his own authority. Indeed, Trump revels in defying traditional constraints on executive power, even when

2. Arthur M. Schlesinger Jr., *The Imperial Presidency*, New York: Houghton Mifflin (1973).

3. See generally, Robert Dallek, *The Lost Peace: Leadership in a Time of Horror and Hope, 1945–1953*, New York: HarperCollins, 2010.

4. Ryan Alford, *Permanent State of Emergency: Unchecked Executive Power and the Demise of the Rule of Law*, Quebec: McGill-Queen's University Press, 2017.

5. The president holds this power under Article II, Sec. 2 of the U.S. Constitution.

it works against his personal and political interests to do so.[6] His supporters find this irreverence refreshing; his detractors find it dangerous. However one regards such attacks, it seems fair to say that they are not by accident. One of the most controversial exercises of executive authority under the Trump administration to date has been the infamous "travel ban,"[7] In the repeated attempts to issue such a ban, and defend it against constitutional challenges in federal court, it is hard to see the president as acting solely from a desire to impose a new restriction on immigration for the purpose of furthering U.S. national security. It is telling that the measure has never been written in a way that might maximize the chances of its being found, and were it not for the unanticipated windfall to the administration of the presence of a new, highly conservative Supreme Court Justice, the ban would likely have been struck down by the that court as unconstitutional. However, most of the professed aims of that executive order could have been accomplished with more constrained and carefully written provisions designed to withstand constitutional challenge.

Until the Supreme Court stepped in, one might have suspected from the way the ban is that the order was designed to court challenges to its legality, and therefore to precipitate a showdown with federal courts. But to what end would this show-down have been manufactured? The likely motive has to do with executive power itself: the courts pose a constraint, and the president wants to challenge that constraint, for the same reason that he goes out of his way to antagonize members of Congress as well as the press, both of whom serve as a "check" on and a "balance" to that authority. The same might be said for the battles the president has fought with foreign leaders, particularly with those historically allied with the U.S. Trump's rejection of diplomacy, and his attacks on those with whom he should by rights share political power, arguably has as its aim the challenging of constraints on his own authority. With this president, it is the perfect storm: a character trait that rejects limitations to personal power, combined with an increasing sense of entitlement on individuals who hold the office of the president.There are numerous examples of the president rejecting any constraint—even that of logic and truth—that might serve to limit his power. Trump or the Trump administration attempted to dismantle the ethics office of the federal government; weakened the State Department by eliminating offices and failing to fill positions; placed individuals as the heads of the various federal agencies who would weaken the authority of those agencies;

6. Cases in point would be Trump's repeated attacks on the FBI, when he is in the middle ofbeing investigated by the very same agency, or his attacks on the media when he craves favorable treatment, or his attacks on Republican members of Congress, when he is seeking their collaboration on various legislative and other initiatives.

7. See Executive Order 13769, which was superseded by Executive Order 13780. The former was found to be unconstitutional in State of Washington and Minnesota v. Trump, No. 2:17-cv-00141 (W.D. Wash. 2017); upheld on appeal, Washington v. Trump, 847 F.3d 1151. However, in a December 4, 2017, decision, the Supreme Court provisionally allowed the second Executive Order to go into effect.

tweeted threats against other nuclear powers and leaders of "rogue" states; attacked perceived traitors at home and abroad; rejected diplomacy in favor of bellicose threats; cast insults far and wide, even against traditional allies of the United States; members of the Trump family, as well as of the administration, refused to divest themselves of their personal financial holdings in compliance with the traditions of presidential ethics and freedom from conflicts of interest; and lied about simple and straightforward factual matters, such as the size of the crowd on Inauguration Day. Although the administration came into power with a clear substantive agenda, what most characterizes the administration's actions in its first months as "imperial" is not its substantive commitments, but its systematic attacks on all sources of restriction on executive authority, whatever the source—Congress, the judiciary, state and local government, the press, international norms of diplomacy, or the public at large.

What led us to a presidency where attacks on the very constraint posed by facts and simple expressions of dissent are spurned as treasonous and unpatriotic? This chapter will argue that the features of the Trump administration that so openly challenge rule of law values crystalized immediately after the attacks on 9/11. Did the new, dramatically increased threats to national security justify this level of concentration of power in the hands of the White House? As Schlesinger so aptly wrote, strong leadership from the executive branch "was necessary to overcome the tendency toward inertia" of a government divided into three structurally coequal branches.[8] As he also describes, however, the need to overcome inertia "has produced a conception of presidential power so spacious and peremptory as to imply a radical transformation of the traditional policy."[9] The real risk with capacious executive power is both that it will attract demagogues and that leaders with unscrupulous morals will exploit the office of the president for personal gain. Thus the lack of boundaries on executive authority leaves the highly vulnerable to leaders with distorted and self-serving personalities, which in turn leaves the country open to foreign interference.

We can describe the threat to the continued robustness of the rule of law and democratic governance by saying that it reflects a decline of foundational, democratic values, coupled with the weakening of traditional legal, political, and moral limitations on the power of the executive branch. The former supplies the connective tissue that ensures that any formal limits on executive authority, primarily legal constraints, will be faithfully applied. With an erosion of both the ethical self-imposed constraints on public leaders, and the lack of robust legal constraints on presidential authority, the ferocity of the attacks on the rule of law by the current administration are no longer surprising. The latter is equally important, however, as the weakening of the institutions with the power to keep presidential ambition in check is an essential part of governance according to the rule of law.

8. Arthur M. Schlesinger Jr. *The Imperial Presidency*, Boston: Houghton Mifflin (1973) at viii.

9. Ibid.

II. POLITICAL AUTHORITY AND THE RULE OF LAW

Let us take a step back to identify what, precisely, is meant by "the rule of law" and its importance for democratic governance. The concept of the rule of law is the idea that control over power in a society governed by this ideal must flow from a legal framework, not from an individual or a group of individuals. In particular, the framework must serve as a constraint on the exercise of governmental power. For law to serve as constraint, however, what the law is must be, itself, immune to exercises of that authority. Like the husband or wife sent by his/her spouse with a grocery list to the store, the items in the cart must match the items on the list; adjusting the list to fit what happens to be in the cart would bring about the correspondence between cart and list from the wrong direction. Similarly, the law cannot be "adapted" or "altered" to justify the antecedently conceived exercises of authority.

But mere adherence to legal rules as constraints is only one critical element of maintaining the rule of law in advanced, democratic societies. A second critical component of the rule of law is that the political leaders of that society accept the normative validity of such laws *from the internal point of view,* as legal philosopher H.L.A. Hart put the point. That is, political leaders must do more than follow and enforce legal standards with a fairly high degree of accuracy. They must, in addition, regard such rules as binding on them, as non-optional standards by which to order their own conduct. They must, in short, regard themselves as obligated by the laws, norms, and standards that provide the hedge against the expansion of their own authority.

The concept of the rule of law is thought to have a particular relationship to democratic governance, and indeed arguably constitutes the very core of democratic ideals. Unlike other militaries, for example, our military swears to defend the Constitution, rather than to defend the country. The oath of office taken by the president and the members of his cabinet, as well as members of Congress, require the same. To understand the rule of law more clearly, we might say that a society governed by the rule of law must meet two conditions: first, that those in power occupy their positions because there is a legal framework that gives them their authority, and second, that the ways in which they wield their power once they have that authority take place within the confines of law and traditional legal practice.

In his famous work *The Concept of Law,* Hart distinguished these two aspects of governance by identifying a difference between what he called "primary rules" and "secondary rules."[10] Primary rules are rules of conduct that pertain to the permissibility of everyday behavior. The substantive rules of the criminal law are the most standard example of primary rules, and primary rules are universally present in every society, even rather primitive ones. Secondary rules, by contrast, are rules that pertain to the authority of officials to make or alter primary rules. These tend to be a feature of more developed legal systems. Thus the provision

10. H.L.A. Hart, *Concept of Law,* Third Edition, Oxford, England: Oxford University Press, 2012, ch. V.

in Article II, Section 1 of the U.S. Constitution that the president must be born in the United States is a secondary rule that pertains to the criteria under which someone can validly hold that office. So is the rule in Article V of the Constitution that requires a two-thirds majority of the House and Senate to adopt an amendment to the Constitution.[11] Secondary rules can be rules regarding the holding of official positions or rules regarding the creation or alteration of secondary rules: in either form they are rules that pertain to other rules, rather than rules that pertain directly to conduct.

Making use of Hart's helpful framework, we can say that a society governed by the rule of law is one in which the secondary rules of the system, and the officeholders whose positions are defined by secondary rules, must themselves be governed at all times by law. Thus a secondary rule that said that "the President of the United States shall be the supreme lawmaker, and anything he proclaims as law is law," would not be a system governed by the rule of law, as it would make the president not subject to the law. He could, for example, declare all primary laws inapplicable to himself, and there would be nothing then constraining him from violating the most basic rules of the system. Or he could declare a law that said that in case of conflict between his pronouncements and the laws on the books, the former would hold sway. He could also declare that the conditions for holding office for the president were now suspended, so that he could declare himself the permanent president, without need for renewal by the next election, for the foreseeable future. In this sense, democratic governance is dependent upon conformity to laws, both at the secondary and at the primary level. This jurisprudential framework may help to explain the deeper connection between democracy and the rule of law.

Second, political leaders must regard their own compliance with the secondary laws of society as mandatory or obligatory. Most relevantly, they must regard the secondary rules by which they hold their own power as an obligatory limitation on that power, and they must see that limitation as part and parcel of the authorization they have to rule. It would seem to follow from this discussion that the duty of public officials to act in conformity with the law and protect its authority would be paramount to the preservation of democratic governance. Yet this point has been less than clear, both to practitioners and to legal scholars. When national security appears to be subject to great threat, it is widely believed that we have to choose between protecting the country and adhering to the law. In such instances, the best interests of the country may seem to come first; legal adherence is a luxury when the country's security is at stake.

Though practitioners and academics alike will avow that upholding the law is, in the long run, in the best interests of the country, they often maintain that particular situations require us to deviate from this perspective, particularly when what may seem necessary to protect the country in the here and now conflicts with what the law requires. We cannot protect the country without violating the

11. Constitution of the United States, Art. V.

law, they maintain, or at least bending it to our purposes, and so we must tolerate a little lawlessness in times of crisis.

Moreover, it is asserted, the Commander-in-Chief power with which the president is endowed under Article II, Section 2 enshrines this flexibility into law, instilling it in the Constitution in a way that makes it superior to ordinary legislation.[12] This way of thinking over the past fifteen years, and indeed starting even earlier with the Cold War, has produced a slow but steady expansion of executive authority, and with it a slide into a mode of governance that poses a significant threat to the idea that the president and members of his administration are beneath, and not above, the law. The Constitution, on this view, becomes the vehicle for its own destruction, as the power of the president is understood so expansively that it is no longer consistent with the basic legalistic framework the Constitution has always been understood to guarantee. It is the slide into the "Imperial Presidency" Schlesinger warned us about so many years ago, or, as some have put the point more recently, a slide into a "constitutional dictatorship."[13]

III. NATIONAL SECURITY SINCE 9/11: TORTURE AND TARGETED KILLING

I argued earlier that the current imperial presidency represents the culmination of a process that has pushed at the boundaries of executive authority for many years, but most notably since 9/11. How, more precisely, has this occurred? The process began with the extraordinary rendition program of the Bush administration could not have been accomplished without the rejection of numerous sources of constraint on executive authority—federal statues, international law, and judicial precedents. Of particular concern was the willingness of Bush administration officials to distort legal doctrine for the purpose of establishing the legality of these interrogation practices, along with the lack of acceptance of contrary and dissenting power. Subsequently, the Obama administration declined the opportunity to remedy these violations by choosing not to prosecute or even investigate individuals who offered up misleading legal doctrine for the purpose of justifying a practice they knew to be illegal. When law is not used to vindicate violations of the rule of law, the violation becomes part of the fabric of our democratic practices. It fades into the background as a legitimate exercise of authority—an acceptable distortion for the sake of accomplishing supposedly legitimate aims.

This difficulty is compounded by a failure on the part of professional organizations to discipline or revoke the professional licenses of lawyers, doctors, and other

12. Constitutional scholar John Yoo, for example, believes that any piece of ordinary legislation that may seem to limit the president's Commander-in-Chief power is on its face unconstitutional, since it violates the constitutional entitlement of the president to do what he thinks necessary in an emergency to secure the country, such as the power of making war. John Yoo, *The Powers of War and Peace: The Constitution and Foreign Affairs after 9/11*, Chicago: University of Chicago Press, 2005, ch. V.

13. Sanford Levinson & Jack M. Balkin, *Constitutional Dictatorship: Its Dangers and Its Design*, Minnesota Law Review, Vol. 94, at 1789 (2010).

professionals who lent their services to supporting the government's agenda with regard to rendition, detention and interrogation, otherwise known as the RDI program. Psychologists readily lent their services to the RDI program, as did medical doctors, government lawyers, and other professionals. The aim was to create, implement, and then justify the infliction of torture and other forms of harsh treatment under the program euphemistically known as "enhanced interrogation." None of the principal architects of this illegal program has ever been prosecuted for their activities, and even informal inquiries into the program have been few and limited in reach.[14] The failure to identify and punish government leaders and their private sector counterparts who engage in violations of international and federal law leaves an open wound that festers. Silence suggests acquiescence and provides a signal that as long as governmental authority is exercised in sufficiently concentrated doses, there will be no repercussions for violating and falsifying the constraints of law.

It is not by accident that in 2010, the newly inaugurated President Obama declared that we must "look forward, not backwards" in deciding how to respond to the revelations about the RDI program, and he made the decision to grant immunity to those who had instituted the program.[15] Why Obama took this position is not clear, but perhaps he did not see it as politically expedient to investigate and punish members of the previous administration. To hold the lawyers and other Bush era officials accountable for violating federal law in acts of leadership would open a Pandora's Box, as well as set a precedent for constraining future presidential initiatives undertaken in the name of national security. Indeed, even the articulation of a legal standard for the exercise of governmental authority in national security matters seems threatening to executive authority, and not surprisingly the Obama administration declined to do so as it undertook to close Guantanamo and thereafter convert the RDI program into a targeted killing program instead.

The failure to investigate and punish the authors of the torture program on the part of the Obama administration was no mere accident of politeness. To the extent the targeted killing program had a legal basis, it was one that duplicated and relied on the distorted legal framework developed by the Bush administration to justify torture, namely the concept of unlawful combatancy, and the lack of clarity around the rights and entitlements of individuals so identified, even those among them who were American citizens.[16]

14. The two main inquiries that have been conducted are the Senate Armed Services investigation, which looked at the involvement of the military into the RDI program, and the Senate Select Intelligence Committee Report, which examined the CIAs role in that program. What is missing is an investigation into the conduct of government lawyers, which would likely take place under the Senate Judiciary Committee.

15. See Glenn Greenwald, *Obama's Justice Department Grants Final Immunity to Bush CIA Torturers*, The Guardian, January 31, 2012, at https://www.theguardian.com/commentisfree/2012/aug/31/obama-justice-department-immunity-bush-cia-torturer.

16. For a discussion of the relationship between the extraordinary rendition program and the targeted killing program, see Claire Finkelstein, *Vindicating the Rule of Law: Prosecuting Free Riders on Human Rights, in When Governments Break the Law: The Rule of Law and the*

The most significant test for the Obama administration's view of its own authority over unlawful combatants emerged in a highly classified memo written by the Office of Legal Counsel (OLC) dealing with the case of Anwar al-Awlaki, the American Muslim cleric who became a member of al-Qaeda on the Arabian Peninsula (AQAP).[17] Through a leak, Nasser al-Awlaki, Anwar's father, caught word that his son had been placed on the Joint Prioritized Effects List (otherwise known as the JPEL list), meaning that Anwar was now a legitimate target of U.S. Special Operations Forces and could be killed on sight. Unlike individuals sought by law enforcement officials, those on the JPEL list are not afforded an opportunity to argue their cases in court or to attempt to prove their innocence. They are treated instead like combatants, meaning that they can be summarily killed regardless of whether they are posing an immediate threat. In December of 2010, Nasser filed suit in the United States District Court for the District of Columbia against Barack Obama, Robert Gates (then secretary of defense), and Leon Panetta (then director of the CIA), to request an injunction to have his son removed from the JPEL list, and to show cause why he was placed on the list in the first place.[18]

The district court rejected Nasser al-Awlaki's assertions, on the ground that whether Anwar could be targeted was a "political question," over which the court has no jurisdiction.[19] It explained that questions of the permissibility of targeted killing, even of American citizens, is politically committed to the political branches of government. The court therefore declined to rule on the merits of the assertion that Anwar al-Awlaki's death sentence, pronounced without the due process guarantees of the criminal process, constituted a violation of his rights under the Fifth Amendment of the Constitution. The court's response was to say that even if there is a violation of al-Awlaki's due process rights, Article III courts are not empowered to vindicate those rights. The court was thus inclined to see any constitutional restrictions on the right of the executive branch to conduct targeted killings as tantamount to a court's attempt to call battlefield operations: it would be highly impracticable for every military decision to be subject to court review, and the court apparently felt it could not distinguish among different types of military operations. In the court's view, all are off limits to judicial review.

This same view was echoed in a White Paper leaked to the press summarizing the OLC memo on whether Americans who were "senior operational leaders of al-Quaeda" and who were operating "outside the zone of hostilities" could

Prosecution of the Bush Administration (Austin Sarat and Nasser Hussein, eds.) New York and London: New York University Press, 2010.

17. Office of Legal Counsel, Department of Justice: Memorandum for the Attorney General Re: Applicability of Federal Criminal Laws and the Constitution to Contemplated Lethal Operations against Shaykh Anwar al-Aulaqi, July 16, 2010.

18. Al-Aulaqi v. Obama, 727 F. Supp. 2d 1 (2010).

19. Ibid. at 44 & ff.

be targeted as combatants in the war on terror.[20] The White Paper articulated conditions under which such targeting could occur, namely that the threat posed by the relevant individual is "imminent," and that capturing him is "infeasible" without undue risk to American military personnel. Under these conditions, the geographical location of the target and his citizenship are irrelevant. In addition, the memo maintains that courts do not have jurisdiction over such cases, and they are not empowered to hear due process claims arising out of such targeting.

Assuming that the White Paper is an accurate summary of the larger underlying memo on this subject, the document is surprising in several important respects, but one in particular stands out in the context of the present discussion. The White Paper eliminates the right to judicial process, and indicated that even if there was a violation of Al-Awlaki's constitutional rights, Article III courts are not competent to consider the matter, given that national security is at stake. This means, if taken seriously, that a mere assertion of national security by the executive branch will make the government's decision to kill an American citizen judicially unreviewable. Moreover, to put it in HLA Hart's terminology, the secondary rule by which the court must constrain the exercise of its authority where targeted killing decisions are concerned was first articulated by the executive branch itself, namely in the famous White Paper dealing with this subject. The Al-Awlaki decision, which was legally unprecedented, poses a substantial threat to basic liberties if the logic of that case is taken seriously.

What does this imply in the context of our larger discussion of executive authority and the rule of law? The measure of executive authority must be taken by examining the constraints on that authority. The ability of a democracy to maintain such constraints, and the ability of such constraints to function as neutral, non-manipulable standards, especially in difficult times, is the best indicator of the health of the rule of law in a given society. By this indicator, the United States has not been doing well. I shall turn now to the second important measure of adherence to the rule of law in advanced, democratic societies, and this is the willingness of the political leaders to accept and internalize the rule of those constraints, as Hart would say, "from the internal point of view." This brings us to the topic of the personal ethics of political leaders.

IV. PERSONAL ETHICS, PUBLIC LEADERS, AND FOREIGN INFLUENCE

As discussed above, the willingness of political leaders to be constrained by the law is an essential feature of the rule of law. For a society governed by rule of law values, however, this feature is a necessary, but not sufficient condition. A second critical feature is internal: those officials must accept those laws from the internal point of view. But internal acceptance of constraints is a function of a person's character, not his or her behavior. The second challenge to maintaining the rule of law, then, is characterological: the personal ethics of public leaders

20. Memorandum of the Office of Legal Counsel.

must be sufficiently evolved to support and accept internal restrictions on their own power.

It should be clear from what I have said thus far that I consider this second point a major challenge with the current administration. The lack of moral character of the president, as well as a number of the individuals with whom he has surrounded himself, have had a corrosive effect on public faith that law will be perceived by public leaders as a constraint. The financial conflicts of interest of the president and several of his cabinet picks are just the most obvious example, but the unwillingness to abide by norms of public decency in personal interactions also feeds the impression that the administration is committed to the Nietzschian principle that the acquisition of power is a virtue, weakness a vice. It is not by accident that so many members of the Trump administration have turned out to be compromised by their conflicts of interest and the lack of disclosure of their financial entanglements.

The Trump administration's consistent defense of the actions of its senior officials and inner circle in terms of mere legality reflects an extreme commitment to the view that the president and members of his administration may do anything in the exercise of their authority that is not flat out illegal—a view of executive branch authority that would have been unthinkable even in the Nixon era. That this argument is offered by serious people illustrates the alarming immunity to criticism of the chief executive and a deep reflection of the "imperial presidency." This conception of executive power is the natural handmaiden to the corrosion of public morals, one that rejects any constraint on executive authority based on character or virtue. The imperial conception of executive authority, combined with the rejection of the relevance of ethical norms to the legitimate exercise of political power, constitutes the gravest threat to the rule of law and democratic values in U.S. history.

But how, more precisely, are the assertions of executive authority related to the impoverished conception of personal ethics on display in the Trump inner circle? While previous administrations pushed at the limits of executive power, there was a difference: the motive for doing so was not usually to promote the selfish personal interests of the president and those of his close associates. Now personal ethical violations can emerge from the shadows with impunity because the president's rejection of personal ethics for himself, as well as for those who surround him, represents the ultimate expansion of executive authority. We are witnessing the rejection of every constraint that might keep presidential power in check, even that of maintaining a pretense of virtue and impartiality in the public eye.

In a society governed by the rule of law, what would happen following the revelation of Donald Trump, Jr.'s emails, which divulged a previously secret meeting between members of the Trump campaign and Russian representatives for the purpose of tilting the election in the direction of Donald Trump, is that members of the campaign would be arrested and tried for their criminal conspiracy to violate campaign finance laws, as well as for lying to investigators, and a host of other legal violations. The president might himself be arrested, or at least impeached, for being implicated in an illegal conspiracy to subvert the 2016 presidential election with foreign assistance. Arrests and impeachment would help to repair the damage done by these flagrant violations of law, since the infliction of legal penalties is the most effective tool for reversing the damage corruption inflicts on the rule of law.

That would be only a beginning, since beyond punishing for violations of our election and national security laws, we will still have to grapple with the ethical damage being done to the younger, more impressionable generations, many of whom do not remember what it's like for public servants to serve as ethical role models. Lying is perhaps the most striking moral failure of the current administration, though it has been imposed on an unsavvy public by many politicians, is far from irrelevant or trivial in thinking about damage to the rule of law. Faced with persistent and pathological lying, there can be no trust of public leaders at any level of government, and without trust there can be no legitimate political leadership.

Ethical character and integrity on the part of public leaders provide the glue that holds the rule of law in place, once mere compliance with legal norms has been achieved. Such virtues help cement fidelity to law, as well as ensure that adherence to law is an ideal worth holding. It is perhaps a surprising, but one might hope ultimately uplifting, result of the current political crisis that we are seeing with increased clarity the importance of personal ethics for preserving the rule of law. What we are learning is that personal ethics will ultimately prove as critical for preserving the rule of law as narrow compliance with the letter of the law. This should ultimately come as no surprise, however, since we often judge the merits of a law by its morality, but never judge the merits of morality by whether the course of action it recommends is convergent with legality.

How are the bid for an imperial presidency and the lack of ethical commitment related? The connection is not as easy to trace as one might suppose. Politicians are people who want power. Sometimes they want that power to realize substantive agendas; sometimes they want it for its own sake, and are willing to sacrifice their agendas to acquire it. So the most obvious connection is that politicians are willing to violate personal ethics to acquire power, and the more determined they are to acquire that power, the more they are willing to ignore ethical constraints. This is admittedly a bit too simplistic. The deeper connection must be articulated more subtly: while all politicians want power, what distinguishes great leaders from mediocre or downright corrupt leaders is the willingness the former have to build that power by making use of, rather than rejecting, existing legal and ethical sources of constraint. It is this critical ability that distinguishes a legitimate leader from a rogue politician.

The current administration seems unlikely to learn the art of building power through self-constraint. Constraint, therefore, will have to come from without. Fortunately, law has been a highly effective tool in liberal democracies for remedying violations of itself; law, unlike people, has the unique power to be "self-correcting." If the other institutions of our democracy are willing to constrain the trend toward imperialism of our executive branch, the correction will likely be effective in reversing the damage to the rule of law of the post-9/11 era. Following ethical constraints, unlike legal constraints, is thus mostly a matter of self-policing on matters of ethics and integrity. Can self-discipline of this sort reasonably be expected of politicians? Is it even rational for public leaders? As in the famous example of Ulysees, who tied himself to the mast to avoid jumping ship to heed to the call of the Sirens, self-constraint may make a person stronger, not weaker. A truly strong leader leads through self-constraint and the building of trust, both in his private and in his public relations. When we can trust our political leaders to self-constrain, we are able to trust them to govern in the best interests of the country. This is not, or should not be, an extra badge of honor for government officials. It should be the first and most fundamental qualification for being a guardian of the public welfare.

The above discussion of the expansion of executive authority in the United States is part of a larger trend, in which democratic institutions are losing ground across the globe. We have become aware of the scope of the Russian efforts to influence American politics through the dissemination of so-called "fake news" and cyber attacks on electoral systems in the U.S. and Western Europe. The French experienced similar attacks to those experienced in the run-up to the French election. The Russians may have played a role in whipping up support for the British exit from the European Union, and there are compelling reports of Russian attempts to influence elections in the Netherlands, France, Germany, Spain, and Italy, to name a few. Dictators and right wing governments are on the ascendency, such as the governments of Turkey, Venezuela, and now Italy. While delving into this critical topic in detail is beyond the scope of the current chapter, it should be clear from what has been said that there is a connection between vulnerability to foreign influence and adherence to rule of law values and norms of public morality: what is emerging is that the United States has made itself vulnerable to outside attack through the compromised nature of its public leaders.

This is not new with the current president. The Bushes, both father and son, were compromised by the ties of their own family with the Saudis, and their ability to safeguard the nation against the dangers of radical Islam may have been placed in jeopardy as a result. Before George W. Bush, President's Clinton's ability to safeguard the nation was compromised by his own personal ethical problems, and arguably even Hillary's bid for president faltered, among other things, in part on her ability to stand up with optimal force to the misogynistic attacks of her opponent. Obama's own commitment to close Guantanamo may have risked his ability to think clearly about his duties to the country, and his anticipated bid for re-election may have compromised his willingness to hold others to account for prior misdeeds.

The crisis in our domestic law and our vulnerability to interference by foreign, illiberal powers are not distinct phenomena. Painting with broad brush strokes, we can say that the two internal factors discussed above—lack of adherence to nonpartisan ethical norms and progressively weakening constraints on presidential authority—have made us vulnerable to external manipulation by foreign powers. Thus a complete picture of the damage done to the rule of law in recent years, culminating with the Trump administration, must combine all three factors in its description of our current political climate. This was precisely the worry that the framers of the Constitution had in designing the U.S. system of government. As John Jay wrote in *Federalist Paper 4* in addressing the topic of foreign adversaries:

> [W]hatever may be our situation, whether firmly united under one national government, or split into a number of confederacies, certain it is, that foreign nations will know and view it exactly as it is; and they will act toward us

> accordingly. . . . If, on the other hand, they find us either destitute of an effectual government (each State doing right or wrong, as to its rulers may seem convenient), or split into three or four independent and probably discordant republics or confederacies, . . . what a poor, pitiful figure will America make in their eyes! How liable would she become not only to their contempt but to their outrage, and how soon would dear-bought experience proclaim that when a people or family so divide, it never fails to be against themselves.

Jay is addressing the practicalities of government—how well it functions, how efficient it operates—but he is also addressing the values of a system such as ours. Where civil liberties are weakened, and our people divided, we can more easily be "played" off one another by a foreign adversary. The same observation can be made about adherence to the rule of law: where our legal boundaries fail, foreign powers will know it, and will be inclined to exploit our internal divisions to their own benefit. This is indeed what has happened with Russia, and we are currently paying the price.

V. CONCLUSION: DEMOCRACY AND RULE OF LAW VALUES

There is a temptation by many political leaders to think that strong national security cannot be achieved without at least bending the constraints of law. This appears to be coupled with the belief that when we act on behalf of national security, we are always acting under emergency conditions, and that therefore bending the rules is both necessary and justified. For the most part, history belies these assumptions. Homeland defense is benefitted, not hindered, by strong rule of law values, alongside well-developed personal ethics in the leaders who apply, interpret, and enforce the laws. These traits must be systemic and exercised across a significant proportion of public leaders, and tied to stable institutions in which such leadership can flourish. Because so much of current presidential authority is left to the softer, discretionary powers of public officers, there is a nontrivial relationship between character and the ability of government to safeguard our national defense. It will unfortunately never be possible to codify these facets of character into legal requirements for holding office, and we are therefore left to look to the culture and practices of a nation to instill these traits as criteria for public leaders.

The present administration is a laboratory for testing the importance of the link between personal ethics and national security, or at least the converse, namely the detrimental impact that weak personal ethics has on the ability of leaders to protect the country's critical interests. The obvious financial interests of the current president and so many members of his inner circle have repeatedly placed him at loggerheads with the best interests of the country, since the failure to adhere to ethical norms regarding conflicts of interest has left the nation unprotected from self-interested policymaking. It is important to understand that it is not just that the best interests of the country fundamentally conflict with the personal financial interests of many of those associated with the current administration. More profoundly, there is compromise and risk as soon as public leaders are not immunized in their public actions from those who would use their positions to advance their personal welfare. Though politicians may not be optimally oriented toward the good of the country, the rules by which they hold their offices should reduce incentives for making policy for purposes of self-benefit to the greatest degree possible. When such rules are ignored or unenforced, there is extreme vulnerability to corruption, and even matters of dire public welfare may be sacrificed to considerations of private benefit.

In the current situation, these compromises of public integrity have led to extreme vulnerability with regard to foreign influences, particularly with regard to Russia and the Kremlin's interest in weakening democratic institutions across the globe. Because rule of law values lie at the core of democracy, this confluence of interests between the Kremlin and Trump administration officials' personal interests strikes at the heart of U.S. democratic governance. It will also threaten our internal compliance with rule of law values. Both because of outside and inside forces, weakening expectations around moral leadership will dilute the degree to which we are a society of laws, not men, and hence permanently risk our ability to defend democratic values.

9

A Two-Level Account of Executive Authority

MICHAEL SKERKER

National security programs create challenges for advocates of popular sovereignty—the idea that "we the people" broadly, should govern ourselves. In a democracy, the people elect officials to govern them and hold these officials accountable, in theory, by monitoring their actions and subjecting the officials to regular re-election. Thus, transparency appears to be a precondition for popular sovereignty. Alex Guerraro lays out the challenges for this kind of accountability in his chapter in this volume, particularly with respect to national security issues. Few citizens know what their officials are doing; the issues at hand are exceedingly complicated, and in the national security realm, certain deliberations, decisions, and actions often have to be kept secret to preserve their efficacy. Thus, a paradox: in a system where the people are sovereign, people elect officials in part, to keep them safe; national security actions may require secrecy, but secrecy undercuts the legitimacy of government action in a system where the people are sovereign. The purpose of this chapter is to determine whether inhabitants of a liberal state—a type of state tracing the legitimacy of its coercive actions to the consent of the governed—also need to know the internal protocols and legal findings of the government agencies ostensibly serving them. To put this question another way, what, if anything, may government agencies in liberal states keep secret?

This chapter will proceed in four sections. It is first necessary, in Section I, to articulate a moral foundation for security operations—law enforcement, military, and intelligence operations—conducted by a state domestically and internationally. The argument for grouping these types of operations together is that they are all oriented to maintaining a secure and peaceful domestic society. Moreover, liberal states divvy up security responsibilities among different agencies in various ways, so it would not serve the purpose of this chapter to restrict the conversation to one agency or activity. A moral foundation will express the rationale for security services such as law enforcement, military, and intelligence agencies to

Sovereignty and the New Executive Authority. Claire O. Finkelstein and Michael Skerker.

engage in operations. This foundation will also provide a possible justification for maintaining secrecy if secrecy is necessary for the success of security operations. Section II will ask if public scrutiny of security services is necessary. Section III will ask if laypersons are competent to scrutinize the operations of security services. After it is determined that public scrutiny is both appropriate and possible, Section IV will consider whether and how security services can effectively deliver security while also making internal protocols, legal rulings, and operations public. I conclude that many types of security operations can survive public disclosure at a certain level of generality. A relatively small number of morally permissible operations must be kept secret when their disclosure would directly or indirectly endanger security personnel or the success of operations.

I. MORAL FOUNDATIONS FOR SECURITY OPERATIONS

A. Institutions, Collective Responsibilities, and Professional Duties

The purpose of this section is to develop a moral foundation for a state's security operations. I will initially rely on technical work done by Seumas Miller to explain the moral foundations of institutions.

Human beings have positive and negative claim-rights by virtue of their natural properties. These rights impose reciprocal positive and negative duties on all others. One person can meet her positive duties toward another by delivering morally required goods and services in circumstances when positive rights are apt and the duty-bearer is in the morally relevant position to deliver those goods and services. For example, many argue that all humans have a positive claim-right to the basic goods for a decent life such as food, shelter, and medical care. If this is true, it follows that a very poor person without the means of providing for herself (perhaps because of disability or scarcity in the local environment) may demand assistance from a well-off person with the power to help her. While anyone *can* demand anything of anyone, the structure of rights suggests that the well-off person is duty-bound to positively respond to the poor person's demand. All humans also have negative claim-rights against being murdered, assaulted, robbed, raped, deceived, and so on, which all others (not merely those in the patient's proximity or those with certain means) can meet by refraining from such rights violations and by protecting her from them.

Individuals also have joint moral rights insofar as they are members of certain groups. These are rights that attach to individuals but only as group members: for example, a right of national determination or a right to secede. They are based on properties individuals have as individuals, such as a right to direct one's own life, as well as on properties they have as group members.[1] A joint moral right of special relevance to this chapter is the right to security, by which I mean a right to live in an environment that is free of rights violations to a degree that people are not unduly inhibited from pursuing different personal and joint projects. This

1. Seumas Miller, *The Moral Foundations of Social Institutions* (Cambridge: Cambridge University Press, 2010), 68.

right will be unfulfilled in most complex societies absent institutions to deter, investigate, and punish rights violations as well as a culture (partly shaped by the relevant institutions) where most people are disinclined to intentionally commit rights violations.

If a person is well-off and can buy the necessities of life for himself, his positive right to these goods does not impose duties on others. The fact that everyone, well-off and not, needs these goods creates a collective moral responsibility to create them.[2] Thus, if for example, a group of shipwreck survivors find themselves on a deserted island, it is intelligible for them to say "Somebody *should* go gather fruit," where the "should" has normative, and not just instrumental weight. The person engaged in these activities, or in producing such goods in a complex society, has a certain moral privilege to her actions, to be further refined below.

The aggregation of individual rights, joint moral rights, and aggregated human needs create collective moral responsibilities to protect and address those rights and fulfill those needs. Collective moral responsibilities are moral responsibilities of groups to attend to these rights and needs because only groups can effectively meet them. Groups are not supra-individuals with special group-sized responsibilities. Collective responsibilities attach to individuals but only if they are members of certain types of groups.

Typically, these collective moral responsibilities are acquitted by creating and supporting institutions to address the relevant rights, such as schools, hospitals, businesses, churches, and militaries.[3] Governments are meta-institutions tasked with coordinating the activities of institutions. These institutions are essentially teleological, set up to foster, create, and protect the collective moral goods (e.g., health, education, security) that protect rights and fulfill morally important needs.[4]

The collective moral responsibility of society is largely, though not completely, transferred to the professionals who work in morally vital institutions. For their part, laypersons should support the work of these institutions (subject to certain limitations, below) by cooperating with institutional actors, obeying relevant laws, supporting the institutions though tax payment or charity, and refraining from attempts to undermine them. They might also be morally required to directly assist institutional actors in cases when they cannot cope with exigent circumstances, such as helping clean out debris after a natural disaster.

The end of these institutions are collective goods so professionals have a joint moral duty to comply with their professional imperatives (a joint moral duty is a moral duty to do something that can only be done in a group).[5] Thus professional imperatives are not simply like the obligations of a member of a club, instrumental to the club's end, but moral duties, with the weight to compete with other moral

2. Miller, 68.

3. Miller, 57, 77, 80. See also Paul Camenisch, *Grounding Professional Ethics in a Pluralistic Society* (New York: Haven, 1983), 52–55.

4. Camenish, 54–55.

5. Miller, 80.

duties, since they meet others' positive rights, protect negative rights, and produce the goods to meet morally important needs.

A professional duty to meet the collective moral right of security is too vague to be action-guiding for professionals such as police and service personnel. At first blush, we can see that many steps to deliver security could be unacceptable to the community supposedly benefited by the state agents, for reasons ranging from brutality to ineffectiveness. I propose we take advantage of the criterion of universalizability inherent in most schemes of rights and duties to further delineate relevant professional duties. Since a key component of deontological morality, on most construals, is the equality of human persons, one way of working out the scope of attendant schemes of rights and duties is through universalization tests. In order to identify rights and their scope of legitimate exercise, philosophers imagine everyone in the world who is capable of bearing rights as having the putative right under discussion and potentially planning to act or actually acting on the right to the proposed degree. Plans or actions that cannot be logically or practically universalized, or rules for actions or permissions to act that cannot win actual or theoretical consent by those potentially affected by the action, are morally impermissible. Non-universalizable rights-candidates fail and thus lack correlative duties.

I propose that the contours of security professionals' duties to contribute to security be specified by imagining the professional behavior winning the universal, hypothetical consent of all the parties affected by the agents' action. In non-philosophical settings, people invoke hypothetical consent when they consider what an acquaintance or a stranger would find consent-worthy when the agent is unable to communicate with the other party. Considerations of what an acquaintance would consent to might be based on particular knowledge of the person's preferences. Considerations of the same question in relation to a stranger must turn on assumptions about what any person would have rational grounds to find worthy of consent. We assume someone experiencing a medical emergency would want to be given first aid, we assume someone who has passed out from hunger would want to be fed intravenously, we assume someone being attacked would want to be defended, and so on. This strategy does not give the agent a wide range of action-guiding directives but will be limited to actions geared toward protecting generic human interests or moral qualities. The agent has rational grounds to think that anyone would consent to proportionate actions taken to save the person's life, limb, and property and to protect her rights because every person has rational grounds to demand and seek the preservation of these interests and rights in her own case. An actual person might not want to live, be fed, or have anyone harmed on her account but has rational grounds to demand satisfaction of ofher rights. She cannot blame a stranger for assuming her desire for rights protection absent some express sign to the contrary.

Philosophical discussions of hypothetical consent sometimes idealize the consenters and/or the context for consent in order to screen out biases, idiosyncrasies, and immoral views actual people may have, and nonideal factors characterizing actual debate on moral issues such as ignorance, limited time, intimidation, and other non-rational group dynamics. These thought experiments are conducted by some in an effort to identify a fundamental framework for all of interpersonal morality or for identifying just political institutions. My use of hypothetical consent will be less ambitious than both of these projects, using it instead to identify the contours of extant professional duties.[6] As argued above, I agree with Miller that the properly constituted professional duties of morally vital institutions are moral duties. Hypothetical consent is one way—not necessarily the only way—of working out the proper constitution of professional duties. To be clear, I am not using hypothetical consent to ground professional norms, but rather, as a heuristic to work out the unvarying norms entailed by professional duty and the derived professional tactics, that vary with context as applications of the norms.[7] Professional morality is ultimately grounded in the collective moral responsibility to protect people's joint moral rights, aggregated individual rights, and aggregated needs.

I will refer to the hypothetical consent of all affected by potential state actions below without specifying which social contract school's notion of consent is being invoked: the consent of idealized consenters operating according to ideal communication rules, of actual people following ideal communication rules, or of actual people unconstrained by ideal communication rules.[8] It is appropriate to

6. I am sympathetic to both projects but lack the space here to work out a full-blown contractualist theory or refine the political contractualist model I developed in chapter 2 of *An Ethics of Interrogation*.

7. There is considerable debate in the contractualist literature as to whether hypothetical consent can ground norms. See Ronald Dworkin, *Taking Rights Seriously*, (Cambridge, MA: Harvard University Press, 1978), 37–53; Jean Hampton, *Political Philosophy*, (New York: Westview, 1996), 66; Hannah Pitkin, "Obligation and Consent–II" *The American Political Science Review* 60.1 (1966): 3952, 56. Cf. John Rawls, *Political Liberalism* (New York: Columbia University Press, 1993), 85. For a further overview of standard critiques, see Nicholas Southwood, *Contractualism and the Foundations of Morality* (Oxford: Oxford University Press, 2010), 135–137.

8. A significant point of debate in the social contract literature is whether the people the theorist imagines to debate rules governing their future interaction have a certain common moral makeup, such as a disposition to find common ground or ignorance about the interests of the parties they represent in dialogue. "Contractualists" hold for certain initial moral constraints about dialogue while "contractarians" do not place such restrictions on dialogue partners. The moral parameters of the contractualists ensures that the ideal dialogue results in moral principles, John Rawls, *A Theory of Justice* (Cambridge, MA: Belknap Press, 1971), 120. Contractualists can be further divided into those who conduct thought experiments involving idealized contractors operating according to ideal communication rules and those who argue that interpersonal morality is constituted by actual people debating according to ideal communication rules. The former group includes Kant; Rawls; John Harsanyi, "Morality and the Theory of Rational Behavior," in *Utilitarianism and Beyond*, ed. Amartya Sen and Bernard Williams, (Cambridge: Cambridge University Press, 1982); and Thomas Nagel, *Equality and Partiality* (New York: Oxford University Press, 1991). The latter group includes T.E. Scanlon, *What We Owe to Each Other* (Cambridge, MA: Belknap Press, 1998) and Jürgen Habermas, *The Theory of Communicative Action* (Boston, MA: Beacon Press, 1985). The benefit of the unconstrained nature of the contractarian dialogue is that dialogue partners are imagined to reach agreements that are in the parties' interests to respect regardless of the parties' level of desire to behave morally. Contractarians include Hobbes and David Gauthier, *Morals by Agreement*,

refer to even the last type of contract as involving hypothetical consent since the relevant theorists anticipate what actual people have rational grounds to endorse based on their self-interests. We need to engage in some kind of philosophical construct to model what large numbers of people would endorse since referenda on professional duties are neither feasible nor necessarily morally salient. The duties of security professionals need to be considered in reference to large numbers of people—all the people in the world—since service members or intelligence officers' actions can benefit all the inhabitants of their states and of allied states and potentially pose threats to the combatants and noncombatants of any state that threatens their state or allies or any state or region hosting irregular militants or pirates.

It is gratuitous to devote space here to defending one of the above contractualist theories first, because the collective moral responsibility grounds the relevant professional norms instead of hypothetical consent, and second, since I suspect[9] all contractual starting points would yield the same results regarding the contours of state agents' duty to facilitate a community's security.[10] A large group of actual people unconstrained by communication rules as well as a group of actual people so constrained might well endorse the same security-seeking tactics identified by the theorist based on a thought experiment involving idealized contractors and ideal communication rules since the options for professional duties for police and service personnel are fairly limited and the proper choices, whether one engages in egalitarian moral reflection or self-interested calculation, clear. Whereas the duty to assist the needy, respect people's privacy, or respect people's autonomy might be executed in many different ways in different contexts, inhibiting consensus on the constitution of such duties, the sorts of options we might put before real or idealized consenters regarding security-seeking norms are less numerous and less sensitive to cultural differences. Military norms, for example, turn on broad questions designed to produce clear action-guiding norms about the use of force such as "May military targets that are not vital to the attacker's strategy be attacked?," and "May military targets be attacked if there are risks to noncombatants?" We can readily predict how idealized or actual people would

(Oxford: Clarendon Press, 1978); Christopher W. Morris, "A Contractarian Account of Moral Justification," in *Moral Knowledge?,* ed. Walter Sinnott-Armstrong and Mark Timmons (Oxford: Oxford University Press, 1996), 215–243.

9. One cannot do more than anticipate what the second type of contracts would yield in its Habermasian construal.

10. Miller argues that state agents in democracies should be constrained in their pursuit of collective goods by the community consent embodied in local law, 248. He acknowledges that professional duties cannot also be considered moral duties if there are gaps between law and common morality. Therefore, I think that hypothetical consent does not suffer in a comparison with a reference to extant law as a moral guide, since Miller has to invoke idealized democratic law anyway to explain how institutional duties are also moral duties. Miller also refers to the teleological end of the institution to give content to professional norms guiding their behavior in areas left unspecified by law. My model provides state agents with a specific model for determining the parameters of their professional duty.

respond to questions involving their physical safety and so will not expect gaps between the anticipated consensus of a large group of people unconstrained by communication rules, people bound by egalitarian communication rules, and idealized consenters whose hypothetical consent is based on axiomatic preferences for the full enjoyment of their rights, and the like.

B. The Security Standard

Hypothetical consent can be used to expose the contours of professional norms and tactics by way of a formal framework I call the security standard.[11] The framework can be used to expose the contours of the professional norms of all the morally vital institutions, but I will here focus on governmental institutions tasked with maintaining the security of the state. Since government measures taken to protect people from rights violations usually include types of coercion, there is a risk that measures aimed at protecting innocent people will also violate those persons' rights. It therefore will not suffice simply to say that all protective actions by security services are permitted.

The security standard endorses norms and tactics. Within the professions, professional norms are general rules for institutional actors that are largely rule-consequentialist in their logic. The norms lead to the morally vital collective goods the institutions are designed to meet when all or most institutional actors adhere to the norms. Norms are morally rich as they deal directly with core human rights or moral goods. They are general, capacious, and communicative to practitioners and outsiders of the values of the profession.

Tactics are instrumental applications of norms and unlike norms, can vary with context. For example, the military norm of discrimination might lead to military units choosing lighter munitions or prohibiting indirect fire when confronting insurgents in densely populated areas. Discriminate tactics will depend on the physical environment, available technology, enemy behavior, and the like. Viewed the other way, the underlying and unifying principle of conscientiously chosen tactics is expressed in a norm. I will only focus on tactics in this chapter.

The security standard is composed of two major rules for picking tactics—two rules for expressing the contours of security-seeking state agents' professional duty. First, we can see that a rule would win the consent of all affected that directed state agents to adhere to tactics reliably, efficaciously, proportionally, and efficiently leading to the institutions' goals of security instead of tactics unreliably, inefficaciously, disproportionately, and inefficiently doing the same. Since security-oriented tactics ranking favorably in these four practical categories may infringe on people's rights, we can imagine consent accruing to a second rule

11. I apply the security standard to police tactics in *An Ethics of Interrogation*, chs. 2–3, 5 and to intelligence collection tactics in "Moral Concerns with Cyberespionage," in *Binary Bullets*, ed. Bradley Strawser, Fritz Allhoff, and Adam Henschke (Oxford: Oxford University Press, 2016), 251–276; "Intelligence Ethics and Non-coercive Interrogation," *Defense Intelligence Journal*, 16.1 (2007): 61–76.

selecting the most rights-respecting among the most reliable, efficacious, proportional, and efficient tactics.

With these two rules, the security standard endorses tactics surviving a three-stage winnowing process. The standard (1) canvases locally available tactics aimed at meeting the joint moral right of security; (2) isolates the most reliable, efficacious, proportional, and efficient tactics; and (3) endorses the most rights-respecting among the tactics meeting the practical metrics of (2). The practical elements of (2) are aimed at achieving the collective good of security while the deontological element of (3) acts as a brake, excluding practically effective tactics that come at too high a moral cost. Essentially, the security standard is a way of balancing affected parties' interests in the effective and efficient delivery of certain collective moral goods with the parties' interests in protecting other goods and rights potentially jeopardized by institutional actors' behavior.

Norms and tactics can "score" better or worse according to the security standard. A tactic with no conceivable causal connection to the end sought is imbued with zero justificatory weight. Some tactics are so brutal that the negative portion of a proportionality calculation can be assumed to outweigh any good done. A tactic that is efficacious only 10 percent of the time similarly fails the security standard. Such a low score on any of the criteria disqualify the tactic. In such a case, the state agents employing the tactic are not acting within the scope of their duties. A promising tactic has to be at least more efficacious and reliable than not (>50 percent) and must be proportionate. A tactic is proportionate if the harm done does not exceed the good accomplished or preserved through the action. Efficiency is context-dependent and so does not lend itself to a categorical or scalar assessment. The efficiency element has to be compared across different tactics and can potentially be a significantly lower scoring element than the other three without disqualifying the norm or tactic.

The rights-respecting element of the security standard is weighted greater than the combined practical elements, so a tactic that is reasonably successful in the practical sense can be excluded if it infringes on rights to a great degree. The basic calculation is that people cannot be modeled as consenting to a cure that is worse than the disease afflicting them. These are situations where the tactics meant to protect rights actually harm rights to a greater degree than they were being harmed or were likely to be harmed when the tactics were contrived. This is obviously going to be an inexact comparison since one needs to consider the impact of a security-seeking tactic, such as compelling plane passengers to pass through metal detectors, with the product of the calamity hopefully forestalled (terrorist attack) multiplied by the likelihood of its occurring. The implication here is that a given tactic might be consent-worthy in one environment but not in another, as the likelihood of certain kinds of rights violations changes.

Given a competitive total score, a contending tactic has to be compared against others. A lower scoring tactic is not consent-worthy if an agency can engage in a better-ranking tactic. The security standard provides moral grounds for people to constantly press for better tactics on the part of state agents, comparing their state's tactics with those used by agents of other states. State agents fail in their duty if they persist in using outmoded tactics that are less practically effective or more rights-infringing than available alternatives.

The security standard endorses the extant phenomenon best meeting its criteria, giving legitimacy to security standard-compliant tactics already in use. Legitimate tactics are tactics expressive of state agents' professional duties, provided that state agents engage in these tactics in an upright manner. Obviously, state agents using permissible tactics for non-official purposes are acting outside of their duty (e.g., a soldier engaging in permissible collateral killing purely out of bloodlust or a police officer repeatedly charging his ex-wife with picayune traffic offenses).

In sum, the security standard answers the question for state agents: In what does my professional duty consist? State agents should use the security standard in assessing which norms to cultivate and which tactics to use. They should also constantly seek norms and tactics that are more reliable, efficacious, rights-respecting, etc. Legislators should hew to this standard when crafting laws meant to reform security agencies. The internal counsel for such agencies should interpret the letter of existing laws according to the spirit of the security standard. The public has a duty to use this standard to oversee the protocols of state agents dealing with foreigners (discussed in the next section). Tactics falling short of this standard, given economically and technically feasible alternatives available to the government, can be reasonably criticized and targeted for reform.

Hypothetical consent accrues to domestic government actions aimed at securing a domestic environment relatively free of rights violations. These actions include actions by military and intelligence operators aimed at defeating external threats to a state's security. There are two types of action, broadly speaking, of relevance to this enterprise: investigative and strategic. Investigative actions (undertaken by any sort of agency) approach targets who may be security threats in order to determine if they are in fact threats. These targets include domestic and international criminal suspects, foreigners who might have information of national security interest but who are not clearly identified members of foreign security agencies, and foreign civilians who may be irregular militants (e.g., insurgents, international jihadists). Strategic actions are actions taken against known adversaries such as foreign service members, intelligence officers, and clearly identified irregular militants. Strategic actions lack the tentativeness and gradualness appropriate with investigative tactics as they presuppose a clearly identified adversary; they are oriented to getting the best of that adversary.

Since all the people in the world can be modeled as consenting to a regime of outward-facing security-seeking actions, model consenters' (in one notional state) consent to foreign operations by their security services also potentially justifies action by foreign agents targeting them. This dynamic can best be explained by discussing its domestic parallel. Hypothetical consent is permissive when it comes to the justification of police tactics meant to keep model consenters safe. Considerations of how to secure the safety of consenters justifies a series of actions aimed at rights violators or potential rights violators. At the same time, a principle of reciprocity urges restraint of police tactics since it justifies police behavior targeting the consenter if that person is suspected of perpetrating or planning rights violations. So the consent that we imagine people extending to domestic security-seeking tactics takes into account that they might be the target of those tactics. The same reflexivity must apply to outward-facing security-seeking tactics.

Regarding investigative actions, model consenters of one notional state must use themselves as reference points, asking whether they can consent to their state agents using tactics abroad that, via the principle of reciprocity, they must also permit foreign agents to use against them. Using this approach, the rule of thumb should be that security agencies should use the same investigative tactics abroad that they use domestically. For example, if the security standard indicates that warrants are necessary for a security service to intercept a domestic inhabitant's communications or that a domestic criminal suspect has to be warned about a right to remain silent in police interrogation, the same treatment should apply to a foreigner targeted by the security service. There might be exceptions if the foreign target is significantly different than a domestic one or if it is not feasible to extend the same treatment to foreigners as to domestic inhabitants. As examples of the former type of difference, the sophisticated encryption technology foreign intelligence officers use might prompt different monitoring tactics than appropriate for domestic criminal suspects. As an example of the latter kind of difference, certain types of up-close, manpower-intensive surveillance feasible for a domestic security agency might not be feasible in an adversary state. In this case, an intelligence agency might want to opt for satellite or drone surveillance—a tactic that might be more privacy-infringing since it permits seeing over walls shielding targets from street-level surveillance. If this more privacy-infringing tactic is consent-worthy under the security standard, the model consenter potentially permits her adversary's security agencies to do the same in her country.

The approach outlined here creates a universal norm for security operations. Foreign security agencies can be criticized for failing to meet the security standard when it is in their power to meet it. An example would be if an intelligence agency bugs the room of every foreign tourist, even though it is capable of targeting select foreigners of intelligence value. Regarding a similar concern, one might wonder if state agents should not adhere to local standards of security operations when operating abroad. This concern might seem particularly germane in cases when it appears expedient to treat foreign combatants or intelligence targets in a less deferential manner than domestic criminal suspects and the adversary state (where operations will occur) already treats its own people roughly. Yet one obviously does not want one's state agents using less reliable or less efficacious tactics (e.g., such as torture) abroad even if they are in a foreign state whose own security forces use less reliable and efficacious tactics. While one would want one's state agents to emulate foreign practices better than their own when operating abroad, practical limitations may make this impossible.

Regarding strategic actions aimed at state agents, we conceive model consenters are first as civilian benefitees of military and intelligence agency protection. The principle of reciprocity dictates that foreigners can benefit from the same protections, so model consenters consent to outward-facing strategic actions by their military and intelligence personnel aimed at foreign state agents, with two limitations. First, military and intelligence tactics are only consent-worthy from the perspective of civilians if they can consent to being collaterally harmed by them when those tactics are targeted at their own state agents. Thus in a military context, tactics imposing a certain level of risk on foreign civilians are only consent-worthy if consenters can consent to the risk of being collaterally harmed when foreign militaries use the same tactics in operations in the consenters' homeland. So, for example, the security standard endorses the traditional tenets of jus in bello—just warfighting. Tactics must discriminate between military and nonmilitary targets, and not cause more damage than is warranted by the military value of a target. If people of one notional state can be modeled as consenting to other states' militaries deploying to war to defend their domestic inhabitants, even if the consenters' own state is the unjust aggressor, they would not consent to foreign tactics pursuing a just cause in an unnecessarily destructive manner, targeting civilians or causing more civilian casualties than are proportionally offset by the good of achieving tactical goals. (Proportionality is an optimal rule integrating two imperatives permitting both sides to pursue important tactical goals while minimizing collateral damage.)

This modeling exercise suffices to limit military and intelligence operations insofar as they affect noncombatants. One would also need to model hypothetical consent from the perspective of a military or intelligence professional in order to determine the limits of military and intelligence operations insofar as they affect state agents. This follows because state agents properly direct strategic actions at other state agents. In some cases, overlapping justifications would yield the same limitations as the noncombatant-based consent exercise. For example, noncombatants cannot be modeled as consenting to being directly targeted in military operations since such actions violate their rights[12] and service personnel cannot be modeled as consenting to directly targeting civilians because such targeting is neither a reliable nor efficient means of achieving a military victory (e.g., killing civilians instead of enemy service personnel leaves the enemy's military capacity intact). There would also be tactics failing the security standard that can only be modeled from a service member's perspective only germane to him, such as tactics using chemical weapons or napalm against massed infantry. I will not pursue service personnel-based consent-modeling further here.[13]

In all, the security standard prompts a cautious approach, particularly with respect to foreign operations, because a wide range of concrete practices could be justified if the security standard permits security services to conduct foreign operations employing the most reliable, efficient, rights-respecting, etc. tactics available to the service. The best locally available tactics justified by the security service will vary depending on a given state's wealth, size, technological prowess, and ingenuity. If the standard then effectively permits all security actors to "do their best," the standard

12. I am condensing a long argument here. Noncombatants' rights are violated because direct targeting of them fails the security standard.

13. I develop the security standard and its associated military norms in much greater detail in chapter 8 of the forthcoming *The Moral Status of Combatants*.

allows situations in which, for example, wealthy country A's intelligence services conduct very discriminate, sophisticated, targeted, and automated intercepts of foreign intelligence target's communications—so that very few innocent people have their privacy violated—while also permitting poor country B's intelligence services to conduct relatively crude, indiscriminate intercepts that violate the privacy of far more innocent people. So too in the case of war: the military of wealthy country A may cause far less collateral damage with precision munitions than the military of country B, despite the fact that B's military is trying just as hard to be discriminate and proportional. Thus, before engaging in a tactic promising a degree of collateral damage, an agency needs to consider if the inhabitants of its own state can be modeled as tolerating the levels of collateral damage associated with its adversary's reciprocal response. It could follow that that peer or near-peer adversaries might be permitted tactics a powerful state is not permitted when fighting a much weaker adversary.

II. IS PUBLIC SCRUTINY OF SECURITY OPERATIONS APPROPRIATE?

A. Dynamics of Oversight

Having articulated a moral standard for judging the operations of security operations, it is next important to consider the implementation of this standard. Is it enough for security operators to self-regulate according to the security standard or for their agencies to self-regulate through the actions of internal auditors, such as staff lawyers and inspectors general? Or must the public conduct oversight of these operations in order to ensure compliance with the security standard, or at least conduct oversight of the internal protocols and legal findings setting the parameters for operations?

In order to answer these questions, it is first important to clarify the practical dynamics of oversight relative to consent. It is a less pressing matter to assign and specify a duty of oversight as a distinct activity in cases of explicit consent when consent immediately precedes the contracted activity, such as the purchasing of an item at a store. It is also less pressing when consent is tacitly given throughout the duration of the relevant activity, since consent can be revoked at any time (by explicitly objecting), such as in the provision of a service involving the client's participation or active enjoyment such as an out-patient medical procedure, massage, or haircut, or in some consensual activity such as gameplay, debate, sex, etc. In these cases, oversight of the service provider's or activity partner's activities by a concrete, particular consenter is simultaneous or nearly simultaneous with consent to the activity. By contrast, hypothetical consent only creates abstract standards; compliance with standards has to be conducted empirically. In that case, concrete, particular individuals can and should offer their explicit consent to consent-worthy activities or explicitly dissent to activity failing this standard. So, from a practical perspective, government transparency is important since there is usually a lag between the execution of a putatively consent-worthy governmental action and the effect on an inhabitant or foreigner. There will also be a significant number of people unaffected by government actions targeted at others. These temporal and participatory gaps inhibit real-time oversight concurrent with ongoing tacit consent. Therefore, just from a practical point of view, government transparency about its operations and post hoc review by some competent parties would be necessary to ensure compliance with the security standard. I will argue that this transparency—and the public oversight that comes with it—is not necessary to legitimize government programs but necessary to ensure that personnel in politically legitimate programs do not become corrupt or incompetent.

The legitimacy of national security actions comes from consent-worthiness in my theory, rather than the explicit consent of a state's inhabitants or citizens or openness to publicity. Explicit consent is not the source of legitimacy despite playing a paradigmatic role in social contract theory. Early social contract thinkers appealed to the notion of the consent of the governed to explain how a government's freedom-impinging actions could be consistent with citizens' freedom, despite the difficulty in explaining exactly how citizens or inhabitants transfer their consent to government officials. There are few opportunities for unambiguous explicit consent to government policies, and even the best candidates, such as oaths of citizenship or votes in referenda, prompt questions about the scope of consent and implications of being in the voting minority. Further, the popularity of a government policy does not necessarily have anything to do with its morality.[14] Therefore, if government transparency is necessary for the

14. The best (i.e., least ambiguous) candidates for expressing consent are ones that rarely occur. Signing a new Constitution, swearing an oath to one, or voting for one in a referendum are suggested as paradigmatic instances of consent to a government invoked in the classic notion of the social contract (John Locke, *Second Treatise on Government* § 89; Thomas Hobbes, *Leviathan*, ch. 17; Michael Walzer, *Obligations* (Cambridge, MA: Harvard University Press, 1970), xi). The obvious difficulty is that such events have not often occurred in recorded history (David Hume, "Of the Original Contract," in *Moral and Political Philosophy*, ed. Henry Aiken (New York: Hafner Press, 1948), 356–372, 362), and probably none have occurred with unanimous consent—a criterion the early contract theorists demanded (A. John Simmons, *Moral Principle and Political Obligation* (Princeton, NJ: University Press, 1979), 72). Further, it is not clear how being bound to one's ancestors' oaths or votes is consonant with the autonomy the doctrine of consent is meant to safeguard (Hume, 360). Immigrating and taking oaths of citizenship or naturalization would seem to express explicit consent (Harry Beran, "In Defense of the Consent Theory of Political Obligation and Authority," *Ethics* 87.3 (1977): 260–271, 262; C.W. Cassinelli, "The 'Consent' of the Governed," *The Western Political Quarterly* 12.2 (1959): 399; Walzer, xi), but most inhabitants of a country are born there and never participate in such events (Cassinelli, 398; Rawls, 13; M.B.E. Smith, "Is There a Prima Facie Obligation to Obey the Law?," *Yale Law Journal* 82 (1972–1973): 950–976, 960). Ritualistic performances such as swearing allegiance encounter difficulties of motivation, vagueness, and scope. Compulsory performance of such rituals cannot express genuine consent. If swearing allegiance is not compulsory, what sort of political obligation accrues to non-swearers? If the performance is voluntary, the ritualistic nature of the performance militates against the likelihood that participants grasp the contractual import of their mantras. Further, is one swearing allegiance to a particular leader, a system, or a particular canon of laws? If allegiance is sworn to the third item, this further argues against the prospect that consent is knowing, given the size and complexity of a canon of laws (Cassinelli, 402).

legitimacy of government programs, it is not on account of legitimacy stemming from inhabitants' explicit consent.

Let us now turn to the openness to publicity standard. This standard of political legitimacy would reject any policy that could not be revealed without destroying its efficacy. Many contemporary exponents of the standard draw from Immanuel Kant's signal articulation of the idea in *To Perpetual Peace*. Kant argues that "all actions that affect the rights of other men are wrong if their maxim is not consistent with publicity."[15] He means that an action is immoral if the general rule guiding the action cannot be known by all without that widespread knowledge making the execution of the action impossible. Performing the action would be impossible because the action's success inherently depends on the maxim (the general rule guiding the action) remaining covert in the way that a lie's success depends on its remaining covert or because it would necessarily create universal opposition in the manner of a person's announcement of his policy of murdering anyone he dislikes. Laws compliant with this publicity standard must be accessible to inhabitants, that is. they could actually go to a library or the internet and read the statute. An attendant feature of permissible positive law is that the law would not necessarily create opposition once it was studied.

Policies need to be *open* to oversight on this line of thinking in order to meet the conditions for citizens' consent (they do not actually need to meet with their consent, for the reasons already articulated). Concealed policies are not even candidates for political legitimacy because of an absence of the conditions necessary for citizen endorsement of the actions—even if the law would have been popular.[16] By way of analogy, a man wrongs a woman if he has intercourse with her while she is too drunk to give informed consent, even if she would have given her consent if sober. David Luban convincingly argues that Kant's openness to publicity principle[17] does not preclude all forms of secrecy. "First-order secrets" cannot be revealed without frustrating the action or identity the secret is meant to conceal, for example, "John Smith is actually an undercover officer." However, "second-order secrets"—secrets about secrets—can be revealed without destroying the relevant first-order secret. "The police department utilizes undercover officers" can be publicly disclosed without jeopardizing undercover operations and without creating necessary public opposition. It therefore passes Kant's openness to publicity principle.[18] Since the second-order secret passes the principle, the related first order secret may be permissibly concealed on

15. Immanuel Kant, "To Perpetual Peace," appendix II, [381] 135, ed. Humphrey.

16. David E. Pozen sympathetically outlines this view, "Deep Secrecy," 62 *Stanford Law Review* 257 (2010): 286.

17. I will use the term "openness to publicity" to express the political application of the publicity principle. The broader publicity principle embedded in the Categorical Imperative captures an aspect of the possible universalization morally sound maxims display: they can still be efficacious even if universally known.

18. David Luban, "The Publicity Principle," *The Theory of Institutional Design*, ed. Robert E. Goodin, (Cambridge: Cambridge University Press, 1998), 154–198, 191.

Kantian grounds. However, a relevant third order secret such as "the government will keep all police activities secret" cannot be revealed without creating public opposition—since this gives the government unchecked power[19] and abnegates duties of inhabitants described below.[20]

I do not find this reading of the openness to publicity standard compelling in all cases because I can think of (and will discuss below) intuitively permissible security-seeking tactics that lose their efficacy if the *fact* of their use is revealed. These are second-order secrets that need to remain secret in order to be effective. The security standard can justify their use. All this will be defended further below, but for the sake of argument now we will entertain the possibility that the existence of some government programs is legitimately kept secret. However, since the personnel assigned to a program are vulnerable to groupthink, blind-spots, corruption, nepotism, and perverse incentives, proper guidance of these programs can only be promoted with external oversight of some sort. Thus, I will proceed below, taking a practical view of the openness to publicity standard as the relevant rationale for public oversight. On that view, external oversight or the possibility of external oversight is not constitutive of a program's legitimacy, but important in order to ensure that legitimate programs do not become corrupt. Section III will address the obvious tension between the need to oversee a program that cannot persist if its existence is publicly revealed.

B. The Public's Interest in Oversight

We can now expand on the idea that government programs practically need external oversight in order to ensure compliance with their moral authorizations. Again, government programs (inclusive of their personnel) are not self-monitoring and do not win real-time tacit or explicit consent from state inhabitants. Who should perform this oversight? The public has interests, rights, and duties relevant to oversight of government security services that would be trespassed if state gents err, overreach, or become corrupt.

First, an inhabitant has an interest in ensuring that his own rights are not being violated by the government. One is obviously in a privileged, though still fallible, position to judge whether one is being wronged by another. Some might also term this interest a duty, though duties to the self—such as a duty not to be made servile—are less widely recognized than duties to others. This duty to the self can be supported by an associated duty to others in the following way. It is likely that the government will perform the same rights-violating actions against others if one does not protest the government violating one's own rights. Thus, allowing the bad behavior to continue unchecked fails to protect others.

One also has a right to oversee government activities for the reason that a contracting party has a right to see the work he has purchased. A taxpayer has

19. Luban, 191.

20. Pozen refers to the concealment of second-order secrets, "deep secrets," and regards them with deep distaste because the public does not even know to ask about them, Pozen, 274.

a right to see the services he subsidized with his tax monies. The purpose of this type of oversight of government actions is to combat fraud and waste.[21]

Regarding duties, inhabitants of liberal states alienate certain powers to state agents to use on their behalf. Principals are morally responsible for their agents' behavior when that behavior is consistent with the principals' orders so the principal has a duty to ensure that her agent is doing things she is morally required to see accomplished and not doing things she herself is morally forbidden to do.[22] This applies both to direct agents, who do relatively low-skilled actions the principal could have done herself such as gardening, babysitting, and proofreading, and to free agents, highly skilled actors such as lawyers or accountants the principal relies on for their expertise and ability to make independent judgments.[23] Obviously, the moral impetus for the public to oversee state agents is greater than the impetus to oversee private agents because of the potential harm these free agents can do utilizing the powers of the state.

There are two specific duties the public has to meet when overseeing state agents. First, people have a collective moral responsibility to contribute to a secure environment, a responsibility largely met when they contribute to the creation or sustaining of relevant state institutions.[24] A component of sustaining state institutions includes ensuring that state agents are indeed working to secure this kind of environment.[25] Second, since the coercive means state agents use to prevent rights violations perpetrated by state inhabitants against each other can themselves violate people's rights, the public must ensure that its agents are pursuing the end of security in ways conforming to the security standard. In other words, the public has a duty to ensure that its agents pursue the moral end of security (creating an environment relatively free of rights violations) without violating deontological concerns making state security morally valuable.

21. These points are famously made by Jeremy Bentham, discussed by Amy Gutmann and Dennis Thompson, *Democracy and Disagreement* (Cambridge, MA: Belknap Press, 1996).

22. A principal is not responsible for something her agent did completely of his, the agent's, own accord, having nothing to do with the agency transferred to him by the principal.

23. Free agents bear a heavier burden of independent moral responsibility than direct agents for electing tactics the principal does not have the training to fully understand. Practically, principals can usually not exercise real-time oversight of free agents because of a lack of relevant expertise, and so will likely focus on consequences, which are intelligible to a layperson in a way tactics are not. Oversight will then likely be expressed in reform efforts rather than proactive guidance. For example, the average civilian, supportive of a given military operation, does not have the expertise to decide what weapon systems should be used in a particular attack, but can demand to know if some more discriminate tactics or technology is available after a large number of civilian casualties are incurred in an operation.

24. This might sound strange, but another example of a negative duty creating a subsidiary positive duty would be a the duty not to harm others leading to a positive duty to ensure one's car is in good working order, one's gun is securely locked, and one's pool is fenced.

25. Other relevant positive duties include paying taxes and complying with all but egregiously unjust laws of any state one lives in or visits.

Since the behavior of state agents abroad can incur responses from foreign state agents, it is in the public's self-interest and consistent with their concern for their neighbors to oversee their agents' behavior and object to unnecessarily provocative or otherwise immoral behavior abroad. Assuming that behavior abroad potentially creates a reasonable foundation for in-kind foreign responses, the public should object to practices that exceed the security standard marking what they would tolerate being done to themselves. This limitation has to be considered in kind rather than degree, given that a certain kind of operation releases the adversary government from engaging in the same kind of operations even if they can only perform it in a cruder fashion than the first government. Thus, for example, the public should object to their security agencies intercepting foreign civilians' private communications electronically if they are unwilling to countenance less-sophisticated foreign agencies doing the same to them by steaming open envelopes.

III. IS THE PUBLIC COMPETENT TO OVERSEE SECURITY OPERATIONS?

The public has a duty to oversee state agents, yet may not be competent to execute this duty. Usually, duties imply the duty-holder's power to perform the duty but this is not always the case. For example, one may find it hard to observe the duty not to unjustly harm others when operating a new vehicle or tool and learning too late that it is difficult to control.

In many cases, the general public is not competent to technically assess the internal protocols of security agencies. One would often need as much knowledge as an expert practitioner to know if a weapon system, a computer code, or interrogation technique is the most reliable, efficacious, proportionate, efficient, and rights-respecting available. However, the general public is competent to assess whether the effects of a given tactic raise moral concerns. For example, the public does not know if stopping and frisking random young men in high crime areas is really the most efficient or reliable method of inhibiting gang violence, but does know that this tactic is disruptive to neighborhood life and offensive to innocent people accosted by police. This concern is enough to begin a conversation with state agents about whether this tactic really is the best available, and if so, whether the good done is really worth the harm.

In order to assess the actions of state agents, the public needs a good understanding of not only the actions of state agents but of the threats the agents' operations are designed to meet.[26] For example, one cannot assess the proportionality of a response unless one understands the danger being faced. Concerns related to the public's knowledge of state agents' operations will be addressed in Section IV. The public's being informed about the threats security agencies are trying to meet creates a different problem, particularly in the international arena. In some

26. William E. Colby, "Intelligence Secrecy and Security in a Free Society," *International Security* 1.2 (1976): 3–14, 9.

cases, a detailed picture exposes sources and methods of intelligence gathering to the state's adversaries.[27] The adversary can learn about the threat-publishing state's technological capacities such as its satellite or other aerial reconnaissance resources (and flight paths), based on the imagery released, and its signal intercept (SIGINT) capacities, based on the electronic communications released. This knowledge both helps the adversary prepare to destroy or jam those assets in case of war and helps the adversary hide the strategic assets that have been shown to be vulnerable. More dangerous still, is the direct threat posed to undercover operatives or their intelligence assets who are the sources of the sensitive information describing the foreign threat. There will be sensitive programs in the adversary state's defense and intelligence apparatus known only to a few, and the process of elimination conducted by counterintelligence agents when such programs are compromised can be brutal and swift.

So there will be times when a government would need to describe a threat in order to justify expenditures or operations at a level of specificity it cannot use without jeopardizing sources and methods of intelligence collection.[28] These are moments of irreducible tension between the need for oversight and the security aims civilian oversight is meant to secure. A government's concealment of a sensitive threat assessment amounts to a third-order secret: a secret policy justifying keeping secret a program encompassing secret operations. Again, Luban does not think concealing third-order secrets can be justified as it gives unchecked power to officials.[29] I recognize the risk in permitting third-order secrets, but think external oversight should be omitted in this case where oversight meant to check compliance with a standard threatens to contravene the goals of that standard. My reasoning follows below. By way of analogy, extensive standardized testing of students should be curtailed if it gets in the way of their education. Again, according to my theory of political legitimacy, lack of oversight does not inherently nullify legitimacy. Lack of oversight is a practical, rather than a constitutive, problem in that it creates risk of corruption.[30]

Whether the keeping of these kinds of third-order secrets—the revelation of which would compromise important security standard compliant operations—is itself in keeping with the security standard is difficult to assess. Keeping these secrets is obviously an efficacious and reliable way of preserving operations that would be compromised by publicity. Efficiency seems to be a non-applicable variable. Proportionality is hard to assess given all the relevant unknown variables.

27. Thompson notes this possibility in Dennis Thompson, "Democratic Secrecy," 114 *Political Science Quarterly* (1999): 186.

28. Thompson, 182.

29. Luban, 191.

30. I think the security value of these secrets outweigh the Millian values Gutmann and Thompson argue are associated with public debate about government actions: the promotion of political cooperation in the face of disagreement that comes from the possibility of consenting to governmental actions, the promotion of citizens' moral perspectives, the extension of respect between disagreeing citizens, and the self-correcting nature of deliberation, 100–101.

Keeping the secrets is not *obviously* disproportionate, comparing the benefits promised by the program with the disvalues of omitting the truth to the public and running risks of corruption.

Regarding the rights-respecting element of the security standard, the public generally has a right to know what its government is doing in its name and so any kind of government secret would seem at first prejudicial to the public's rights. This right to know is relevant to the protection of other rights since government programs failing the security standard may be abusing more substantive rights among the people affected. Yet clearly, there are limits to the public's right to know. The public does not have a right to know personal information about government employees such as their medical histories or financial details (with the possible exception of top elected officials). The public does not have the right to know first-order secrets that will endanger state agents. State agents have an institutional right linked to their professional roles to be spared from unnecessary or frivolous endangerment by their own governments. Their rights trump the public's general right to know about government programs when it comes to particular agents' involvement in the program. Yet we cannot simply conclude that it does not wrong the public to conceal third-order secrets in order to protect the agents involved because the program may be doing the public such a disservice due to its practical inefficacy and disregard for human rights that a proportionality calculation indicates that the good done by exposing the program outweighs the disvalue of exposing agents to harm. To be clear, this is probably a rare case where the mere revelation that a particular type of program exists would expose agents to risk (whereas usually, second-order secrets such as "the police use undercover officers in counter-narcotics operations" can be revealed without exposing particular agents to undue danger).

If the program is security standard-compliant, then the security standard indicates that its existence can be permissibly concealed because of the risk to the state agents involved. Ideally, if responsible members of government recognize that the program is a failure, they will pull their agents from the field, halt the program, and announce to the public what went wrong. Failing official measures, a whistleblower would ideally alert field agents before revealing the program or only reveal the program if agents were not currently deployed, counting on the government's subsequent protection of the agents from possible foreign reprisals. Failing all those ideal scenarios, a whistleblower may reveal the program to the detriment of field agents if the proportionality calculation is strongly in favor of revelation.[31]

The other justification for concealing third-order secrets is that revelation would lead the adversary to close otherwise fruitful intelligence-gathering channels. I have argued that the purpose of publicizing government programs generally is to give the public an opportunity to verify that the programs are

31. In particularly odious programs, agents' right not to be endangered may be offset by their culpability in immoral actions they should have known were immoral and inefficacious, for example, torture.

security standard-compliant. Advocates for the concealment of third-order secrets regarding security standard-compliant programs are effectively holding that the government should be trusted with designing security-seeking programs and then unilaterally determining whether their existence should be concealed. Skeptics worry that all programs need to be publicized (even while keeping tactical applications secret) in order to avoid corruption. Roughly, it seems that concealment of third-order secrets violates the rights of the public if the program is being corruptly run but does not violate their rights if concealment facilitates a vital and properly run national security program. Revelation of the latter type of program would in fact fail the government's duty to protect the public. The problem, of course, is that secrecy prevents the public from knowing which situation obtains. We need some kind of publicly available data to use to model the consent of all affected parties to the concealment of third-order secrets. I will tentatively conclude that concealment of third-order secrets passes the rights-respecting element of the security standard if there are significant national security threats facing the state. We can model all affected parties as agreeing ex ante to a premise permitting a state facing significant national security threats to engage in third-order secret keeping—effectively, to engage in secret government deliberations about which programs to initiate based (ideally) on the security standard and which programs will have to be concealed from the public.[32] Barring a clear, present, and significant danger, it may well be too risky to give a government the power to conceal third-order secrets.

If we go down this road, the government's knowledge of certain threats will have to be kept secret, as will the intelligence-gathering operations meant to assess the threats; and the contingency plans developed to meet them. The expenditures on personnel and equipment designed to counter the threat would also have to be kept secret if their nature is so specific as to tip the hand to the adversary, for example, if country A buys chemical-resistant suits for all its service personnel, adversary country B will realize that its secret chemical weapons program has been exposed.

State agents have to operate on their own recognizance in cases where third-order secrets are legitimate. This situation does open the door to corruption and abuse and so necessitates the careful vetting and training of recruits to security agencies. Disclosures of sensitive threat assessments and secret operations *would* be indicated by the security standard if corruption and incompetence hindered state agents from actually securing their state.[33] An imperfect compromise designed to mitigate the tension between security and oversight would be to have an oversight body of legislators assigned to the agency who themselves

32. This consent extends to targets of intelligence collection, who can be modeled as consenting to their own government engaging in reciprocal intelligence collection and secret-keeping.

33. This argument creates a standard for whistle-blowing. Revealing threat assessments or programs whose efficacy depends on secrecy is not appropriate, but revealing gross abuses by state agents in the prosecution of these programs may be appropriate, provided one meets some criteria similar to those appropriate for civil disobedience.

were sworn to secrecy. This option is imperfect because overseers committed to secrecy have no legal way of alerting the public or their colleagues outside of the select committee if the security services ignore their concerns and the wider legislature does not act on their necessarily vague, unclassified recommendations.[34]

IV. WHICH GOVERNMENT PROGRAMS ARE PROPERLY KEPT SECRET?

Section III broached the key question of this chapter: what types of government actions are properly classified and kept out of public view? We now have a formal answer implied by the foregoing discussion of threat assessments. Operations, expenditures, recruitments, protocols, internal legal rulings, and threat assessments meeting the security standard but which cannot be revealed without jeopardizing the relevant operations should be classified. This section will specify the programs meeting this criterion. A surprising number of military and intelligence operations can be revealed to the public, at least at a certain level of generality, without harm to national security. In order to make substantive recommendations about what sort of secrets should be classified, I will consider five typical activities of intelligence agencies and three typical activities of the military. I will assume that some tactics within these categories can meet the security standard without working out specific justifications. Analysis of concrete activities will produce five stock rationales arguing for, or against, secrecy.

SIGINT—the key question to consider when judging security operations is whether disclosure of government actions will directly or indirectly endanger state agents or civilians and whether disclosure will lead adversaries to cease activities from which the government is currently garnering useful intelligence. Cyberespionage is consistent with public disclosure at a certain level of generality (i.e., second-order revelations). It can be revealed that state agents attempt to collect classified information from adversaries' computer networks and even that a particular foreign agency is targeted. This follows, because, in the digital age, every technologically-sophisticated state assumes its adversaries are attempting cyberespionage and every such state is engaged in cyber defenses including encryption, information assurance activities, and intrusion and malware detection. I will call this assumption that the adversary is already engaged in defensive operations the Defense argument. First-order disclosures that would compromise a specific operation should remain secret, for example, "agents posing as defense contractors plan to use zip drives infected with the XYZ virus to install a back door in the Quds Force network this July."

Secrecy is appropriate with respect to more traditional SIGINT involving the collection of communications via the interception of various kinds of microwave and other electromagnetic transmissions. Disclosure of a state's ability to capture certain kinds of transmissions can lead to their enemy halting usage of that technology, such as al-Qaeda's alleged halting of satellite phone communications

34. Pozen makes a similar point, 332.

after the media revealed that US agencies could monitor the calls and also use their signatures for targeting purposes in 1998.[35] I will call the adversary's abandonment of tactics in reaction to its enemy's abilities the Avoidance argument. This is a key example of a program that I believe passes (or could pass)[36] the security standard but the existence of which must be concealed lest the purpose of the security standard not be met. Revelation of the second-order secret that the United States is intercepting al-Qaeda satellite phone calls makes the program inefficacious. This is the case even if the adversary has no choice but to use the form of communication in question, because they will presumably communicate less than they would have otherwise. The need for secrecy is mitigated to a degree if the intercept capability is understood to be less than comprehensive such that the adversary can wager that there is a reasonable chance that his communication will slip through the collector's net (call this the Randomness argument). Once it is widely known that an agency can collect a certain kind of communication signal, secrecy is still appropriate regarding operations collecting transmissions from particular targets. Al-Qaeda closed down a communication channel after it was leaked that NSA monitoring had led to an intercepted order from Aymin al-Zawahiri to al-Qaeda in the Arabian Peninsula leader Nasser al-Wuhayshi to attack US embassies in the Middle East.[37] It should also be noted that while SIGINT raises privacy concerns, the elimination of SIGINT as an intelligence source forces agencies to rely more on human intelligence (HUMINT). HUMINT is far more fraught than SIGINT in that it involves the penetration of undercover agents into enemy territory, the corruption of foreign intelligence assets, the enabling and financial support of criminals, and the interrogation of detainees.

HUMINT—the most traditional occupation of intelligence officers is "turning" intelligence assets, that is, convincing members of adversary states with access to security-sensitive information to reveal the information. Secrecy about HUMINT operations is unnecessary on a general level because of the Defense and Randomness arguments. Publicly revealing that undercover intelligence officers from state A are attempting to turn assets in state B tells state B nothing it did not already assume and was not already attempting to root out with its own counterintelligence operations. Secrecy should be maintained with respect to specific operations along the lines of "an intelligence officer posing as the Agricultural minister from country A is attempting to turn Gen. X in the Strategic Air Command." Obviously, both the undercover agent and the prospective intelligence asset are endangered by disclosure. Assuming that the undercover agent is

35. Whether the leak directly led to al-Qaeda's change in procedure is contested. Cf. "Bush Account of a Leak's Impact Has Support," David E. Rosenbaum, nytimes.com, publ. December 20, 2005 and "File the Bin Laden Phone Leak Under 'Urban Myths,'" Glenn Kessler, washingtonpost.com, publ. December 22, 2005.

36. As noted in Section III, a civilian has a limited ability to assess whether a given operation has better available tactical alternatives.

37. "Qaeda Plot Leak Has Undermined U.S. Intelligence" Eric Schmidt and Michael Schmidt, newyorktimes.com, September 29, 2013.

conducting a just mission, his life is of moral value apart from the inherent value of all people; his being compromised puts his state at greater risk (this is the case even if he fails in his mission but is able to escape safely). I will call this the Danger argument.

Covert Operations—paramilitary operations conducted by undercover (i.e., nonuniformed) operators including assassination, incitement, and sabotage—bear some similarities to HUMINT operations. General disclosure that agents may conduct covert operations in an adversary state is permissible because of the Defense and Randomness arguments. Specific disclosures are forbidden because of the Danger and Avoidance arguments. The Danger argument would apply in all cases while the Avoidance argument would be particularly apt in the case of sabotage, such as when state A ensures that the rare components for some weapon system or computer network procured by the adversary security services are defective or contain listening devices or malware. The adversary would know not to install the components if the plan was disclosed.

Interrogation—there is an argument to keep interrogation tactics secret because adversary agents may be able to prepare for them, thus reducing their effectiveness. This argument is more germane for non-coercive stratagems than coercive tactics (which do not pass the security standard anyway). It would be useful for security agents or irregular militants to know that interrogators of their adversary typically engage in certain kinds of emotional manipulation, for example, playing on detainees' fears, sense of loyalty, resentments, etc., or that interrogators offer fake incentives, for example, promises to assist detainees' family members or to forgo sentences in exchange for information. However, the Defense and Randomness arguments suggest that disclosure is not overly problematic. Knowing that adversary interrogators might play on detainees' concern for their families or comrades does not eliminate the fact that detainees will be concerned for their families and comrades. Given that emotional backdrop, even the savvy detainee who is dubious of the interrogator's attempts at rapprochement might seize on the possibility that *this* interrogator is telling the truth about helping family members or minimizing the suffering of comrades.

Cryptography—the fact that a security agency tries to break its adversary's codes can be revealed because of the Defense and Randomness arguments. The Defense argument can justify disclosure of attempts to break the encryption of particular networks so long as the adversary already knows that other states are aware of the network. For example, disclosure that agency A is attempting to break the codes protecting the computer networks of its adversary's nuclear facilities is permissible but not if the adversary thinks its nuclear program is still clandestine. As with SIGINT, specificity may lead to the adversary closing down networks protected by insecure encryption.

The following three subjects pertain to the military.

Battleplans—standing contingency plans can be disclosed at the level of generality where they would be obvious to potential adversaries, for example, a Russian tank invasion of the Fulda Gap will be met with NATO armor and air assets (the precise number of assets used should remain classified). There is also little incentive to keep secret even less obvious plans from weaker adversaries who do not lack the resources to respond to the battleplans. For example, there is no reason to keep secret, contingency plans to attack an adversary with stealth bombers if neither the enemy state nor its allies have any way of detecting these bombers (call this the Asymmetry argument). Otherwise, specific battle plans for imminent operations must be kept secret because of the Danger argument.

In certain cases, foreign aggression can be deterred through an adversary's ambiguous plans for response. Chinese officials might suspect that the United States will not really go to war to defend Taiwan, but the possibility that the United States would may be sufficient to deter aggressive moves to restore Taiwan to mainland control. Noninterventionist plans should be kept secret in cases where deliberate ambiguity serves as a deterrent to hostilities. In a similar case, plans to omit reciprocal responses should be classified if deterrence is maintained by the adversary's logical assumption that a certain action would earn a reciprocal response. For example, British ballistic missile submarines are said to have handwritten notes from the prime minister with orders of what the captain should do if Britain is attacked with nuclear weapons. It is appropriate to keep these instructions classified since adversaries' reasonable assumption that British submarines would retaliate in case of nuclear attack serves to deter a rational adversary.[38]

Deterrence maintained by false, explicitly announced policies is a harder case. For example, in the run-up to the Gulf War, the Bush administration supposedly made it known to Saddam Hussein through diplomatic channels that a chemical attack on Coalition forces would be met with an American nuclear strike. I suspect this was a false threat. There are obvious moral concerns involved with a government lying to its own people if a false threat is made more publicly. There is a considerable literature on this subject raising some of the above-mentioned issues regarding government secrecy, which I will not address here except to touch on a point relevant to the security standard. There is less impetus to disclose the truth about a covert false threat if the ultimate rationale for government transparency is to reform policies inconsistent with the security standard. This is because the actual policy is not inconsistent with the security standard. Whether the policy of making false threats to adversaries is consistent with the security standard depends on its prudence. While lying to an adversary may initially seem less problematic than lying to a domestic audience, false threats may increase tensions and make the adversary more aggressive and more entreprenurial with its intelligence operations. Yet one can also imagine cases where lies are prudent instances of deterrence.

Troop movements—in cases of active hostilities, troop movements have to be kept secret because of the Danger argument.

Location of military assets—during peacetime, the location of strategic assets designed to deter a peer adversary, such as Cold War-era American and British ICBMs, has to be kept secret on account of the Defense argument. This argument also applies to any military assets in active theaters of war. The location of assets designed to deter or to respond to weaker adversaries often do not need to be

38. Luban makes a similar point, 164.

classified because of the Asymmetry argument. For example, the drone operators stationed at Creech Air Force base in Nevada, engaged against operations against the Taliban in Afghanistan, do not need to fear an enemy lacking any expeditionary capabilities.

V. CONCLUSION

In liberal states, security services should seek to secure an environment relatively free of rights violations to inhabitants by using the most reliable, efficacious, efficient, proportionate, and rights-respecting tactics available. This standard undergirds just coercive actions by state agents and should guide internal reviews of policies and interpretation of relevant law. The public has a duty to oversee the activities of government security agencies in reference to the security standard. Nonetheless, the security standard takes precedent over oversight in cases when disclosure would neutralize the efficacy of security-seeking tactics. Secrecy is indicated for government policies meeting the security standard when revelation of these policies would directly endanger state agents or indirectly jeopardize national security by drying up intelligence sources. These areas of secrecy open up opportunities for corruption and abuse, risks that can partly be mitigated by oversight from a select group of citizens (legislators, judges, perhaps even ordinary citizens who have security clearances). These select committees are imperfect solutions to the basic tension between security and secrecy because their inability to disclose their privileged information limits their ability to end immoral or wasteful programs when they are in the minority of their committees or when the security services ignore the committees' objections. I believe this tension is an irreducible risk attendant to liberal societies, akin to the possibility of intolerant religions flourishing under a government guaranteeing freedom of religion or illiberal parties coming to power in a democratic process. The solution to the security dilemma, as in the other inherent difficulties of liberal systems, is the cultivation of the virtues of citizens and public servants.

10

Transparency and Executive Authority

CHRIS NATICCHIA

Missiles fired from an unmanned aerial drone killed Anwar al-Awlaki, an American citizen alleged to be an al-Qaeda operative, in Yemen, on September 30, 2011. Although the U.S. government's targeted killing program was officially unacknowledged, the *Washington Post*, citing unnamed military sources, reported as early as January 2010 that al-Awlaki had been placed on a secret kill list drawn up by the Joint Special Operations Command.[1] Suing on behalf of his father to uncover the legal and factual basis for placing al-Awlaki on the list, the American Civil Liberties Union lost twice: first, in December 2010, when a court dismissed the suit by asserting that the elder al-Awlaki lacked standing and that the subject matter involved a "non-justiciable political question," then again, in September 2011, when a court rejected a Freedom of Information Act request for records from the Central Intelligence Agency, which refused to confirm or deny its participation in the program.[2] Three weeks later, al-Awlaki was dead.

Meeting in secret, deferred to by courts, its decisions shielded from public review, its actions officially unacknowledged, the Joint Special Operations Command essentially possesses the power to create a body of secret law that determines which targeted killings are consistent, and which inconsistent, with the Fifth Amendment's prohibition on deprivation of life without due process.

Similarly, in June 2013, *The Guardian* reported that a top-secret decision of the Foreign Intelligence Surveillance Court ordered a telecommunications

1. Dana Priest, "US Military Teams, Intelligence Deeply Involved in Aiding Yemen on Strikes," *Washington Post*, January 27, 2010.

2. Lisa Hajjar, "Anatomy of the US Targeted Killing Policy," *Middle East Research and Information Project* (vol. 42): MER 264 (Fall 2012). The *political question doctrine* holds that courts may not decide cases that involve political questions, which are questions properly (legally) settled by legislative or executive decision (typically involving the conduct of foreign affairs and national defense).

Sovereignty and the New Executive Authority. Claire O. Finkelstein and Michael Skerker.

company, Verizon, to supply the National Security Agency with "all call detail records . . . created by Verizon for communications (i) between the United States and abroad; or (ii) wholly within the United States."[3] "Under the terms of the blanket order," reported *The Guardian*, "the numbers of both parties on a call are handed over, as is location data, call duration, unique identifiers, and the time and duration of all calls. The contents of the conversation itself are not covered." *The Guardian* later reported that the National Security Agency could also legally obtain other electronic communications, such as "email, video and voice chat, video, photos, voice-over-IP chats, file transfers, social networking details, and more," from Apple, Google, and other internet companies under another blanket order, without having to request them from the internet providers, without obtaining an individual court order, and without barring access to the content of the communications.[4] As with the Joint Special Operations Command, the Foreign Intelligence Surveillance Court essentially possesses the power to create a body of secret law—determining which surveillance activities are consistent, and which inconsistent, with the Fourth Amendment's protection against unreasonable searches without a particularized warrant based on probable cause.

These recent developments in national security law raise philosophically important, politically urgent, questions. To what extent (if any) can secret laws ever be justified? If they are ever justifiable, under what conditions?

Specifically, I want to consider what the *social contract* tradition contributes to our understanding of these issues. The social contract tradition, in my view, offers us the richest, most theoretically interesting, perspective from which to consider them. My thesis will be that, however it may appear to the contrary, the social contract tradition *does* justify, under certain conditions, secret laws. The challenge is to identify what those conditions are. Its ability to identify those conditions demonstrates the resourcefulness of the social contract tradition.

I. THE CONCEPTUAL INCOHERENCE THESIS

Judging from the views of Aquinas, Hobbes, and Fuller—philosophers whose outlooks are about as diverse as the philosophers themselves—to speak of *secret* laws makes no sense at all. Like the notion of a round square, the notion of a secret law is conceptually incoherent. Since a law is, essentially, a public command of some sort, a "secret law" is simply a contradiction in terms. It is not merely an invalid law. It is no law at all. Call this position the *conceptual incoherence thesis.*

"[T]he definition of law," writes Aquinas, "is nothing else than an ordinance of reason for the common good, made by him who has care of the community, and *promulgated*."[5] As Aquinas explains, "in order that a law obtain the binding force

3. Glenn Greenwald, "NSA Collecting Phone Records of Millions of Verizon Customers Daily," *The Guardian*, June 6, 2013.

4. Glenn Greenwald, "NSA Prism Program Taps In to User Data of Apple, Google, and Others," *The Guardian*, June 7, 2013.

5. Saint Thomas Aquinas, *Summa Theologica* (1273), Question 90, Article 4 (emphasis added).

which is proper to a law, it must needs be applied to the men who have to be ruled by it. Such application is made by its being notified to them by promulgation. Wherefore promulgation is necessary for the law to obtain its force."[6] Similarly, Hobbes claims that "the Law is a Command, and a Command consisteth in declaration, or manifestation of the will of him that commandeth, by voice, writing, or some other sufficient argument of the same."[7] Although the law of nature, which, known by reason, need not be written, differs, "it belongeth to the essence of all other Lawes," he maintains, "to be made known, to every man that shall be obliged to obey them, either by word, or writing, or some other act, known to proceed from the Soveraign Authority."[8] Finally, Fuller insists that "a failure to publicize, or at least to make available to the affected party, the rules he is expected to observe" results in a failure to make law.[9] It "does not simply result in a bad system of law; it results in something that is not properly called a legal system at all."[10] This follows from the fact that, on the one hand, there is an obligation to obey the law, but, on the other hand, "there can be no rational ground for asserting that a man can have a moral obligation to obey a legal rule that does not exist, or is kept secret from him."[11] So it seems as though Aquinas, Hobbes, and Fuller hold the conceptual incoherence thesis.

If the conceptual incoherence thesis is true, then, not only does it make no sense to speak of secret laws, it makes no sense to ask whether they can be justified, and if so, under what conditions. If secrecy is incompatible with a command's status as law, then there is no such thing as secret laws, properly speaking, and consequently, we cannot sensibly ask whether they can be justified.

Yet there are dissenting voices too. Locke, for instance, seems to imply that, although rational individuals would not consent to be governed according to secret laws, the notion of secret law nonetheless involves no conceptual misfire. He admits that "no Body can be under a Law, which is not promulgated to him; and this Law being promulgated or made known by *Reason* only, he that is not come to the Use of his *Reason*, cannot be said to be *under this Law*."[12] It does not follow from the fact that one is not "under" a law (be it natural or civil) that the command or requirement or directive given fails to qualify as a law (nor does Locke claim that it follows).[13] A law that is not promulgated, Locke seems to allow, still qualifies as a

6. Ibid.

7. Thomas Hobbes, *Leviathan* (1651), ch. 26, para. 12.

8. Ibid., para. 15.

9. Lon Fuller, *The Morality of Law* (New Haven, CT: Yale University Press, 1964), excerpted and reprinted in Joel Feinberg and Hyman Gross (eds.) ,*Philosophy of Law* (5th ed.) (New York: Wadsworth, 1995), as "Eight Ways to Fail to Make Law," pp. 88–91, at 90.

10. Ibid.

11. Ibid.

12. John Locke, *Second Treatise of Government* (1690), para. 57.

13. Ibid., paras, 57–60.

law, even if it does not have binding power over its putative subjects. This explains why Locke feels the need to *argue* that secret laws are unjustified rather than simply dismiss them as conceptually incoherent. "Men give up all their Natural Power to the Society which they enter into," he argues, "and the Community put the Legislative Power into such hands as they think fit, with this trust, that they shall be govern'd by *declared Laws*, or else their Peace, Quiet, and Property will still be at the same uncertainty, as it was in the state of Nature."[14] To suppose that they would agree to be governed by secret laws, he suggests, is to imply that they would irrationally court danger: "For all the power the Government has, being only for the good of the Society, as it ought not to be *Arbitrary* and at Pleasure, so it ought to be exercised by *established and promulgated Laws*: that both the People may know their Duty, and be safe and secure within the limits of the Law, and the Rulers too kept within their due bounds, and not to be tempted, by the Power they have in their hands."[15] So while it is clear that Locke deems secret laws unjustified, he does not appear to endorse the conceptual incoherence thesis.

If Locke is right, we *can* intelligibly ask whether (and if so, under what conditions) secret laws can be justified. Yet even if the conceptual incoherence thesis is true, we can nonetheless ask a related question by performing a simple substitution. Call a *directive* a type of command that directs officials to enforce requirements on citizens regardless of whether citizens know, or can know, what those requirements are. In that case, we can still ask whether secret *directives*, issued by duly-constituted democratic authorities, can be justified. My aim here, then, is to examine whether such secret laws or directives can be justified, and if so, under what conditions.[16]

II. THE WEAK TRADITION THESIS

Despite initial appearances, it is not obvious that the social contract tradition condemns secret laws or directives as such. Consider the views of Hobbes, Locke, Rousseau, and Rawls, for instance. On the one hand, as we have just seen, Hobbes himself holds the conceptual incoherence thesis, in which case it makes no sense at all to speak of secret laws, let alone whether they can be justified. On the other hand, were we to consider whether Hobbes would endorse secret *directives*, it seems that he is committed to accepting them, at least in principle. Hobbes's absolute sovereign is the sole legitimate judge of the means to the peace and common defense of the society that it governs. "[W]hosoever has right to the

14. Ibid., para. 136.

15. Ibid., para. 137.

16. For expository convenience, I will discuss only secret laws and directives, even though the concern involved is broad enough to include other types of secrecy, such as secret exercises of executive discretion or prerogative (the power, Locke claims, "to do several things of their own free choice, where the Law was silent, and sometimes too against the direct Letter of the Law, for the publick good" (ibid., para. 164)), and secret legal processes (such as the process that the Joint Special Operations Command undergoes in vetting potential names for inclusion on the kill list).

end," writes Hobbes, referring to the ends of peace and common defense, "has right to the means; it belongeth of right, to whatsoever man, or assembly that hath the sovereignty, to be judge both of the means of peace and defence."[17] In principle, these means could include (in the judgment of the "man or assembly that hath the sovereignty") governing through some secret directives. So it seems false to claim that Hobbes is committed to condemning secret directives as such.

Although Locke does not endorse the conceptual incoherence thesis, he also denies that secret laws can be justified. Nonetheless, Locke too seems committed to accepting some secret laws, despite his explicit claims to the contrary.

On the one hand, one central defect of the state of nature, according to Locke, is its lack of known, settled, public laws.[18] For that reason, he suggests that allowing the government to operate by secret laws and then vesting it with enormous power wouldn't trade the inconveniences of the state of nature for the security of political society. On the contrary, it would replace "what Mischiefs may be done . . . by *Pole-Cats*, or *Foxes*" with the prospect of being "devoured by *Lions*."[19] Accordingly, when individuals leave the state of nature and consent to join political society, they transfer only that portion of their right of self-government necessary to preserve humankind and society: "The first *Power, viz. of doing whatsoever he thought fit for the Preservation of himself*, and the rest of Mankind [the right of self-government], *he gives up* to be regulated by Laws made by the Society, so far forth as the preservation of himself, and the rest of that Society shall require."[20] The transfer of power then is *limited*.

On the other hand, even *this* limit could include within its scope some secret laws, if *in fact* such laws were necessary for the preservation of the consenting individuals and their society. Although this might raise a problem for citizens when they attempt to evaluate whether their government observes its entrusted powers, later I will suggest a way of overcoming this problem that is consistent with Locke's view, broadly construed. If this is right, then it seems false as well to claim that Locke is committed to condemning secret laws as such.

Rousseau seems committed to accepting some secret laws or directives too. Claiming that "the general will studies only the common interest while the will of all studies private interest, and is indeed no more than the sum of individual desires," Rousseau then asserts that "if we take away from these same wills, the pluses and minuses which cancel each other out, the sum of the difference is the general will."[21] However we interpret this (much-discussed) claim, the idea that the general will ascertains the common interest (and that a just society observes

17. Hobbes, *Leviathan*, ch. 18, para. 8.

18. Locke, *Second Treatise of Government*, para. 124.

19. Ibid., para. 93 (emphasis in original).

20. Ibid., para. 129 (emphasis in original).

21. Jean-Jacques Rousseau, *The Social Contract* (1762), book II, ch. 3, para. 2.

the general will) is purely formal, and therefore consistent with accepting some secret laws or directives, at least in principle, in certain conditions.[22] In fact, the conditions under which such laws or directives would be acceptable, for Rousseau, seem similar to the ones under which they would be acceptable for Hobbes and for Locke: that is, when essential to the peace, common defense, or preservation of society, assuming them to be in the common interest. Nor does Rousseau rule out the possibility of accepting some secret laws when he discusses law in general. "Yet what, in the last analysis, is law?" he asks. "If we simply try to define it in terms of metaphysical ideas," he answers, "we shall go on talking without reaching any understanding."[23] Answering more concretely, he says, "when the people as a whole makes rules for the people as a whole," when "the matter concerning which a rule is made is as general as the will which makes it . . . *this*," he emphasizes, "is the kind of act which I call a law."[24] Since Rousseau includes no publicity requirement in his definition of law, his position does not commit him to condemning secret laws as such.[25]

Finally, Rawls allows that when ranking his principles of justice in lexical order, liberty may still be permissibly restricted, but only for the sake of liberty—and particularly when a less extensive liberty is required in order to "strengthen the total system of liberty shared by all."[26] The precedence of liberty, he argues, "means that liberty can be restricted only for the sake of liberty itself."[27] It may not be restricted for compensating social and economic goods. One type of situation in which this occurs is when the basic liberties are "less extensive though still equal." In this case, if "liberty is less extensive, the representative citizen must find this a gain for his freedom on balance."[28] This may occur, Rawls suggests, when social conditions are not ripe for fully realizing the basic liberties and when restrictions might enable those conditions to improve to the point where they can be fully realized, or when emergency circumstances exist in which temporary restrictions protect the enjoyment of these liberties against longer-term loss.

22. Rawls, for instance, understands the notion of common interests in Rousseau as shared fundamental interests in self-love, security, and property, and the general will as expressing laws that would secure these fundamental interests for each citizen. This specification of the formal idea is not inconsistent with accepting some secret laws or directives. See John Rawls, *Lectures on the History of Political Philosophy*, ed. Samuel Freeman (Cambridge, MA: Harvard University Press, 2007), p. 230.

23. Rousseau, *The Social Contract*, book II, ch. 6, para. 3.

24. Ibid., book II, ch. 6, para. 5.

25. In particular, they are consistent with secret laws in a specific sense that I introduce later in this Section: they are consistent with a promulgated *secondary* rule (which "the people as a whole [can make] for the people as a whole") that explicitly embraces government powers to make some secret primary rules in areas publicly identified by the secondary rule.

26. John Rawls, *A Theory of Justice* (Cambridge, MA: Harvard University Press, 1971), p. 250.

27. Ibid., p. 244.

28. Ibid.

Either way, appealing "to the interests of this representative man," Rawls argues, is "to invoke the principle of the *common interest*."[29] While this is consistent with restricting liberties through public laws, it is also consistent with restricting them through secret laws. Conceivably, a less extensive though equal liberty of this sort (under some secret laws) might be necessary for protecting the full realization of the basic liberties in the long term. Hence, Rawls seems committed to allowing some secret laws imposing restrictions on liberty that, under more favorable social conditions, his first principle of justice would condemn.

In contrast with Hobbes, Locke, Rousseau, and Rawls, however, Kant appears to reject secret laws as such. On the one hand, he famously (or notoriously) denies that there exists any right to revolution, rebellion, or resistance.[30] On the other hand, he nevertheless insists that "since every human being still has his inalienable rights, which he can never give up [in the social contract] even if he wanted to and about which he is authorized to judge for himself," it follows that, if he judges that his ruler violates them, "the wrong that in his opinion is done to him occurs only from the supreme power's error or ignorance of certain consequences of his laws."[31] For that reason, he maintains, "a citizen must have, with the approval of the ruler himself, the authorization to make known publicly his opinions about what it is in the ruler's arrangements that seems to him to be a wrong against the commonwealth."[32] But of course it would be impossible for him to do this in the case of secret laws. Combining these two points, Kant writes: "In every commonwealth there must [therefore] be *obedience* under the mechanism of the state constitution to coercive laws (applying to the whole), but there must also be a *spirit of freedom*, since each, in what has to do with universal human duties, requires to be convinced by reason that this coercion is in conformity with right, lest he fall into contradiction with himself. The former [obedience] without the latter [freedom] is the occasioning cause of all *secret societies*."[33]

Call the view that the social contract tradition (generally) condemns secret laws or directives as such the *tradition thesis*. We have seen that the tradition thesis

29. Ibid., p. 246 (emphasis added).

30. Immanuel Kant, "On the Common Saying: That May Be Correct in Theory, But It Is of No Use in Practice," 8:298–303 (1793), and Kant's *Metaphysics of Morals*, 6:320, both in Mary J. Gregor (transl.), *The Cambridge Edition of the Works of Immanuel Kant: Practical Philosophy* (New York: Cambridge University Press, 1996).

31. Immanuel Kant, "On the Common Saying: That May Be Correct in Theory, But It Is of No Use In Practice," 8:304.

32. Ibid., 8:304.

33. Ibid., 8:305 (emphasis in original). See also passages tending to reinforce this rejection of secret laws in Kant's "An Answer to the Question: What Is Enlightenment?," 8:35 (1784), also in Gregor's translation. "If I have a book that understands for me, a spiritual advisor who has a conscience for me, a doctor who decides upon a regimen for me, and so forth"—which invites the addition, "an executive, legislator, and judge who will make unknown laws for me"—"I need not trouble myself at all. I need not think, if only I can pay; others will readily undertake the irksome business for me"—which invites the addition, "nor need I think, if only I *obey*."

is false; few contractual thinkers consistently condemn secret laws. Yet even if it were true—even if, say, every member of that tradition consistently and unequivocally condemned secret laws as such—we could still distinguish a *weak* version of that thesis, the generalization that its members consistently condemn secret laws as such, from a *strong* version, the view that the social contract tradition itself is committed to condemning secret laws as such. While some prominent contractualists condemn secret laws, I will argue that a contractualist need not be committed to this position.

So even if the conceptual incoherence thesis is true, we can still intelligibly ask whether (and if so, under what conditions) secret directives would be justified, and even if the weak tradition thesis were true, we could still investigate whether social contract doctrine might provide a justification for them. The most promising candidate for such a justification, it seems, is *a promulgated secondary rule that explicitly embraces government powers to make some secret primary rules* in areas publicly identified by the secondary rule. Those secret primary rules would then qualify as secret laws or directives whose justification ultimately derives from contractarian reasoning.

If such a secondary rule can be justified at all, I want to suggest, the most likely areas that it will publicly identify as appropriate for secret lawmaking will be *thresholds*—the criteria that trigger the enforcement of directives whose efficacy consists in their remaining secret. Criteria for identifying who may be the target of a drone strike, or whose outgoing telephone call numbers may be placed on a list, are examples of thresholds. Were these criteria publicly revealed, the information could become known to the targets or callers, who could then change their behavior so as to avoid identification, defeating the purpose of the law. The law of thresholds is the most promising area for justifiable secret lawmaking if such lawmaking is ever justifiable at all. I will close my discussion by considering whether contractarian reasoning can justify more sweeping secrecy, where the secondary rule itself is secret, and the programs that it authorizes—such as drone strikes and metadata collection—are themselves secrets, not just their thresholds.

III. THE STRONG TRADITION THESIS

According to the strong tradition thesis, the social contract tradition itself is committed to condemning secret laws as such, regardless of whether (as the weak tradition thesis asserts) members of that tradition have generally condemned them. However, if we can defend a social contract view that endorses a promulgated secondary rule that explicitly embraces government powers to establish a secret law of thresholds, the strong tradition thesis is false.

Any plausible social contract view, I will assume, endorses broadly liberal principles of justice: basic rights and liberties familiar from the liberal tradition, protections for the integrity of the person, and adherence to the rule of law. The issue, then, concerns how to adjust these rights and liberties against government powers. As Rawls suggests, a social contract view can attempt this task at a second, or constitutional, stage of a social contract, after the selection of principles of justice at a first stage. Although the parties to the contract's second stage are still under a veil of ignorance, Rawls suggests, they possess more information than at the first stage.[34] In what follows, I propose to construct a contractual choice situation for a constitutional stage that, while indebted to Rawls's methodology, departs from its specific commitments where appropriate and adds to it where it is silent.

A. The Parties' Interests and Knowledge

In order to construct this contract, we need to identify the interests of the parties and the knowledge that they possess. As a first approximation, we can attribute three interests to them. Call one of these interests a *security* interest.[35] This security interest consists of three more specific interests: a national security interest, a domestic security interest, and a personal security interest (these are not meant to be mutually exclusive). The national and domestic security interests deal with large threats, the personal security interest, smaller ones. The national security interest is an interest against external aggression, the domestic security interest an interest against internal aggression, and the personal security interest an interest in not being harmed by a common criminal (citizen-on-citizen violence) or an abusive police officer (government-on-citizen violence).

Besides the security interest, the parties also have an *evaluation* interest, an interest in being able to evaluate, for themselves, the justice, fairness, and efficiency of their political institutions and laws. This interest is implicit in one of the two moral powers that Rawls ascribes to the parties in the original position, a capacity for a sense of justice, a capacity to understand, apply, and act from a public conception of justice,[36] since the parties are said to have corresponding "highest-order" interests in developing and exercising these powers.[37] Accordingly, in the first stage of his domestic contract, the original position, this interest requires freedom of the press (among other freedoms), given the instrumental importance of such freedom for evaluating the conception of justice manifested by their political institutions and laws—and hence for developing and exercising their capacity for a sense of justice.[38] The *basis* for this interest, let's say (in a manner that Rawls

34. Rawls, *A Theory of Justice*, pp. 195–201.

35. While Rawls himself does not explicitly stipulate a security interest, one is implicit in the parties' interest in primary goods, which require personal security to enjoy, and which a particular primary good, the right to integrity of the person, presupposes. However, as this characterization suggests, this appears limited to an interest in personal security, which is narrower than the security interest stipulated here. Since a broader security interest is needed to address the issues under discussion, I make it explicit here.

36. Rawls, *Political Liberalism* (New York: Columbia University Press, 1993), p. 19.

37. See Rawls, "Kantian Constructivism in Moral Theory," in Samuel Freeman (ed.), *John Rawls: Collected Papers* (Cambridge, MA: Harvard University Press, 1999): 303–58, pp. 312–13.

38. "We look for social background conditions and general all-purpose means normally necessary for developing and exercising the two moral powers and for effectively pursuing a conception of the good." These include "basic liberties (freedom of thought and liberty of conscience,

himself would hesitate to say), lies in our autonomy, in our interest in choosing our own way of life, and in understanding and influencing the social conditions that constrain or facilitate our choices—conditions that include our political institutions and laws. Presumably, at the next, constitutional, stage of the contract, the parties, in furtherance of the evaluation interest, need to operationalize the rights that it supports by determining their particular scope, given the other interests that they possess (such as the security interest).

Finally, in addition to security and evaluation interests, the parties have a *privacy* interest. Privacy in this context refers to a right of individual sovereignty over certain personal decisions, free from government interference, and is meant to be a stronger right than a right over one's confidential information or over a particular area (such as one's home) or territory. While confidentiality over personal information and freedom from interference in, say, one's own home are instrumental to enjoying sovereignty over one's personal decisions, they do not exhaust the scope of the privacy interest as understood here.[39]

Now as Rawls constructs the constitutional stage, his two principles of justice have already been selected and the task for delegates to this "constitutional convention" is to fashion procedures optimally designed to lead to legislation that satisfies them.[40] As we saw, the veil is partially lifted: while the delegates remain ignorant of their particular roles and circumstances, they nonetheless know general facts about their own society, such as "its natural circumstances and resources, its level of economic advance and political culture, and so on."[41] Specifically, they know "the beliefs and interests that men in the system are liable to have and of the political tactics that they will find it rational to use given their circumstances."[42]

In our construction of the constitutional stage, then, let's adopt this knowledge condition and add it to our initial stipulation of the parties' interests. These seem like reasonably weak stipulations as starting points.

B. Provisional Fixed Points

Now in order to approach the question of whether secret laws (specifically, thresholds) can be justified, I want to start first by considering some areas where

etc.)"—the "etc." plausibly including freedom of the press—as these "allow for the development and exercise of the sense of right and justice." See ibid., p. 313.

39. Here I intend to follow the useful suggestion of Ronald Dworkin. See Ronald Dworkin, *Life's Dominion: An Argument about Abortion, Euthanasia, and Individual Freedom* (New York: Alfred A. Knopf, 1993), pp. 53–54. Although Rawls himself does not appeal to a privacy interest in the sense used here, one is implicit in many of the primary goods (specifically, many of the rights and liberties) in which the parties do have an interest, in his view. Again, in order to address the issues under discussion, I make this interest explicit here.

40. Rawls, *A Theory of Justice*, pp. 196–98.

41. Ibid., p. 197.

42. Ibid., p. 198.

government secrecy is firmly accepted—as provisional fixed points, we might say. For instance, it seems generally accepted that government legitimately possesses the power to classify certain information and intelligence-gathering methods. Presumably, this power derives from citizens' security interest.[43]

However, this power can also be clearly abused: for example, by classifying information that is merely politically inconvenient to disclose, or using methods such as waterboarding to extract intelligence information. So the exercise of this power must assume that its scope extends only so far. How do we determine the limits?

Within political institutions, the need to determine limits argues for empowering courts to decide whether certain classified information or intelligence-gathering methods must remain classified. We must have institutional mechanisms, in other words, for determining what the limits are and for deciding whether they have been observed. Accepting on faith executive assertions that it operates within its proper limits is unacceptable. A neutral, politically insulated, mechanism, such as courts, seems like the best venue for the needed assessments.

Still, this leaves open what their criteria should be for making the assessments. Clearly, they should consider citizens' security interests. But just as clearly, they should consider their evaluation interests too. In any case, I intend at this point only to indicate the general kinds of considerations that courts should take notice of in reaching decisions on these matters as a first step toward examining the more complicated issue of secret laws. Can we say anything more precise?

It's tempting to claim that, if classification is *necessary* for security, then the security interest should trump whatever other interests come into competition with it. While apparently true, this claim raises two problems. First, the assertion of necessity is not self-certifying: we still need an institutional mechanism for assessing the assertion. Second, it seems that nothing (strictly speaking) is ever necessary for security—unless a threat to security is immediately imminent. Classification, one might plausibly claim, is usually *instrumental*, but not necessary, for security—and its instrumental value is a matter of *degree*. So even if it is true that, if classification is necessary for security, the security interest should trump, this claim is unhelpful in the cases that we (and courts) are most likely to face.

Once we concede that classification is typically merely instrumentally valuable for fulfilling the security interest, though, it's tempting to claim that we should use a *balancing* test, where courts consider the *strength* of the security interest and weigh it against competing interests. The notion of a balancing test, however, seems implicitly utilitarian: we weigh the various interests in the utilitarian scales and fulfill the strongest set of interests. Unless we are willing to embrace a utilitarian balancing test, then, we must say something more precise once we turn our attention to secret laws.

43. If we are Lockeans, we might say that this power is part of the individual right of self-government that gets transferred to government as necessary to preserve oneself and society.

So a constitutional stage social contract must tell us how to weigh these competing interests, so as to determine the proper scope and limits of the classification power. But of course this assumes an affirmative answer to the threshold question whether classification of any sort is permissible in the first place. For these provisional fixed points, we granted that assumption for the sake of argument. We now have to account for it.

We can account for it as follows. Notice that including security as a basic need is consistent with Rawls's allowance that "the first principle covering the equal basic rights and liberties may easily be preceded by a lexically prior principle requiring that citizens' basic needs be met, at least insofar as their being met is necessary for citizens to understand and to be able fruitfully to exercise those rights and liberties."[44] Being "lexically prior" suggests something about the principle's *force*, and, correspondingly, the force of the security interest.

If we were to follow Rawls in this regard, the security interest would be quite strong—in fact, strong enough to trump competing interests, including any evaluation interest. In that case, even if the delegates accept (as I have argued they should) the weaker claim that classifying information or intelligence-gathering methods is at best instrumentally useful for fulfilling the security interest (rather than the stronger claim that it is necessary for fulfilling it), they would surely grant *some* such constitutional powers, since any competing interests that such powers might thwart could never outweigh the security interest that trumps them. Nonetheless, knowing "the beliefs and interests that men in the system are liable to have and of the political tactics that they will find it rational to use," neither will they be such fools as to leave this power unchecked. Realizing its invitation to abuse, but recognizing the need to grant some such powers, they can protect their other interests (such as their evaluation interest when the executive makes an implausible security interest assertion) through an act of delegation.[45] They can delegate to courts the responsibility for reviewing requests to declassify information while keeping the information classified during the review. Through this act of delegation, courts perform, for citizens, the Lockean task of evaluating whether government observes its entrusted powers. So the delegates are not forced to choose between (on the one hand) granting classification powers while extending a blank check to those who exercise it and (on the other hand) granting no such powers at all.

However, we should *not* accept the view that the security interest trumps all competing interests. If it were true, then anything that tended to satisfy the security interest, no matter how trivial, would automatically outweigh the evaluation interest, no matter how seriously compromised. The only way to make sense of

44. John Rawls, *Political Liberalism* (New York: Columbia University Press, 1993), p. 7. By "basic needs," Rawls is likely referring to subsistence needs, but the phrase is consistent with counting other pressing needs as basic, too (such as security).

45. It would also include their *personal* security interest when both (1) the executive makes an implausible security interest assertion, and (2) their personal security interest would be threatened by government exercise of the (falsely) claimed power.

the view that some acts or policies so seriously compromise the evaluation interest, but so trivially affect the security interest, that they ought to be rejected is to hold that the two interests can be weighed in the same scales, that they are commensurable. On this view, the security interest could still possess much greater weight than other interests, but it would no longer *automatically* outweigh them. By allowing the possibility of some sacrifice in the security interest, admittedly, the delegates would place at risk the satisfaction of one of their most basic needs. But permitting "trade-offs" at the margins with security seems intuitively acceptable provided that *enough* security is already guaranteed.[46]

Within the contract, then, the security interest should possess less force. It no longer automatically outweighs competing interests. It no longer trumps. It is weaker, but still strong. Endowed with this interest and their general knowledge of the world, the delegates consider whether to grant some constitutional powers to classify information or intelligence-gathering methods. Recognizing the dangers that they may face, they can readily envision a range of situations in which such powers would be instrumentally useful for fulfilling their security interest. Assuming that their general knowledge is substantial enough, they can further envision a range of situations in which the powers would be so instrumentally useful for fulfilling their security interest, and the security involved so compelling, that their security interest, while not trumping competing interests, would surely outweigh them (however they are weighed). Such situations are *conceivable,* and, given the delegates' general knowledge, likely to be encountered over the course of a lifetime. Finally, they can always delegate to courts responsibility for reviewing requests to declassify information while keeping the information classified during the review—an institutional mechanism for evaluating whether government observes its entrusted powers. For these reasons, it seems likely that the delegates would grant these powers.

So it appears that we can account for these two provisional fixed points at the constitutional stage. When we examine secret laws, though, we are considering classification powers that go beyond classifying information or

46. Interestingly, Rawls himself seems to permit much *greater* trade-offs, and much greater risks, with security, despite his suggestion that "basic needs" (presumably including security) receive "lexical priority," even over the two principles of justice. For this suggestion, see *Political* Liberalism, p. 7. Also see his general discussion of the clear and present danger rule in *Political Liberalism,* pp. 348–56, especially pp. 354–55: "[P]olitical speech is by its nature often dangerous . . . This is because the free public use of our reason applies to the most fundamental questions, and the decisions made may have grave consequences. Suppose a democratic people, engaged in a military rivalry with an autocratic power, should decide that the use of nuclear weapons is so contrary to the principles of humanity that their use must be forsworn and significant steps taken unilaterally toward reducing these weapons, this done in the hope that the other power might be persuaded to follow. This could be a highly dangerous decision; but surely that is irrelevant to whether it should be freely discussed and whether the government is constitutionally obligated to carry out this decision once it is properly made. The dangerousness of political speech is beside the point; it is precisely the danger involved in making this decision which must be freely discussed."

intelligence-gathering methods. We are considering the power to classify some laws themselves. Does the preceding reasoning extend to secret laws?

C. Beyond Provisional Fixed Points

In fact, the potential dangers they face are the same—the parties know this. Further, just as they can readily envision a range of situations in which classification powers would be instrumentally useful for fulfilling their security interest, so too can they envision situations in which the power to make some secret laws would be instrumentally useful. In fact, their familiarity with classification powers facilitates their ability to envision this. In particular, secret thresholds will be instrumentally useful. Since nothing precludes secret thresholds, in a range of situations, from being so instrumentally useful for fulfilling their security interest, and since nothing precludes the security involved from being very compelling, nothing will preclude this interest from outweighing any competing interests, including the evaluation interest, in such situations either. Endowed with the information and powers of reasoning that they possess, the delegates, considering these facts and the interests of the persons they represent, would likely grant the power to establish secret thresholds too.

Clearly, just as the power to classify information and intelligence-gathering methods can be abused, so too can the power to establish secret thresholds. The power to classify information can lead officials to classify information that it is merely politically inconvenient to disclose—or that affects the security interest only marginally—while classifying it affects the evaluation interest substantially. Similarly, the power to classify intelligence-gathering methods can be abused, so as to hide from public view, for instance, methods that amount to torture. But while these powers can be abused, their potential for abuse, in each case, does not argue for denying them altogether. It argues for having credible institutional mechanisms in place to protect against abuse. While even the most credible institutional mechanisms will fall short of being perfect, this fact alone does not argue for denying these powers altogether either, unless those institutions fail significantly.[47]

Given these considerations, it will not follow from the fact that the power to establish secret thresholds can be abused that we should deny that power altogether. Yet the risks are real, and they significantly impact our other interests. For example, the Foreign Intelligence Surveillance Court issues classified rulings, creating a body of secret law that determines, by implication, which surveillance activities are consistent, and which inconsistent, with the Fourth Amendment's protection against unreasonable searches without a particularized warrant based on probable cause. Similarly, the Central Intelligence Agency's targeted killing program ("drone strikes") maintains secrecy in its procedures and criteria for placing an individual on its target list, secrecy that courts have deferred to, creating a body of secret law that determines, by implication, which killings are consistent,

47. On this topic, see especially the article by Claire Finkelstein in this volume.

and which inconsistent, with the Fifth Amendment's prohibition on depriving people of life without due process of law. These are both examples of thresholds. Just as we count on our courts to protect our evaluation and other interests by countermanding violations of the power to classify information and intelligence-gathering methods, so too must we count on them to protect these interests by countermanding violations of the power to establish secret thresholds.[48] We count on them to make sure that the executive branch remains within its proper limits on exercising these powers. Having offered a contractarian argument that justifies granting the powers, though, can we extend that argument to determine what the limits on those powers should be?

IV. THE FINE PRINT: CONFER BUT CONSTRAIN

Even if the conceptual incoherence thesis is true, we can still sensibly ask whether conferring a power to issue secret directives would be justified. Even if the weak tradition thesis is true, we can still ask whether the social contract tradition itself is committed to condemning secret laws as such. However, if the preceding argument is sound, it is *not* committed to condemning them as such. So the strong tradition thesis is false. We *can* offer a social contract argument that justifies conferring some powers to make secret laws, at least in the area of thresholds. In particular, it justifies a promulgated secondary rule that explicitly embraces government powers to make some secret primary rules in areas publicly identified by the secondary rule. These primary rules comprise the law of thresholds.

Assuming that social contract reasoning does justify conferring some powers to make some secret laws, what constraints or limits should there be on their exercise?

Call these conditions the *constraining conditions*. The constraining conditions are precisely those in which the evaluation interest is justifiably overridden. We will consider five principles as candidates for these conditions, with the parties at the constitutional stage selecting one of them. Before stating the principles, though, let me say more about the evaluation interest.

Previously, we stated that the evaluation interest is an interest in our being able to evaluate the justice, fairness, and efficiency of our political institutions and laws for ourselves. However, we also stated that, in some instances, this interest can be protected through an act of delegation. The delegation is to courts, which perform, for citizens, the Lockean task of evaluating whether government observes its entrusted powers—in this case its secret powers. Presumably, government observes its entrusted secret powers when the evaluation interest is justifiably overridden. By contrast, when the evaluation interest is not justifiably

48. The Electronic Privacy Information Center reports that, from 1979 to 2013, the Foreign Intelligence Surveillance Court (which hears only the government's requests for surveillance and not any adversary) has denied just 0.03 percent of the over 34,000 government surveillance requests. This fact admittedly creates the appearance of bias in favor of the government. See https://epic.org/privacy/wiretap/stats/fisa_stats.html (accessed June 2, 2018).

overridden, government exceeds its entrusted powers, and in those cases courts should order disclosure.

Clearly, the delegation to courts of responsibility for safeguarding evaluation interests is a decided second-best. Courts can err—or be corrupt. Since courts are among the political institutions that we have an interest in evaluating, we have an interest in evaluating their performance in constraining government's secret powers. Yet our ability to evaluate their performance will inevitably be limited since they may not be able to disclose the full set of facts that would enable us to do so.[49] Of course, we could always set up a further court, a court of appeals (such as a Foreign Intelligence Surveillance Court of Review), with authority to re-evaluate the evidence. But this would merely push the problem back a level, for we could always raise the same questions about the performance of this court of appeals.[50] Nonetheless, this is the position that we are pushed to once we accept the justifiability of some secret laws.

In order of increasing strength, consider these five principles as candidates for constraining conditions:

1. *Security-trumps principle*: the evaluation interest is justifiably overridden when and only when a security interest comes into competition with it.
2. *Balancing principle*: the evaluation interest is justifiably overridden when and only when a security interest comes into competition with it and outweighs it.
3. *Weak security crisis principle*: the evaluation interest is justifiably overridden when and only when a compelling security interest competes with it, or the evaluation interest, generally presumed to be strong, is weak instead.
4. *Strong security crisis principle*: the evaluation interest is justifiably overridden when and only when a compelling security interest competes with it.
5. *Evaluation-trumps principle*: the evaluation interest is never justifiably overridden; no laws or directives may be secret.

49. Consider the Foreign Intelligence Surveillance Court (FISC). In an opinion released by the FISC that rejects a 2007 ACLU motion to release FISC orders on NSA surveillance of international terrorism suspects, Justice John Bates writes: "The FISC is a unique court. Its entire docket relates to the collection of foreign intelligence by the federal government. The applications submitted to it by the government are classified, as are the overwhelming majority of the FISC's orders. Court sessions are held behind closed doors in a secure facility, and every proceeding in its history prior to this one has been ex parte, with the government the only party. In the entire history of the FISC, just two opinions have been publicly released. (This opinion makes it three.) Other courts operate primarily in public, with secrecy the exception; the FISC operates primarily in secret, with public access the exception." See https://www.aclu.org/files/pdfs/safefree/fisc_order_2007_1211.pdf (accessed June 2, 2018).

50. The actual Federal Intelligence Surveillance Court of Review is empowered only to consider *denials* of government surveillance applications by the FISC. In other words, only the *government* has a right of appeal.

If the argument up to this point has been sound, we can safely reject the first and last principles: the security-trumps principle and the evaluation-trumps principle. If some secret laws are justifiable, as I have maintained, then we must reject the evaluation-trumps principle. Further, in order to make sense of the view that some acts or policies so seriously compromise the evaluation interest, but so trivially affect the security interest, that they ought to be rejected, we must hold that the two interests can be weighed in the same scales, that they are commensurable. But this implies that we must reject the security-trumps principle as well. That leaves just the balancing principle and its two alternatives, the security crisis principles, weak and strong. Since the balancing principle, with its implicit utilitarian rationale, can be rejected only if we can provide a stronger contractarian justification for one of its security crisis rivals, we should focus on that issue alone—that is, whether a stronger contractarian justification can be offered for one of the security crisis rivals, and if so, which one is best supported.

Rejecting the security-trumps principle implies that the security and evaluation interests are commensurable and may therefore be weighed in the same scales. Whether this supports the balancing principle depends on whether the parties, as agents of construction, have reason to give *special priority* to one of these interests. Special priority is weaker than *lexical priority*, which implies that the lexically prior interest automatically trumps all interests lower in priority, although lexical priority is one form of special priority—in fact, the strongest form possible. If the parties do have reason to give special, but not lexical, priority to one of these interests, then the two interests, though commensurable, and weighable in the same scales, are not simply to be balanced.

Without following Rawls in every detail, I believe that, on this matter, his remarks on the priority of liberty are particularly instructive as a starting point—and can be extended to support giving special, but not lexical, priority to the evaluation interest. In discussing the priority of liberty, Rawls remarks that, once society achieves an adequate level of material prosperity, "the marginal significance for our good of further economic and social advantages diminishes relative to the interests of liberty."[51] At a certain point, "it becomes and then remains irrational from the standpoint of the original position to acknowledge a lesser liberty for the sake of greater material means and amenities of office." The reason for this, he argues, is that "only the less urgent [wants] remain to be met by further advances," while "a growing insistence upon the right to pursue our spiritual and cultural interests asserts itself," and we "aspire to some control over the laws and rules" that regulate our association, either by participating directly in their framing or indirectly through representatives.[52] For these reasons, his first principle of justice receives lexical priority over the second.

Now it seems plausible to maintain that just as when society achieves an adequate level of economic prosperity, we can justify giving the first principle of justice special priority over the second, so too, when society achieves a sufficient

51. Rawls, *A Theory of Justice*, p. 542.

52. Ibid., pp. 542–43.

level of background security, we can justify giving special priority to the evaluation interest, *without* making it lexically prior to the security interest. On the one hand, just as "the marginal significance for our good of further economic and social advantages diminishes relative to the interests of liberty," as Rawls insists, so too, it seems, does the marginal significance for our good of further security diminish relative to our interests in autonomy. In other words, just as, at a certain point, it becomes irrational to sacrifice liberty for greater material means, so too does it become irrational to accept sacrifices in our autonomy for greater security. If "a growing insistence upon the right to pursue our spiritual and cultural interests asserts itself" as society advances materially, as Rawls claims, and we "aspire to some control over the laws and rules" that regulate our association, so too, it seems, as society's security advances, do we aspire to exert greater control over our laws and rules—and hold greater interest in understanding and influencing the social conditions that constrain or facilitate our choices. All of this supports giving special priority to the evaluation interest.

Yet, on the other hand, unlike desires for further material goods, which "are not so compelling as to make it rational for the persons in the original position to agree to satisfy them" by compromising the first principle of justice,[53] desires for greater security are often quite rational, even when prompted by dangers that are not so severe as to undermine the adequate development and exercise of two moral powers, or threaten the assumption of sufficient background security. Imagining significant security threats that fall just short of that mark, but that still affect how confidently they can pursue a determinate conception of the good, the parties have reason for the security interest at least to *register* when it comes into conflict with the evaluation interest, even under the assumption of sufficient background security. In order for it to register, though, the evaluation interest cannot receive lexical priority over the security interest.[54]

If this reasoning is sound, then we have reason for the parties, as agents of construction, to give special, but not lexical, priority to the evaluation interest when it comes into conflict with the security interest. Though commensurable, and weighable on the same scales, the two interests are not simply to be balanced, as the balancing principle holds.

Rather than balancing the two interests when they come into conflict, we can give special priority to the evaluation interest through a *presumption*. When the two interests come into conflict, the evaluation interest will presumptively override the security interest, unless that presumption is defeated. The question then becomes what defeats the presumption. The two remaining principles offer

53. Ibid., p. 543.

54. Another way of stating this point may be to claim that the security interest admits of *satisficing*. Once society achieves a sufficient level of background security, the security interest is satisficed. Beyond that point, the security and evaluation interests are weighable in the same scales, and are therefore commensurable. But their weights as such are not then to be treated *equally*, as the balancing principle holds. Rather, beyond that point, the evaluation interest is to receive special, but not lexical, priority.

different defeating conditions, and the parties at the constitutional stage select one of them.

The parties at the constitutional stage know the following facts:

1. Threats exist against their society.
2. Of these threats, some are omnipresent.
3. Of these, some are grave.
4. Of these, some are credible.
5. Of these, some are imminent.

Define a *compelling security interest* as one that seeks to protect individuals from omnipresent, grave, credible, imminent threats. Both the weak and strong crisis principles insist that compelling security interests defeat the presumption in favor of the evaluation interest. The difference between the two principles is that the weak crisis principle also allows the presumption to be defeated when the evaluation interest, generally presumed to be strong, is weak instead. The intuitive idea is that the evaluation interest's strength is variable, depending on the strength of the other interests that are affected by a secret law. For example, the personal security interest affected by those who are potential targets of lethal drone strikes is no doubt much stronger than the privacy interest affected by those whose phone and email metadata is stored for potential, later, investigative use. So, in the first case, the evaluation interest is much stronger than it is in the second. If the evaluation interest is weak enough in either case, the presumption in its favor may be defeated by the security interest, even when the security interest does not qualify as compelling. In contrast, when the presumption (under either principle) is not defeated, then courts should order disclosure, exposing the thresholds to public discussion. Unless drone strikes, for example, protect citizens against imminent threats, then courts should order disclosure of the criteria for being placed on the list of targets, so that citizens may evaluate them. Similarly, unless the privacy interest in one's phone and email metadata is judged to be weak, courts should order disclosure of the criteria for collecting them as well, so that citizens may evaluate them too.

Acting as trustees for the evaluation, security, and privacy interests of the individuals they represent, the parties then select among the two remaining principles.[55] The main question is whether they would agree to grant the power to enact secret thresholds to courts when the evaluation interests affected by keeping them secret are relatively weak. Since both principles allow compelling security interests to defeat the evaluation interest, this is the only difference between them.

Clearly, there are trade-offs either way. If they grant the power, they themselves would be unable to evaluate or publicly discuss the thresholds, but they would gain a measure of security. If they deny the power, they themselves would be able

55. Technically, they can select from among the five principles listed, plus others salient candidates that might be formulated.

to evaluate and publicly discuss the thresholds, but they would lose a measure of security. Now the crucial point here is that, in theory, this problem admits of a solution: it is determined by the selection of the parties, from the standpoint of the representative equal citizen. The setup of the contract limits the feasible options. And though their selection might ultimately rest on an appeal to intuition, such an appeal is nonetheless constrained by the contractual circumstances. It is not an appeal to mere *unguided* intuition.

Determining whether there are significant conflicts of intuition among people on this matter is obviously then of the first importance. Nonetheless, I believe that, considering extremely weak evaluation interests against security interests falling just short of compelling threats (such as ones lacking imminence), the parties would probably judge that it is worse (1) to sacrifice the marginal security for the sake of preserving their ability to evaluate those thresholds themselves, than it is (2) to sacrifice the ability to evaluate those thresholds themselves for the sake of marginal security. Accordingly, the parties would probably select the weak over the strong security crisis principle.

Regardless of their decision, whichever principle they select provides a basis for justifying a law of thresholds—a *secret* law of thresholds. Does it justify more than this? Does it justify, for example, keeping the very existence of entire programs secret, such as the drone program itself, or the collection of metadata? While my primary concern here has been to identify the most plausible candidates for secret laws (thresholds), it's fair to ask whether the reasoning can be extended to justify more controversial cases of secrecy, such as this one. However, it's hard to see how such sweeping secrecy could be justified, because for the government (more precisely, the executive) to hold entire programs secret seems to imply that there could be no judicial review at all of them—no institutional mechanism at all for evaluating the security and evaluation interests—since the submission of such programs for such review involves disclosing their existence. To maintain the secret, the judicial review itself would have to be secret. Would the parties to the contract nonetheless confer *that* power? Here I assume that there is a distinction that the parties to the contract would acknowledge. Endowed with their general knowledge of the world, which includes their knowledge of the potential for abuse, the parties could well reason that the potential for abuse is markedly higher with powers to keep entire programs secret (with secret judicial review) than it is with powers to classify information, intelligence-gathering methods, or thresholds. If the difference is significant enough—and they judge that secret judicial review does not qualify as a credible enough institutional mechanism for ensuring that the executive branch observes its proper limits—then that would be grounds for denying the power altogether.

V. CONCLUDING REMARKS

As a principle of adjudication, the weak security crisis principle imposes significant constraints on the use of secret laws or directives. By design, those laws or directives must be limited to protecting citizens against imminent threats, or else the evaluation interests at stake must be extremely weak in the circumstances they govern. If either of these conditions is violated, then courts should order disclosure, and the public should be allowed to evaluate the justice, fairness, or efficiency of the laws.

The social contract tradition, then, does not categorically forbid the making and enforcement of secret laws. Such laws are consistent with the views of virtually all of its most famous members, and more important, they can be positively supported by an appropriately constructed social contract. But the support that such a contract offers is admittedly modest. It is support in principle. Secret laws can be justified *in principle* by contractarian reasoning. In practice, however, the occasions in which secret laws are justified are significantly constrained. Further, if experience shows that courts are unwilling or unable to police those constraints, then those occasions will become even more limited. The value of the social contract tradition is that it provides us with a standpoint from which to think systematically about what those constraints should be.

11

Secret Tribunals and the Limits of Sovereignty

LARRY MAY

The question of the legitimacy of secret tribunals has arisen again due to the FISA Courts in the United States claiming to be a necessary and legitimate means of combating terrorism. I will examine the importance of the idea that a defendant is granted notice and the ability to confront his or her accuser. And I will also examine how significant is transparency and publicity for the justification of tribunals. I will argue that secret tribunals, in most cases, violate the proper limits on sovereignty and render the sovereign state that employs secret tribunals illegitimate.

Historically, as well as in contemporary times, secret tribunals have operated to deny a detainee or defendant due process. The justification offered for this denial of due process is that it is necessary to achieve some other goal such as security from terrorism, anarchy, or heresy that risk significant disruptions of society. Yet, while security is an important value of any society, obtaining security at the expense of justice and equity leaves the sovereign with a severe problem of legitimacy. Only in rare cases, so I will argue, can the problem of legitimacy be overcome or balanced by obtaining security. If the sovereign's rule is unjust and inequitable the legitimacy of such sovereigns cannot be sustained. And the lack of transparency in secret tribunals opens the door for the greater likelihood of abuse. These issues have been debated over the centuries but are now more important than ever as various Western governments, most notably the United States, claim that they need secret tribunals in order successfully to fight terrorism.

As will become clear later in the text, it is possible to have secret tribunals that operate within the rule of law. The problem is that it is very difficult to tell whether

Sovereignty and the New Executive Authority. Claire O. Finkelstein and Michael Skerker.

a secret tribunal is or is not operating within the rule of law—the secrecy of the tribunals disrupts the transparency that is normally needed to ascertain whether procedural fairness is guaranteed in the tribunals. The chief difference between secret and non-secret tribunals is that the former but not the latter make it nearly impossible for an outsider to tell whether the tribunals are operating fairly. And this, as obvious as it seems, is the crux of the problematic nature of secret tribunals.

I. A BRIEF HISTORY OF SECRET TRIBUNALS

In Plato's *Republic*, there is a defense of what are called "noble lies," stories that are meant to teach the public their stations in life.[1] The fact that these stories are not true is something that must be kept secret, argues Plato, lest the intended effect be diminished. And Plato's *Laws* ends with a description of what is called "the Nocturnal Council," which "shall be compelled to meet each day, from dawn until the sun has risen."[2] While the council meets at night it is unclear whether all of their proceedings are formally held in secret. Yet, the idea of a court that meets when everyone else is asleep has animated later critiques of secret tribunals, the most notorious of which occurred in Germany and England at the end of the Middle Ages.

In Germany, the Secret Court of Westphalia was established at least as early as 1267 by a secret society of Fehmenotes who prosecuted serious crimes, especially having to do with treason and serious forms of robbery.[3] These crimes were associated with the lawlessness that had gripped most of Germany since 1024, where "anarchy and feuds prevailed to an alarming extent; the castles of the nobles became dens of robbers; and law and justice were nowhere to be found."[4]

These secret courts employed torture and also went to extraordinary lengths to hide the proceedings and the identities of the members of the court.

> Certain and instantaneous death was the portion of the stranger who was seen at any place where a tribunal was sitting, or who dared so much as look into the books which contained the laws and ordinances of the society. Death was also the portion of any member of the society who revealed its secrets; and so strongly did this terror, or a principle of honor, operate that . . . no motive had ever induced a single one to be faithless to his trust.[5]

The terrorizing of the population was part of the method of maintaining secrecy for this tribunal.

1. Plato, *The Republic*, 415a–c, Jowett translation.

2. Plato's *Laws*, 951d8, translated by Thomas Pangle, Chicago: University of Chicago Press, 1980, p. 353.

3. See Thomas Keightley, *Secret Societies of the Middle Ages*, 1837, p. 340.

4. Ibid., p. 337.

5. Ibid., pp. 333–34.

As far as the procedures of the tribunal are concerned, there was no notice given to the defendant that he was being investigated or what the charges against him or her were.

> At the time when we have most reason for supposing these tribunals to be instituted the Germans were familiar with the language of the civil and canonical laws; the Fehm-gerichte departed from the original maxims of German law, which was—no accuser, no judge[ment], and in imitation of those foreign laws, proceeded on common fame, and without any formal accusation against persons suspected of crime or evil courses.[6]

There was no notice, formal charges, or the opportunity to confront one's accuser, contrary to law and custom at this time in Germany. The secret nature of these tribunals in Germany extended to the very fact of even whether the tribunals met or not. There is though now good evidence, although probably not available at the time, that these tribunals did meet, but they lacked transparency in nearly every aspect of the workings of these tribunals.

At about the same time as these German tribunals were first operating, the barons in England were in revolt against King John for somewhat similar practices. The barons refused to contribute to the war chest of the king until such practices were stopped. And so it was at Runnymede in 1215 that King John was forced to sign the Magna Carta outlawing such practices as were employed by secret tribunals.

Two of the most important provisions of Magna Carta are directly addressed to such practices as secret tribunals. Chapter 39 (29) guaranteed a set of basic rights for those who have been accused of a crime or other violation of the law.

> No freeman shall be taken or imprisoned or desseised or exiled or in any way destroyed, nor will we go upon him nor send upon him, except by the lawful judgment of his peers or by the law of the land (*per legem terrae*).

Here we have the requirement that there be a lawful judgment of one's peers before liberty or property can be taken.

Indeed, it is common to say that the right of habeas corpus received one of its first significant protections here in Magna Carta. Habeas corpus is the right of a person who is detained to be brought out of prison and have his or her jailer publicly declare what are the charges against him or her that would justify this imprisonment. If no valid charges were announced, then the detainee must be released. This right, which can be traced at least to the century before Magna Carta, is often said to be the foundation of all of the rights of citizens against their government. Indeed, this is the only right that is mentioned in the main body of the United States Constitution, perhaps giving it pride of place over the rights listed in the

6. Ibid., p. 344.

amendments to the Constitution, including the right to free speech, religion, and press, as Justice Kennedy wrote for the majority in the *Boumediene* case.[7]

In the seventeenth century, commenting on Chapter 39 (29) of Magna Carta in the second part of his Institutes of the Laws of England, Edward Coke said:

> That no man be taken or imprisoned, but *per legem terrae,* that is by the common law, statute law, or custom of England; for these words *per legem terrae,* being towards the end of this chapter, do refer to all precedent matters in this chapter, and this hath the first place, because the liberty of a man's person is more precious to him, than all the rest that follow, and therefore it is great reason, that he should by law be relieved therein, if he be wronged, as hereafter shall be showed.[8]

Coke was the most significant chronicler of the laws of England, as well as chief justice of the King's Bench. The clear implication of Coke's interpretation is that secret proceedings are outlawed by Magna Carta.

In addition, in Chapter 38 (28) of Magna Carta, one of the most important components of the rule of law is enunciated:

> No bailiff (*balivus*) for the future, shall upon his own unsupported complaint, put anyone to his "law," without credible witnesses brought for this purpose.

Most commentators agree with Coke who said that "*balivus*" here refers to all officials of a government: "under this word *balivus,* in this act is comprehended every justice, minister of the king, steward and bailiff."[9]

Chapter 38 (28) contains a strong statement that no person of whatever office shall be able to make of himself "the law." As the phrase is normally used, it refers to the principle that we should have a system of laws not men. The rule of law is understood to be opposed by the rule of men. There is an assumption here that people left to their own devices without restraints will abuse the system for their own gain. And Chapter 38 (28) makes it clear that the king "was no longer to take the law into his own hands: the deliberate judgment of a court of law must precede any punitive measures to be taken by the king against freemen of his realm."[10]

Despite Magna Carta, I now will discuss a case in Medieval England, the Star Chamber court. The Star Chamber court often met in secret and dealt very harshly with defendants, employing ingenious forms of torture, as well denying

7. Boumediene v. Bush, U.S. Supreme Court, 553 U.S. 723, decided June 12, 2008.

8. Edward Coke, *The Second Part of the Institutes of the Laws of England Containing the Exposition of Many Ancient and Other Statutes,* p. 45.

9. Coke, *The Second Part of the Institutes,* p. 44.

10. William Sharp McKechnie, *Magna Carta: A Commentary on the Great Charter of King John,* Glasgow: James Maclehose and Sons, Second edition, 1914, p. 381.

them basic procedural rights. Yet, Edward Coke seems to praise the Star Chamber court, calling it a "most honorable court,"[11] even as he also praised Magna Carta in the strongest of terms. In part this seeming inconsistency can be partially explained by Coke's belief that the Star Chamber court was acting primarily against threats to the realm and hence could operate under different rules than normal courts.

In addition, at the end of the seventeenth century, Thomas Hobbes spoke somewhat supportively of the Star Chamber when he declared:

> As for cutting off of ears, and for the pillory, and the like corporal punishments usually inflicted heretofore in the Star-chamber, they were warranted by the statute of Hen. VII, that giveth them power to punish sometimes by discretion. And generally it is a rule of reason, that every judge of crimes, in case the positive law appoint no punishment, and he have no other law of the King, then do consult the King before he pronounce sentence of any irreparable damage to the offender: for otherwise he doth not pronounce the law, which is his office to do, but makes the law, which is the office of the King.[12]

Yet, Hobbes also seems to support the closing of the Star Chamber court by the Long Parliament.[13]

William Blackstone, writing in the eighteenth century, put the rights of Magna Carta's Chapter 39 (29) at the top of the most fundamental of rights in England. He defended the fundamental right to public trials as follows:

> To bereave a man of life, or by violence to confiscate his estate, without accusation or trial, would be so gross and notorious an act of despotism, as must at once convey the alarm of tyranny throughout the whole kingdom. But confinement of the person, by secretly hurrying him to gaol, where his sufferings are unknown and forgotten; is a less public, a less striking and therefore a more dangerous engine of arbitrary government.[14]

Blackstone was reacting to such institutions as the Star Chamber court in England that was used from the late fifteenth century until the middle of the eighteenth century. Blackstone proposes that the term "star chamber" originated from the practice of requiring contracts signed by Jews during the time of Edward I to be lodged in a special room that was later the place where this notorious court sat.[15]

11. Edward Coke, *Institutes of the Laws of England*, Part IV, c. 1644, chapter 5, p. 65.

12. Thomas Hobbes, *A Dialogue between a Philosopher and a Student of the Common Laws of England*, 1671, EW VI, p. 124.

13. Thomas Hobbes, *Behemoth*, EW VI, p. 256

14. William Blackstone, *Commentaries on the Laws of England* (1765), Chicago: University of Chicago Press, 1979, vol. I, pp 131–32.

15. Ibid., vol. IV, p. 263, note a.

Blackstone refers to the Star Chamber courts as "the most dangerous and unconstitutional,"[16] and says that the power of the sovereign to institute such tribunals "is usurped."[17] Here is a reference by Blackstone to the idea that secret tribunals are beyond the limits of sovereignty. In part his critique of the Star Chamber court is that it usurped the normal operation of sovereignty in England in that properly passed legislation could by these courts be secretly overturned without a further act of Parliament. It is interesting to note that critics of the Star Chamber court also criticized the Chancery Court, as well as other equity courts, often on the same grounds. I will return to this issue in a later Section of the chapter.

The third historical example is the Inquisition courts. The courts of the Inquisition were part of the Roman Catholic Church's attempt to deal with heresy starting in the twelfth century and extending into the nineteenth century. Heretics, whose ranks included Galileo, were seen to be a threat to the Catholic Church's ability to serve its mission of protecting the souls of its members. Yet, the secrecy of the proceedings and the horrific torture employed by the Inquisition made it eventually synonymous with the abuse of power, in this case the power of the Church supplemented by the sovereigns of France, Spain, Portugal, and other countries.

There is a common feature to the Secret Courts of Westphalia, the Star Chamber court, and the Inquisition courts. All were initially established as a response to a perceived emergency, the anarchy of especially difficult times in the Middle Ages. In the Middle Ages the threats of anarchy and overthrow of civil authorities were notorious, as was the threat to the authority of the Church. Yet, the tactics and procedures of these tribunals also constituted a threat of abuse by the sovereign authorities. In some cases the very act of establishing secret tribunals undermines the legitimacy of the sovereign. In other cases, sovereignty is only undermined when abuses occur in the secret tribunals. And in the case of the Star Chamber, the perceived abuses did in fact count heavily in bringing down the English monarchy in the middle of the seventeenth century, as well as the beheading of a monarch. Secret tribunals, even though they have been defended as necessary for the preservation of sovereignty, have also been seen as serious challenges to the legitimacy of sovereignty as well.

II. WHY, AND WHEN, SECRECY IS A PROBLEM

What is secret is typically hidden, and intentionally so. As a result the opposite of what is secret is that which is intentionally revealed, transparent, and open to public view. When things are intentionally hidden it is often because the person who did these things is afraid of being negatively evaluated. And often the negative evaluation of secret tribunals is due to an abuse that has taken place or can be perceived to have occurred. But it is sometimes the case that also secrecy plays

16. Ibid., vol. IV, p. 422.

17. Ibid., vol. IV, p. 430.

an important role in providing justice or securing peace. Indeed, there is nothing about secrecy that is wrong in itself. Yet, every time there is secrecy people become suspicious that what is kept secret is likely to be an abuse or wrong.

Let us discuss some cases of secrecy in government that seem not to be a problem. In discussions between state leaders it is often important that their candid assessments of one another's positions not be open to public scrutiny, especially to being publicized in mass media. Indeed, even that there were high-level discussions between two state leaders can itself be so likely to be misinterpreted that the meeting itself should be secret, not merely the content of the meeting. Secret meetings are one thing, but secret tribunals are quite another as we will see in subsequent sections of this chapter.

Another interesting case of seemingly positive secret proceedings concerns something that occurs sometimes in normal trial proceedings. In camera proceedings are a staple of Anglo-American procedure as are proceedings *in limine*. It is sometimes necessary to have such proceedings in order to protect the rights of parties to a suit, or more commonly to protect third party witnesses. The classic case here is the examination of evidence in camera to see if it is indeed significant to the case, where the evidence, if publicly disclosed, is likely to harm someone's reputation or otherwise cause harm to third parties. And when judges, acting *in limine*, investigate "sealed documents" about the lives of minors, the point of the proceedings is to protect the child, not to abuse the rights of the defendant.

One further case where a secret trial might be required not just permitted is where the material that is the subject of the suit is such that if revealed it could cause grave harm. Consider the case of a United States magazine editor working for *The Progressive* who tried to publicize how to construct a hydrogen bomb but was prohibited from doing so by the government. In a trial to determine whether the government's prior restraint was justified, one of the main issues was whether the magazine was correct in what it purported to report about how to construct the bomb. If the trial were to take place in public the very subject of the suit would also become public, thereby thwarting the government's attempt at prior restraint before it could be determined that the government's restraint was contrary to law. And if the government had been right then the public trial would have disclosed how to build a hydrogen bomb that any student of chemistry could have successfully accomplished.[18] Such considerations have played a prominent role in the defense of secret tribunals today, such as in the Energy Department's secret proceedings in cases such as that of *The Progressive* magazine. Today we are also faced with the Foreign Intelligence Surveillance Act (FISA) courts established after September 11, 2001, to deal with cases involving the threat of terrorism and other national security issues.

To contrast the above cases with cases where secrecy is indeed problematic, we return to the three examples of questionable secret tribunals discussed in the previous section (the Secret Tribunals of Westphalia, the Star Chamber court, and the Inquisition's courts). Secrecy was seen as important for obtaining something

18. See United States v. The Progressive, 467 F. Supp. 990 (W.D. Wisc. 1979).

more important than transparency, namely security. Transparency might be such that enemies will gain an advantage and will more easily be able to achieve their objectives. Notice that in the case of the Inquisition, the threat was to public morals, or less charitably to the supremacy of the Catholic Church in Southern Europe, not to the physical security of the populace. The "security" concerns are very different though if it is the physical security of the populace that is said to be threatened as opposed to the threat to public morals.

In the cases of the Westphalian courts and the Star Chamber, the threat was more closely related to the populace's security, although it was very unclear why what was needed was a secret court rather than one that issued especially cruel sentences, in order to accomplish the deterrent objective of stopping lawlessness. Depriving someone of due process rights at trial does not necessarily deter anarchy or mass robbery. Indeed, it is not clear why the harsh sentences meted out by these tribunals would not better deter if the proceedings were public, where everyone in the society is made aware of the costs of anarchy, as opposed to a private trial where such knowledge is not commonly disseminated. In the Inquisition's courts, the public safety rationale was much less clear since heresy does not have a close relationship to anarchy or civil upheaval.

The case of deprivation of procedural rights so as to confront terrorism is today the main source of worry about secret tribunals. Unlike in camera proceedings, secret tribunals determine *guilt* in secret, which almost always works out to the disadvantage of that defendant. The only third parties who are potentially affected by secret tribunals are those citizens who might be exposed to the security threat if the acts of the defendant are publicized. Yet the potential harm to the society from some forms of terrorist violence is quite large and most societies would go to considerable lengths to prevent such violence. If secret tribunals would decrease the likelihood of terrorist violence then we have a seemingly strong reason in favor of some secret tribunals.

But again, I would stress that the deterrence of violence due to terrorism would rarely require a secret criminal tribunal. An in camera proceedings as part of a public trial could deal with names of informants, and other sensitive matters, without making the whole criminal proceedings secret. And in any event the threat of terrorist violence is very difficult to predict, and the idea of a terrorist threat is subject to be abused by government leaders. Indeed, the abuse of the Star Chamber Court was so notorious that, as I said, it precipitated a political crisis over sovereignty in England in the seventeenth century. This is why transparency rather than secrecy is thought to be important in such cases. In the next section I will address the value of due process that is almost always thwarted by secret tribunals as has been recognized at least since the time of Magna Carta.

III. DUE PROCESS AND SECRET TRIBUNALS

In this Section I will focus on two values: (1) public notice of the charges against a defendant, and (2 public confrontation with the defendant's accusers. Both of these values are absent in secret court proceedings. In their essay, "Notice and the Right to Be Heard: The Significance of Old Friends," Stephen N. Subrin and

A. Richard Dykstra defend the value of notice in terms of efficiency in court proceedings and dignity of the defendant. One of the general values of transparent and public court proceedings is that the presence and participation of the defendant makes it more likely than otherwise that the fact-finding will be more effective since the defendant will have a vested interest in bringing out as many relevant facts as he or she can. And the public will be more likely to provide oversight of the prosecutor.[19]

A second general value of notice and public hearings is that they will be more likely to at least have the appearance of legitimacy and will actually be more likely to produce just results, thereby supporting the dignity of the defendant. The dignity of the person is important for Sabin and Dykstra because when people feel that their dignity is respected they are less likely to rebel or otherwise undermine the functioning of the state. This admittedly functional analysis can be supplemented by a more explicitly moral defense of both notice and public hearing.

From a moral perspective, the dignity of the defendant is not merely important for the peace of mind of the defendant. Dignity is of crucial relevance because even the worst offender is still a human being who is deserving of minimal respect as a person with dignity. In the Universal Declaration of Rights as well as in the Bill of Rights of the U.S. Constitution, procedural rights are the backbone of our more substantive rights, and survive even serious challenge in times of emergency or crisis.[20] Public hearings where one can confront one's accuser will not allow the accuser's word to drown out any possible rebuttal by the defendant.

Blackstone, writing in the eighteenth century, put his finger on one of the most important due process considerations for secret tribunals. The treatment of people who have been removed from public scrutiny leaves these detainees with little or no recourse when abuse occurs. I quoted Blackstone earlier to this effect: "But confinement of the person, by secretly hurrying him to gaol, where his sufferings are unknown and forgotten; is a less public, a less striking and therefore a more dangerous engine of arbitrary government."[21] Blackstone here indicates that the sufferings or abuse of a person, when hidden, cannot offend the public, and hence the public does not call for a further investigation. For this reason secret proceedings are more dangerous than public acts that inflict suffering on a prisoner or other detainee. Without public oversight, those who would use the reins of government for their own personal purposes will not have to worry that they will be found out.

19. Stephen S. Subrin and A. Richard Dykstra, "Notice and the Right to Be Heard: The Significance of Old Friends," *Harvard Civil Rights-Civil Liberties Law Review*, vol. 9, 1974, pp. 449–80, especially pp. 454–55, reprinted in *Procedural Justice*, edited by Larry May and Paul Morrow, Burlington, VT: Ashgate, 2012, pp. 287–318.

20. See James Nickel, "Due Process Rights and Terrorist Emergencies," in his book *Making Sense of Human Rights/*,Malden, MA: Blackwell, Second edition, pp. 106–22, reprinted in *Procedural Rights*, edited by Larry May and Paul Morrow, Burlington, VT: Ashgate, 2012, pp. 407–24.

21. William Blackstone, *Commentaries on the Laws of England* (1765), Chicago: University of Chicago Press, 1979, vol. I, pp. 131–32.

Secrecy masks the arbitrariness or abuse of a sovereign ruler or the ministers of that ruler. And so it is important to restrict secret proceedings to those where the rights of citizens are least likely to be abused by such proceedings. In camera proceedings as only one part of an otherwise public trial are designed with this principle in mind. Only those matters that are strictly necessary for protecting the rights of others or for maintaining security of the state are open to in camera proceedings—everything else must be open to public scrutiny. Once we are no longer dealing with emergency exceptions, the value of public oversight is more important than comparatively minor advantages gained from closed proceedings.

It is especially important that when a person's liberty or life is in jeopardy, a public trial should be held rather than one that is secret. Life and liberty are the most important values of persons. When liberty or life can be taken from a citizen without his or her participation in a trial, or without public oversight of that trial, the sovereign authority has gone beyond its proper limits. In the next Section I will mount an argument in defense of this claim.

IV. SOVEREIGNTY AND DUE PROCESS

There is an often unrecognized connection between the legitimate claims of sovereignty and the claims of due process. Sovereignty is itself only legitimate, for instance, if rulers have a right to issue binding laws that are coercively enforced. And the right to issue binding laws is grounded in the sovereign having been granted the right to rule by the express or implied consent of the citizenry. Whether one supports a social contract approach, as I just suggested, or some other, there is a process that must be followed for a sovereign to attain the right to rule. And this due process constraint on sovereign legitimacy is related to the due process constraints on the functioning of the judiciary, discussed in the previous Section. Due process is aimed at guaranteeing that the exercise of power by the sovereign and the making of judgments by the courts are non-arbitrary.

There is a second way that due process and sovereignty are related. Decision-making by the judiciary can affect the legitimacy of the sovereign lawmaker. When judicial decisions appear arbitrary, or when it is considered to be likely that they are arbitrary, trust in government more generally is eroded, affecting the sovereign lawmaker as well as the law interpreter and applier. Due process concerns can thus affect the legitimacy of the sovereign in these two ways.

Due process generally concerns a set of procedures that attempts to eliminate arbitrariness in various kinds of decision-making, whether by the sovereign legislator or by the judiciary. All decision-making, to be legitimate, must conform to whatever reasonable rules govern that forum of decision-making. And while due process is not often discussed in terms of sovereignty, it is my view that due process is just as relevant for sovereignty as it is for judicial decisions.

Earlier in this chapter I pointed out that some seventeenth century critics of the Star Chamber court compared it to other equity courts, tarring them all with the same brush. Equity considerations sometimes appear as if they are contrary to due process in that legal rules that were properly enacted are found inapplicable to particular cases, because of the unfairness that would result if the laws were applied. Yet this is seemingly in contravention of the rule of law. But in fact equity is an important component of due process in that, as theorists have recognized since Aristotle, the application of some rules to particular cases results in a kind of unfairness that is often undreamed of by the original lawmakers.[22]

Let me contrast the equity court of Chancery with the court of the Star Chamber in seventeenth century England. Chancery's proceedings were public and the rules employed were well articulated, if not always well understood by the general citizenry. Chancery courts could overrule the King's Bench or common law courts, but only when the ruling by these courts was seen as clearly in contravention of basic fairness. Chancery and other equity courts are only seen as acting contrary to due process and the rule of law when equity courts are not acting according to considerations of fundamental fairness. Mechanical application of law to facts is not what the rule of law requires. And equity courts have historically been places for correcting the application of law to facts that does not square with the intent of the lawmakers or with fundamental fairness. For instance, equity courts were where one went if one was about to be evicted because of nonpayment of rent, but where one's nonpayment was simply due to the fact that one was in jail temporarily at that point.

The Star Chamber proceedings, in contrast to equity courts, were often not public. And while they could also overrule King's Bench and common law courts, the reasons for such overruling were also shrouded in secrecy, and seem not to be influenced by considerations of fundamental fairness. Rather, the most charitable accounts of what drove these courts was a concern for thwarting public unrest and heresy, which were thought to be destabilizing factors in the society. There is here a major difference between the Star Chamber and equity courts such as the Chancery Court in terms of the rule of law.

Equity courts "overrule" other courts only in the sense that they play a role in providing a check against abuse or unfairness of other courts. But this is not a true overruling of the law since the equity proceedings are supposed to make sure that judicial rulings accurately reflect the spirit of the law. This is not at all what the Star Chamber court did when overruling other courts. At Star Chamber the concern for the integrity of the law was not the issue; rather the claim was that the security of the society was at stake. Yet, as indicated earlier, it remains problematic what kind of security interests were actually at stake. Very different considerations apply for instance between the physical security versus the security of public morals

The Star Chamber court and our contemporary FISA courts are similar in that while they can act independently, and even contrary, to normal courts, the basis of the rulings is security not the spirit of the laws that have been enacted. And hence many of the same objections made against the Star Chamber court can also be leveled at the FISA courts. Most significantly both types of court place the liberty or even the life of a citizen in jeopardy without public oversight.

22. See Aristotle, *Nicomachean Ethics*, penultimate section of Book V.

Lon Fuller tried to capture the elements of the rule of law with his eight desiderata that must at least partially be satisfied for a proper legal system.[23] Among these desiderata include a failure to make the laws public and a failure to make the announced rules congruent with the actual administration of the rules. Both of these rule of law constraints seem to be clearly violated in the institution of secret tribunals. The publicity requirement is obviously violated when tribunals are secret. Here secrecy makes it unclear how a person is to govern his or her behavior so that he or she does not run afoul of the law.

The congruence requirement may be satisfied but there is virtually no way to know for sure that this is so, at least not if one is outside the Star Chamber, or other secret tribunal's legal framework. And here is where one might need to supplement Fuller's approach. Congruence is very important, but so is the need for the public to see whether there is congruence or not. This is perhaps somewhat to blur the publicity and congruence requirements. But the point is that prior to seeing the value of congruence between the announced rules and the administration of the rules one must be in a position to determine whether or not congruence has been satisfied, and secret tribunals generally block this.

V. THE LIMITS OF SOVEREIGNTY

Even for philosophers who are supporters of strong sovereigns, there are significant limits on sovereignty having to do with justice and equity. In the past, some have tried to defend secret laws and tribunals with reference to equity. Such a strategy is bound to fail in most cases. In this final Section I will provide a more sustained argument for the conclusion that there must be significant limits on sovereignty, including a prohibition on secret tribunals, by working within a Hobbesian framework, since Hobbes is often seen as one of the philosophers most sympathetic to strong sovereignty.

As I said earlier, on one of the most prominent views, the legitimacy of the sovereign depends on having received the right to rule over the citizens either from their express or implicit consent. And so the question of the limits of sovereignty can be addressed, at least as a first approximation, in terms of what the citizenry would find to be an acceptable exercise of sovereignty. The issue that has confronted us in this chapter is whether secret tribunals have legitimacy, understood in terms of the acceptability of these tribunals to the citizenry. And the question now to consider is whether the citizenry would indeed support secret tribunals during times of terrorism or the risk of anarchy.

Issues of security generally are the proper purview of the sovereign. After all, what the sovereign is primarily supposed to do is to provide for the peace and prosperity of the society. And here it is clear that some trade-offs between security and rights would be acceptable to the citizenry as long as the trade-offs were not too limiting of rights and these limits were largely temporary. If the limitations on liberty were severe or permanent it is not initially clear why anyone would find

23. Lon L. Fuller, *The Morality of Law*, New Haven, CT: Yale University Press, 1964, p. 39.

this to be acceptable. In other words, while attaining peace is important, as has often been noted, it is a just peace that is sought, not a bare peace.

Hobbes is often portrayed as a philosopher who supported severe limits on the liberty of the citizenry to achieve security and peace. But Hobbes speaks of the duty of the sovereign to secure peace in terms of a peace that involves a wide array of liberties and conditions of happiness. And it is also Hobbes to whom one can turn to see a defense of equity considerations in his *Dialogue between a Philosopher and a Student of the Common Laws of England*. In this work, Hobbes identifies the conceptual restraints of equity on the sovereign with the way that the equity courts of his day corrected the law in various ways, especially as the laws had been interpreted by common law and King's Bench courts. As I have argued in detail elsewhere, Hobbes recognized the importance of the rule of law for the proper rule of a sovereign.[24]

The rule of law is important from a Hobbesian perspective because even if it is necessary, or seems to be necessary, to restrict liberty of citizens in order to respond to an emergency, it is important that at least minimal rule of law restraints remain in place even during such times of crisis, since they provide a way back to a robust rule of law when the emergency has passed. Without retaining some rule of law restraints, a temporary limitation on liberty could easily turn into a permanent loss of liberty. Equity provides such rule of law restraints by its guarantee that only good laws will be promulgated by the sovereign lawmaker. Secret tribunals can be initially justified by the deference that sovereigns are owed by the citizenry when societal peace is jeopardized. But this deference is lost in permanent, or greater than temporary, tribunals that are conducted without retaining at least minimal rule of law conditions.

Let me end by summarizing the main lines of argument of this chapter. If one counts publicity or transparency as a rule of law restraint on sovereignty, then secret tribunals obviously violate the rule of law. Of course some temporary loss of publicity or transparency can be justified as I said. But a serious problem is the requirement that Lon Fuller calls "congruence." Here is a requirement that the application of the rules must match the expressed content of the laws. But congruence as a rule of law restraint on sovereign authority only has teeth if there is some way to tell if the laws are indeed being applied in a manner that matches the content of the laws. And yet the secret nature of secret tribunals makes it nearly impossible to tell whether the congruence requirement of the rule of law is satisfied. On Fuller's view, that I also support, each of the eight desiderata must be at least partially satisfied. Secret tribunals cannot even partially satisfy the publicity or transparency requirement.

Here we find one of the main problems with secret tribunals: it is very difficult to tell whether these tribunals are indeed satisfying even minimal rule of law restraints. It is possible that all of the rule of law restraints are satisfied by secret tribunals, with the exception of the publicity or transparency requirement.

24. See Larry May, *Limiting Leviathan: Hobbes on Law and International Affairs*, Oxford: Oxford University Press, 2013.

But because of the failure to satisfy publicity or transparence it is normally not possible to tell whether the other rule of law requirements have been met. And it is equally important that it is very difficult to tell whether the other rule of law restraints will be met in the future by the government once the emergency has passed. This is a structural problem with secret tribunals that brings them into conflict with the rule of law in virtually every case. Given that sovereignty is only legitimate when it is subject to rule of law restraints, secret tribunals are structurally almost always in conflict with legitimate sovereignty.

PART FOUR

Horizontal Sovereignty

International Relations and War

12

Logically Private Laws

Legislative Secrecy in "The War on Terror"

DUNCAN MACINTOSH*

I. INTRODUCTION

Wittgenstein taught us that there could not be a logically private language—a language on the proper speaking of which it was logically impossible for there to be more than one expert. For then there would be no difference between this person thinking she was using the language correctly and her actually using it correctly. The distinction requires the logical possibility of someone other than her being

* This chapter began as a discussion paper for the conference, "On the Very Idea of Secret Laws: Transparency and Publicity in Deliberative Democracy," sponsored by the Center for Ethics and the Rule of Law (CERL) at the University of Pennsylvania Law School. For helpful comments I'm indebted to my fellow participants at the conference, especially Claire Finkelstein and Jens Ohlin; to my students in my advanced class on the theory of rational decision; to a colloquium audience at Dalhousie University; to Greg Scherkoske and Sheldon Wein for useful conversation; and, again, to Wein, for written comments. I'm grateful to Finkelstein and the Board of Directors of CERL for involving me in their activities. This has required me to stop thinking only abstractly as a philosopher and to grapple with real-world problems with a view to policy and practice. Happily this began at the same time as my marriage to a person of alternative political vision and great practical wisdom—thank you, L. Finally, I want to express my admiration for the people I meet at CERL conferences—academics, journalists, people in the military, the defense industry, the intelligence community, in government, and in law. Regardless of the sides they have taken on issues or the roles they have played in events, they have been reflective people of integrity trying to figure out what to do in the fog of war. Never was this exemplified more than by Chris Inglis, who, while he was Civilian Director of the National Security Agency, made common cause with us at the aforementioned conference for two days as we all sat around a table trying to get it right.

Sovereignty and the New Executive Authority. Claire O. Finkelstein and Michael Skerker.

expert enough to criticize or corroborate her usage, someone able to constitute or hold her to a standard of proper use.[1]

I shall explore the possibility of something opposite-sounding about laws, namely, that there could in principle be laws whose existence, legitimacy, goodness, and efficacy depend upon their being private, in this sense: their existence is kept secret from those who legitimately benefit from the laws and yet who would misguidedly destroy them were they to come to know of them; and it is kept secret from those who would illegitimately benefit from being able to circumvent the laws, and who could circumvent them if they knew of them. The secrecy of the laws increases their efficacy against bad behavior, and since were the public to come to know of these laws the public would lose its nerve and demand that the laws be rescinded, it prevents the public from destroying laws that are in fact in the public interest. These laws are therefore in a way logically private: they cannot at the same time exist, have the foregoing virtues, and be public.

After proposing conditions under which such laws ought to be enacted, I moot logical objections to the very idea that there could be such laws, practical objections to their workability, and moral objections to their permissibility. I conclude by suggesting that, while we normally think of secret laws as creatures of the executive branch, things functionally equivalent to secret laws could also be created by other branches of government and societal institutions, and that all of this would be compatible with the form of sovereignty that is democratically grounded in the will and interests of the people.

II. THE DEFINITION AND ANALYSIS OF LOGICALLY PRIVATE LAWS

In my terms, a law is secret to the extent that it is not widely known. But a law's being logically private involves further conditions. A law is logically private just in case its not being widely known is essential to its existence, efficacy, goodness, and legitimacy. So something is only such a law if its becoming public would rob it of these characteristics. Merely secret laws, on the other hand, would not be so threatened in these respects, and might even be enhanced.

Logically private laws must stay secret if they are to continue to exist because if they were made public they would be voted away. They must stay secret in order to have efficacy because they have their effects by means of stealth and ambush. They must stay secret in order to be good laws, because one condition on their being good is that they have good effects; to have effects at all by their operation they must stay secret (as we just saw), and so to have effects that are good they must stay secret. But further, their becoming public would have indirect bad effects, effects owing not to consequences of their operation, but to consequences of public reactions to their very existence. Their publication could cause social unrest and destabilize governments, something that might happen were the public to

1. Ludwig Wittgenstein, *Philosophical Investigations* (G.E.M. Anscombe, trans.) (Oxford: Blackwell, 1967).

come to know, for example, of secret laws allowing them to be spied upon, and of laws preventing the disclosure of the existence of the technical means to do this, something we saw in the Edward Snowden case. Their publication could threaten international relations, something that could happen if secret treaties between nations were to become public. And their publication could allow criminals to escape regulation, something officials feared would happen were terrorists to learn of the laws allowing their electronic communications to be monitored. Finally, logically private laws must stay secret in order to have legitimacy. Again, this is for several reasons. First, their legitimacy depends on their having, or at least being plausibly expected to have, good effects, which they can have only if they are secret. Second, they are authorized by rules (e.g., the Constitution), institutions (e.g., the executive branch), and persons (e.g., the president) who are themselves authorized to do the sorts of things secret laws authorize only in secret. Secret laws are born of the recognition that some things are both defensible (as, say, being in the national interest) and inherently such that they can only be done clandestinely, and they are birthed by the democratically vetted creation of rules and institutions authorized to act in secret. Spying, for example is the activity of coming to know something about someone without that person knowing you've come to know.

I'm tempted to make it a condition on a private law's being a good law that it has the aim and effect of improving compliance with public laws, and to suggest that part of what makes private laws legitimate in a democracy is that the laws compliance with which private laws aim at improving are themselves voted into place publicly, after public deliberation, in a noncontroversial expression of democratic values and in accord with democratic principles. But this may be too strong. For some public laws are not good laws—they are not in the public interest—and it may be that sometimes a secret law could be justified by the very fact that it would undermine compliance with a bad public law. Think of JFK trying to undermine racist laws: for all I know he might have promised pardons to officials who would act in violation of public laws in order to subvert those laws, thereby making it a secret law that it is okay to act to prevent the enforcement of racist laws. Or think of prosecutors in Chicago trying to "get Capone." A similar problem would afflict the suggestion that secret laws are good only if they compel behavior in accord with the values the citizenry publicly holds. For again, these values might in a given instance be bad values. And I can imagine situations where a good leader would enact secret laws with a view to changing or going against public values. Racist values would be an example.

Of course it seems there could also be secret laws with the properties that their being unknown is a harm to those whom good law should not harm, and a benefit to those whom good laws should not benefit. This would happen if, for example, corrupt or ideologically extreme agents infiltrated the government and enacted secret laws benefiting their cronies or alike-thinkers and harming the public interest. The secrecy of the laws would allow these people to proceed unmolested and would prevent the public from awakening to privations of its own interest. And of course one objection to permitting secret laws is that if our institutions permit the former, good secret laws, they will be at risk of becoming corrupted and resulting in the latter, bad secret laws. More on this in due course.

III. APPROPRIATE CONDITIONS FOR ENACTING LOGICALLY PRIVATE LAWS

Assuming for now that good such laws are conceptually intelligible, under what conditions should they be enacted? There are two: conditions of universal justice and conditions of absolute war.

By conditions of universal justice I mean this: Suppose there is a total set of arrangements that would be best for everyone, a deal that offers everyone a higher expected utility than any other deal. But suppose there are people incorrigibly too stupid or ignorant to recognize the deal for what it is, or too weak-willed to do their part in it. Suppose their behavior would ruin the deal for themselves and others. Those who can't recognize the deal for what it is might directly act against it, while those too weak-willed might balk at the severity of the laws needed to deal with the former sorts of people, and so might themselves wrongly worsen the deal for everyone. But now suppose there are arrangements that would save the deal for others and even for these problematic people because, although the arrangements might result in the secret manipulation of these people's circumstances, or in their incarceration or death, the arrangements still give them a better chance of a good life than would any other arrangements that also constituted a best deal for everyone else. Finally, suppose these arrangements would have to be brought about by secret means for the reasons stated in the definition of logically private laws, namely that otherwise people who benefit from them would, from stupidity or weakness of will, destroy the arrangements, thereby worsening the deal; and the people meant to be dealt with by the arrangements could evade them, again, worsening the deal. Then such laws should be instituted.

The other conditions where such laws should be instituted, conditions of absolute war, are when some deal is best for some people, another deal is best for other people, but no deal is best for all, and each deal puts its people at war with the people of the other deal. Then by right of self-defense each group would be justified in trying to enact such laws to try to win in the battle with the others.

IV. INSTANCES OF SECRET LAWS

In the American context the following have been offered as instances of secret laws: it not being made public what the criteria are for being on a drone kill list, or when a kill will occur; there not being a public trial for an alleged terrorist; there being nonpublic presidential orders, for example, orders authorizing interrogation techniques that would be widely seen as torture, or authorizing the killing of an American citizen, or the violation of the privacy of citizens, or orders forbidding disclosure of violations of that privacy or of the existence of means to its violation; or, speaking more generally, there being private presidential authorizing of exceptions to publicly proclaimed principles in what is arguably a kind of legalized hypocrisy; or there being secret treaties between nations.

I suggest that sometimes any of these things can be the proper object of good logically private laws. But are they even prima facie cases of laws at all, let alone private laws? Yes, for in the United States, under certain conditions—especially in war or to defend the country, and especially if Congress has declared war so that the president's Commander-in-Chief status is invoked—the executive branch of government has the power to make things law by judicially unobstructed decree so that, for example, presidential edicts are then eo ipso laws.[2]

V. POSSIBLE OBJECTIONS

We all have as our default intuition the idea that law must be public in every dimension. I now explore reasons this might be thought to be true, reasons formulated as possible objections to what I'm proposing, and I try to meet those objections.

For example, don't laws have to be enacted by a lawful authority? Sure. But that doesn't mean their enactment has to be public—duly elected representatives

2. My education in this matter (I'm neither an American nor a lawyer) began in conversation with Claire Finkelstein and Jens Ohlin. Quite separately from what they've told me, I note that the U.S. Constitution gives the president the right to pardon certain offenses, which means that he can in effect make it legal for people to do various things that are not normally legal, since he can save them from legal consequence (at least so long as he himself can avoid impeachment). And since the president could promise to do this privately, it would be a secret that this person's action has become legal. (I overstate for effect here. In fact all the president can do is secretly make it that this person's action will have no federal legal consequences. But that is troubling enough.) For a more thorough review of the sorts of things that can count as secret law, see Dakota Rudesill, "Coming to Terms with Secret Law," *Harvard National Security Journal*, vol. 7 (2016), pp. 241–390. It is of course controversial just when the president has this sort of power, and just how extensive it is or ought to be, controversial both in the abstract and as a matter of interpretation of the Constitution as the document that authorizes this power. As a Canadian and so an outsider to how Americans think about such matters, I have been struck by two things: first, that so much of the debate in America about whether there ought to be secret laws is conducted as debate about whether the U.S. Constitution permits them, rather than about whether they can be good things in themselves. It is like seeing religious people trying to engage in moral reasoning by interpreting biblical text. Second, I am struck by the vehemence of the disagreement. On casual reading it seems to me a reasonable understanding of the Constitution to see it as saying the president can do what he judges necessary to defend his country. I can also see how reasonable people, with the benefit of other contexts, might read it another way. But the astounding thing is that so many on each side of the debate think the other side is crazy, evil, incompetent, or criminally irresponsible. Recall the controversy surrounding the readings of the Constitution offered by John Yoo when he worked in the Office of Legal Counsel during the administration of President George W. Bush. Perhaps this vehemence is explained by the fact that the real issue isn't what the Constitution says. It is whether one should favor things such as secret laws, or the actions that some of such laws have aimed to make legitimate—torture, spying on one's own citizens. These are polarizing questions. And when the debate about them is conducted in terms of whether the Constitution permits them, the question how to read the Constitution becomes likewise polarized. In much of this chapter, I shall be arguing about what follows concerning the legitimacy of secret laws from a reading of the Constitution as in effect permitting the president to enact them. But there is of course a debate to be had about whether the Constitution should be amended to prohibit such laws. That debate might be decided by reflecting independently on the goodness of such laws.

could oversee the enacting of the law by duly enacted processes and just keep quiet about it.

But mustn't laws be public to make a difference? Well, some people must know of them, namely those who are to implement them. But not everyone. For laws can affect lives in ways other than by people deliberately obeying them. It can be enough that people exist within the social structures the laws create, for example, without people having to be aware that these structures are the product of a given law. Think of secret treaties between governments: a peaceful co-existence of countries is secured, so their citizens enjoy peace; but the law securing this is private and unknown to the public that enjoys it. Perhaps for many years the countries' populations hated each other over past conflicts and are not ready to forgive, even though forgiveness would be in everyone's interest. Their leaders see this and so deceive their populations with secret treaties while publicly posturing in the attitudes their populations demand. There are current examples in the politics of the Middle East.

Another way a law can be both nonpublic and yet influential is by its existence being merely suspected: this could induce people to comply with the law without it being publicly known that it actually is the law. Think of totalitarian regimes such as Russia and China where it's never quite clear what you can say about the government, and where the worry that saying a certain thing won't be tolerated inhibits saying it. Even in liberal democracies with strong traditions of freedom of speech there is the category of legally regulated hate speech, but it is not always clear in advance what sort of speech would be so categorized. And the worry that a given utterance would be so categorized inhibits those who might otherwise engage in language behavior at the borders of hate. Here the law is in effect secret because it won't be known until after the fact and judicial mooting whether a given uttering was illegal. This is sometimes thought to be a feature of common law—the law allowing citizens to sue each other, creating a situation where the defendant doesn't know that what's been done is illegal unless and until a judge finds for the plaintiff—in contrast to criminal law, where it is supposedly clear in advance what will count as a violation of law.[3]

But surely a law must be in the public interest in order to be a good law. And doesn't this require that the public be consulted in order for its interests to inform the content of the law? So doesn't this require that the public approve of and so know of the law? No and no. Even if a law must be in the public interest to be a good law, it doesn't follow that the best or only way to produce such a law is by public consultation in the deliberative production of law. Instead it might be better done by social experts and technocrats who privately poll or otherwise discover the public interest, and who thereafter are the only ones who know of the law.[4]

3. Famously Jeremy Bentham protested against the legitimacy of common law precisely for this feature. See his "Truth versus Ashhurst," in *The Works of Jeremy Bentham* (W. Tait, Edinburgh, 1843), vol. 5, pp. 233–37, especially p. 235.

4. For a more thorough mooting of this possibility see Alexander Guerrero, "National Insecurity: Democracy, War, and Popular Sovereignty," this volume; and Alexander Guerrero, "Against

But mustn't the law express the public will in order to be legitimate? Let's say yes. (Although the public will might be evil on a given matter and so not something that should find its way into law—more below). But doesn't this require the public to know of and expressly approve the law? No. Again, the public will might be discovered other than by collectively and overtly asking the public. And sometimes a law might more fully express the public will if it is arrived at by a process not involving public, deliberative democracy. This might happen where the public is distracted into misunderstanding its own will by demagoguery, superficialities of personality and appearance in a public figure, or local, temporary, unrepresentative events. As an example of that last phenomenon, in Canada capital punishment is illegal. The issue sometimes comes up, however, usually in response to some horrible crime that inflames the public. But the leaders of Canada's political parties have long had a little-known pact never to let legislation be proposed reinstituting capital punishment. They think it would not express the better angels of their citizens' natures—their true wills.[5] Likewise for the abortion issue. Abortion is legal under many conditions in Canada, and the parties' leaders try to head off private members' Parliament bills to make it illegal.

But if a law is secret, won't there be slippery slope dangers of its abuse? Mightn't a given clear case of something's being appropriately kept secret create a penumbra of endorsement extending to some less clear case? But then better not to have the category of secret law at all. Such slippery slopes won't necessarily occur, however. For there could be oversight by elected representatives who do not apprise the public of what they are doing. Besides, publicity of laws is no guarantee against slippery slopes. The public can become inured, can uncritically fail to make distinctions needed to block slides down the slope from good laws to bad; and in these instances perhaps better that matters be controlled by professionally critical thinkers habitually on guard against this sort of thing. At any rate, perhaps the best insurance against such things is good general education of those who will eventually have legislative power, and electing to these offices people of good character, broadly democratic and liberal values, and critical intelligence.[6]

Elections: The Lottocratic Alternative", *Philosophy and Public Affairs*, vol. 42 (2014), pp. 135–78.

5. I learned of this from my old Canadian Political Science professor, Hugh Thorburn, who for a generation trained students at Queen's University, many of whom became prominent in Canadian government and civil service.

6. In this I agree with Michael Skerker's chapter in this volume. A student of mine from Iran suggested to me that whether secret laws in a given country would be a good thing would depend on the character of the country. In Canada or the United States it might be acceptable to have the possibility of them because there is a strong tradition in these countries of respect for the public interest in formulating and administering law, a respect inscribed in the political nature of the citizens of such countries by their upbringing and education. But the possibility of secret laws would be dangerous in countries where these traditions are not well established.

But surely fairness, and so the ultimate legitimacy and goodness of the law, requires that the law be published in order to give people fair warning before they violate it and incur punishment?[7] Not necessarily. First, suppose we don't expect the law to deter. And suppose the reason for the law isn't to attempt deterrence. Instead it is to make legitimate the use of force to deal with behavior that we expect some people to attempt whether or not there are laws against it. In that case it's not clear that any sort of fair warning is required, especially if this would only make it more likely that these people would succeed.

Thus it is not always true that the main or only point of a law is to improve behavior by people coming to obey the law upon learning that it is the law (whether from respect for the institution of law, from agreement with a given law and its aim, or from fear of punishment). Rather, the means by which a law improves behavior can be by its authorizing officials to directly intervene in problematic people's behavior. A law might authorize officials to directly control the behavior of those whose behavior other, public laws are supposed to regulate. In extreme cases it might even authorize officials to incarcerate or kill those who would violate the public laws. Laws therefore don't necessarily operate by their publicity having a direct effect on their target population; they can also or instead operate by inducing officials to act to control the target population. The officials obey the secret law for the usual reasons people obey a law; but the people on whom they act behave a certain way by being compelled to so behave.

There is a precedent in the literature for a less radical version of this idea: Meir Dan-Cohen points out that our legal culture is consistent with the possibility of some rules being known (audible, in Dan-Cohen's terminology) only to judges and enforcers of law (decision rules)—while other rules (conduct-rules)—are known (audible) to everyone.[8] The decision rules may contain information about, for example, leniency in sentencing. If this information was widely known, it would make the conduct-rules less likely to be followed, for people would expect lenient sentencing and so wouldn't fear punishment enough to comply with the law. (Perhaps a good conduct-rule would be "don't steal," while a good decision rule might be "give lenient sentences to those who stole from need.") And yet it might be a good thing that the laws constituted by conduct-rules be followed. This would justify the acoustic separation of which Dan-Cohen speaks. That is, it would justify keeping it a secret from the general public just what the decision rules are. Apparently even now many laws are so worded as to give instruction not to citizens, but to judges. For example the law against murder is in effect phrased

7. Think again of Bentham, "Truth versus Ashhurst" (1843); or Lon L. Fuller, "Positivism and Fidelity to Law—A Reply to Professor Hart", *Harvard Law Review*, vol. 71 (1958), pp. 630–51; or of the view that it is of the essence of law that it be promulgated, a view expressed in Thomas Aquinas, *Summa Theologica*, Question 90, article 4, corpus, in Saint Thomas Aquinas, *The Treatise on Law* (R. J. Henle, S.J., ed. & trans., Notre Dame: Notre Dame University Press, 1993), p. 145.

8. See Meir Dan-Cohen, "Decision Rules and Conduct Rules: On Acoustic Separation in Criminal Law," *Harvard Law Review*, vol. 97, no. 3, January 1984, pp. 625–77, esp. pp. 625–37.

like this: "the act of murder shall be punished by a sentence of no less than ten years in prison"; it is not worded like this: "No one shall commit murder."[9]

But surely for something to exist and operate in a society qua law, the law must be publicly known? Otherwise, the role this thing is playing isn't that of a law. This is false, partly for the reasons just discussed, but also because most of (what everyone would regard as paradigm) law is nonpublic in the following senses: most people don't know exactly what the laws are, people who violate laws don't know if or exactly when they will be arrested, and they don't know exactly what punishments they will face. The last fact is partly from ignorance of the rules about punishment, and partly because often the matter requires a judge's or jury's decision in order to become determinate. This is true not just of common law, where it obviously holds, but also criminal law. After all, criminal law provides a range of possible punishments and then the judge's or jury's judgment chooses from that range. Moreover, most laws are not exactly understood by most people. Some laws are so complex that some people could not understand them even with instruction. And most people don't know exactly what happens to most law violators.

And yet no one can argue that it is a moral surprise when they are found to have broken a good law, when they are arrested, and when they face a punishment. (It is at best strategically surprising, and for laws designed to effect control of terrorists the element of strategic surprise is a necessary part of effective enforcement.) That is, moral outrage from those accosted by agents of the law when it is good law is not appropriate, and is untypical. Remarkably, when the laws are good one can work out what they are—by which I mean what is in their spirit, not their exact letter[10]—by asking what they ought to be. One doesn't need to be told. And it is one's sense of what the laws ought to be that informs one's expectations and one's sense of justice about the matter.

Lon Fuller claims the explanation of public knowledge of the law is that some people trouble to learn the law explicitly and their expertise percolates into society broadly.[11] I'm suggesting a different epistemology for public legal knowledge, one more a priori. Moreover, Fuller's theory of our knowledge of laws requires that people can simply choose to inform themselves of them. But in the case of secret laws this would be impossible. For even those permitted or obliged to learn of the laws as, say, members of oversight panels, would be sworn to secrecy—they could not be a source of knowledge for the public. And if I'm right that secret laws can be legitimate, then neither does their legitimacy require that people in the general public have the right to become informed about them by means of

9. Thanks to Claire Finkelstein and Sheldon Wein for pointing this out to me.

10. One reason one can't always work out their exact letter owes to a phenomenon Sheldon Wein pointed out to me: even in a society of saints there would be the possibility of dispute about who has a right to what, and the fact who has the right is in part rendered determinate by the process of a judge adjudicating the matter and coming to a decision. Until then there is no fact about what the right is and so no fact to be known either.

11. See Lon Fuller, *The Morality of Law* (New Haven, CT: Yale University Press, 1964).

inspection, whether directly by themselves, or indirectly from experts who became such by inspection. Fuller's epistemology would, however, go some way toward explaining the public's general knowledge of morality, justice, and the basic ideas of what the rule of law involves, the things from which I've been saying the public infers its legal obligations and its expectations about what laws exist. But part of the explanation is also that the public's attitudes and dispositions are part of what constitute morality and justice.

Indeed, because of all of this, terrorists, like everybody else, know in some sense what the general law is and what it ought to be. And they don't even disagree with us about this: they agree that what they do is ordinarily wrong. They don't even think it ought to be legal for them to do what they do in pursuit of their cause. They just think their cause justifies breaking laws. Of course they don't agree with every law of, say, the United States or Canada; and they may want certain additional laws, for example, about the behavior of women. But they agree in general that there should be laws against killing, theft, torture, slander, libel, etc. And they are generally in favor of the rule of law, even where they disagree about particular laws. In effect, even those punished by a secret law would probably satisfy the Hobbesian condition on the justice of punishment that the punished consent to their own punishment—they recognize the illegality of what they do, and the appropriateness of punishing it. They might have been prepared to sign a social contract enshrining these laws prior to finding themselves inclined to violate them. And a common motivation in terrorists is precisely resentment at the nonenforcement of laws by whose violation they are victim in the legally hypocritical and corrupt states in which they live.

There is an esoteric but plausible idea from Wittgenstein relevant to this issue. Before him it was thought that people learn things such as the rules of language or the laws of the land by being given some description of these things plus a few examples—of proper and improper language use or conduct in accord with the law—and then generalizing from this data to what behaviors the rules and laws require. Unfortunately, due to the phenomenon of the underdetermination of theory by data, any number of conjectures about what the rules and laws require are compatible with any finite set of examples. The examples cannot suffice to dictate how rightly to carry on from them. So it cannot be that this is how people learn the rules/laws, and this cannot be in what knowledge of them consists. Rather, "knowing the rules/laws" is just a matter of being disposed to carry on from the examples in ways that will not be objected to by the community whose rules and laws these are. What is involved is a prior shared tendency of people to carry on in the same ways from the same precedents. And this may—indeed, must—preexist instruction by example, else examples couldn't instruct.[12] So our agreeing to a practice can't be our literally following a law conceived as a verbal instruction. It's not like, when people behave law-abidingly, they do so purely in consequence of having the law books before them and running their finger under

12. For more on this reading of Wittgenstein, see Saul Kripke, *Wittgenstein on Rules and Private Language: An Elementary Exposition* (Cambridge, MA: Harvard University Press, 1982).

the sentences describing the law as if following a recipe. Even when it seems like this is all that's going on—for example, when trying to follow difficult rules about income tax—in the background there is a shared tendency, itself not learnable by induction over example cases, that makes possible this sort of legal behavior by close reading of the relevant law.

I am a law-abiding citizen. Yet I do not know a single law of my country. I couldn't recite a single one of them. (What about the law against jaywalking? Don't we all know that? Well, what is that law? Is it "don't cross except at intersections?" "Don't cross except within five feet of an intersection?" What if it's a really long block? Is the law "except where a block is over one third of a mile long, don't cross except at an intersection?" I would be astounded if any of you know the answer.)

And yet in spite of my ignorance of the laws, I am inveterately law-abiding. I have the ability to behave legally. We're all like this. But as we have just seen, this is not by virtue of our having had the law proclaimed to us and our having heard, understood, recalled, and complied with the proclamations. Therefore it cannot be a condition on something being the law that such an instruction is made public—proclaimed—as an explicit rule. Rather, a law is in place if (1) it has been enshrined in the right way,[13] whether we know of this or not; (2) we would all generally go on in the same way (in our making judgments of what is and isn't legal, not necessarily in the sense of invariantly complying with such judgments, something we each might sometimes have reason not to do); and (3) we would not be morally astonished to discover that there is a law written down about this somewhere, that some due process made it official. As for the jaywalking law, we are all generally able to go on in its spirit—we get the idea that if you recklessly walk into traffic you are at fault, and we can evaluate arguments about what would and wouldn't count as such recklessness.

I suspect a lot of the controversy about nonpublic laws isn't really about their secrecy. It's about their content, that is, about whether they are correct laws, that is, about how we ought all to carry on given how we've carried on in the past, and given the new circumstances we face. The controversy is really about a failure of national consensus concerning the correctness of the behaviors these laws authorize.

We've all heard it alleged how President Bush authorized torture, how Presidents Bush and Obama authorized using technology to spy on citizens' communications, how both ordered that this technology and this use be kept from the public—how they in effect made it illegal to disclose these things. (These are the laws Edward Snowden allegedly violated.) And now, after the whistles have been blown, there is outrage.

But imagine instead that President Bush had secretly outlawed torture rather than permitted it. Or that Presidents Bush and Obama had secretly outlawed

13. Think of H.L.A. Hart's idea that, as Sheldon Wein explained it to me, "every legal system consists of both primary rules (ordinary laws), which get their validity by being made in the proper way, and secondary rules (rules about how one makes, enforces, and interprets primary rules), which get their validity by being recognized as the appropriate way of making primary rules."

using technology to monitor electronic communication between citizens. We'd all be applauding; we'd think these were wonderful uses of presidential authority in war, good secret laws, laws rightfully kept secret in order not to embolden the enemy, and so on. Unless of course there had been a sequence of even worse 9-11s, and evidence that if only the presidents had required torture and spying, all of it could have been prevented. Then we'd be castigating them now for their failures of moral courage, for their excessively tenderhearted reluctance to order the hard things, to be our Dark Knights, to take moral stain upon themselves in order to keep us all safe.

But surely if we all think and act publicly as if the law was one way when secretly it's another, then our law, our nation, and we ourselves insofar as we are represented by and think of ourselves as endorsing our law and our nation, are hypocrites. And isn't hypocrisy in law a decisive objection to something's being good law? Relatedly, the law is an ambassador for the people whose law it is, and shouldn't they know what laws their system is creating? Worse, if their system's laws are conflicted, isn't that a problem for citizen self-concept and self-identity?

I begin with the hypocrisy issue. I suggest that, first, arguably what's going on isn't hypocrisy; and second, if it is hypocrisy, it's not bad in this instance. Suppose American public policy forbids torture; suppose President Bush secretly authorizes waterboarding. There is a dispute about whether that's torture. Let's say it is. Is America now hypocritical? Not necessarily. America may in effect be saying, "we think torture is generally bad, we think it shouldn't be used in ordinary times, we think we should all work to bring about a world in which there are no times so extraordinary that its use would ever be called for; but for now, in this imperfect world, in these extraordinary times, we'll use it if we have to." This is a consistent message, and it is not trying to have anything both ways. Nor would the following message be hypocrisy: "we can use torture for our cause because our cause is good, but you can't use it for your cause because your cause isn't good." Since in one case the ends justify the means and in the other, not, the cases are different and there is no hypocrisy.

But suppose the message is literally, "do as we say, not as we do," with the acknowledgment that we are proposing to use torture secretly in exactly the same circumstances as we publicly forbid it. This might be hypocrisy. But is it necessarily bad? Suppose torture would in fact advance our cause, and suppose our cause is good. And suppose torture would only advance our cause if we were generally against it, and generally seen to be against it (even if we're not in fact against it in this very limited case). Then our multiple, conflicting messaging could be a good thing. It allows those who oppose torture to endorse us for our public stance on the issue. It allows those who think an exception needs to be made in these extraordinary times to endorse us for our secret realpolitik—secret in this sense: it is suspected that we engage in the practice, there is some evidence of this but nothing conclusive, it is officially denied, and those of us who do engage in it on behalf of our state are legally barred from revealing that we do this. Our secret-ish realpolitik makes our enemies fear us—which, incidentally, makes it less likely we'll actually have to use torture, because the suspicion that it might be used will be a deterrent—and our public stance makes our potential allies more disposed to ally with us, since they like to think of themselves as people against torture; and their allying is for a good cause, and, incidentally, also makes the need for torture less likely, because now the enemy sees it faces overwhelming force and so will more likely give up. For all of these reasons, consistency is overrated as a feature of good law. (Perhaps the reason it is overrated is that it is assumed people will read conflicting elements of law as summing to unfollowable instructions—"do x, but don't do x," a paralyzing command. But in fact they uptake different parts of the law in different ways, prioritizing one part in one context, a different part in another.)

Something similar might be said about whether consistency is always good and necessary for the ambassadorial function of law, and for our relation to it in our self-conception and self-identity as citizens: grayed out, ambiguous, ambivalent, or even conflicted identities aren't necessarily always bad.[14] In fact, tolerance for vagueness, ambiguity, and even contradiction might sometimes be as much a mark of good law and politics as it is of a psychologically healthy person.

I said a good logically private law has the property that, were it to become public, it would wrongly be voted away—the electorate would demand that it be rescinded. But surely if a law would be voted away were it to become public, it must by that very fact be a bad law? Not necessarily. After all, sometimes the public in a moment of clarity messages to its government that it wants something done—wants a war won, for example. But it is known that the public can experience fading resolve and weakness of will during war. This is why in war the government invariably propagandizes the enemy as more evil than they really are, the war as going better than it really is, the number of casualties as less than they really are. Now suppose that in the public's initial moment of clarity the president enacts laws that have a good chance of winning the war. In order to protect the public from its own failure of will perhaps the laws should be kept secret. Paradigms are laws suspending rights to privacy, public trial, and freedom from torture.

Received wisdom is that 9/11 is an example: the nation is attacked and the president, with popular support from a terrified population, announces that he will handle it, but of course, he can't say all the things he'll be doing because full disclosure would aid the enemy. The president then decrees to national security agents that it is legally permissible for them to spy on all citizens (in hopes of catching terrorists among us); and that it is illegal to tell citizens that the technology exists to make this possible and is being so used (for then terrorists could evade the technology, and the citizenry would lose the resolve embodied in their Commander-in-Chief and insist that the violations of citizen privacy stop). Further, the president decrees that it is legally obligatory secretly to try citizens for conspiracy to commit terrorist acts where the convicting evidence would, were it to become public, make citizens aware of the foregoing technology and its use. And the president decrees that, for similar reasons, it is legally permissible to secretly impose punishment on those convicted—for example, death by drone

14. I say this contra Christopher Kutz, "The Repugnancy of Secret Law" (ms., offered for consideration at the CERL conference mentioned in note 1, above.)

for those tried in absentia, where this is the only way to prevent a terrorist act; or incarceration without habeas corpus—that is, without right to a public trial and demonstration of guilt.

Note that there are logically possible logically private laws that don't involve coercion, torture, or any other such negative thing. Suppose Presidents Bush and Obama had instead used executive authority to nonviolently eliminate all conflict, making it part of secret law to pay off terrorists with enormous amounts of money instead of using these resources on kinetic weapons in physical wars; or had used the money in expensive and secret social work, psychotherapy, education, subsidies, and so on, proceeding on the assumption that most of America's enemies are such because they are afraid; ignorant; ill-educated; traumatized from past conflict; hopeless; under-affiliated; confused by self-defeating, self-oppressing ideologies infused in them by problematically illiberal cultures; under-schooled in the self-liberating tools of critical thinking; or justly resentful of past hegemonic actions by Western powers. Suppose the presidents had decided to deal with all of this with "love bombs," not real bombs, soft skills rather than weapons. And suppose the public would never have accepted this, thinking that the attacks on America were unjustified and should be met with retaliation and revenge, not paternalistic indulgence, therapy, restitution, and constructive nation-building. Again, there would have been an argument for making these sorts of legal initiatives private. After all, were they publicized, the public would have objected; and unscrupulous people would have tried to horn in on the benefits. So it is not just prima facia vile things that may have to be stealthed in secret laws for the laws to be efficacious. This means the issue of secret laws is not itself a left/right issue, for there could be secret laws preferred by left-wingers and bleeding hearts, others preferred by right-wingers and hawks.

Now some further analysis of the possibility that good law need not be able to pass public scrutiny. I said sometimes laws must be secret to protect those whom they are meant to benefit from their own weakness of will. Here the secrecy functions much in the same way as, in the Greek myth, do the instructions Ulysses gives to his crew-mates. Ulysses wants to hear the song of the Sirens. But he knows the song would seduce him into crashing his sailboat on the rocks, killing everyone on board. So he orders his men to tie him to the mast, plug their ears, and not free him until the boat is safely past the Sirens. This may seem like arranging unfreedom, for Ulysses will not be free to take the action that would result in his crashing his boat, even though he will want to. But arguably his preparations in fact make him freer and give him strength of will: in forgoing the freedom to sail toward the rocks he gives himself freedom to hear the Sirens' song in safety. And of course at the outset he would prefer being tied and hearing the song to not being tied, hearing the song, and crashing. So in the end he gets exactly what he wanted at the outset. True, while hearing the song he wants desperately to be untied and to sail to the Sirens on the rocks. But this is precisely the self-destructive impulse from which he has saved himself.[15]

15. The classic treatment of this idea is Jon Elster, *Ulysses and the Sirens: Studies in Rationality and Irrationality* (Cambridge: Cambridge University Press, 1979).

In the case of national security, we know we want procedures that will keep us safe, but we also know we'll want to undo them if we ever see them in action. At the outset we want security more than freedom, yet we know that once we see the freedom infringing policies in practice, our resolve will fade and we'll prefer freedom to security. So, like Ulysses, and judging now that even then security would be more important, we take steps to ensure that we'll never be in a position to undo the initiatives—we "tie ourselves to the mast" by allowing the result of the initiatives to be stealthed. So even though we'd undo secret laws the president might enact if we were offered the option, that doesn't mean the laws are illegitimate; for they express our will.

It might be objected that nothing like this explicitly happened for President Bush's response to the events of 9/11. Americans didn't say, "protect us from terrorists, even to the extent of enacting secret laws to save us from our own weak wills." On the other hand, Americans are governed by the Constitution, a document in force unless two-thirds of the House or of state legislatures vote to overturn it, which did not happen. And it contains a clause that, arguably, authorizes the president to do what he thinks necessary to defend the country. So in accepting the Constitution Americans are in effect authorizing him to do that. And if he decides this requires secret laws, then Americans have in effect authorized him in that, too. Just not explicitly. So again, all of this expresses the will of Americans. And again, even though Americans might try to rescind the laws if they came to know of them, that doesn't mean the laws are now illegitimate.

There is, of course, a discussion to be had about just how blanket legitimate authorizations can be. Must we have envisioned that one option the president might use would be secret laws in order for his enacting them to be an expression of our will? I'm not sure. But even if once we discover that he's done this we would want to amend the Constitution to preclude such laws, that wouldn't necessarily entail that his enacting secret laws before this was illegitimate or did not express our will as it then was. For the goodness of the Constitution, and of any given law, aren't things that need to be revisited each time they are applied in order to be legitimately applied and to express our will. Reconsideration is required only upon extensive experience of problems with them.

The Ulysses scenario was a case where, in making a plan to advance a current desire of ours that we endorse—the desire to hear the Sirens—we seek to prevent being befallen by a desire we do not now endorse—the desire to sail toward the rocks. The plan will result in our will being expressed even if it will also result in our going against a new desire we expect to have. But there are other sorts of scenarios in which we expect our desires to stay the same, and yet it still might express our will to put in place a plan that will have us go against those desires. These are sometimes called paradoxical choice situations. Here our irrevocably committing to doing an action would advance our desires, but our actually performing the action to which we have committed would not. Suppose we are Americans who believe it would most benefit us to live in a nation which, if ever it is attacked, will respond at the dictates of the president—we think this will make attack less likely because enemies will fear his vengeful-mindedness. But we also believe that, once attacked, our judgment would be better than his on what should be done—he'd make war by means including the suspension of principles we favor (the right to a public trial, the publicity of laws, and so on), while we would preserve the principles. Here, it would advantage us to be committed to matters being governed by the president, but it would not advantage us to actually have him govern post-attack. Would it be rational for us to form the commitment? And would it be rational for us to act in accord with it if we are attacked, allowing the President to govern? Or would it be more rational for us to violate the commitment, seeking to oppose him? Which would best express our true will?

Some will say that we should commit, for that would be to our advantage earlier, and that we should violate the commitment if we're attacked, for that would be to our advantage later. But if we intend to violate the commitment, arguably we can't rationally sincerely make it; so that advice is unfollowable.

Others will say that, since we should violate the commitment, we cannot rationally make it, for it cannot be rational to commit to something it would be irrational to do. So we should not make the commitment, and this means there will be no occasion of having to decide whether to act on it.

I suggest, following David Gauthier,[16] that there is a case for making the commitment, since that will best advance our desires (in the sense of making them more likely to be satisfied), and for acting on the commitment, even though acting on it will not advance our desires. It would be rational to act on it because it is rationally obligatory to fulfill any commitment it is to rational to make, and it is rational to make the commitment because doing so will advance our desires.

It would then be rational for us not to seek to undermine the president, refraining from trying to penetrate any secret laws he may enact, taking steps to prevent our accidentally discovering them, and refusing to publicize discoveries we may make. The idea is that an action is rational not in virtue of the fact that doing it would best serve our desires, but because disposing ourselves in some way to do the action would have this effect. Gauthier argues that is rational to do whatever maximizes our expected utility (advances our desires) to commit to doing even if doing it doesn't itself maximize—here the disposing takes the form of making a commitment, and making the commitment has good effects separate from those of acting on it. It makes our enemies even more afraid to attack, for they will know Americans will back their president.

I have elsewhere argued that there is a problem with Gauthier's view: if it's rational to form whatever disposition it advantages our desires to form and then to do whatever it advantages us to become disposed to do, after the nation is attacked, won't it advantage our desires to dispose ourselves to act on our own judgment instead of the president's? After all, that's still what we desire. And won't it then be rational for us to act against the president, since that has become what is advantaging for us to be disposed to do? So Gauthier's view can't really explain the possibility of rationally forming and fulfilling these sorts of commitments.

16. See David Gauthier, "Deterrence, Maximization and Rationality," *Ethics* 94 (1984): 474–95; and David Gauthier, *Morals by Agreement* (Oxford: Clarendon Press, 1986).

But I think there's a fix for this: the correct theory of rationality would have it that it's rational to do whatever it was maximizing to form a desire to do, whether or not the thing to be done was initially desired—here, our disposing ourselves to support the president if attacked takes the form of our undergoing an alteration in our desires, and altering them advances our initial desires even if acting on the new desires might not. For example, prospective attackers will be more fearful, because they will see that we now desire to support our president if attacked. We won't have to somehow make ourselves do this against our own desires; doing it will be exactly what we (have come to) desire, thus making it even more certain that it will be done. Should the nation be attacked, we will now support the president, since we will have undergone a change in our desires so that this is what we desire to do. And it would not advance these new desires to readopt the old ones, for the latter would have us do things we no longer desire to do. So unlike on Gauthier's rationale, on mine there would be no reason to backslide. Thus people would genuinely find it rational to support the president, including not trying to sleuth out secret laws.[17]

On the assumption that something is democratically grounded if it would be endorsed by the will of the people, and on the assumption that their will is whatever it would be rational for them to commit to given their desires, all of this would mean that secret laws might have democratically grounded legitimacy and would therefore not be objectionable on democratic values. If Gauthier's proposal can be repaired in its own terms, such laws are legitimate even if they go against our current desires, provided that those desires justified us in a commitment to a process—presidential decision-making—that could have resulted in them. While if my variant on Gauthier's proposal works, if, through the operation of the variant's conception of rationality, we now have desires that are expressed by the existence of the laws—because we've come to desire to see the president's decisions prevail—then the laws are democratically legitimate even if their existence would not have expressed the desires we had before disposing ourselves toward the laws by undergoing a revision in our desires. For it was rational to have undergone the revision. So the new desires are now ones appropriate to have. And the secret laws are legitimate because their existence expresses legitimate desires.

But suppose a law is one citizens would vote to rescind were they to learn of it, and the government keeps the law secret because it thinks the law to be in the public interest. Wouldn't this be excessively paternalistic of government?[18] Not where I'm advocating secret laws, since citizens there in effect ask for them in the pre-attack situation. And given the foregoing points about how this in effect

17. Thanks to Claire Finkelstein and Jamaal Hyder for asking about and helping me to more fully elucidate the relevance of Gauthier's ideas here, and to contradistinguish them from the ideas figuring in the Ulysses case. On the approaches of Gauthier and myself to the rationality of forming and fulfilling commitments, see my "Assuring, Threatening, a Fully Maximizing Theory of Practical Rationality, and the Practical Duties of Agents," *Ethics*, vol. 123, no. 4 July (2013), pp. 625–56.

18. Thanks to Sharon Lloyd for the question.

empowers and expresses the citizenry's true will, we shouldn't see this as the government paternalistically overriding the will of its citizens.

But situations change—laws that once were of moment become obsolete, the terrorist threat is overcome—and it's time for things to return to normal. Or maybe there is still a threat but the nation matures in its conception of it, sees it more proportionately. After all, only 3,000 people lost their lives, the number of terrorists is small as is their capacity to harm us, perhaps we can afford to have the nation's agenda be less focussed on the threat, maybe we overreacted, maybe our war-conception of how to respond is only making things worse, etc., etc. These changes, whether of fact or of our attitudes to the facts, mean that secret laws properly have a half-life—their correctness tends to decay.

But doesn't that rebut the rationale for them in the first place, the rationale that secrecy is required to prevent reconsideration that would undermine the resoluteness needed to attain our original goals? No. For that rationale only justified steps to make the laws persistent on certain assumptions about what the facts of the situation were. If the facts change (for example, if the threat that the laws were invented to deal with has been eliminated), or if the facts weren't as originally thought (for example, if it turns out that the threat was never factually as bad as it seemed, or if our reaction was out of proportion)—then of course the laws should change, and the justification for stealthing them to preserve them evaporates.

There is an irony here: insofar as secret laws tend to work, they tend eventually to be vilified. The secret laws allowing torture of enemies and spying on citizens, for example, might eliminate the terrorist threat directly by means of the legally enabled behavior of officials in law enforcement, government, and the military against the enemy—the officials torture and spy, and so prevail. Or the laws might succeed by creating a mindset that encourages officials to behave boldly and yet in ways perhaps strictly legal even without the laws. Officials feel like, whatever they must do to eliminate the threat, they won't face reprisals—"if we're now allowed to torture," they think, "surely we're allowed to do this other thing that's just short of torture," a thing there might naturally be some question about but which might yet have been okay by pre-threat laws. (I'm not sure how many of the interrogation methods the so-called torture memos authorized after 9/11 were ever used—perhaps only ones that would have been at least borderline acceptable even without the memos.) Either way, the laws will later tend not only to get renounced, but also retro-actively condemned as overreactive, unnecessary, or otherwise under-pretexted and pernicious. Part of this is owing to the fact that people tend to overreact to unexpected bad events and then, once they digest them, see them more proportionately and recriminate upon the initial reaction. Another part owes to the fact that initially one worries the bad thing is a harbinger of worse things. But if the extreme steps initially taken reduce the likelihood that further bad things will happen, the harbinger argument disappears and again the initial steps seem like overreactions.

At any rate, the fact that the laws had to be enacted and enforced secretly doesn't mean they should be permanent. Trying to save a population from being weak-willed is one thing. Failing to recognize that its will has rationally changed is another. Leaders have a duty to periodically review secret laws and ask whether there is still good reason for them. In this, secret laws are like any other laws.

Next I want to explore a concern raised by Christopher Kutz.[19] Kutz says: "I argue that a distinction between two forms of secrecy—between direct secrecy, where the fact of secrecy is itself known, and meta-secrecy, where the secret itself is unknown—provides a key to the puzzle. When the state makes clear the bounds of its secrets, it remains committed to a conception of limits to the ruler's power, and hence to one of the central bases of legitimacy. Meta-secrecy obscures the limits of state power, and so undermines the state's claim to legitimacy." Aren't my logically private laws instances of meta-secrecy and therefore the illegitimate artifacts of a government itself illegitimate?

Well, some of them may be instances of meta-secrecy, but I don't think they go too far, for I don't think meta-secrecy is the thing Kutz thinks. I agree that the state loses legitimacy if it accepts no limits on its power. But the mere fact that not only does the state have secrets, but it is a secret that it has secrets, is not automatically an overreach of power. After all, it is fully consistent with there being oversight by elected officials, the judiciary, and branches of government that were designed to ride herd on each other. Further limitations are imposed by the requirements of re-election for all levels of government, so that people in the know get voted out, and new people get voted in who might vote differently about whether to continue secret policies, and who might demand penalties for their predecessors if their actions are found indefensible. Apparently Kutz thinks that when laws are secret—not just in content, but in their very existence—the law issuer has no limit on its power. But as we've just seen, the two issues are separate.

Perhaps it is true that, as Wittgenstein might tell us, there is only such a thing as something legitimately being a law if there is a distinction between someone saying it's a law and it's actually being a law. And a state features rule of law rather than rule by decree only if there is a distinction between the president saying that something is a law and it's actually being a law. His mere saying that it's a law can't make it so. But these conditions are met by the fact that the lawmaker in my picture is duly elected, is enacting secret law by provisions in the Constitution—itself democratically created—and has those laws examined by the judiciary and oversight committees from elected bodies of government, is accountable to these bodies, and so on. This means it is not sufficient for something becoming law that the president so decrees it; all these other hurdles must be overcome. Of course if we take all these hurdles and call them the government, then if the government says something's a law, then it is. But this is exactly as it should be and cannot be called the state accepting no limits on its power. Rather, its accepting limits is its producing laws by a process that includes these checks and balances.

Similar considerations afford a reply to objections along Wittgensteinian lines to the very idea of a logically private law. For example, Julian Sanchez objects that, when the president proposes to do something and consults the Office of Legal Counsel (OLC) to see if it is legal, he can keep asking different people in that

19. See Kutz, "The Repugnancy of Secret Law."

office until one of them tells him it's legal. So there is really no constraint from law on the president. *He* decides what's lawful, by waiting until he likes an answer.[20] Likewise Claire Finkelstein worries that there is merely the illusion of constraint in the process the executive uses to review its own orders, when really it's like one hand giving the other money. And if there is any constraint in this process it is only self-constraint, which is no constraint at all.[21]

But I suspect Sanchez and Finkelstein underestimate the degree to which there is external constraint on the president's impulses. It's not really like he can keep asking people in the OLC until someone says he can do what he proposes. For it's not guaranteed anyone will ever say he can do it, and even if someone will, that doesn't mean their saying it is ungrounded and so not in principle regulated by some constraint. Instead, things would be fine if they went like this: The president asks, "Am I allowed to order secret spying (or waterboarding, or whatever)?" and his counsel consults the Constitution, or asks someone at OLC to consult it, and they say, "Yes, Mr. President, you can do whatever you want in defending the nation." But if the Constitution had said otherwise then his counselors would have said otherwise, too (probably). And if it looked like what the president was proposing had nothing to do with defending the nation (e.g., the waterboarding was really to get information out of a business competitor of a friend of the president's), then (probably) someone would have told him he can't do that. So there is constraint. And it is not mere self-constraint. The constraint is provided by the externally determined drawing of a perimeter within which the president may act at will, and, in so acting, make it that something is law.

Sanchez and Finkelstein have similar worries about the reluctance of the judiciary to obstruct decisions of the president in defense of the country. But there are similar replies: the judiciary relies on the Constitution, which it reads as giving the president certain powers in these situations. This is not the judiciary refusing to hold him to rule of law. It is the judiciary believing that he has the legal right to so maneuver.

Speaking as an external observer of governance in the United States, I note that while there are all sorts of rules and institutions supposedly informing and constraining what the president can do, what it comes down to is this: if those in the ruling classes in the various branches of government don't object, then he can do what he wants. But that's obviously not the same as saying he can just do what he wants, for he has the ruling classes to answer to. In fact, there is no system of governance of which this is not true. For it is not laws that ultimately constrain people. Only people constrain people.

20. Julian Sanchez, "Wittgenstein, Private Language, and Secret Law", *Cato at Liberty* blog, http://www.cato.org/blog/wittgenstein-private-language-secret-law Nov. 1, 2011, last accessed May 30, 2018.

21. Finkelstein worried about this in her "On the Very Idea of Secret Laws: National Security and the Rule of Law," presented at the 2014 Penn Faculty Retreat. I don't know if she still stands by this worry. But either way it's a concern worth mooting.

In sum, the president is not acting without the constraint of law. There is real constraint afforded by the OLC: if he can't find someone to agree with his proposed conduct, then it's unlawful. And there is oversight by judges, congressional committees, and so on. And the president will eventually be replaced, by due process, by someone who might revoke his orders, or even punish him for malfeasance.

Of course Sanchez and Finkelstein know all of this. I suspect therefore that their real objection is that the constraints on the president are not *timely*—he can have things done and only have to pass scrutiny later—by oversight committees, by his successors, and so on. And by then it is too late. I acknowledge this concern, but I'm not sure secrecy is the problem. For something similar can happen for any part of government that is required to take action in haste, including parts that operate transparently. And arguably the whole point of the privileges given the president by the Constitution is to allow him to be able to shoot first and be asked questions later. The alternative of fighting wars by the method of committee is too plodding.

It is also worth speculating that, if the president is given the right to do what he wants in defense of the realm by the Constitution, then in such cases, his dictate *is* the law. He is an exception to the idea that something cannot come to be the law by someone saying it's the law. Or more precisely, he is an exception to the idea that the difference between rule of law and rule by a man is that in rule by law, no man makes the law. In these cases, some man does. But of course only with a lot of background rule-of-law conditions in place making this possible and legitimate.

Now a few more words about Kutz's position. Perhaps Kutz thinks full legitimacy requires full accountability—accountability to everyone whom the law is to govern. Now in one sense the process I've just described yields that very thing—we elect people who elect people who oversee secret law for us, so there is accountability all the way down. What there is not is every person to whom the laws are to apply perusing the laws and voting on them. But that is not a reasonable ambition of legitimate government. For one thing it's impossible—see above on the competence of people as existing under laws. And for another thing it's not conceptually necessary to the distinction between legitimate and illegitimate law. As the philosopher, Hilary Putnam, tells us, what is needed for distinctions marked in language to be real is the possibility of expertise upon them. But not everyone needs to be an expert: only some people, with others disposed to defer to their judgment. He calls this the distribution of linguistic labor. The world is divided into natural kinds, for example—substances such as gold and water—and we have words for these kinds; but we are not all expert on what counts as instances of each kind, and so on what instances deserve to be called by the names that are the words for those kinds. I can't tell the difference between gold and fool's gold, but an expert can, and we all recognize that there are or could be such experts. And because of these factors, the distinction between those natural kinds is a real distinction in my language. The same for genuine and non-genuine law, good genuine law and bad genuine law. What makes it true that something the president decrees to be a law actually is a law is that it is a law only if it passes oversight by the foregoing institutions. And some of those are operated by experts on the constitutionality of prospective laws. Moreover, all of those bodies, the president included, are accountable to tests for something being not just a genuine law but a good one, one in the public interest. So here too there is a distinction between the president saying something is a good law and its actually being one. And none of this requires explicit consulting of every person to whom a law is to apply.[22]

At least the foregoing is true provided we are talking about matters whose nature is not constituted by collective opinion about them. If there is a criterion for something's being x, and if it is possible for several people to be experts on whether the criterion for something's being x is met, and if the criterion for something's being x is not everyone's thinking it's x, nor the majority's thinking it's x, then it isn't true that everyone needs to vote that something is x for it to be x. If legitimate laws are like this, then it isn't true that something is a legitimate law only if everyone voted to make it a legitimate law. But of course, the possibility of secret laws raises this very question about the legitimacy of laws. In the next Section I consider more fully, and in the context of the democratic conception of sovereignty, whether laws can be legitimate only if voted on by everyone.

VI. SOVEREIGNTY, LOGICALLY PRIVATE LAWS, AND SECRET LAWS FROM OTHER BRANCHES OF GOVERNMENT AND SOCIETAL INSTITUTIONS

On then to some reflections on the relation between secret laws and sovereignty. In a democratic society the citizens are the sovereign, in two senses: laws are to serve their interests (rather than, say, the king's), and something is a law only if the citizens so decree, whether directly by referendum, or indirectly by electing representatives to make judgments and vote for it. In secret law, arguably the interest of citizens is sovereign—the laws are supposed to be in the collective interest. And if the laws are created by people voted for by the citizens, then arguably the citizens decree them, at least indirectly. Especially if all elected officials maneuver in ways constrained by the Constitution.

But secret laws are an extreme instance of the more general fact that what would be in the interest of citizens, and what they do or would vote for, can come apart. And since it could happen that citizens make mistakes and fail to vote for the laws that are in their interest, it appears that we have conflicting criteria of the democratic legitimacy of a law. John Stuart Mill resolved the conflict in this way: he thought that, sooner or later, if laws are decided by the direct vote of those who have interests at stake in them, the result will be laws that serve their interests.

22. Note that all of this is separate from the issue mooted above of how people come to know of the law. That legal facts depend on the possibility of there being such a thing as an expert about what is law does not entail that people come to know of laws only by consulting experts; nor does it entail that every person knows of the law.

And many theorists of legitimate government think that the only guarantee that laws will be in the interest of citizens is the requirement that citizens be the ones who decide laws by direct voting.

Arguably the system we in fact have represents a compromise between the interest test and the citizen vote test for the democratic legitimacy of laws: it recognizes that laws should reflect the interests of citizens, but it also recognizes that not all citizens are always the best judges of their own interests and how to serve them. For citizens vary in the time they have to pay attention to issues, their capacity to understand them, the soundness of their judgment about them, and so on. As a partial solution to these problems we have representative democracy. Decisions are made not by referendum, with each person voting on each issue. Instead, decisions are made by representatives elected for their perceived possession of the character traits, values, and knowledge that would make them good curators of the interests of citizens. The fact that in our system some people are empowered to enact secret laws can be seen as just the logical extreme of this compromise—these people have been elected for their presumptively good judgment and for their commitment to the interests of citizens, and have been elected to offices in a governmental system presumptively required to act in the interests of citizens; and sometimes this is thought to require secret law, especially where the very publicity of law and the process resulting in it would compromise the public interest.

I suggested that, if the Constitution gives the president the right to enact secret laws, then since the Constitution was voted into place, as was the president, democratic legitimacy flows from the people, to the Constitution and president, thence to the laws. But how far can such legitimacy flow? Could the president order others to create whatever secret laws they deem necessary but also order these people not to tell him what they are? Perhaps he wants deniability; or he fears capture and doesn't want knowledge the enemy might wring out of him. Would these laws be democratically legitimate?[23] On the one hand, (let's say) the Constitution makes the president the ultimate (even if constrained) authority in these circumstances—the "Decider in Chief." Arguably then the president fails his constitutional duty if he deputizes others to decide secret laws. On the other hand, if he picks people of good character, people he expects to express his values, to respect the Constitution, and so on, and if he gives them broad guidelines he wants followed in their choosing of laws, then arguably he's just being a good delegator, an effective executive; and, again, the resulting secret laws have democratic legitimacy.

The president's enacting secret laws could be democratically legitimate because both he and the Constitution that regulates him were democratically created. But there are other sorts of officials in other sorts of government structures who were voted for, officials and structures permitted or required by the Constitution to

23. My thanks to Vaughn Black for this question.

engage in their characteristic functions. Could this ever give *those officials* the right or duty to maneuver in secret in ways that would mean we are tacitly governed by de facto secret laws in their respective domains?[24]

In America, several institutions comprise the democratic corpus, each charged with offering checks and balances against the others: the executive branch, composed of the president and the cabinet; the judicial branch, composed of the Supreme Court and lower federal appellate and district courts; the legislative branch, composed of the House of Representatives and the Senate; the Fourth Estate comprising journalists; the police, prosecutors, and ordinary judges; arguably the military, comprised of generals, the joint chiefs, and so on; and perhaps even the defense industry—the so-called military-industrial complex—comprised of private corporations some of whom are virtually branches of government due to getting the bulk of defence contracts and having security clearances, with a mutuality of influence between them and the official government through lobbying, the employment by the defence industry of former government employees and vice versa, plus the shared recognition that America and its businesses are closely allied in interests, actions and consequences. I suspect that each of these institutions—the Congress, the judiciary, etc.—could, with democratic legitimacy, operate with secret pacts biasing society in various directions, this in effect comprising the creation of logically private laws.

For example, suppose the members of the Supreme Court conspire to use a certain principle to decide cases. They agree to always decide them in ways legally plausible given book law and precedent, but wherever those constraints leave latitude, agree to slant the decisions toward, say, wealth equalitarianism. They make a pact to never tell anyone about this, and like members of the French Resistance who sustained the appearance of cooperating with German invaders, they decide enough cases in ways against this principle that no one suspects its existence.

Arguably the resulting decisions would be law, since if what the Supreme Court decides isn't law then nothing is. And arguably it's legitimate law, at least case by case, since the Court ensures that all its decisions are defensible in ways standardly legally plausible. But the cumulative effect of these decisions is a pattern. Can individual legal rulings be questioned for contributing to a pattern? Does it matter whether the pattern forms with conscious intention? Certainly those who vote in appointing justices seek to detect patterns, both in recent decisions by the Court, and in past legal judgments by nominees to the Court; and they aim to vote in people whose legal opinions will create the patterns they favor. Arguably this is their prerogative. But when someone with an interest in how a judge or a whole court tends to vote detects a pattern, they do not thereby have a basis for invoking legal censure or punishment. What I'm talking about is a private pact among members of the Court to generate a pattern.

24. Something like what I'm about to develop is also suggested in Rudesill, "Coming to Terms with Secret Law"; but I apply the thought more radically, and to institutions additional to the ones he considers.

At any rate, for all I know, this is exactly what happens. There are only a handful of Supreme Court justices so it wouldn't be difficult for them to conspire. In fact it would be difficult for them not to influence each other, difficult for them not to form a school of thought. And if patterns in their decisions emerged simply from their inevitable mutual influence as colleagues, surely there could be no legal objection.

Moreover such activity would meet the conditions on logical privacy of law. For this sort of legal decision-making might be challenged were it to become public, its method of achieving its effects is stealth, there is a constitutional basis for the activities of this group; such goodness as may inhere in this sort of legal decision-making may depend on its secrecy, and its effects could be in the public interest. So it meets all conditions for being good logically private law.

Something similar could happen if the Fourth Estate—the community of journalists who comprise the free press protected by the Constitution—conspired to interpret certain recently passed laws in certain ways, and in so doing, in effect influenced what laws people in the country are following—a law interpreted this way, or a law interpreted that way. As with members of the Supreme Court making sure their decisions are legally plausible case by case even while having a predetermined judicial direction, so the media could ensure that they meet sound journalistic standards case by case even while taking the interpretation of the law as reported in a predetermined direction. After all, just as correct judicial decisions are underdetermined by book and case law, so every law is subject to interpretation in its reportage, and more than one way of reporting the law will be defensible by journalistic standards. (Besides, the Constitution only makes provision for freedom of the press; it doesn't tell the press how to interpret what it reports.) The result would be that journalists, in nuancing the reporting of laws in certain directions, are in effect making it the case that we are hearing of and following laws so nuanced—secretly nuanced laws.

Or suppose police officers or prosecutors conspire to do only token enforcement of certain laws, in effect making the law as implemented different from the laws on the books. Again, in each case let's say their decision is defensible—it's often gray whether a given case merits arrest or prosecution; it's just that in our thought experiment there is a prearranged cumulative tendency in play. Here each journalist, police officer, or prosecutor is doing something in her rightful purview. And maybe all of it is in the public interest, saving people from what would otherwise be their worst tendencies. And of course, the jig is up if any of this ever becomes public. So all of this has the defining characteristics of logically private law.

And again, for all I know, it's exactly what happens, in ways more or less deliberate and explicit. For all of these organizations hold conferences and conventions, their members drink together, they have friends in the business, they talk about the direction of the country, about how they think of the law, about whether they think certain laws are good, worth enforcing, and so on. They may not think of themselves as in some coordinated and Machiavellian way seizing control of the country. But perhaps they don't need to be thinking of their professional interactions as like this in order for what they do to count as the manufacture of secret law (or the secret manufacture of law).

What are the implications of all of this for sovereignty? Obviously it is even less plausible to demand that all of the foregoing sorts of decision be made instead by referendum: we're not going to have Supreme Court decisions by referendum, newspaper stories written by referendum, decisions on whether to arrest or prosecute this or that minor law violator by referendum, and so on. This is for any number of reasons, all decisive, for example, that there are too many of these issues for it even to be possible given limitations of time to have the nation vote on all of them, many of them require specialized expertise so that the nation voting to decide would be to wrongly let ignorance do the deciding, some of them involve processes designed to produce verdicts precisely when the public itself is divided on the issue and so when voting could not resolve the issues because it would just keep producing ties. So either these things cannot be democratically grounded, or it is not necessary to democratically grounded sovereignty that all decisions about law be fully directly publicly taken in the sense of figuring in governance by referendum.

But in what sense could the foregoing activities be democratically legitimate? How can they be seen to represent the collective will?

The question is urgent, both because the nation will continually face pretexts for secret law enacted by the executive branch, and because, as I've just suggested, so much of the operation of all the institutions of the democratic corpus probably feature elements of secret law in their operation and effect, whether by the conspiracy of the agents who operate these institutions, or by the cumulative effect of individual decisions of such agents even if not so expressly motivated. If we cannot find a way to see these as democratically well-founded, the recognition of the foregoing practices stands as a prima challenge to the legitimacy of the very institutions supposed to constitute our democracy.

I suspect the problem is not as intractable as it seems. For suppose a society with secret laws would be more workable and would better serve everyone's interests than a fully publicly governed society: Wouldn't we all vote for it? And if certain arrangements for taking further decisions are voted for, aren't the decisions from those arrangements themselves democratically taken? The argument that they are is that the mechanism of their production was voted for. The argument that they are not is that no voting is operant in the actual method by which further decisions are taken. But we've just seen that, to the degree a system of governance is not exhausted by the method of referendum, there will always be that argument against the democratic legitimacy of its decisions; and yet we've also seen that the method of referendum simply cannot assure the respecting of the interest of citizens. The non-referendum methods can do that, however; therefore they are to be preferred. And the decisions in which they issue therefore count as democratically grounded by two measures: first, they serve the interest of citizens; second, they are the only practicable method of doing so. Indeed, I suspect that the fact that we would assent to the preceding argument itself transmits consent to the deliverances of the resultant process.

If it still seems doubtful that secret laws from these sources and processes could be justified as expressing our will, even if we don't know of them and haven't directly voted for them, then consider the following. Suppose for all you know there is an angel prepared to subtly bias social arrangements in ways advantageous to the general welfare. Wouldn't you be happy to have this happen? Wouldn't you now be prepared to say a prayer asking this angel to make things better? Now suppose Supreme Court justices, or journalists, or congressmen and senators, or police officers and prosecutors, or leaders of major corporations, are in effect doing this very thing. (Angels work in mysterious and subtle ways, maybe through ordinary people.) Surely their doing it is an expression of your will even if you don't know they're doing it. Of course there is the argument that nothing guarantees they'll do this, and the point of having arrangements be made by collective, informed decision is to make it more likely that arrangements will be to the advantage of the collective. But suppose you thought some people know better than you what would make things best go in the ways you'd prefer if you weren't subject to bad information, bad judgment, and so on. Wouldn't you want them to subtly bias things in good directions, even if you in your ignorance or bad judgement or weakness of will, wouldn't directly make their decisions?

Yet it could still reasonably be argued that the foregoing processes and results are democratically legitimate only if we can guarantee that matters will be arranged in the best way. Is there any way to make this happen without our directly voting for each arrangement? Yes: we need only vote for educational systems inculcating the value of the public interest into anyone likely to be in authority. This is something citizens already do. They use their best judgement in voting for educational systems and government representatives who are like this. And they encourage arrangements in which those who wind up being justices, police officers, prosecutors, journalists, and so on broadly have this agenda. We recognize, too, that many different ways of choosing laws, and of interpreting, policing, and reporting them, are consistent with that agenda. In fact, the checks and balances the various institutions in our democracy are designed to provide on each other can be understood as, among other things, seeking to ensure that all of these interpretations serve the agenda of citizen interest.

13

Sovereignty and Associative Obligations

AARON JAMES

> When in the Course of human events, it becomes necessary for one people to dissolve the political bands which have connected them with another, and to assume among the powers of the earth, the separate and equal station to which the Laws of Nature and of Nature's God entitle them, a decent respect to the opinions of mankind requires that they should declare the causes which impel them to the separation.
>
> —PREAMBLE OF THE U.S. *DECLARATION OF INDEPENDENCE, July 4, 1776*

The modern world is organized by a territorial state system.[1] What began as a deal struck among kings at Westphalia would in time become an entrenched, world-wide social practice—a social practice in which political authority is divided over distinct portions of the earth's surface.

In medieval times, lines of authority and loyalty had no general territorial basis.[2] If the state system defines modernity, it places territory at the heart of

1. For relevant discussion, I thank Oliviero Angeli, Richard Arneson, Margaret Gilbert, Jeff Helmreich, Violet McKeon, Kevin Olson, Daniel Pilchman, Mathias Risse, Amanda Trefethen, the UCSD political theory group, and especially the members of my graduate seminars at NYU in the fall of 2013 and at UCI in spring of 2015.

2. John Gerard Ruggie, "Territoriality and Beyond: Problematizing Modernity in Relations," *International Organization*, 47, 1 (Winter 1993): 139–74. As Ruggie explains (p. 151), "The distinctive feature of the modern system of rule is that it has differentiated its subject [i.e., the organization of human collectivities] collectively into territorially defined, fixed . . . mutually exclusive [functionally similar, political centralized] enclaves of legitimate [and supreme]

Sovereignty and the New Executive Authority. Claire O. Finkelstein and Michael Skerker.

political authority. But while this is now a basic reality of human social existence, the social contract tradition, despite being closely associated with modern political thought, has never fully reckoned it. As I will explain, social contract thought has largely neglected an important possibility: that societies incur a distinctive class of "associative obligations" to one another by virtue of their territorial political union.

Recently, several conservative American legal scholars have challenged the authority of international law.[3] Concerned about the increasing reach of international organizations, *the conservatives* (as I'll call them for convenience) roundly reject the authority of much that has come to be regarded as international law, by what is assumed to be a fundamental appeal to "popular sovereignty." Although the conservatives are not especially clear about the principled basis of that idea, what they do say is arguably either affirmed in the social contract tradition, or at least not clearly precluded by it. And if only because all moderns accept an ideal of popular sovereignty in one form or another, the question for those who would disagree with the conservatives is therefore not how they could possibly be right, but how and why they mishandle a fundamental insight.

In this discussion, I propose to answer the conservatives in a way that develops underappreciated resources of the social contract tradition. Whether in Hobbes, Locke, and Rousseau, or, more recently, in Walzer, Rawls, and Nagel, the tradition has often begun from a domestic social contract and an ideal of popular acceptance and then worked outward. In this regard, the conservatives mainly follow suit. I suggest that a quite different approach is not only more appropriate to the modern world, but also a better fit with the social contract tradition's basic form of moral and political argument.

dominion." He adds: "As such, it appears to be unique in human history," especially in contrast with the territorially fluid medieval order, and anything yet to emerge in its place. Aside from his own historical survey, on this last point he cites Robert David Sack, *Human Territoriality: Its Theory and History* (New York: Cambridge University Press, 1986).

3. See especially Jeremy Rabkin, *Law without Nations? Why Constitutional Government Requires Sovereign States* (Princeton, NJ: Princeton University Press, 2005), as well as *The Case for Sovereignty* (Washington, DC: American Enterprise Institute Press, 2004). For more specific concerns about the U.S. constitutional order, see Julian Ku and John Yoo, *Taming Globalization: International Law, the U.S. Constitution, and the New World Order* (New York: Oxford University Press, 2012). For a human rights focus, see Curtis A. Bradley and Jack L. Goldsmith, "Customary International Law as Federal Common Law: A Critique of the Modern Position," *Harvard Law Review,* 110 (1997), 815–76; "UN Human Rights Standards and US Law: The Current Illegitimacy of International Human Rights," *Fordham Law Review,* 66 (1997), 319–39; and "Treaties, Human Rights, and Conditional Consent," *University of Pennsylvania Law Review,* 149 (2000), 339–468. On the undemocratic nature of international lawmaking, see John McGinnis and Ilya Somin, "Should International Law Be Part of Our Law?," 59 *Stanford Law Review* 1175 (2007). For constitutional arguments written within the U.S. Bush administration, see John Yoo and Robert J. Delahunty, "Memo 4. January 9, 2002," *The Torture Papers: The Road to Abu Ghraib,* eds. Karen J. Greenberg and Joshua Dratel (New York: Cambridge University Press, 2005) (especially on the sources of U.S. law). For a more general, but perhaps supportive rational choice challenge to international "legalism," see Eric Posner, *The Perils of Global Legalism* (Chicago: University of Chicago Press, 2009).

The territorial state system is a kind of social practice that raises questions of justification in its own right, in part for the deep way it shapes or "constructs" domestic social contracts, in a historical process of coevolution. When we apply a practice-based method for answering those questions, I claim, we see how popular sovereignty comes with external conditions. We see how, by virtue of their distinctive, territorial political union, sovereign states could incur associative obligations to follow international law as it emerges over time, even as a matter of state custom, quite aside from any given state's consent.

I. THE QUESTION OF TERRITORIAL AUTHORITY

The main norms of the territorial state system are so familiar that one could easily mistake a modern invention for the natural state of humanity. Three kinds of social norm are particularly central:

(i) Each of many distinct but functionally similar political states is granted jurisdictional rights over a specified territory (i.e., a set of (Hohfeldian) powers to regulate its borders, set rules for the use of its resources, govern supremely over its population, issue money, and so on.[4] (These are often called norms of territorial "supremacy");

(ii) Each such authority is permitted to repel outside attackers, but also subject to default expectations of noninterference across territorial jurisdictions (which may be qualified by secondary norms that permit intervention, under specified conditions).[5] (I.e., the norms of "non-intervention");

(iii) Further rules or understandings specify what types of functionally similar "states" could qualify for membership in the system, as a bearer of its rights and subject of its obligations. (Such "membership criteria" may evolve, being shaped by international standards within

4. I might emphasize that territorial rights are not strictly speaking property rights, but rather powers to set property rights. For discussion, see Anna Stilz, "Why Do States Have Territorial Rights?," *International Theory* 1 (2), 2009, 185–213; "Nations, States, and Territory," *Ethics* 121 (3), 2011: 572–601. Lockeans such as A. John Simmons, "On the Territorial Rights of States," *Philosophical Issues* 11, 2001: 300–26, attempt to explain state territorial rights in terms of natural property rights, but also admit that this is a revisionist project.

5. Even "sovereignty" as a default legal standing hardly means that states are equal in capability or functioning in real practice. We can agree with Stephen Krasner, in *Sovereignty: Organized Hypocrisy* (Princeton, NJ: Princeton University Press, 1999), that conventional models of legal sovereignty are unrealistic. We can also agree with David A. Lake, in *Hierarchy in International Relations* (Ithaca, NY, Cornell University Press, 2009), that power relations are often shaped not simply by coercion but by special authority relations, for example, as between the United States and Mexico, and Nicaragua and both the United States and Mexico. That is, it can still be true among particular states that, as Lake puts it, "the right to rule rests on a social contract in which the ruler provides a political order of value to the ruled, who in turn grant legitimacy to the ruler and comply with the restraints on their behavior necessary for the production of that order" (p. 3).

a secondary practice for "recognizing" a political group as member by other member states).[6]

Though Thomas Hobbes was mainly preoccupied by the British Civil War, he more than anyone gave us the image of separate societies, sprung up like mushrooms, each with its own security contract but at war with each other. And yet the publication of Hobbes's *Leviathan* came a few years after the new territorial state system was instituted at Westphalia, in 1648, in a development that would change the nature of war itself.[7] First established in the name of peace, the system took hold in Europe. After three sordid centuries of conquest, bloodshed, subjugation, two world wars, and a post–World War II era of decolonization and ossified borders,[8] it has become global in reach. It now ranks among the most consequential institutions in world history, for setting basic territorial limits on the possible form of political aspiration for people the world over.

Whatever doubts one may have about whether states follow rules in their dealings with one another—even if only as a public basis for criticism, sanction, and occasional punishment—the territorial system itself is the "constitutive" backdrop against which international rules and all state choices function.[9] In the modern age, every existing society and every government has been deeply shaped by the underlying territorial division of political authority, even as domestic developments (e.g., the rise of democracy) have also shaped it "from below," in a process of coevolution.

Philosophers sometimes pose the question of political authority as a simple one of how a person could be subject to someone else's rule. How, as the question is sometimes put, could a person be obliged to comply simply on a putative ruler's say-so? How, if at all, could legal commands be other than the coercive threats of a mobster?

This simple framing is perhaps apt for medieval times, but too simple for the modern political order. Under the state system, the right to rule is territorial in the first instance, and only secondarily a matter of ordering personal choices. A state is

6. Practices of recognition are arguably central to the territorial order, as suggested by Ruggie, "Territoriality and Beyond," p. 162.

7. Even warfare changed markedly. Ruggie ("Territoriality and Beyond," p. 163) distinguishes the "constitutive wars," such as the Thirty Years' War that gave rise to the Peace of Westphalia, from subsequent "configurative wars" in which "the nature of the units was accepted but their territorial configuration remained contested" (including the Wars of Succession in the eighteenth century and the Seven Years' War of 1756–1763). A still later phase of "positional" wars, were merely strategic and tactical, interrupted by rebuffed quests for universal empire.

8. Daniel Philpott, in *Revolutions in Sovereignty: How Ideas Shaped Modern International Relations* (Princeton, NJ: Princeton University Press, 2001), emphasizes two main "revolutions," at both Westphalia and in postwar decolonization.

9. Realists such as Kenneth Waltz, in *Theory of International Politics* (Reading, PA: Addison-Wesley, 1979) would agree, since powerful state incentives of self-help are seen as created by the state system's effective operation. I resist Waltz's view on practice-based grounds in Aaron James *Fairness in Practice* (New York: Oxford University Press, 2012), ch. 3, pp. 82–87.

in the first instance presumed to have jurisdictional title to set law and policy concerning a whole population's existence, composition, and terms of cooperation (e.g., in decisions about immigration, residence, citizenship status, money, population growth, basic rights, standard of living, etc.) over a more or less specified land and/or water area of the earth. Because the system has come to span the globe (excepting a few ungoverned spaces, etc.), almost every person is now a subject of some state or other. But which persons are ruled by which states is determined entirely by location. A person is subject to a given ruler's authority only according to where on earth he or she happens to be or have been, by birth or travel from a birthplace. The medieval order settled who rules whom by loyalty, commitment, and conscience, and only incidentally by location. The modern practice treats location as the crucial condition—no matter how loyal or committed to obedience a person might otherwise be. The American Francophile won't be a proper subject of French rule until he or she is on French territory, for example.

If early versions of the system settled who rules a territory by dynastic succession, we moderns have long rejected the divine right of kings. Any state, we assume, must earn the right to rule in the eyes of its subjects, in accord with what is naturally called a social contract. State sovereignty comes with a general condition of "popular" acceptance: all who reside within the state's putative borders, being subject to its exercise of coercive power, must in some sense accept, or be able to find acceptable, the state's claim to legal authority, in both procedure and substance.

And yet, if this basic idea of "popular sovereignty" is our historical inheritance from the social contract tradition, the tradition has never fully and definitively answered the fundamental question of state authority, which is equally about the territorial state system that sets boundaries for domestic social contracts, and whether it is itself a source of law and obligation.

The question remains: If a state is to enjoy the various rights of sovereignty, can a domestic social contract suffice on its own? Or are the sovereign's powers of rule over a particular part of the earth's surface, with a firm presumption of noninterference, *also* subject to external conditions? And might such conditions include compliance with larger state practices, or widely affirmed principles, which are commonly regarded as international law? Might even sovereigns face obligations that flow from the more basic social system that divides political authority over distinct territories in the first instance?

II. POPULAR SOVEREIGNTY, WITHOUT CONDITIONS

Recently, amidst heated public arguments over U.S. unilateralism in foreign policy, some conservative American constitutional legal scholars have claimed that that U.S. sovereignty is subject to *no* external conditions, not even well-established international norms often regarded as standing law.[10] In their view, although treaties undertaken by the United States are a source of binding law

10. See the references in note 2.

(albeit subject to unilateral interpretation and revision by the U.S. executive), the norms standardly regarded as customary law—including customary state practice and widely affirmed principles—are not legally authoritative, even when states generally affirm or obey them from a sense of obligation. At most, such customary norms offer moral recommendations, helpful guidelines, or aspirational ideals. As the idea might be elaborated, while such norms might inform political debate, they do not generate "content-independent" reasons for state action; they do not bind in the mere social fact of their having become widely endorsed or followed in state practice, irrespective of their moral content, not even by defeasible presumption.

For the conservatives, what is crucial—both necessary *and sufficient* for the enjoyment of the sovereign's rights over a territory—is that those who reside within a state in some sense generally "accept" its right to rule. Whether acceptance is of unwritten rules or understandings, or of a formal constitution that specifies agreed-upon forms of government, some such constitutive agreement sets all sources of authoritative law for those involved.[11] And so if the United States' founding agreement *only* mentions treaties undertaken by the United States itself as among law's sources, as the conservatives propose, it follows that no external decisions, or standards for decisions, could limit its right to decide for itself, in domestic and foreign policy.

This position would be of little fundamental interest if it were a nothing more than a bald assertion of U.S. special privilege. Some of the conservatives do argue dogmatically, in contempt for opposing positions. Yet their more principled appeal to the ideal of general acceptance, especially as approximately realized in constitutional democracies, at least places them in good company. Hobbes, Locke, and Rousseau each can be plausibly said to have located the source of political authority entirely within a domestic social contract.[12] In our own day, Michael Walzer at least accepts a strong natural right of territorial collective self-determination.[13] John Rawls either agrees or failed to take an unambiguous position on the relationship between domestic and international sources of law.[14] In recent writing, Thomas Nagel largely agrees with the conservatives' position.[15]

11. See Rabkin, *Law without Nations?*, pp. 39–41. As Ku and Yoo put it, in *Taming Globalization*, p. 4, "The Constitution provides the exclusive source of sovereign power to the U.S. government." They also cite Akhil Amar, "Of Sovereignty and Federalism," *Yale Law Journal* 96 (1987): 1427, 1429–65 (1987) and Gordon Wood, *The Creation of the American Republic, 1776–1787* (Chapel Hill: University of North Carolina Press, 1969).

12. As suggests in *Law without Nations?*, chs. 3–4.

13. Walzer, in *Just and Unjust Wars*, p. 54, does offer a Hobbesian reason why the collectivized right to life gives rise to a natural right of a group over a territory. It is not clear that he takes this or any other natural right to be the general ground for all international legal authority, however, since a variety of interpretive and moral considerations inform his analysis.

14. *The Law of Peoples* (Cambridge, MA: Harvard University Press, 1999).

15. "The Limits of International Law," in *Secular Philosophy and the Religious Temperament: Essays 2002–2008* (New York: Oxford University Press, 2010). For parallel views about socioeconomic

Are domestic social contacts the *sole* source of political authority? Not according to several forceful lines of argument. A first line defends the authority of treaty-based international organizations—even when their administrative rulings outstrip what state signatories of the original treaties may have envisioned. Such rulings, it may be said, nevertheless serve informational, advisory, and deliberative functions in ways that facilitate domestic democracy.[16]

In part, the point here is simply that the increasing scope of international administrative law does not imperil domestic social contracts. The conservatives do seem to worry about this, but in any case they can simply reply that their position is finally about fundamentals: when a ruling body such as the International Monetary Fund, International Labor Organization, or World Trade Organization does outstrip the narrow purposes that states consented to in a founding treaty, the result, they maintain, is *merely* helpful advice. It is not genuine *authority* of the sort that would flow directly from state consent. As they might explain, states would have to be given reasons for action irrespective of the wisdom or morality of its content, and this is not the case when the narrow, originating intent of a treaty is being outstripped.[17]

However, a second reply works more plainly on the conservatives' own terms, by advancing a more expansive interpretation of the United States' social contract. In the Declaration of Independence, the U.S. Founders publicly declared the causes of their separation. They did so out of avowed respect for the "decent opinions of mankind." And was this not a tacit, pre-constitutional recognition of mankind's decent opinions as a possible source of law? Those decent opinions might well be reflected in treaties, state custom, or the rulings of international

justice, see "The Problem of Global Justice," in the same collection and in *Philosophy and Public Affairs*, 33 (2) (2005): 113–47.

16. See, e.g., Robert O. Keohane, Stephen Macedo, and Andrew Moravcsik, "Democracy-Enhancing Multilateralism," Institute for International Law and Justice Working Paper No. 2007/4 (New York: New York University Law School, 2007); Allen Buchanan, *Justice, Legitimacy and Self-Determination: Moral Foundations for International Law* (Oxford: Oxford University Press, 2003), esp. pt. III; Allen Buchanan and Russell Powell "Constitutional Democracy and the Rule of International Law: Are They Compatible?," *The Journal of Political Philosophy* 16 (3) (2008), pp. 326–49 and "Fidelity to Constitutional Democracy and to International Law," *The Routledge Handbook of International Law*, ed. David Armstrong (Cambridge: Cambridge University Press, forthcoming); Mattias Kumm, "The Legitimacy of International Law: A Constitutionalist Framework of Analysis," *European Journal of International Law*, 15 (2004), 907–31 and "Constitutionalism and the Cosmopolitan State." *New York University Public Law and Legal Theory Working Papers*, October 1, 2013. http://lsr.nellco.org/nyu_plltwp/423; Samantha Besson, "Whose Constitution(s)? International Law, Constitutionalism, and Democracy," in *Ruling the World: Constitutionalism, International Law and Global Governance*, ed. J. Dunoff and J. Trachtman (forthcoming 2018); Joshua Cohen and Charles Sable, "Global Democracy?," *NYU Journal of International Law and Politics*, 34 (7) 2005: 763–97 and "Directly Deliberative Polyarchy," *European Law Journal* 3 (1997): 313–42.

17. Cohen and Sable, "Global Democracy?," pose a basic challenge to the assumed "principal/agent model" of authority, suggesting the authority of public deliberation. This is consistent with the reply to the conservatives I develop below.

administrative bodies. To the extent they are (as the first line of reply suggests), international law would be binding by the Founders' own admission.

Moreover, since the Declaration predates the U.S. Constitution, international law would be presumed to set limits on the very terms of a written domestic constitution. And so as the decent opinions of mankind change over time in response to new problems, even a written constitution would have to be constantly refreshed according to the emergent international norms that reflect decent opinions about how new problems are best resolved.[18]

This reply to the conservatives presents an interpretive challenge. A different, specifically *moral* reply would simply reject the conservatives' positivistic view of law. The assumption is that bare moral principles for international conduct do not qualify as binding law. But from a natural law perspective, for example, states have significant natural duties that constrain when positive law counts as genuine law. And such duties may require compliance with state legal custom as solutions to international problems emerge in practice over time.[19]

Here the assumed moral duties can be very modest—for instance, a weak Grotian or Lockean proviso for natural resource use. Natural persons, in order to exist at all, must be somewhere, usually relatively close to the earth's surface. Likewise, political communities comprised of such essentially embodied, located persons must also be located in a habitable space, usually a land area suitable for common affairs. According to one proviso, however, no individual or group is entitled to live in any area of physical space, while claiming rightful permission to use its natural or social endowments, without leaving "enough and as good for others" (e.g., by leaving enough for them to meet their basic needs[20]). So to the extent a state claims borders that do not leave enough and as good for outsiders, its claim to exclusive use is rightly limited, by force if necessary. As a condition

18. The conservatives may mean to suggest that the United States would suffer an *unfair burden* in being asked to comply with international law, because of threats to its distinctive constitutional order. But this would not present a fundamental challenge to the authority of international law; it would be a moral argument about what international law ought to be, or how it is fairly understood, while nevertheless binding.

19. According to Ronald Dworkin, "A Philosophy for International Law", *Philosophy and Public Affairs* 41 (1) (2013): 2–30, any coercive government "has a standing duty to improve its legitimacy," which includes "a duty of mitigation" "to pursue available means to mitigate the failures and risks of the sovereign-state system" (p. 19). This, the "true basis for international law," "includes an obligation to try to improve the overall international system," when (and only when?) "a state can help to facilitate an international order in a way that would improve the legitimacy of its own coercive government" (p. 17). A "further fundamental structural principle"—"the principle of salience"—requires compliance with established state practices that "improve the legitimacy of the subscribing state and the international order as a whole" (p. 19). For a similar view, which more explicitly appeals to natural duty, see Mattias Kumm, "Constitutionalism and the Cosmopolitan State," *New York University Public Law and Legal Theory Working Papers*, October 1, 2013, at http://lsr.nellco.org/nyu_plltwp/423.

20. For different versions of this idea, see Mathias Risse, *On Global Justice* (Princeton, NJ: Princeton University Press, 2012), chs. 6 and 7, and Cara Nine, *Global Justice and Territory* (Oxford: Oxford University Press, 2012).

of its legal right of sovereignty, it might be legally obliged to redraw its territorial boundaries, accept immigrants, and pay compensation to the deprived others (e.g., in a transfer scheme).[21]

My own view is that the foregoing replies suffice to refute the conservatives' position. They show, at very least, that the conservatives' uncompromising position is inadequately grounded as a thesis of fundamental political philosophy. Yet I take it that none of the foregoing replies answer the conservatives in a way that speaks to what might have made their position seem credible initially. None of them fully reckon with the social contract tradition's general ambivalence about the sources of domestic and international authority. I hope to do that in the remainder of my discussion. By developing a neglected possibility, I will offer what I take to be the most important reason that the conservatives go wrong about the social contract tradition itself.

On the *practice account* I will outline, the moral and the legal rights of a sovereign state may well be sensitive to its domestic social contract, as the conservatives claim. Even so, they are *also* conditioned by the *associative* obligations that any political group incurs by availing itself of the rights afforded by a larger territorial division of authority.

This general thought can be developed in two levels of analysis. At a first level, we point to and assess a general social practice—in this case a practice that defines a bundle of sovereignty rights over territories, assigned to specific claimants in a way that is supposed to serve valuable ends. At a second level, we assess more specific governance practices or procedures by which specific territorial assignments are given or revised. Neither level of analysis seeks recourse in natural rights or duties, whether of nations or of individuals. But because territorial rights are part and parcel of a political social practice, they can come with "associative obligations" for a state conduct, including obligations to follow emergent treaty and customary law, quite aside from a given state's consent.

III. PRACTICE-SENSITIVE JUSTIFICATION

The "constructivist" school in international relations tells us that states and their officials define their interests by "identities" tied to their larger state relationships. So even if international relations are "anarchic" in the trivial sense that there is no world state, in a sociological sense they nevertheless are not a "state of nature," but rather a kind of (perhaps adversarial) social understanding.[22]

21. The more demanding the proviso, the more demanding the limits on state sovereignty might be. Locke's own expansive reading of spoilage allowed the dispossession of Native Americans. They lacked ownership rights over the land for letting it "lie wast," and so could be displaced by European farming techniques that made the land more bountiful. Contemporary conservatives might argue that, whatever Locke thought, America has in the meanwhile been especially good for the world, and so that any proviso-demands have been satisfied.

22. As, for example, according to Alexander Wendt, "Anarchy Is What States Make of It: The Social Construction of Power Politics," *International Organization* 46 (2) (1992): 391–425, and

This thought is highly suggestive for political philosophy, but also of limited or unclear significance. The question remains of how such points of sociology might bear on moral obligations, as a matter of principle. As Hume might say, even the "is" of de facto *acceptance* of putative principles, as a sociological fact, does not entail the "ought" of either the right to rule or its limits. For why should the principles be accepted in the first place? What error is made when a state dismisses a consensus, claiming a moral right to go its own way?

To bridge the gap, we can follow John Rawls's elaboration of the social contract tradition's central insights, and, in particular, his practice-sensitive method of justification. On this method, moral principles are justified ultimately by moral reasoning, but for, and from, an independently identified and interpreted social practice.[23] As I understand the method, it works through three main stages (in whatever order aids in the search for reflective equilibrium): "individuation," "framing characterization," and "substantive argument."

A. Individuation

At the first stage, we individuate a candidate social practice. We single out an object of social interpretation, at first in relatively uncontroversial terms, with reference to various interpretive "data points" or "source materials" that any further conception of the social activity should take into account and explain (or "explain away").

In the present case, the territorial state system can be roughly singled out in the relatively uncontroversial sociological terms offered above. To elaborate, one might further distinguish the state from other social formations. For example, Hedley Bull does so by contrasting the system-bound state with a mere "independent political community," which "merely claims a right to sovereignty (or is judged by others to have such a right), but cannot assert this right in practice." This, he suggests, "is not a state properly so-called."[24]

Social Theory of International Politics, New York: Cambridge University Press, 1999. On "constructivist" accounts more generally, see Judith Goldstein and Robert O. Keohane, eds., *Ideas and Foreign Policy: Beliefs, Institutions, and Political Change* (Ithaca, NY: Cornell University Press, 1993).

23. Aaron James, "Constructing Justice for Existing Practice: Rawls and the Status Quo," *Philosophy and Public Affairs* 33, 3 (2005): 281–316; *Fairness in Practice,* ch. 1; and "Why Practices?," *Raisons Politiques* 51, August (2013): 44–61.

24. *The Anarchical Society*, pp. 8–10. Bull adds: "The Germanic peoples of the Dark Ages, for example, were independent political communities, but while their rulers asserted supremacy over a population, they did not assert it over a distinct territory. The kingdoms and principalities of Western Christendom in the Middle Ages were not states: they did not possess internal sovereignty because they were not supreme authorities within their territory and population; and at the same time they did not possess external sovereignty since they were not independent of the Pope or, in some cases, the Holy Roman Emperor. In parts of Africa, Australia and Oceana, before the European intrusion, there were independent communities held together by ties of lineage or kinship, in which there was no such institution of government. Entities such as these fall outside the purview of 'international relations,' if by this we mean . . . the relations of states in the

Even at this stage, the social object identified cannot simply come to a mass of disparate actions, unwittingly coordinated conduct, or coordination that is separately intentional but lacking any common aim or end. The object must be a candidate "social practice," in at least the following minimal sense: the conduct of different agents is more or less effectively coordinated by widely understood social expectations, as rationalized and adjusted by some shared, or at least presumed, purposes.

Here the attributed aims can merely be "presumed"; they needn't be actually endorsed, widely, or even at all. Mere "ideational" endorsement can coordinate conduct, even without genuinely shared purposes under the following condition. If enough of the agents accept that *enough of the other agents endorse* a purpose, even if few or none of them *in fact* accept its necessity or value, the agents may still more or less effectively coordinate around the presumed end. In that sense, the coordinated group "presumes" the end. [25]

In the case of the state system, we do observe such coordination on a worldwide scale. Most people, most collectives, and most of their officials at least act *as if* a state system exists. Most assume that its basic norms are widely accepted and followed, and largely comply on the presumption that enough others are doing likewise (in what may be collectively self-fulfilling expectations). And political actors can and do rationalize or adjust norms of state conduct according to presumed purposes -- whether through state policy, treaties, international administration, political argument, or trend-setting action—all without a global state. [26]

B. Framing Characterization

At the second stage of the method, we work up a general characterization of the practice, in light of its distinctive structure and (presumed legitimate) purposes. Here social interpretation can be "constructive," as long as any use of moral terms comports with canons of interpretation (e.g., consistency, coherence, explanatory power, simplicity, etc.).[27]

strict sense.... But where states are in regular contact with one another, and where in addition there is interaction between them sufficient to make the behavior of each a necessary element in the calculations of the other, then we may speak of their forming a system."

25. This is consistent with degrees of "cooperativeness" and perhaps corresponding degrees of stability in different settings. How cooperative a group is may depend on such varying factors as: how widely a social purpose is actually endorsed; whether and to what degree people personally intend to comply, and for what reasons; whether people are motivated by moral concerns; and whether and to what degree people also have genuinely shared intentions, joint commitments, or shared identities, etc.

26. Such governance may well amount to what Krasner calls an "organized hypocrisy" (in *Sovereignty: An Organized Hypocracy*), because states routinely violate the norms they say they affirm. But the ideational affirmation that lip service perpetuates means that people worldwide are more or less generally organized, in a generally governed system, all the same.

27. Aaron James, "Constructing Justice for Existing Practice," 3 (3)(2005): 281–316.

Again following Hedley Bull, here we might characterize the state system as a kind of anarchical *society*, which is animated by common values, purposes, and rules.[28] In addition, we can more fully characterize particular norms, their degree of centrality to the practice under some general description, and the general purposes that rationalize the overall structure—casting each of these, as charity permits, in a favorable light.

So, for example, here is a modest first point of interpretation: Westphalia's strict norm of nonintervention is but one possible "regulative" norm, rather than a "constitutive" norm of the larger state system. It is not a properly "constitutive" norm, in the sense that it needn't be approximately upheld simply in order to have a *state system* at all, as opposed to a fundamentally different social animal. The same sort of general social practice can equally run on a norm of *default* noninterference among different territorial authorities. Whatever kings and princes once presumed, the norm of nonintervention can be qualified by any number of secondary norms of state conduct without threatening the more general territorial division of authority. So perhaps outside interference in a state's affairs is governed by secondary norms that say when, how, and in what form it is permitted (e.g., in view of human rights standards, or procedural norms, such as requirements to secure UN or at least wide multilateral authorization). But, the idea goes, this is but an improved version of the territorial division first instituted at Westphalia. It isn't an abandonment or "withering away" of the basic territorial system itself.

Likewise, as a matter of interpretation, we can say that having some membership criteria or other is properly constitutive of a state system, but equally allow membership norms to have very different regulative elaborations. Traditionally, statehood was thought to be settled by the effectiveness of a political group's control over the use of force in a territory. This can be seen as an outdated understanding of what substantive grounds are necessary and sufficient for being duly "recognized" as a state with full standing in the international legal system.[29] Instead, we can see the decision by associated states whether or not to recognize new claimant groups as having legal standing (e.g., in regime change or secession) as subject to more demanding regulative permissions or expectations, in view of publicly established substantive governance tests. This, we may say, is mainly an improved version of the old, but distinctively modern territorial practice.[30]

28. Bull, *The Anarchical Society*, pp. 13, 15. This is an interpretive step beyond a mere "system of states" as he defines it on p. 9.

29. For discussion see James R. Crawford, *The Creation of States in International Law*, Oxford Scholarship Online, Feb. 2010, at http://www.oxfordscholarship.com/view/10.1093/acprof:oso/9780199228423.001.0001/acprof-9780199228423.

30. More generally, along with qualifications on nonintervention, the class of such readily adjustable "regulative norms" also arguably includes the whole multiplicity of norms that have risen to prominence in the postwar era, including treaty, administrative, or customary law, publicly established human rights standards, and other public bases for "good standing" and demands for public accountability.

The Treaties of Westphalia suggest at least one larger, presumed purpose in all of this: peace, or at least improved security. The resulting Peace of Westphalia did manage to reduce the outbreak of war and violence on the continent of Europe. And the original agreements' putative aim of relative peace is surely one we can endorse in a presumptive or at least provisional way. The basic territorial system, despite its rank injustices, including the innumerable evils of its colonial expansion over centuries, can at least lay claim to legitimacy in its provision of general security, if only in its postwar version. For all its horrors, the system did eventually bring the virtual end of territorial conquest. It finally at least helped to dramatically reduce war and violence (in conjunction with any number of other factors). Even as further revisions may be urgently needed, the state system now appears to be at least capable of advancing peace over the longer haul, much as Kant once dreamed.[31] And if we add, with Hobbes, that global anarchy would be an intolerable hell, and if, with Kant and Rawls, we find prospects for a stable world state too uncertain, then we can tentatively presume that the state system roughly as we know it—subject to progressive improvement and perhaps major revision—is at least not morally illegitimate. It is not akin to the practice of slavery—not so patently unjustifiable that it should be abolished rather than further improved.

As a matter of political sociology, so much is widely assumed. The aim of peace, or at least of relative security, at least finds general ideational endorsement. If peace often proves elusive, enough people accept that enough others accept the aim of peace and security as necessary or worthwhile, such that it generally organizes reasoning about apt rules of conduct, choices made in light of them, and the lip service routinely paid to them in public argument. The vast majority of people arguably also do genuinely care about security and the reduction of war and violence (even terrorists often seek order, albeit in a new form). This is the well-understood aim of the territorial state, but also of the more basic division of the world into territorial states.

Beyond peace and security, several further aims present candidate aims of the state system, especially in its postwar understanding. These include the aims of securing conditions for: stable possession, the establishment of (individual or collective) property rights, and the conservation of resources; societal economic development and plenty; collective self-governance and self-determination; and the realization of basic civil, political, and economic rights and larger social justice (perhaps variously understood).

An interpretive argument is required in order to attribute any, let alone all, such aims to the state system. Yet much will depend on one's interpretive methodology. In particular, how far should we defer to established social understandings when they seem to conflict with our personal moral or interpretive judgment as theorists? Arguably, an adequate *interpretation* of a social practice will attend

31. Though perhaps not for the reasons of economic interdependence that Kant suggested in *Perpetual Peace*. The success of the postwar effort to secure the conditions of peace arguably founded upon the rise of democracies, since democratic governments seem, as a rule, not to wage war on one another, as argued by Michael W. Doyle, *Liberal Peace: Selected Essays* (New York: Routledge, 2012).

to shared understandings of the agents involved in some measure. How *they* interpret their shared aims or organization will partly determine what they are doing together, much in the way an individual's intentions partly determine the nature of his or her action. Yet, as theorists, we can be deferential to participant interpretations to different degrees, depending on our theoretical objectives.[32] A relatively "catholic" interpretation will hew closely to obvious, deeply entrenched, or at least well-established social understandings. A relatively "protestant" interpretation will rely more heavily on the interpreter's own understandings and evaluations in making sense of a social structure. Perhaps deeper moral aims or principles are invoked in the name of interpretive charity. (Note that both methodologies can be "constructive," differing only in how much deference is paid to the interpretations of a practice's participants, irrespective of the theorist's own substantive judgment.)

The aims of peace and security seem most amenable to a "catholic" defense. And yet the postwar system may well offer ample resources (e.g., in any number of international conventions) for the full list of aims suggested earlier.[33] The attribution may still fall short well of our own best, freestanding ideas of justice; a proposed framing characterization is supposed to be an interpretive characterization of a state system that is anyway there, rather than a pure moral recommendation about how things ought to be, ideally speaking.[34] Even so, to the extent we follow a relatively "protestant" methodology, placing less weight on established meanings, we have a freer hand to interpretively attribute any number of moral aims to the state system, including those just suggested, and perhaps others as well.

C. Substantive Argument

At the third stage of the method, we engage in substantive moral reasoning about what principles of conduct apply, as framed and guided by the specified framing conception. Here I assume the domain of deontological morality that T. M. Scanlon calls "what we owe to each other," in which case we argue for regulative principles for a practice, among feasible alternatives, by considering what principles different parties can reasonably complain of.[35] First, we specify relevant interests or claims of all affected parties (persons or collectives, specified in light of the practice in question). Taking each party one by one, we then compare the different complaints or objections they could fashion to candidate principles, objecting on their own behalf, in view of their relevant interests or claims.

32. James, "Why Practices?"

33. See, e.g., Bull's *Anarchical Society*.

34. For related discussion of "ideal theory," see James, "Constructing Justice for Existing Practice" and "Why Practices?"

35. T. M. Scanlon, *What We Owe to Each Other* (Cambridge, MA: Harvard University Press, 1998).

We take the strongest (i.e., the "reasonable") complaint to rule out a given principle, in favor of some feasible alternative. Finally, we treat the principles that are not subject to any stronger countervailing complaint as normatively conclusive requirements for how the practice must be organized if it is to be justifiable to each and every one involved.

Here our working assumption is that putative natural rights, per se, have no relevance or force. They only become relevant when considered as relevant interests or claims and weighed into the moral reasoning just described. So for clarity's sake, we can tentatively assume away all "natural rights." The question is: What, if anything, is left?[36] To be sure, as long as one's reasoning is duly sensitive to the practice under evaluation,[37] certain relevant interests or claims might well be *called* "natural rights" in a stipulative sense. But this adds nothing to their justification or status as rights in the relevant practice; the case for their relevance would still have to be made. And it would have to be made in view of the distinctive nature and consequences of the territorial state system, as suggested below. And the argument couldn't appeal directly to the "natural" rights one would possess in a hypothetical "state of nature," as John Locke for example suggested.

IV. MORAL ASSOCIATIVE OBLIGATIONS

The idea, then, is that a social practice such as the state system must be justified in its own right, in view of its own consequences. And even if, for the sake of argument, we leave aside Grotian or Lockean natural rights (and indeed any principles that apply in the absence of the practice), we can still say that whole societies owe things to one another by virtue of their territorial and decentralized political union.[38]

The argument for such obligations can begin from claims about the state system's distinctive consequences, especially the familiar perversities due to its politically decentralized and territorial nature.[39]

36. James, *Fairness in Practice*, ch. 1. For discussion of "internal" and "external" values, see also Charles Beitz's contribution and my reply in our discussion of *Fairness in Practice* in the *Canadian Journal of Philosophy*, 44 (2) (March 2014): 286–304.

37. Such reasoning and the resulting principles are "practice sensitive" in the sense that our interpretation of the practice shapes our substantive evaluation at each stage, and that the whole set of interpretive and moral considerations is seen as *sufficient* to justify a basic, normally conclusive regulative principles of conduct. Absent further argument, no further principles are assumed to apply (although they may well apply, given further argument).

38. I take these to be specifically international obligations, for states, in contrast with "cosmopolitan" principles that apply individuals in different societies. It is of interest that this kind of position is possible, but little turns, for present purposes, on the difference. To the extent associative state obligations capture the central moral demands of global justice, we can question whether arguments from natural rights or cosmopolitan principles should be seen as peripheral rather than central concerns of political philosophy.

39. See, e.g., Dworkin, "A New Philosophy," pp. 17–19.

One tendency, for example, is that people are largely left in the hands of their sovereign, being subject to heightened risks of abuse, given the difficulties of, and presumption against, outside intervention. What people gain in being freed from wars and invasions, they may lose in domestic tyranny or oppression. Even in a relatively decent regime, people may suffer persistent political exclusion or underrepresentation.

In theory, such risks of abuse could be managed if states could effectively coordinate effective interventions. But any such efforts are also hobbled by the general dysfunctions of decentralized politics. The policies of different sovereign governments can be amazingly difficult to coordinate, even in obvious matters of common concern. Cross-border externalities, from trade or pollution policies, easily appear to be someone else's problem, or perhaps devolve into mutual "beggar my neighbor" policies and recriminations. Perhaps states could move to a cooperative equilibrium of mutual forbearance provided scarcely more than adequate assurances and yet bitter or shortsighted diplomats fail to provide them for years or decades on end. Nor are the problems limited to low-stakes issues. Even the most urgent commons problems (e.g., the spread of serious disease, regional pollution, or global problems such as climate change) may not readily marshal collective state action.

Still further difficulties directly reflect territorial privileges. Certain established international privileges give illegitimate rulers title for the legitimate sale of a country's resources, and the right to borrow in its name. This can in turn create perverse incentives for domestic corruption and persistent underdevelopment (i.e., rulers that control the oil faucet are prone to enrich themselves and underinvest in society, whether in infrastructure, education, industrial diversification, or public health).[40]

And of course the mere existence of enforced borders may itself generally exclude individuals and societies from natural and social resources, including bare means of physical subsistence. The adverse consequences of exclusion may not be readily compensated for by the general benefits of dividing the world into territorial states. Many willing migrants will be excluded from greener pastures, while whole societies may suffer unfavorable conditions for development, because of a worsening climate, or because poor geography has left them far from trade routes, or because they've inherited poorly governed institutions, in part due to perverse incentives created by the international system. Sinking island nations find themselves shopping for a home, with no unclaimed territory on the planet available for settlement (except perhaps at the price of a king's ransom).

Let's assume that some such consequences can be attributed to the state system, itself or in one of its versions. Then we can imagine societies objecting to how they are treated under the shared practice. Consider again the strict Westphalian norm of nonintervention. Those vulnerable to domestic abuse by their rulers have

40. Thomas Pogge, *World Poverty and Human Rights* (Cambridge: Polity Press, 2002), pp. 4–6, and Leif Wenar, "Property Rights and the Resource Curse," *Philosophy and Public Affairs* 36, 1, 2008: 2–32.

powerful reason to have states generally held to account according to some public standards for decent treatment. And though kings and princes may protest, no one can reasonably demand that states enjoy immunity to *any* accountability-seeking conduct. Especially if permissions to intervene are designed so as to be consistent with and serve the system's aim of facilitating general security, they would not generally be open to reasonable complaint. In that that case, we can conclude that a social practice that divides political authority on a territorial basis is indeed subject to certain principled permissions. When a state fails to adequately comply with appropriate standards of domestic conduct, it is permissible for other states to hold it to account in some appropriate way, whether by the use of force, economic sanction, public criticism, or demands to provide a public justification (as appropriate to the situation in question, subject to further practical considerations).

To take a different example, we might similarly justify an associational obligation of foreign assistance. Think of any of the untoward general tendencies cited earlier. The societies that suffer disadvantages might in each case complain of any version of the state system in which better advantaged societies fail to reliably provide them with important and necessary forms of assistance (whether in the form of emergency relief, security or development assistance, or, where feasible, diplomatic, economic, or military intervention). Barring special justifications for inaction, this objection will often be reasonable. For relatively advantaged societies will usually lack a comparably strong complaint against a principle of assistance (because the resulting sacrifices are sufficiently low and perhaps shared over large populations).

So stated, this argument does not yet make reference to an aim of the system. It does not yet mark a clear break from arguments from natural duty (such as a general duty not to harm). But when such an aim is invoked, the argument is more plainly addressed to the social practice as an associative obligation, in view of the social understandings that make it a common enterprise. This is significant in several respects.

First, it bears on the substantive assessment of different potential complaints. When an argument makes reference to an aim of the system, and so to the general kinds of goods it aims for or "promises," a society can more forcefully object when it is being avoidably deprived of benefits of those kinds. For one thing, the bare *relevance* of the grounds can't be reasonably contested (as they might if the moral claim were simply to greater happiness). If an aim of the common practice is to secure conditions for peace, security, stable possession, and societal prosperity, for instance, but many societies are avoidably deprived of those conditions through no fault of their own, it will not be reasonable to disqualify those benefits as irrelevant to the common association. They are, after all, part of its very point. Underprovision of those "promised" goods is grounds for relevant, potentially weighty complaint, which may be decisive if sufficiently strong counter-objections are not forthcoming.

Likewise, countervailing objections based in the cost of compliance for measures that provide those goods in particular may themselves appear irrelevant, or at least much less weighty than they might otherwise be. When the costs are demanded in the name of the system, a system in which the societies addressed already participate, the objection will have force it might not have had if instead made in the name of aims that cannot be attributed to the system. (At least in some such cases, others may reply: "That is all well and good, and fine in a perfect world, but beyond the purview of our association.") Such objections will be especially weak in the mouths of the system's chief beneficiaries. In many cases, as with nearly all advanced societies, the societies asked to sacrifice for the sake of the system's fulfilling "promises" will be largely compensated by enjoyment of benefits that also fall under the aims of the practice. So they won't be in a particularly good position to object to being asked to bear moderate or even significant costs so that other societies, as members of the common association, can enjoy the system's promised benefits as well.

Further, specific arguments aside, when principles are justified under a practice's aim, they have special authority over its members. A principle of assistance, say, would count as a proper principle of *the system itself*. It would not simply be an independent moral demand (such as a natural duty of assistance).

And in the same way, *any* interpretively attributed aim of the system (i.e., peace, collective self-determination, economic development, or basic domestic social justice) could support demands for fair treatment under the common practice and corresponding obligations for the states in a position to effect reform. Such "internal" principles may be said to give all relevant parties effective "standing to demand" fulfillment of what they require, seen as a general status that nonmembers of the system would not enjoy. (Although "standing" as a member might be more or less meaningful and effective to the extent the principles in question are in fact socially recognized, even if only in the ideational sense.)

V. MEMBERSHIP OBLIGATIONS

All of this gives us certain associational principles. To whom are they addressed? In the first instance, they are addressed to participants in the territorial state system, seen as social practice. But then it remains a further question how states come to count as participants in the state system— especially if that comes with costly obligations. Why is any particular domestic political group seen as properly addressed with the reasons for action justified along with general expectations of state conduct?

A first, limited point concerns the acceptance of benefits. In general, to the extent a political group does successfully operate as a state with the effective powers of "vertical" sovereignty, ruling supremely over a territory, along with relative freedom from outside interference due to the forbearance of outside powers ("horizontal" sovereignty), it avails itself of social opportunities created by a larger system. This might suggest that state obligations are merely a matter of "fair play," of giving fair return to others for benefits received. But this would be a serious oversight.

A "fair play" approach is by itself consistent with the Hobbesian or Lockean image of largely independent, sovereign societies, who come together on occasion to make limited agreements for mutual benefit. This encourages the idea that the world situation is analogous to distinct fleshy persons bound by common rules, who could instead go their separate ways in a primordial state of nature. Yet the situation is rather different. Any particular territorial state that claims a right of sovereignty (whether "vertical" or "horizontal") is a "construction" of the larger territorial order, being both historically and constitutively related it.[41] Even if all states cut off all interaction with those beyond their territory, they would still do so within the larger social system that partitions rule in territorial units; we would still have the distinctively modern form of world order that calls for its own justification.

Here the appropriate contrast is not with persons, but with certain groups, especially as politically organized. Families, religious groups, and ethnic groupings, for example, are often spread across different state territories. But in general, few such groupings within a territory (perhaps among a set of rivals) can or will lay claim the rights to rule that the larger system affords, instead of simply going about other business. The groups that do are expressly laying claim to rights the state system affords (e.g., from a megaphone at a rally, or in a Declaration of Independence). A mere *claim* to rightful rule may or may not be credible; the group with the megaphone may have little real chance of effectively controlling the use of force, for example, and an initially credible declaration of independence might devolve in a blood feud. But when a particular political group does exercise the prerogatives of state governance in a putative collective's name in some real measure (e.g., it at least controls the use of force, directs traffic, provides social services, etc.), it can be said to have made a credible claim to the right of sovereignty as created and defined by the social system, in the sense that other states can appropriately treat the group as a candidate for legal recognition. Other states must then decide either to officially "recognize" the group as enjoying the sovereign's rights to rule, or to withhold such recognition (perhaps in hopes that, with suitable reform, or a quite different claimant to power rising, a better government will prevail).[42]

41. In passing, Dworkin's "A New Philosophy" (p. 19) suggests that each state "derives its moral title to govern a particular territory from the arrangements that make up th[e] international system" and that states therefore have "independent" reason to promote the system's legitimacy. Here Dworkin may mean to invoke an associative obligation of the kind I am developing. But the comment is not obviously related to Dworkin's proposed duty of each state to promote its own legitimacy and the related "duty of mitigation." He may have intended a connection by also mentioning, in the same passage, "the unchecked state sovereignty system," which "impairs or threatens the legitimacy of the individual states that make up the system." Perhaps, because of this general tendency, legitimacy for any one state turns out to require institutions that promote the legitimacy of all states.

42. Even here, an *express* declaration of the right to rule does not seem essential. It suffices when a group does successfully operate as a state, in effect availing itself of the social opportunities created by the larger state system. It then becomes an apt candidate for legal recognition. At the same time, such groups do often at least tacitly claim the system's right to such operations—a claim that becomes explicit when the group invokes the system's privileges, perhaps in the face of rival powers or outside interference.

In this sense, then, state political obligations are membership obligations. They are addressed to the state system's participants (states, their officials, and their publics), and justified, if at all, as reasons for action *in virtue of their (perhaps minimal) participation* in the larger social practice that the state system is. Still further practice-independent or natural duties might require participation in the first place. But associative obligations will be incurred only once participation is underway.

In that case, whether or not other states formally "recognize" a political group as a member of the legal system, when a group does have a credible claim to rule with the rights the larger system affords and meets the minimal requirements for participation, it is thereby saddled with all of the associative obligations that fall to that system's members. The associative obligations that follow from any principles justified for the practice and its participants can then be properly addressed to the claimant group as giving it genuine reasons for action. At least in the distinctive practice that the territorial state system is, making an effective claim to the rights it affords is all it takes to incur both its obligations and general liability for their fulfillment.

For present purposes, these are offered as plausible proposals. If they require a fuller defense, here I merely emphasize that they are meant to apply *only* to membership obligations in the distinctive practice that the state system is, and not necessarily among natural persons.[43] By design, the state system recognizes large-scale collectives as artificial persons as its official members. So obligations justified as membership obligations do not necessarily address or oblige mere persons residing in or visiting a territory. Instead, they can be seen as addressed directly to states and their officials, and to the politically organized group that claims state prerogatives, especially to its elite representatives. Persons residing in or visiting a claimed territorial area will be addressed only indirectly, if at all, perhaps depending on what particular relation they bear to the group that happens to rule. (Perhaps they must be not only counted as citizens, but acting within assigned political roles, e.g., as voters).

This allows for the important possibility that a newly obliged proto-state and its elite representatives might not yet be sufficiently legitimate to authoritatively command compliance from its de facto subjects; if they aren't far enough beyond mobster rule, those living on the claimed territory may have no reason to comply beyond reasons of expedience. A *duty* to obey or at least respect the law may await the proper constitution of a decent social contract. A chief obligation of the claimant proto-state may be precisely that it should, with all deliberate speed, meet such legitimacy conditions (perhaps as specified by comparisons with other societies or international standards for good domestic governance).

43. Obligations of "fair play" in a cooperative practice among natural persons may be subject to more stringent conditions. We can still ask: Is mere benefit from a practice sufficient? Or is benefit sufficient if the practice is very important (unlike Nozick's famous public address system)? Must noncompliance (e.g., by free riding) impose a cost upon others? Must the benefits be voluntarily accepted, regardless of how important the practice is? If so, against what background options?

VI. ASSOCIATIVE LEGAL OBLIGATION

Assume, then, that some such account of how membership obligations are incurred can be adequately defended. The main point for present purposes is that we can now present an answer to the question of why even customary international law binds. An argument for this conclusion can be presented in two premises.

We have discussed the first premise, the thesis that states have moral associative obligations. By virtue of laying credible claim to the right to rule within a larger territorial system of authority, each state has sufficient reason to do what is asked of it under moral principles justified for that larger social practice.

The second premise of the argument is that international law is a *relatively effective remedial practice*. We might call this the Law as Remedy Thesis:

> Under normal circumstances, if states are to reliably fulfill their associative moral obligations, they must generally comply in good faith with contemporary (and perhaps evolving) international standards of state conduct, including the standards set in widely signed treaties, administrative rulings, customary state practices, and widely affirmed principles.[44]

In conjunction with the first premise, it follows that compliance with international law is the sovereign's obligation. The development of international law limits the right of state sovereignty rather than being fundamentally limited by it, contrary to the uncompromising view taken by conservative American constitutional lawyers.

Here one might worry that we have obscured a real difference between law and justice. Natural law theories will of course deny that there is any general and fundamental difference. On Dworkin's version, the content of law is determined by appropriate (and perhaps "constructive") interpretive reasoning, perhaps by appropriately placed judges.[45] So to the extent that the best interpretation of international legal practice calls upon moral principles, whether natural or associative, they shape what legal rules require.

44. Dworkin's principle of salience adds the proviso that a state must comply with emergent state practices "only if a more general practice to that effect, expanded in that way, would improve the legitimacy of the subscribing state and the international order as a whole" ("A New Philosophy," p. 19). The Law as Remedy Thesis makes a stronger claim, namely, that compliance with emergent state practices *does* generally advance the fulfillment of state associative obligations. But below I offer an interpretation of good faith compliance that allows states to also make quasi-legislative judgments in light of expectations of injustice.

45. Dworkin, in "A New Philosophy" (p. 14), imagines a hypothetical court charged with such interpretive judgments. One could also simply point to U.S. federal judges who have treated customary law as U.S. common law under the Alien Tort Statue. Amanda Trefethen (UC Irvine dissertation) proposes that legal norms must either have agreed-upon applications or be settled by *established* domestic or international courts (though perhaps while drawing broadly on principles for the larger system, as Dworkin suggests).

On the other hand, the foregoing argument can also grant that law is a social fact, and in that sense accept a kind of legal "positivism." For one thing, we can leave aside all appeals to natural duty, as suggested; associative state obligations can be justified quite aside from direct appeals to natural rights or principles, and so to the extent they are justified for and from a kind of social system, they depend on the social fact of its existence for their application.[46] We might further burnish a practice account's positivist credentials by adding that the territorial system of authority sets very basic social preconditions for the effective rule of law in both domestic society and international relations. It may even be said, without great implausibility, that the system's entrenched norms amount to an implicit and perhaps incomplete (small-c) "constitution" for international *and* domestic legal systems.[47] The state system might be counted as a "constitution," at least, in the sense that its norms are not only presupposed in international dealings but also potentially of central importance to any more specific determination of what less deep norms count as legally binding. They can in that way be counted as a "source of law," in international *or* domestic legal interpretation.

Still, the key question is what we should say when international laws and practices are unjust. When particular treaties or state customs run afoul of deeper moral associative obligations (or other moral principles), should states invariably comply with them anyway, setting justice aside? If so, law would seem to have authority of its own. And yet invariable compliance may not seem to be what any state should actually do in practice. In that case international law may seem not to have authority of its own, and so would not count as "law" properly speaking.

One solution, consistent with the Law as a Remedy Thesis, is to further specify what it is to "comply in good faith." First off, we might say, officials comply in good faith only if they treat contemporary international standards as presumptive, even if defeasible, requirements in their policy deliberations. Law has "authority" over state deliberations, in at least that psychological sense. When prevailing legal rules are given appropriate consideration, we can admit that a state fully complies when its chosen policy is consistent with a plain, uncontroversial reading of them. But, we may add, a state can also "comply in good faith" by acting otherwise, when its officials judge that all policies consistent with standing law would allow a significant injustice, to their own society or to another. In that case, the officials comply in good faith when they: (1) adopt an appropriately remedial policy; (2) publicly propose an appropriate reinterpretation of relevant international standards, along with a highly credible justification for the proposed revision; and (3) respond to review and censure by qualified representatives of the international legal community (including, e.g., international judges, lawyers, scholars, and other state

46. At least barring further argument: similar principles well might be defended without reference to the practice in question, and so be regarded as "practice-independent." But even this would not show that such principles were the same principles, or somehow more basic than principles justified for the practice; they may simply be different principles, with similar requirements.

47. Philpott, *Revolutions in Sovereignty*, ch. 2.

officials). A state would fail to comply in good faith, then, when it simply fails to give relevant international standards due consideration, or when it adopts a policy that is inconsistent with standing law while shirking one or more of legislative responsibilities (1)–(3).

Here one might object that we have yet to explain how international "law" would have genuine legal *authority*. To be different from mere moral obligation, it may be said, law would have to give states "content-independent" reasons to comply, simply on a norm's say-so, irrespective of its moral failings. But because even moral associative obligations lack this feature, we may not seem to have a kind of genuine legal authority after all.

This objection turns on the plausibility of attributing a particular conception of legal authority to international law in particular. But we arguably need only capture the degree of content-independence that international legal practitioners normally claim for legal norms in practice.[48] In that case, there is a case to make that, normally (i.e., barring extenuating circumstances), states will indeed do better in complying with their associational obligations by complying in good faith with established international standards, on those standard's say-so.[49] In that way, the Law as Remedy Thesis could be offered as an explanation of international law's genuine legal authority. If major differences from domestic legal authority remain, this may only show that legal authority should not be so closely tailored around the case of domestic law. Legal authority is the authority law has in practice. In the international realm, it is the kind of authority that is appropriate for a decentralized political practice, in which states are at once the subjects and authors of their common law.

The conservatives have positivist leanings, and many would presumably object on grounds of state consent. Treaties, they admit, do legally bind the states that undertake them. But how, they may ask, could the suggested wide range of legal obligations fail to infringe upon a state's sovereign rights if they do not flow from its own consent in the treaty agreements it officially undertakes? We can now see how sovereignty would not be infringed, however, for either moral or legal reasons. By morality, the associational rights of state sovereignty, whether "vertical" or "horizontal," would just *be* the legal rights afforded by the international legal system, subject to each state's good faith reinterpretation. And given the Law as Remedy Thesis, law would bind in just the general way it is commonly presumed to, quite aside from whether a particular state has authorized a particular treaty. Customary law claims no basis in any given state's consent. Nor does administrative law, which, again, may run well beyond the wording of treaties that previously established administrative bodies that issue expert rulings on new issues. Even

48. Perhaps as characterized by Abram Chayes and Antonia Handler Chayes, *The New Sovereignty: Compliance with International Regulatory Agreements* (Cambridge, MA: Harvard University Press, 2005).

49. This is to assume a form of Raz's positivistic "service conception," in *The Authority of Law: Essays on Law and Morality*. 2nd ed. (New York: Oxford University Press, 2009). This possibility is developed by Daniel Pilchman (UC Irvine dissertation).

treaties might come to bind states that are not among their signatories when they are widely enough adapted in the treaty undertakings of *other* states.

The Law as Remedy Thesis is in part a general empirical thesis. So one could still argue that *only* state consent in fact works over time as an effective remedial means of fulfilling state associative obligations. But this line of objection is foreign to the conservative's position, once shorn of its natural rights underpinnings. This would in effect admit that the sovereign's rights are not a simple function of its domestic social contract. Sovereign states remain fully beholden to the demands of a larger political union.

VII. TERRITORIAL RIGHTS: TWO LEVELS

We have yet to say how sovereignty rights over particular territories might be assigned to specific claimants. Recent work on territorial rights often begins by distinguishing two questions about state jurisdictional rights over territory and populations. First, why have them at all? And second, when should any given state have jurisdictional rights over a *particular* land area, especially given the claim that persons or societies seem to have to being located in particular places?

In recent work, this first question tends to be posed in order to distinguish it from the second question, which is mainly left unresolved. It is suggested that people do have claims to be in particular places, and not just in some place or other, contrary to utilitarians such as Sidgwick, or other "functionalists." On those views, an established state would lose its right to rule over a territory if it turned out that colonial rule would do better by the relevant functional standard (e.g., promoting overall welfare). But this seems too permissive.[50] Most important for our purposes, much recent work assumes that we should look for a *general, substantive* account of the neglected claims to rule over particular places, albeit perhaps in a "hybrid" analysis in which more than one ground is counted. (Is the relevant ground or grounds ties of a nation to its land?[51] Or an individual's natural right of property?[52] A collective's natural right of property?[53] Or are the grounds an individual's right to secure legal residence, given his or her autonomy and vested relationships?[54]) Finally, we are invited to expect that, provided a general, substantive account of particular territorial rights, we will have answered the first, why-question as well.

50. David Miller, "Territorial Rights: Concepts and Justifications," *Political Studies* 60 (2012): 4.

51. Miller, "Territorial Rights."

52. Simmons, "On the Territorial Rights of States."

53. Although Nine, *Global Justice and Territory*, and Risse, in *On Global Justice*, takes natural rights to be held collectively by all humanity in the first instance.

54. Stilz, "Why Do States Have Territorial Rights?," "Nations, States, and Territory." The larger literature also includes Tamar Meisels, *Territorial Rights* (Dordrecht: Springer, 2005), and Avery Kolers, *Land, Conflict, and Justice, A Political Theory of Territory* (Cambridge: Cambridge University Press, 2009).

The practice account sidesteps this way of framing the debate. It does so by working at two levels of analysis, corresponding to the two questions stated earlier, and by accepting a plurality of grounds at both levels. This first question, of why to have distinct territorial jurisdictions at all, is understood as a question of why a territorial division of authority is basically acceptable, given some presumptively legitimate social purposes. The answer can cite any of several purposes, in what might be called a "pluralistic functionalist" account.[55]

The second question, about claims to particular land areas, is then understood as follows. Assuming we do have a territorial system, on what different bases, or by what procedure for deciding complex cases, should a state be accorded jurisdictional rights over a particular territory and population? To this second question, the practice account proposes a procedural answer. By way of a suitably idealized practice of legal recognition, complicated decisions are made ad hoc, in view of a full and diverse range of considerations, owing to both general state associative obligations and the particularities of societal circumstances. In the remainder of my discussion, I'll further elaborate this second stage of the practice account, and then respond to an objection.

A decentralized political setting, which lacks an effective centralized authority, will have only limited means of assigning specific territories. And yet the assignments must be given and perhaps adjusted, as necessary, if the larger territorial division of authority is to work in practice. Accordingly, world politics has settled upon something of a decentralized method, a rough-and-ready practice of state recognition.[56] The practice assumes a set of established states, which are widely presumed to enjoy the legal rights of membership, and which in effect enjoy legislative powers, to decide both when such rights are to be revoked and newly granted. When new claims to rule are made (often in secessionary movements), the question arises of which, if any, among rival claimants shall be incorporated into the international legal system. The answer is settled in the following admittedly messy way. Each established state decides on its own which political groups, if any, to recognize as a member of the international legal order. Each then announces this publicly, so that other states may consider whether they, too, are willing to admit the group in question as a member. If a new political grouping is recognized first by a few states, and it has good enough fortunes, it might then be recognized by others, and, in time, by enough (even if not all) of the rest, so as to have finally gained membership.

Ideally, each state's recognitional decisions would be morally guided, by the larger aims of the territorial political practice, with each state carefully weighing national self-interest in view of its associative obligations. The true statesman or stateswoman approximates this ideal in real practice. Routine politics is uglier

55. In contrast with a "monistic functionalism," such as utilitarianism, the Scanlonian contractualist reasoning outlined earlier admits of a wide variety of relevant interests or claims, which can also be applied to the present questions of basic legitimacy, as suggested above.

56. For discussion, see Hersch Lauterpatch, *Recognition in International Law* (Cambridge: Cambridge University Press, 1947).

and often corrupt, but there, too, decisions can and arguably often are at least shaped by public accountability for international standards. Prevailing standards shape deliberation and argument about both which claimants to rule are minimally credible, and which groups are headed in the direction of a decent social contract (e.g., given human rights standards and norms for democratic governance). Ideally, in a well functioning practice of assigning membership rights, a state act of recognizing another state takes the form of a quasi-legislative suggestion. The act reflects not simply a descriptive judgment, that basic criteria have been met, but a normative recommendation, offered to other states, that they too ought to do likewise and admit the claimant group as legally sovereign over its claimed territory. All states ought to do so, it is suggested, because both the facts and the weight of appropriate legal standards and moral considerations call for this.[57]

Such proceedings are often a mess. This is perhaps understandable: any decisions about where boundaries should lie, or about which groups are credible and headed in a decent direction, will be made in view of an enormous range of practical considerations. Security prospects are difficult enough to game out, and even fact that a territory has been secured is only the beginning of decent, respectable governance as judged by contemporary standards and key peer political movements. Here one can ask, more generally: What are the various and most important grounds appropriate for territorial reconfigurations, beyond capacity to control the use of force? What considerations of social cohesion, basic requirements of justice, and forms of decent governance, are relevant and central? But here our answer might also be pluralistic: perhaps no single kind of consideration is likely to provide a general answer, as the only or even the main basis for deciding who will best rule. Such inherently complicated decisions, it may be argued, are not amenable to general moral theoretic analysis, even if there are more and less sensible things to think when sensitive experts are staring down particular cases.

In this case, it is natural to prefer a procedural solution, a method that does as well as possible at yielding the best decisions, given the limited options, without pretending that a variety of general grounds can do more than give suggestive guidance ahead of time. And if indeed a plurality of considerations must be delicately balanced, but in a decentralized political setting that lacks an effective central authority, then it is at least sensible to resolve particular questions by roughly the kind of decentralized method that states actually follow. The task then is to characterize its distinctive obligations. States in a decentralized practice of recognition, we may say, ought to be guided by the suggested quasi-legislative expectations mentioned earlier, in view of the larger aims and associative obligations of the territorial system.

This rough model requires further elaboration, but it at least serves to mark out a significant and largely neglected view of the particularities of territorial rights.

57. Lauterpatch, *Recognition in International Law*, argues that this fits real practice, or at least the obligations practice assumes.

Earlier I simply set natural rights and duties aside, for purposes of offering an associational account of a general territorial political practice. Do we need to invoke them now in order to answer the second question about claims to particular land areas? We don't. A recognitional practice that is sensitive to a variety of factors, in view of the complexities of a given case, can explain how particular territorial claims are properly assigned. Indeed, the proposals found in recent literature can be seen as fixing upon important elements of truth, even if no one type of relevant interest or claim could settle a particularity question in a general way. The practice account doesn't *have* to offer a general answer to the question of when a state should have jurisdiction over any particular territory. So it is not open to the various counterexamples proposed against one or the other account. We need only have good enough procedures for making decisions on an ad hoc basis.

Whether any version of going practice is "good enough" is of course open to question. A. John Simmons briefly mentions the foregoing strategy, what he calls a strategy of "indirection." He then objects on grounds of unjust procedure. He explains:

> Instead of trying to directly justify particular distributions of territories to states (by appealing to some nationalist, functionalist, voluntarist or hybrid theory), we might try to justify these distributions *indirectly*—by justifying the international legal order that has made or confirmed (much of) the extant distribution (through its acceptance and its defense of [many] existing territorial boundaries).

He then objects:

> If the international order is not itself well justified, it cannot convey through its history any legitimacy to its recognition of territorial claims by states. And the international order has been and continues to be indefensibly structured around the interests of powerful states, while its lack of enforcement mechanisms undermines its capacity to uphold any judgments of illegitimacy it makes (judgments that are typically forgotten after a suitable period of mourning). . . . A "legal order" with such a history lacks, in my view, sufficient legitimacy to convey legitimacy to the territorial claims by states that it upholds.[58]

Rousseau made much the same point about the international order he observed in his own day:

> As for what is commonly called the law of nations, it is certain that, for want of sanction, its laws are nothing but chimeras even weaker than the law of nature. This latter at least speaks to the heart of individuals, whereas the law

58. "Territorial Rights: Justificatory Strategies," ms. p. 25.

> of nations having no guarantee than its utility to the one who submits to it, its decisions are respected only as long as self-interest conforms to them.[59]

But whatever was true in Rousseau's time, the same points don't plainly apply to what the state system has become in the postwar era. Simmons is quite right that the system needs "sufficient legitimacy," but he's too skeptical about how far things have come.

There's no denying the influence of rank selfishness, power politics, and their enormous injustices. Yet there is at least a serious case to make that the contemporary system is not so radically unjust as to confer no legitimate rights to rule over the territories it assigns, albeit with important exceptions, and anyway on a provisional basis, subject to further, progressive improvement.

While I won't try to offer a serious argument for this point, the following unsystematic reflections should suffice to suggest how the argument could run. In the era of decolonization, borders have been long settled, at least for the most part. (Palestine and Israel, as well as Russia's 2014 venture into Crimea, testify to the general rigidity of borders, as exceptions that prove the rule.) Borders have solidified in the good name of security and collective self-determination (even as, in many cases, liberation from imperial oppression often brought tyranny that is home-grown, and a need for humanitarian or human rights interventions). In more general international legal practice, Rousseau's image of convenient compliance is less apt than it once was. Career-minded international practitioners now routinely give prevailing international standards the serious consideration appropriate to law, subjecting themselves to public accountability, much in the way recommended above (if only to be promoted, or at least not fired).[60] Simmons echoes Hobbes's view that reliable coercive enforcement is lacking. But contemporary international law and practice suggested precisely that more decentralized ways of holding states accountable can suffice for a genuine legal practice.

I might add that here we can be plenty cynical about world politics and the motives of its primary actors. The aims of the state system can organize conduct even when they aren't in fact endorsed, simply for being "ideationally" affirmed. When enough governments and their officials accept that enough other governments and their officials accept the aim of security or collective self-determination, the animating spirits are not general good ill, but the triumph of ideology. For this, it is enough that officials and worldly commentators make their arguments, believing that others are signing on. Officials can then comply with emerging norms, partly for selfish reasons, partly to be in a position to publically legitimate their decisions if or when they are called upon for an argument. Indeed, in a few cases, officials presumably aren't simply paying lip service; they actually do believe in the norms and the values they uphold. And the more officials explain themselves in terms that find approval in public eyes, the more the invoked

59. "The State of War" in Jean-Jacques Rousseau, The Social Contract and Other Later Political Writings, trans. Victor Gourevitch (Cambridge: Cambridge University Press, 1997), pp. 162–63.

60. Chayes and Chayes, *The New Sovereignty*.

norms gain public recognition, and the more they come to shape further official decisions about what will publicly fly and so can or cannot be done.[61]

VIII. THE DECENT OPINIONS OF MANKIND

The American Founders took themselves to be entitled to a separate but equal station among the powers of the earth under "the Laws of Nature." And yet they also felt obliged to declare the causes of the separation. Their claim to self-rule, they seemed to assume, *had to be publicly justified*, with just cause, in the eyes of the decent opinions of mankind.

Perhaps the Founders only assumed that a public *declaration* of the causes of separation was obliged. Once declared, respects to the opinions of mankind were paid in full, with no further duty required. On the other hand, Jeremy Rabkin notes the Founders' oddly specific view of what would seem to be an institutionally defined bundle of powers. In commenting upon the Declaration's penultimate sentence, which defines the powers of states with "lawyerly care," Rabkin explains:

> In joining the ranks of "free and independent states," the Declaration concludes, the United States can now claim "full Power to levy War, conclude Peace, contract Alliances, establish Commerce and to all the other Acts and Things which Independent States may of right do." The Declaration thus seems to take for granted that there is something like a pre-existing law, determining the right of independent states, with some degree of precision.[62]

It is indeed puzzling how the Founders could have taken such precise, distinctively modern legal powers for granted in what is supposed to be a bald appeal to natural, pre-institutional right. This becomes much less mysterious, however, if the Founders were not invoking practice-independent entitlements, but simply laying moral claim to as-yet-unrecognized standing in a larger territorial political practice.

In this case, the rightful basis for separation was not a bare natural right to self-rule, but political injustice—especially the litany of arbitrary British actions that the Declaration enumerates. The Americans presumably had a rightful claim to sovereignty. But as the Founders would perhaps have agreed, it came with strings attached: an obligation to uphold the laws that emerge from the common opinion of mankind, whether then or today.

61. I develop this thought in response to the selectorate theory of politics in Aaron James, "How Cynical Can Ideal Theory Be?," *The International Journal of Political Theory*, 12 (2) (June 2016): 118–133.

62. Rabkin, *Law without Nations?*, p. 72.

14

Contract, Treaty, and Sovereignty

MATTHEW LISTER*

I. INTRODUCTION

International economic law[1] has long had a legitimacy problem. Especially since the 1970s, with the developments coming out of the Tokyo round of GATT trade negotiations, increasing questions about whether this body of law was intruding into the rightful sovereignty of states became common. This criticism has increased in frequency and intensity since the 1970s, growing along with the large number of bilateral investment treaties (BITS), NAFTA, and the start and development

* Earlier versions of this chapter were presented at a conference on sovereignty and executive power at the University of Pennsylvania Law School, at a faculty workshop at the University of Denver Sturm College of Law, at a meeting of the Junior International Law Society, and at a meeting of the Zicklin Center for Business Ethics Research at Wharton. My thanks to Claire Finkelstein, Jens Ohlin, Christopher Morris, Bill Burke-White, Bernard Chao, Alan Chen, Viva Moffat, Michael Siebecker, Amy Sepinwall, Wayne Norman, Alan Studler, Richard Shell, Phil Nichols, Caroline Kaeb, MJ Durkee, Jean Galbraith, Maggie Gardner, Pam Bookman, and Kish Parella for helpful comments on those occasions, and to Govind Persad for very helpful written comments.

1. I shall use the term "international economic law" to cover that heterogeneous body of law relating to trade, investment, international business, and related areas. This is not, by any means, a natural kind, or even a clearly coherent social kind. There are many different types of law, law-making activity, and enforcement procedures covered under this heading, and no one thread running through all of them except that they relate to cross-border economic matters. Still, I think that it is a useful enough grouping to talk about in general terms. Most of the examples I will use relate to international trade regulation, as covered by the WTO agreements—the GATT, GATS, and TRIPS, and bilateral investment treaties or other similar agreements such as NAFTA. This body of law has, I think, important implications for human rights concerns, but is nonetheless conceptually distinct, and I shall discuss human rights issues only indirectly, as one point where my approach provides some possible clarifications and improvements on the current discussion.

Sovereignty and the New Executive Authority. Claire O. Finkelstein and Michael Skerker.

of the WTO, extending now to the proposed Trans-Pacific Partnership (TPP) agreement. In this chapter, I will argue that drawing on insights from contract law provides a means to address these legitimacy concerns.

As international economic law has increasingly reached "beyond the border" and come to regulate areas of life such as public health, environmental regulation, professional licensing, and others that were long the sole concern of domestic governments, the need for greater legitimacy has grown. These worries about subverted state sovereignty via a sharp curtailing of policy space, and the illegitimacy of this body of law, come not only from anti-cosmopolitan nationalists, but also, and increasingly, from those on the "left." For example, in the lead-up to U.S. accession to the WTO, Ralph Nader charged that, if the United States joined the WTO, "Decision-making power now in the hands of citizens and their elected representatives, including the Congress, would be seriously constrained by a bureaucracy and a dispute resolution body located in Geneva, Switzerland, that would operate in secret and without the guarantees of due process and citizen participation found in domestic legislative bodies and courts," and that "if existing or proposed local and state standards can be chilled by a foreign country's formal accusation . . . that the standards are a non-tariff trade barrier, then the evolution of health and safety standards around the world will be stalled or degraded."[2] Similarly, opposition to the TPP (warranted or not) was especially strong among supporters of Bernie Sanders' recent campaign from the left for the Democratic Party presidential nomination, where opposition to intellectual property rules, public health regulations, and investor-state dispute settlement panels were particularly salient.

Despite these worries, developments in international economic law have the potential to do significant amounts of good, increasing trade, furthering development, and increasing cooperation among the states of the world.[3] Yet the gains of globalization are unlikely to be achieved if societies believe that the only way to do this is to make unreasonable and illegitimate incursions into their own rightful sovereignty, limiting their ability to address important issues. If we are to both gain the potential advantages of cooperation in this area and to protect the rightful sovereignty of societies, we must find a way to deal with this tension. It is my contention in this chapter that drawing on insights from contract law,

2. Statement of Ralph Nader before the Senate Committee on Foreign Relations Hearing on the Uruguay Round of the General Agreement on Tariffs and Trade, June 14, 1994. Quoted from John H. Jackson, *Sovereignty, the WTO, and Changing Fundamentals of International Law* (Cambridge University Press, 2006) 317.

3. Some, of course, doubt that the promises of international economic law to further these ends are anything more than hollow, and perhaps are a mere façade for the furthering of the interest of already powerful and wealthy elites. I sometimes have sympathy with adequately qualified versions of these complaints, but think they are, at best, over-put, especially in light of economic growth and huge improvements in living standards in China and, to a very significant degree, Mexico for example. For useful, if slightly dated, discussion of this matter, see Jagdish Bhagwati, *In Defense of Globalization* (Oxford University Press 2004). In this chapter, however, I shall largely not address these issues.

especially relating to remedies for breach, can help solve or reduce this tension. In particular, I will argue that states should be able to craft new remedies to violations of treaty obligations, moving beyond the current rule, which is roughly equivalent to specific performance in contract law. Doing so will encourage more mutually beneficial interaction between societies without unduly limiting the policy space different societies rightfully claim.

I shall argue that looking to contract law can help illustrate how this can be done. Contracts have the seemingly paradoxical ability to allow us to do more of what we want by binding ourselves to certain courses of action. Charles Fried presents the point nicely when he says,

> In order that I be as free as possible, that my will have the greatest possible range consistent with the similar will of others, it is necessary that there be a way in which I may commit myself. It is necessary that I be able to make nonoptional a course of conduct that would otherwise be optional for me. By doing this I can facilitate the projects of others, because I can make it possible for those others to count on my future conduct, and thus those others can pursue more intricate, more far-reaching projects.[4]

This self-binding feature of contracts can not only lead to greater autonomy, it can also produce shared social welfare. As Robert Scott and Paul Stephen say, "The institution of voluntary commitment is the time-honored mechanism for achieving compliance with cooperative goals that benefit the collective interests of parties whose particular interest diverge."[5]

We see here how contracts can help individuals gain goods—increased autonomy or increased welfare—that they could not on their own. In what follows I will show how importing certain insights from contract law and theory to the evaluation of treaties in the international economic realm can help us gain similar advantages for international economic law. That is, I shall show how insights from contract law can help make international economic treaties sovereignty-enhancing and better able to produce joint welfare, rather than sovereignty-compromising. The approach argued for in this chapter, I will show, can help solve the legitimacy problem that international economic law faces, as well as making it more just and fairer.

I shall proceed as follows. I will first give a brief account of the aspects of contracts, treaties, and sovereignty that are most salient and important for my analysis. I do not intend these accounts to provide anything like a theory of any

4. Charles Fried, *Contract as Promise* (Harvard University Press 1981) 18. As I show below, I think this point about the autonomy-expanding power of contracts is independent of Fried's moralized view of contract law, though arguing for this is not the main purpose of this chapter. The classic account of how freedom requires a way to convince other that I will fulfill my agreements is, of course, found in Hobbes's *Leviathan*.

5. Robert E. Scott and Paul B. Stephan, *The Limits of Leviathan: Contract Theory and the Enforcement of International Law* (Cambridge University Press 2006) 60.

of these subjects, but simply to highlight some points I take to be particularly important or relevant for my account. While some points will be controversial, I hope that at least the majority of what I shall say in this Section will at least be plausible, if not fully acceptable to everyone. Next, I shall show how these points about contracts, treaties, and sovereignty come together to show a way to make international economic treaties sovereignty-enhancing by increasing the amount of "policy space"[6] societies have, thereby making international economic law in general more legitimate.[7] Then, I shall illustrate my argument by looking at three examples, the dispute between the United States and the European Union (EU) on the important of hormone-treated beef; the dispute between the United States and Mexico over access to the United States by Mexican truckers; and the dispute between the United States and Antigua over internet gambling. Finally, I will consider other strengths of the "contract" approach and consider three possible objections. Looking at these examples can help show how my approach to international economic law can make it more legitimate by making it sovereignty-enhancing.

II. CONTRACTS

The goal of this Section is to highlight some aspects of contract law that can be adopted to promote sovereignty-enhancing features in international economic treaties (and not to provide a theory of contracts). I follow Brian Bix in thinking that it is a mistake to look for a unified theory of contracts, as there are too many goals and too many uses of contracts to make them susceptible to a single theoretic approach.[8] My interest in contracts is not, then, in the "correct" theory of contract law, but in how we may use contracts to help us achieve important goals that we could not reach acting on our own. In particular, this chapter will not address whether there is a distinctly moral obligation to "keep contracts,"[9]

6. I take this notion from Steven Ratner. See, e.g., Steven Ratner, *The Thin Justice of International Law: A Moral Reckoning of the Law of Nations* (Oxford University Press 2015) 327–28.

7. This is only one aspect of the legitimacy of international law, or even of international economic law. I am not here attempting to give a full theory of legitimacy for even this one area of law, but simply showing one way in which legitimacy may be improved. For an account of international economic law in relation to the goals of human rights protection and peace promotion, see Ratner (n 6) 322–79. There is also a large literature based in international relations theory applied to international economic law. Because this literature is largely at best diagonal to, and often in conflict with the sort of normative analysis undertaken in this chapter, I largely leave it aside. Interested readers are directed to Richard Shell's illuminating paper, "Trade Legalism and International Relations Theory: An Analysis of the World Trade Organization" (1995) 44 Duke L.J. 829.

8. Of course, one might object that this "pluralist" approach to contracts is itself a theory of contract law. I have no stake in that argument. For discussion of this point, see Brian H. Bix, *Contract Law: Rules, Theory, and Context* (Cambridge University Press 2012) 147–62.

9. This is Bix's term, which he prefers to "perform," as it seems less liable to beg the question on the issue here. See Bix (n 8) 141.

or whether "efficient breach" can ever be morally justified. Rather, I will focus on how certain remedies available in contract law are important for protecting autonomy. This is not a theory of remedies, or an argument that any particular remedy is always the correct one. Rather, the central point here is that, if specific performance—the legal duty to perform the actual act contracted for—were the only possible remedy for a breach of contract, then contracts would be much less well suited to help us perform the task of increasing our autonomy in a way that is compatible with the autonomy of others, and of cooperating to produce shared welfare.

It is not hard to see why this is so. If specific performance were the only possible remedy, then many contracts that we do enter into, given the possibility of alternative remedies, would be "too risky" to rationally enter. Sometimes this risk would be economic—if the situation turned out the wrong way, we might be forced to take on losses that were highly disproportional to the potential benefit that was bargained for when making the contract. Sometimes the risk would be to our autonomy—we might be forced to perform some task that we would find personally offensive or degrading, which would violate our other moral or legal commitments, or which would otherwise compromise strong values, despite the fact that our counterparty could be compensated either in ways other than our personal performance, such as through a money payment, or by performance by another person.[10]

Because it would very often be "too risky" to enter into a contract if specific performance were the only remedy available, we have a number of alternatives. We should not expect any one remedy to be the appropriate choice for all types of contracts, and the fact that courts have crafted different remedies for different circumstances seems to support this conclusion. Insofar as the point of contract law is to promote autonomy and build social welfare, insisting on a remedy that would regularly run the risk of forcing people to act in autonomy- and welfare-destroying ways would be perverse indeed, and we can therefore have good reason to not insist on specific performance as the sole or even primary remedy

10. Specific performance is, of course, a more common remedy in civil law countries than in the common law system. However, there is some indication that specific performance is becoming less common, and is sought by parties increasingly rarely even in jurisdictions where it is theoretically more readily available. See Bix (n 8) 99, 107. For a case that nicely illustrates how specific performance can needlessly require a party to face the option of a contempt charge (and fines) or violating other legal obligations, see the Dutch case of Compagnie Europeenne des Petroles SA v Sensor Nederland BV, District Court at the Hague, 1982, 22 ILM 66 (1983). Sensor Nederland, a Dutch company that was wholly owned (via a few steps) by a U.S. company, and thereby subject to U.S. export controls on sales of petroleum exploration equipment to the Soviet Union, was ordered to perform under the sales contract it had made for the equipment prior to the export controls being put in place, or to face significant fines. If the United States had not waived the penalties for violating the controls in this case, Sensor Nederland would have faced the choice of penalties from the United States and perhaps the loss of certain export rights, or significant penalties from the Dutch court, despite the fact that this seems to be the sort of case where monetary penalties would be both possible and appropriate.

for breach of contract. As I shall show, there is a similar situation in relation to international economic treaties.

III. TREATIES

Given the very large number of treaties currently "in force," and the great diversity among them in form, subject matter, and method (if any) of enforcement,[11] it is a mistake to think that we should expect a unified theory of treaties, except perhaps at such an abstract level as to be of little use. This chapter, therefore, focuses on treaties covering international economic relations. There is still a large amount of diversity within this subsection, however, and so even here we should not expect a completely uniform account. For example, this subsection of treaties include bilateral investment treaties, a groups where we should also expect diversity between treaties where both parties are highly develop states and ones where one party is highly developed while the other is developing; very large and complex multilateral treaties covering most of the countries of the world, such as the WTO agreement; regional free-trade agreements that share some features with the WTO agreement and some with BITs; old treaties of "Friendship, Commerce, and Navigation"; treaties relating to certain topics such as trade in civil aircraft or petroleum; and so on. This includes a large percentage of the total treaties in force, but excludes many important and well-known treaties, such as those covering human rights, international criminal law, international humanitarian law, and other similar subjects. It is reasonable to expect these other treaties to have different normative structures, but this will be left aside in this chapter.

I contend that the reasons states enter into treaties, at least of the sort addressed in this chapter, are often very similar to the reasons individuals enter into contracts. That is, doing so allows states to achieve goals[12] that they could not achieve on their own, and allows them to engage in welfare-enhancing forms of cooperation. Because these goals of contracts and economic treaties are similar, we may hope that some insights from contract law will apply to treaties as well.

This chapter is not, of course, the first to treat the similarities between contract law and treaties. Robert Scott and Paul Stephan, for example, have written extensively on the similarities between treaties and contracts and what we might learn from this, but while they focus heavily on the question of enforcement—how what we know about the enforcement of contracts can help us better understand and craft treaties–[13]the focus of this chapter is not enforcement but rather

11. On this point, see Jackson (n 2) 42.

12. There is, of course, some dispute about whether it makes sense to attribute goals or motives to corporate bodies such as states. While there are deep issues here, I will assume that we can make sense of such claims. I will not attempt to establish exactly how this is to be done, but will leave the issue to others and rely largely on common-sense understandings of such attributions. I do not think that anything I say here will be deeply controversial on any understanding of corporate actorhood.

13. See generally, Scott and Stephan (n 5).

remedies. The two issues are related, and there are important parallels between the argument in this chapter and that of Scott and Stephan, but as they hardly discuss remedies at all (even about contracts) there remains important work to do here. Furthermore, Scott and Stephan are primarily interested in the question of "optimal enforcement," where this is the level and method of enforcement of international law that will maximize social welfare.[14] Importantly, what is included in "welfare" is largely left undefined by Scott and Stephan, but whatever it is, its maximization is seen as the point of international law. While increasing welfare (however defined) is an important goal of international law, perhaps especially international economic law, I argue that to understand the behavior of states in relation to treaty formation, we must look beyond a strictly consequentialist approach.

In what follows, I argue that states have reason to craft remedies for violations or breaches of treaties that respect, as far as possible, their rightful sovereignty.[15] The desire for more "policy space," in Ratner's terms, may be focused on increasing welfare, but may also have sovereignty-promoting goals as well. We see a parallel here with contracts. A party may choose to not provide specific performance, even when doing so would maximize social welfare, if doing so would compromise her autonomy in an unacceptable way.[16] Of course, it is also the case that specific performance will itself often not maximize social welfare, though noting this just gives us one more reason to make sure that we have other remedies available.

14. *Ibid.*

15. In very helpful written comments on an earlier draft of this chapter, Govind Persad raised the important distinction between *respecting* a value and *promoting* it, and reminded me that the two need not always go together. It is, of course, possible that respecting the sovereignty of a state in some cases might lead to the state having less sovereignty overall or in the long run. This is something that must be kept in mind when crafting remedies or when setting up systems of international cooperation, assuming we take sovereignty, in the sense assumed here, to be important. As I expect that respecting the sovereignty of states will at least often also promote it, and that respecting this sort of sovereignty has value on its own, I will mostly focus on respecting it rather than promoting it. Additionally, in this chapter we are primarily interested in rightful sovereignty—the sort and amount of sovereignty that a state should have—and not in "promoting" more than that. It will, however, be necessary to keep this distinction in mind and consider particular cases carefully.

16. This leaves open the question of when, if ever, parties to contracts, or treaties, should be able to decide in the contact itself to require specific performance in the case of breach. This has been allowed most often when the subject of the contract is such that money damages cannot provide a substitute. This will rarely be the case in the sort of treaties we are considering here. For discussion of this point, see Bix (n 8) 106–07; City Stores v. Ammerman, 266 F. Supp 66 (D.D.C. 1967); U.C.C. § 2-716. To continue the discussion of the respecting/promoting distinction from the previous footnote, we might accept that the treaty equivalent of specific performance should be allowed in certain cases where it seems that the decision to agree to it was free and fair, but that the default position should be to not make it the default, as it currently is, if it is not explicitly agreed to and bargained over. This will be especially likely to apply in the case of multilateral treaties.

However, a traditional approach to treaties has seen something very similar to specific performance as the primary, or even the exclusive, remedy. (In some cases compensation, in addition to the equivalent to specific performance, might be required, but the "performance" is still necessary to meet a state's obligations under the treaty, as traditionally understood.) Understood slightly differently, treaties have typically treated violations as the breach of a property rule rather than a liability rule, in Calabrisi and Melamed's sense.[17] This understanding is arguably implied by what many take to be the fundamental principle with regard to treaties, pacta sunt servada, or the idea that agreements must be fulfilled, where "fulfillment" means "performance."[18] This approach finds support in the world from important scholars of international economic law such as John Jackson, and arguably in the language of the WTO agreement itself.[19]

In this chapter I will show that in the case of international economic treaties, adopting a "property rule"/specific performance only approach can lead to perverse results. In a way similar to how Scott and Stephan have noted that changes in the method of enforcement may lead to a change in the "activity level" of states in a particular area, either encouraging or discouraging agreements,[20] I will argue

17. See Guido Calabresi and A. Douglas Melamed, "Property Rules, Liability Rules, and Inalienability: One View of the Cathederal" (1972) 85 Harv L. Rev 1089, 1105–16. For a helpful discussion of this point in relation to international investment law, see Ratner (n 6) 354.

18. At one point Hans Kelsen thought that this norm, in international law, might plausibly be thought to be the *grundnorm* for all of law. While Kelsen later modified his view, he continued to hold that this was a norm "of special importance." See Kelsen, *The Pure Theory of Law* (University of California Press 1967) 214–17, 323–24. Kelsen's later view was that the *grundnorm* of international law (and perhaps of all law) is that "the individual [here a state] ought to behave in such a manner as the others usually behave (believing that the others ought to behave that way)". Ibid 216. I make no pretenses to being about to fully understand Kelsen's view, and while he rarely discusses commercial or economic law, whether domestic or international, I see no reason why this later view on the *grundnorm* of international law should be incompatible with the approach I develop here. For discussion of the role played by the norm of pacta sunt servada in the civil and canon law traditions, see Bix (n 8) 115.

19. See the discussion in Jackson (n 2) 149, 168. WTO Charter, Article XVI(4) requires each member to "ensure the conformity of its laws, regulations, and administrative procedures" with the obligations set out in the agreements, and the Dispute Settlement Understanding holds that the obligation imposed on "offending" states is "to secure the withdrawal of the measures concerned if these are found to be inconsistent" with WTO obligations. DSU Art 22(1). Countervailing measures are meant to be temporary and not a replacement for compliance with obligations. DSU Art 22(2). This runs strongly in opposition to the position I shall propose. (I may add that, when I first started thinking of this idea, at a Salzburg Seminar session on protectionism several years ago, and suggested it to David Unterhalter, then-chairman of the WTO Appellate Body, he rejected it out of hand as being incompatible with the understanding of settlements under the WTO agreement. I agree that my proposal is a significant change, but do not think that is reason to reject it.)

20. Scott and Stephan (n 5) 18.

that allowing remedies other than the equivalent of specific performance under economic treaties may encourage a greater amount of cooperative and mutually beneficial treaty-making.

As international economic treaties come, to an ever greater degree, to not just regulate the "external" affairs of state, or traditional matters such as national treatment and most-favored-nation status, but to also reach "beyond the border," and into areas of regulation that once would have been seen to be of clearly domestic concern, this issue has grown in importance. Examples here include environmental regulation, health and safety standards, employment regulation, licensing, agricultural policy, regulation of public morals, cultural policy, and so on.[21] These are areas of regulation that we might think are rightfully within the sovereign prerogative of a state, at least within the bounds set by human rights norms.[22] The worries we may have about this intrusion into plausible areas of state sovereignty become more pronounced when those who make the decisions about such regulations are tribunals or arbitration panels that have minimal, if any, responsiveness to democratic, or otherwise decent, responsive decision-makers.[23] The goal of this chapter is to find a way to use a wider variety of treaty remedies to ensure that economic treaties are sovereignty-enhancing for states in a way that is similar to how contracts may be autonomy-enhancing for individuals, while still encouraging mutually beneficial cooperative activity. Doing this, I contend, will strengthen, and not undermine, the legitimacy of international law. However, before looking at some examples, I will say a few words about the notion of sovereignty that I consider relevant for this project.

21. Environmental regulation, health and safety standards, and agricultural policy were all implicated in the U.S./Canada–EU beef hormone dispute, discussed below. Public morals were at the core of the dispute between the United States and Antigua over internet gambling, and safety standards, employment regulations, and licensing were relevant to the dispute between the United States and Mexico on trucking under NAFTA, each discussed below. Quotas and limits on "foreign" media put in place by countries as diverse as France and China have been overruled by the WTO, arguably impinging on cultural sovereignty. Other examples are numerous, perhaps especially under the GATS and TRIPS agreements, not to mention many regional and bilateral agreements.

22. For a discussion of how human rights norms are directly related to this issue, see Ratner (n 6) 323–47, 349–77. I will briefly discuss the direct relations between the proposals in this chapter and human rights later in the chapter.

23. These concerns about intrusions into the rightful sovereignty of a state are of course most strongly felt when the state is a democratic one, and the domestic decisions interfered with are the result of a legitimate democratic process. I take this to be the paradigm case for us to consider. However, roughly following Rawls, I think that we may extend this analysis, at least to some degree, to non-democratic states who at least mostly respect human rights and are to some sufficient degree responsive to the interests of their citizens. To defend this position would, however, take me too far away from my main interest in this chapter. See John Rawls, *The Law of Peoples* (Harvard University Press 1999) 62–78. For my take on relevant issues, see Matthew Lister, "There Is No Human Right to Democracy. But May We Promote It Anyway?," (2012) 48.2 Stan. J. Int'l L, 257.

IV. SOVEREIGNTY

Traditional notions of sovereignty, often traced, somewhat dubiously, to the Treaty of Westphalia, treat sovereignty as essentially unified, and as granting essentially unlimited authority to act within a state to the sovereign, without the interference of other states.[24] These claims have generally, and rightly, been rejected.[25] But, this is no reason to reject a suitably modified notion of sovereignty, one that accepts moral and legal constraints on state action in certain areas, while holding that states ought to have a high degree of autonomy in setting their internal policies and in charting their own paths in the world.[26] In this sense, sovereignty for states plays a role that is similar in many ways to that played by autonomy for individuals in liberal theories of justice. An autonomous individual in this sense is one whom no one else has a right to tell which ends or purposes to pursue, so long as these ends and purposes are compatible with similar freedom for others.[27] This notion of sovereignty (as the parallel for autonomy for individuals) is inherent, for example, in Rawls's idea of international society as made up of democratic and decent peoples.[28] While the full extent of rightful sovereignty is too large a topic for this chapter, I will, following Ratner, take it to include significant degrees of territorial integrity, political independence, and equality of standing.[29] Working out the proper extent of political independence in relation to international treaties will be one of the primary goals of this chapter.

One consequence of this notion of sovereignty is that many parts of international law will be legitimate only if they are freely consented to by the relevant states. There is a parallel here with more traditional notions of sovereignty,

24. The first clear formulation of this idea seems to be from Jean Bodin. See Bodin, *On Sovereignty* (from *The Six Books of the Republic*) (first published 1576, Julian H. Franklin, ed., Cambridge University Press 1992). In the English-speaking world important versions of this idea are found in Thomas Hobbes, *Leviathan* (first published 1651, Edwin Curley (ed.), Hackett 1994) para XVII 13–15, XVIII, and in John Austin, *The Providence of Jurisprudence Determined* (first published 1837, Wilfrid E. Rumble, ed., Cambridge University Press 1995). All three authors accept that, while the sovereign may be a collective individual, the power of sovereignty cannot be divided, and that the sovereign is legally unlimited in his authority to act within a state.

25. For a useful early attack on Austin's notion of sovereignty, applicable in large degree to Bodin and Hobbes as well, see Henry Sidgwick, *The Elements of Politics* (2nd edn, Macmillan and Co. 1897) 651–58. Various notions of sovereignty are teased out and shown to not depend on each other by Stanley I. Benn in his paper, "The Uses of Sovereignty," in Anthony Quinton, ed., *Political Philosophy* (Oxford University Press 1967) 67–82.

26. For an instructive argument suggesting this conclusion (though not framed in quite this way), see Anna Stilz, *Liberal Loyalty: Freedom, Obligation, and the State* (Princeton University Press 2009) 44–56.

27. For a very helpful discussion on this point, see Arthur Ripstein, *Force and Freedom: Kant's Legal and Political Philosophy* (Harvard University Press 2009) 35–36.

28. See Rawls (n 23) 42–43, and Matthew Lister "Sovereignty" in Jon Mandle and David Reidy (eds.), *The Cambridge Rawls Lexicon* (Cambridge University Press 2015) 800.

29. See Ratner (n 6) 103–263 for detailed discussions of these ideas.

which see it as the basis for the idea that international law depends, in general, on state consent, and in the idea of the "equality of nations"—the idea that each society, regardless of its size or power, has equal standing in international law and decision-making.[30]

We can, however, reject the idea that sovereignty provides states with unfettered authority to act internally (and to make war in the pursuit of state interest) without rejecting it wholesale. When we see this, we must note that we are left with important questions about which decisions ought, rightfully, be left to states to decide on their own, and how much policy space they ought to have in relation to these decisions. This is not a rejection of sovereignty (or, as Jackson seems to suggest, a reduction of it to the question of how to achieve "good governance"[31]) but rather, an attempt to understand its proper scope. Once we see this, we understand that consent retains an important, if not unlimited, role in legitimating international law and institutions,[32] and that those who think consent plays no important role here either have an unduly narrow view of international law, or are confused about its role in relation to sovereignty.[33] The areas over which states ought to have sovereignty, and so where legal actions against the state ought to depend on the consent of the state, are contested, but I will here contend that at least most of the areas covered by international economic law fall into this category. These are areas of life within societies where we may think it is inappropriate to permanently (or essentially permanently, barring difficult and expensive withdrawal from a treaty altogether) remove all decision-making authority from a people and place it in a decision-making or dispute resolution body that lacks democratic or other legitimacy.[34]

In addition to political independence, we may also here see the continuing importance of the idea of the equality of nations (or states—this notion has no essential connection with the idea of a "nation" as that term is often used in political philosophy). Within the area of rightful sovereignty for a state, the mere fact that a majority of other states think that an action is appropriate is no ground

30. For discussion on this point, see Jackson, (n 2) 58 and, at much greater length, Steven Ratner, (n 6) 186–263.

31. Jackson, (n 2) 72.

32. On this point, see Matthew Lister, "The Legitimating Role of Consent in International Law" (2011) 11 *Chicago Journal of International Law*, 663, and, for a slightly different take, Thomas Christiano, "The Legitimacy of International Institutions," in Andre Marmore (ed.), *The Routledge Companion to the Philosophy of Law* (Routledge 2012).

33. Allen Buchanan, in his book *Justice, Legitimacy, and Self-Determination* (Oxford University Press 2004) seems to me to be guilty of the first charge (see in particular 234–47), especially in relation to his near total neglect of international economic law, and John Jackson, (n 2) of the second. (See especially 57–78.)

34. This worry is addressed directly by Gopal Sreenivasan in his paper, "Does the Gats Undermine Democratic Control over Health?" (2005) 9 The Journal of Ethics 269–81. I will below show how my approach can provide answers to many of the problems raised by Sreenivasan without abandoning the real advantages of the GATS and other similar agreements.

for forcing a dissenter to go along, any more than the fact that, say, the majority of my neighbors prefer a certain lifestyle is grounds for forcing me to comply. Of course, states may voluntarily enter into organizations or agreements where majority or weighted majority vote controls, but this itself is no objection to the correct idea of the equality of nations.[35] Rather, this takes us to our next point. In a way that is similar to how individuals may commit themselves to a certain course of action by forming contracts, without this meaning that the notion of autonomy was somehow mistaken or illusory, states may bind themselves by entering into treaties, without this showing that the notion of sovereignty is illusory.[36]

Just as an individual may limit her autonomy in some ways by making an agreement as a means to achieving a goal, a state may limit its sovereignty—its freedom to act in an area where it may rightfully act—so as to achieve some important good, such as increased welfare or a wider total range of options in which to act. Just as the ability to bind one's self in this way may be autonomy-enhancing for an individual, so may the ability to enter into treaties be sovereignty-enhancing for states.[37] However, whether a particular agreement is autonomy-enhancing for individuals or sovereignty-enhancing for states will depend, at least in part, on the types of remedies that are available.[38] This is important in that, if remedies are not carefully crafted, many agreements that could be beneficial—autonomy or sovereignty-enhancing or welfare promoting—will not be entered into, making all parties worse off than they otherwise would be. Additionally, a poor fit between agreements and remedies can lead to a lessening of legitimacy for the agreements that are actually made, especially when less powerful actors or those with fewer resources accept an agreement out of necessity, but then feel aggrieved when there is a dispute over the agreement that requires them to take steps that do not seem to be fair. Remedies that provide more room for divergent policy choices can lessen this sting, even if they will not always fully remove it. Of course, none of this is to say that every actual treaty will turn out to be sovereignty-enhancing for states, any more than that every particular contract an individual enters into will be autonomy-enhancing for her. However, by allowing both states and individuals to have practices of binding themselves, we can, if the

35. For useful discussion here, see Ratner (n 6) 220–63.

36. The claim I attack here is suggested by Jackson (n 2) 71. On Bodin's notion of sovereignty, the sovereign may not bind himself, for if he did, he would no longer be sovereign. This seems to me to show the mistaken nature of Bodin's account, rather than that the very notion of sovereignty is rendered incoherent by the idea of a binding treaty, as Jackson seems to think. Bodin's claim is found in Bodin (n 23), bk. I, ch. 8, p. 358 of the standard pagination, or p. 11 in the edited Cambridge edition, *On Sovereignty*.

37. The classic case of binding one's self so as to be able to achieve a goal one would have otherwise not be able to achieve is that of Ulysses and the Sirens. For helpful discussion of the general phenomena, see Jon Elster, *Ulysses and the Sirens: Studies in Rationality and Irrationality* (Cambridge University Press 1979) 36–85.

38. Of course, this is not the sole consideration. As Scott and Stephan show, enforcement mechanisms are also very important, among other considerations.

practice is properly constructed, both respect their sovereignty (or autonomy) and expect, on average, to enhance it.

V. USING IDEAS FROM CONTRACT LAW TO ENSURE THE SOVEREIGNTY-ENHANCING NATURE OF TREATIES

In this Section of the chapter, I will show how many of these problems can be overcome or reduced if we understand international economic treaties more like we do contracts, and, among other considerations, attempt to craft remedies for a "breach" of a treaty that is in some ways similar to that of breach of contract. This would require a fairly significant shift in how we think of treaties, at least in relation to international economic law. At least on one interpretation, it would mean rejecting pacta sunt servada as the basic norm governing treaties,[39] and it would, for example, involve a major shift in how dispute resolution in the WTO works, at least officially,[40] with a shift from a property-rule paradigm to one more in line with liability rules.

Oliver Wendell Holmes famously argued that the obligation imposed by a contract was not to perform, simplicitor, but rather to perform or to pay damages.[41] Either course of action would fulfill one's legal duty.[42] This has not been the rule or the approach in international law. For example, as noted before, under WTO rules, as currently understood, a state may not fulfill its obligations, if found to be in violation, by accepting certain countervailing duties. These duties are meant to encourage the "offending" state to bring its actions into accordance with its obligations, and until a state does so, it is seen as in violation of its obligations.[43]

Holmes's formulation is often associated with the idea of "efficient breach"— the idea that breach of contract and payment of damages is justified when doing so would produce greater overall welfare than would fulfilling the contract. Though this is a likely scenario for Holmes's formulation to apply, it is not the only possible one. For example, one may decide to breach and pay damages for reasons other than economic gain. The cases most centrally addressed in this chapter will fall into this later pattern, though cases on a closer analogy with efficient breach are also possible. We may usefully characterize the cases at issue in this chapter as presenting a "sovereignty preserving" equivalent of efficient breach. In these

39. This would be so if we do not consider paying damages as "keeping" one's agreement. It is not obvious to me that we should think this, but the converse also does not seem obvious to me.

40. As we shall see below, the shift might well be seen to be less significant in practice, though even here, there would be important differences.

41. Oliver Wendell Holmes, "The Path of Law" in John Oberdiek and Aileen Kavanagh (eds.), *Arguing about Law* (Routledge 2009) 18.

42. Of course, someone might insist that this just shows that, even if Holmes is right, that legal and moral duties come apart here. I am not particularly sympathetic to this line of thought, but also do not think it is central to my concerns in this chapter, and so will not spend significant time on it.

43. DSU Art 22(2).

cases, a state holds that it would compromise important aspects of its rightful internal sovereignty if it were to "perform" under the treaty. In such cases, I contend, the state in question ought to have the option of "paying damages," in some suitably determined way, and to be seen to have thereby fulfilled its obligations under the treaty, just as one who pays damages after a breach of contract has fulfilled her legal obligations.[44] In this case, the "breaching" state is still able to exercise independent control over the area of life that it feels to be essential to it, while the "non-breaching" state is still able to gain the benefit of the bargain, by means of alternative remedies.

Cases closer to paradigmatic "efficient breach" are also possible on my account, perhaps particularly in the sorts of situations discussed by so-called "strategic trade theory."[45] These cases, however, seem somewhat more problematic to me than either standard efficient breach in contract or the "sovereignty preserving" version discussed above, in that there may be more chance of undermining the trade system as a whole in these situations. If so, special care must be used to craft remedies for such cases, though I will leave these aside here.

The approach argued for in this chapter can also help with another important issue that has developed in multilateral treaties such as the WTO agreement, the issue of treaty rigidity. This is an issue that is especially likely to arise in multilateral treaties with many members and where supermajority or consensus voting rules make changes to the treaty difficult to achieve.[46] There is a difficult situation here, related to the "equality of nations" aspect of sovereignty. States have good reason to worry about joining treaties that cannot be changed except with great difficulty, even in the face of changed circumstances, but there is also no universally accepted voting rule that would make change easier to accomplish. Smaller states are unlikely to accept voting that is weighted on population or economic factors, such as that found in the IMF, as it would allow them to be dominated by larger or more powerful states, and larger and more powerful states are unlikely to accept simple majority voting, as this could lead to a small minority of

44. As Bix notes, a significant worry about the Holmes formula is that, at least in a typical American contract case, damages can rarely be expected to make the non-breaching party whole. See Bix (n 8) 116. While this need not be a legal problem, it suggests that paying damages may not fulfill all of one's moral duties, though the question seems to me to be a difficult one. However, this worry seems less pronounced to me in the case of treaties than in contracts, in that states are arguably better situated to expect, and negotiate around, these costs, and to be repeat-players, who sometimes come out ahead, sometimes behind, but who can expect balance in the end.

45. See Paul Krugman, "Introduction: New Thinking about Trade Policy" in Paul Krugman (ed.), *Strategic Trade Policy and the New International Economics* (Massachusetts Institute of Technology 1986) 1–22 for a brief overview of strategic trade theory. Strategic trade theory "claims that much of international trade is the result, not of inherent national advantages, but of 'increasing returns'" that come from large-scale production. These advantages may, in some instances, be created directly by government action. Paul Krugman, *Pop Internationalism* (Massachusetts Institute of Technology 1996) 109–10.

46. See Jackson (n 2) 47 for useful discussion of this point.

the world's population or economic power dictating to the rest. The predictable result is a stalemate. This makes changing exiting institutions difficult, and gives a strong disincentive to forming new institutions, even when doing so would be predictably beneficial.

My approach can help mitigate this problem, even if it cannot solve it. (There may be no complete solution.) By offering greater flexibility to states in meeting the obligations imposed by international institutions, the cost of entering such institutions may be made more acceptable. Conversely, by making the cost of existing institutions more explicit, the approach argued for here may also help encourage increased cooperation for making needed modifications to existing institutions.

VI. ILLUSTRATIONS AND EXAMPLES

I will now turn to three examples of fairly recent and prominent disputes in international economic law to show how my approach may be applied in these situations. By looking at these examples, we can see how this approach can help promote sovereignty while maintaining international obligations, and also get some idea of how remedies might be crafted differently in particular cases. The cases I will consider will include disputes between two highly developed countries or associations of countries, and between a highly developed country (the United States) and a less developed country (Antigua in one case and Mexico in the other.) I will here look at the disputes between the United States and Canada and the EU over hormone-treated beef, the dispute between the United States and Antigua over internet gambling, and the dispute between the United States and Mexico over access to the United States by Mexican truckers.

VII. EU–U.S./CANADA BEEF HORMONE DISPUTE

The dispute between the EU and the United States and Canada over hormone-treated beef lasted over 20 years before finally reaching a negotiated settlement in 2012.[47] The ban started in 1988, when the EU banned the importation of beef treated with certain hormones. These hormones were, at the time, used in approximately 90 percent of U.S.-raised beef, and were considered to be safe by the United States and Canada. The EU, however, claimed that there was not sufficient evidence showing that they were safe. The ban was challenged before a panel of the Dispute Resolution Body of the WTO as a non-tariff barrier to trade. The EU argued that clauses in the Agreement on the Application of Sanitary and Phytosanitary Measures allowed the ban, but this argument was rejected (for somewhat different reasons) by both the original panel and by the Appellate Body of the WTO. Countervailing duties amounting to over $110,000,000 per year for the United States and $11,000,000 for

47. This settlement, importantly, did not result in the EU removing its ban on hormone-treated beef, but rather allowed other alternative measures to be taken.

Canada were allowed by the Appellate Body, to be imposed on a rotating body of EU agricultural products.

This dispute touched on food safety and agricultural policy, two areas traditionally and plausibly thought to be subject to internal state control, and on which societies might reasonably disagree. While food safely and agricultural policy may raise human rights issues, these were not relevant to this particular dispute, making it a straightforward example for the approach of this chapter, which focuses on "policy space" issues that, while important, are less pressing than human rights. The fact that the WTO Dispute Resolution Body and Appellate Body found that the EU had not supplied sufficient scientific evidence to justify its ban of hormone-treated beef under the Agreement on the Application of Sanitary and Phytosanitary Measures does not change this point. Here we have a tribunal with limited, at best, democratic accountability dictating to a society which level of health precautions it must take.[48] If the WTO agreement requires the EU to admit in food products that it does not consider safe, then it will clearly be sovereignty-reducing, cutting into the relevant policy space held by the EU, and thereby give incentives to the EU and its member-states to not engage in such agreements in the future. But, if the United States and Canada cannot depend on the Dispute Settlement Body of the WTO to secure their rights under the Agreement, then these countries, too, would have reasons to be skeptical of such agreements. The approach advocated in this chapter can help solve this problem. Here carefully crafted remedies, which would compensate the United States and Canada for their loss of expected benefits under the treaty while still allowing the EU the ability to set its own health and safety standards, would provide for a sovereignty-enhancing alternative. In the end, this is exactly what happened, providing some implicit support for the theory presented in this chapter. In 2012, after more than 20 years of dispute, the EU and the United States and Canada reached a negotiated agreement, giving the United States and Canada greater access to the "high quality" beef market in the EU in exchange for removing their countervailing duties.[49] This agreement did not bring the EU into compliance with their obligations under the WTO agreement, as set out by the Appellate Body, but rather reached a mutually satisfactory agreement that did not require the EU to give up the ability to make its own decisions on what level of food safety was most appropriate for

48. The point here is not that the WTO agreement lacks legitimacy, in the sense that it was entered into under unfair conditions or the like. My point, as I make in the text following this note, is only that using the current means of enforcing WTO agreements as the only possible type of enforcement will lead to fewer mutually beneficial agreements being made, because they will be seen as unreasonable intrusions into legitimate areas of democratic decision-making.

49. See Press Release from the European Parliament, "Win-Win Ending to the 'Hormone Beef Trade War,'" March 14, 2012, http://www.europarl.europa.eu/news/en/news-room/content/20120314IPR40752/html/Win-win-ending-to-the-hormone-beef-trade-war accessed August 28, 2016.

its citizens,[50] while still providing comparable benefits to trading partners, so as to retain roughly equivalent benefits to those bargained for. If the proposal argued for in this chapter had been in place at the time of the dispute, the conflict could have found a mutually beneficial solution without wasting 20 years on expensive litigation and trust-destroying rotating retaliatory tariffs.

VIII. U.S.-MEXICO TRUCKING DISPUTE

As part of the NAFTA agreement, the United States had an obligation to allow Mexican trucks to deliver goods from Mexico to the United States and return goods from the United States to Mexico. However, this program was delayed for nearly 15 years on the grounds that, according to the United States, Mexican trucks did not meet U.S. safety standards. Mexico, in retaliation, imposed countervailing duties on U.S. goods. Highway and automobile safety is plausibly an area where states should have a high degree of autonomy in setting their own standards, not least because different societies may reasonably differ on the costs and benefits of different measures and what level of risk they are willing to take on. For the sake of argument I will here assume that, in this case, the United States was motivated by actual safety concerns and the inability of Mexican trucks to meet generally applicable standards that were set higher in the United States than in Mexico, and not merely engaging in pro-U.S. trucking protectionist measures. Given this, the United States could reasonably feel that it would be unacceptable to be required to allow trucks that it did not believe to be safe to drive in the United States or to lower its safety standards for trucks. While the NAFTA agreement, which entered into force in 1994, called for cross-border access for Mexican trucks, this access was blocked by legislation in the United States for a number of years. After several years of complaints and failed negotiations, in 2001 a NAFTA arbitration panel unanimously found the United States to be in violation of its obligations and authorized the imposition of countervailing duties amounting to $2.4 billion dollars annually.[51] Importantly, the panel held that "the inadequacies of the Mexican regulatory system provide an insufficient legal basis for the United States to maintain a moratorium on the consideration of applications for U.S. operating authority from Mexican-owned and/or domiciled trucking service providers."[52]

In this case, Mexico imposed countervailing duties on U.S. goods in retaliation. However, more appropriate remedies could have been crafted, such as a comparable exclusion of U.S. trucks from Mexico until the dispute was settled, or requiring the United States to pay an amount into a fund to be used to improve and verify safety standards of Mexican trucks until the appropriate standard was

50. I should note that I largely agree with the Appellate Body that the EU's position was not, in fact, well supported scientifically, but also hold that this is beside the point in this context.

51. See In the Matter of Cross-Border Trucking Services (Secretariat File No. USA-MEX-98-2008-01), Final Report of the Panel, February 6, 2001.

52. *Ibid.* para. 296.

reached. Once the standard was reached, further exclusion of Mexican trucks would not be justified under this approach. Either of these approaches would have better acknowledged that highway safety is an area where states may legitimately disagree, but that, in light of the duties imposed by the NAFTA agreement, certain policies, such as that imposed by the United States, would have higher prices. As matters stand, the United States has agreed to a pilot program to allow Mexican trucks to have access to the United States, if they meet certain safety and reporting requirements.[53] The approach argued for in this chapter would likely have helped reach this desirable end more quickly and with fewer destructive tariffs having been imposed, while still respecting the freedom of each state to determine the proper level of safety for interstate truck and similar activities.

IX. U.S.-ANTIGUA INTERNET GAMBLING

This case provides one of the most interesting possible applications for the approach argued for in this chapter. The dispute started in 2003, when the government of Antigua and Barbuda commenced a challenge before the WTO challenging the United States' total ban on cross-border gambling services, several providers of which were based in Antigua. In 2004, a Dispute Resolution Body (DRB) panel ruled in favor of Antigua.[54] Antigua attempted to reach a negotiated settlement with the United States, but was unsuccessful. The United States appealed the ruling to the Appellate Body of the DRB, but the Appellate Body again ruled for Antigua, though on slightly different grounds.[55] Importantly, the Appellate Body rejected the United States' argument that the "public morals" clause in the GATS allowed its ban on internet gambling.[56] For several years the United States evaded coming into compliance with the ruling, before eventually claiming that it would, instead, withdraw from its obligations under the GATS in this area. Because such a removal of benefit can be made only with appropriate compensation, Antigua asked WTO arbiters for the right to impose appropriate remedies.

Rules relating to "public morality" are plausibly within the rightful sovereignty of a state, and again represent an area where different societies may reasonably disagree. To tell a state that it must accept activities that it considers to be socially harmful is plausibly to make a deep intrusion into the state's ability to engage in self-government. In this case, the WTO Dispute Settlement Body

53. Federal Motor Carrier Safety Administration, "U.S.–Mexico Cross-Border Trucking Piolet Program," http://www.fmcsa.dot.gov/international-programs/mexico-cross-border-trucking-pilot-program accessed August 28, 2016.

54. The exceedingly long full panel decision may be found here: http://www.antiguawto.com/wto/37_WTO_Panel_Report_%2010Nov04.pdf, accessed August 18, 2016.

55. See United States, Measures Affecting the Cross Border Supply of Gambling and Betting Services, WT/DS285/AB/R, April 7, 2005. The Appellate Body report may be found here: http://www.antiguawto.com/wto/Antigua%20_WTO_Appellate_Body_Report_7Apr05.pdf, accessed August 28, 2016.

56. *Ibid.* §§ 277–327.

and the Appellate Body held, not implausibly, that, from the perspective of the WTO agreement, there was no difference between the domestic gambling services allowed by the United States and the internet gambling services provided by Antigua, and so the United States was in violation of its obligations under the GATS agreement by blocking internet gambling operations from Antigua.[57] Antigua was therefore authorized to put in place countervailing duties on the United States. However, the great difference in size between the United States and Antigua made traditional countervailing duties impossible to employ. Even if Antiguans stopped importing any goods from the United States, the United States would hardly notice, and the Antiguans would merely be made worse off. Therefore, an arbitration panel of the WTO took the unusual step of allowing "cross-modal" remedies, allowing Antigua to avoid its obligations under intellectual property laws and the agreement on Trade Related aspects of Intellectual Property (TRIPS) in relation to the United States, and to produce and sell copies of protected materials. Unable to reach any other resolution, Antigua has recently changed its copyright and patent laws to allow such activities.[58]

As in all such cases, the DSB officially sees these measures not as "damages" that the United States may decide to pay if it decides to keep in place its ban on internet gambling, but rather an inducement to encourage the United States to take steps that it has an obligation to meet. Such an understanding has two problems. First, it will require more ongoing supervision from the DSB than is desirable, so as to make sure that the "inducement" is proper and not being abused. If the award to Antigua were instead seen as damages analogous to those in contract law for breach, then it would be reasonable to put the obligation to show that they are no longer necessary, if that were to be the case, on the United States. Second, this interpretation suggests that a state may not rightfully decide, via the democratic process, what its public morals legislation should be, but rather that such decisions may be decided by unaccountable tribunals. While the approach argued for in this chapter allows that such decisions might involve a cost (damages to be paid), it holds that states ought to retain the policy space needed to make such decisions. The current rule is likely to make increased cooperation less likely rather than more likely, as states rightfully think they cannot engage in this sort of cooperation without risking important goods. We see just this result in this case, with the United States taking the then-unprecedented step to fully withdraw a former concession, here to allow cross-border gambling services. Now that this step has been taken, similar moves, weakening the overall trade system, are more likely. If such steps are accepted as regular, or seen as the only way to respond to perceived invasions of rightful sovereignty, the overall trade system will be weakened My alternative approach, which sees the rights granted to Antigua

57. I should add that I think this reasoning is quite persuasive, but also think that these sorts of decisions are most properly made via the democratic process within a country.

58. See "Antigua Adopts New Strategy in On-Line Gaming Battle with United States", Caribbean360, January 24, 2014, http://www.caribbean360.com/business/antigua-adopts-new-strategy-in-online-gaming-battle-with-united-states, accessed August 28, 2016.

to circumvent intellectual property rules otherwise required by the TRIPS agreement as damages, and thereby encourages negotiation over appropriate measures, both recognizes the rights of a state such as the United States to set its own rules in these areas, and makes transparent that certain choices will have costs that the state will have to decide to accept or not. The approach set out in this chapter, therefore, is sovereignty-preserving and does not threaten future cooperation, at least to the degree that is done by the current WTO system.

X. TWO FURTHER ADVANTAGES OF THE "CONTRACT" APPROACH

The "contract" approach to international economic law suggested in the chapter has two further advantages over the existing paradigm and possible rivals. First, it helps show a better, more constructive way to solve certain sorts of worries over the "democracy deficit" found in international economic law than does the current approach (and some possible rival approaches.) Second, it may provide us a framework for thinking about the interplay between international economic law and human rights law. These are both long-standing and multifaceted problems, and I cannot hope to give full treatments to them in this chapter. However, I will hope to show how the approach I suggest here, that of using ideas from contract law to understand international economic treaties, might allow us to make progress in these areas. I will first discuss one example of a worry about conflicts with democracy and then look at human rights.

In his important paper, "Does the Gats Undermine Democratic Control over Health?,"[59] Gopal Sreenivasan argues that international trade agreements may unduly restrict societies from making decisions that ought to be under their own democratic control. In particular, he argues that the GATS "unduly restricts the scope for democratic control" over important aspects of a domestic health system.[60] In doing so, Sreenivasan introduces a distinction that is potentially problematic for my approach, between national sovereignty and democratic legitimacy, and argues that while international economic agreements may promote the former, they often violate the later in a way that is unacceptable. I hope to show that my approach to international economic treaties, seeing them as similar to contracts in important ways, helps disarm this worry and shows it to be misguided insofar as it calls for an approach different from my own.

Sreenivasan is particularly worried about cases where a country enters into an agreement such as the GATS, placing certain restriction on its ability to regulate services. (This self-restraint is in exchange for similar restraint by other countries, it must be added. This element is strangely undiscussed in Sreenivasan's paper, but will be essential for understanding the correct way to deal with these problems. If we fail to see these restraints as bargained-for attempts to achieve mutual advantage, we will misunderstand them. The contract approach helps

59. Sreenivasan, (n 34) 269–281.

60. *Ibid.* 270.

drive this point home.) What is especially worrisome here, Sreenivasan suggests, is that the original decision to "bind" some area under an agreement such as the GATS will persist into the future, limiting the ability of future citizens to make certain decisions.[61]

If it were impossible for a state to remove or withdraw from obligations it had placed on itself via a treaty, then Sreenivasan's objection would be completely convincing. However, as he notes (and as the U.S./Antigua dispute discussed above shows) it is in fact possible for a state to withdraw from its obligations under GATS. Sreenivasan objects, however, to the fact that this may require the payment of compensation, and may only be made after appropriate notice, making the decision to withdraw an expensive one for the state seeking to "unbind" an area formerly bound under the agreement.[62] Sreenivasan argues that this fact leaves democratic legislators with "no power" (or, when he is being more careful, "effectively none") to change their obligations under such an agreement,[63] and holds that this requires that any such agreement must be subject to supermajority decision-making, in a way similar to how a constitutional amendment would be, if it is to be democratically legitimate.[64]

Once we use ideas from contract law to think about international economic treaties, however, we can see that Sreenivasan has gone wrong at several important points. Taking my approach helps us understand why the notification and compensation requirements for "unbinding" an economic sector currently bound by the GATS is completely reasonable and not plausibly antidemocratic in any important sense. Once we see these agreements as similar to contracts, we must note that more than one society or peoples is involved. If a state could withdraw from its agreement without paying appropriate compensation, then it would have the ability to gain from the restraint of others without having given up anything comparable on its own. Of course, such agreements would typically be exploitive and not something that states could legitimately agree to. So, if we removed this aspect from treaties such as GATS, any internal democratic legitimacy gained would come at the expense of others who would have even less democratic influence on the decisions—people in other states—or would lead to less autonomy for peoples overall, because of a reduced ability to take advantage of the sovereignty-enhancing power of treaties. (Here we should recall the earlier quoted remark from Fried on the autonomy-enhancing features of being able to bind one's self in an agreement.) Furthermore, compensation is only required when others have relied on the binding. If there is no reliance, no compensation is needed. This indicates that the compensation is a necessary element of fair dealing here, as we would expect if we saw these agreements not as the one-sided restrictions on behavior that Sreenivasan seems to see them as, but as mutually

61. *Ibid.* 277.

62. *Ibid.* 277

63. *Ibid.* 278.

64. *Ibid.* 280.

beneficial agreements undertaken by multiple parties. That is to say, we should see these agreements as similar to contracts.

This does not mean that Sreenivasan is wrong to suggest that some sort of supermajority affirmation of treaties such as the GATS should be required by state governments. I take no stand on that issue here. It is worth noting, though, that the approach argued for in this chapter offers a method for dealing with conflicts between national democratic decision-making and treaty obligations that is less onerous than the full unbinding of a section of the economy—paying compensation as "damages" to the party whose bargained-for benefit has been abrogated. When we see that this is a possibility, then worries about possible nullification of democratic control are greatly lessened. When we join this point with the recognition that it would be illegitimate in itself to change treaty obligations without compensation, given their contract-like nature, then most of the worries suggested by Sreenivasan dissipate, and the conflict between sovereignty and democracy here is shown to not be as significant a problem as we might have thought.

Next I will show how the approach argued for in this chapter may open up new and fruitful ways to think about the connection between international trade and human rights.[65] One particularly fraught issue is how to react when an obligation under an economic treaty arguably conflicts with a requirement to support human rights. This conflict comes in two main varieties. Either a state may believe that if it fulfills its obligations to other states under an economic treaty, it will potentially violate the rights of its own citizens, or else a state may believe that, in fulfilling its obligations under an economic treaty, it aids in the violation of human rights by another state. This second possibility arises in particular when a state decides whether to impose trade sanctions in response to human rights violations.

One source of significant difficulty in integrating human rights protections and international economic law is the extremely limited explicit authority under existing international economic treaties to abrogate an obligation in the name of protecting, ensuring, or promoting human rights. While it is conceivable that, in WTO cases, GATT articles XVIII (government assistance for economic development), XX(b) (general exceptions necessary to protect human life or health), or XXI (security exceptions) could justify departing from a treaty obligation to promote or protect human rights, or that the various "necessity" clauses found in many BITS and in the customary international law of investment[66] could also do so, there is little explicit authority for this, and even less explicit jurisprudence. While some have called for the explicit integration of human rights law

65. This is, of course, a huge topic with an ever-expanding literature. I can hope to address only a small part of the issue here. For a useful overview of many of the relevant topics, see Thomas Cottier, Joost Pauwelyn, and Elisabeth Burgi (eds.), *Human Rights and International Trade* (Oxford University Press 2005). My discussion here has some similarity to that presented by Steven Ratner. See Ratner (n 6) 323–38. My account is more focused on showing how a particular method (the one argued for here) can address possible conflicts than is Ratner's. I see the two projects as complementary rather than in competition.

66. See here Ratner (n 6) 360–70 for discussion.

and international economic law, the "contract" approach argued for here provides another, less radical possibility.

As Karin Lucke has noted, "All WTO members are parties to at least one of the human rights treaties with a legal obligation to respect, protect, and fulfil the human rights they stipulate."[67] While often reluctant to do so, courts have sometimes been willing to find that a contract is void due to "impossibility" because of an intervening legal obligation that makes performance under the contract in violation of another legal duty.[68] While the analogy between an intervening law that would justify an impossibility defense in contract law and an obligation under a preexisting human rights treaty is not perfect, it does provide a possible justification for not meeting an obligation under an international economic treaty when doing so would conflict with a human rights duty. The parallel is made stronger when we recall that while conflicts between human rights and economic treaty obligation are, in some sense, predictable, individual and specific conflicts are unlikely to be known about at the time a treaty is negotiated. In this way, the future emergence of the conflict is more like the intervening legal obligations that grounds an impossibility defense in contract than we might have first thought. We see here again how taking ideas from contract law can help us better meet our obligations under international economic treaties, by showing how these obligations may be made compatible with human rights norms.

XI. SOME POSSIBLE OBJECTIONS

In this Section I consider three possible objections to the approach argued for in this chapter: first, that it is not significantly different from current practice; second, that this approach would reduce the stability and predictability we seek from international economic treaties; and finally, that the approach would undermine international economic law more generally by encouraging parties to not comply, thereby reducing valuable cooperation.

The first question one might have about this approach is whether it is a significant change from current practice at all, or whether it is merely a relabeling of what actually happens in the WTO at this time. After all, many of the most well-known trade disputes have gone on for years. In the U.S./Canada–EU beef hormones dispute, for example, countervailing duties were in place for nearly 20 years before a negotiated settlement was reached. Why think that this approach is, therefore, importantly different in substance than what we have now?

There is something importantly right in this objection, in that a large part of the approach argued for here is to change how we think about or conceptualize our obligations under international economic law, rather than to suggest very different penalties than have been put in place by the WTO DSB. However, I contend that even this reconceptualization can be significant, insofar as it helps us

67. Karin Lucke, "States' and Private Actors' Human Rights Obligations under International Human Rights Law and the Draft UN Norms," in Cottier, Pauwelyn, and Burgi (n 65) 150.

68. For discussion of this point, see Bix (n 8) 81–83. See also UCC § 2-615(a).

better understand the normative structure of international economic law. First, it helps us see that countervailing duties or the withdrawal of protections are not, in these cases, punishment, but rather costs that a party must pay. Under my approach, when the DSB allows countervailing duties, this is not meant as a punishment for the "offending" state, but as a way to make the costs of the choice transparent, in a way that is similar to the order to pay damages in a contract dispute. The strict liability nature of damages in contract suggests that damages are best seen as costs and not punishment,[69] and something similar, I contend, should be seen in the case of "damages" applied in disputes over international economic treaties. In such cases, a society may more carefully decide which it values more—preventing internet gambling or having additional protection on intellectual property, for example—and evaluate its choices in light of their costs. Insofar as decisions of tribunals are seen as imposing an obligation, and not merely a cost, on a society, this sort of evaluation is not officially open. It is my contention that, by making this structure more transparent and explicit, societies will be able to better evaluate their choices and to be better reconciled to the costs and benefits that come from international cooperation. Here it is worth reflecting again that the actual resolution of the U.S./Canada–EU beef hormones dispute did not involve the EU coming into compliance with its obligations under the WTO agreement, but rather finding a different mutually acceptable solution. The approach argued for in this chapter would encourage such solutions and therefore likely lead to quicker and more mutually satisfying outcomes, causing less damage to the international trade system.

The second objection builds on the idea that one of the important goals of international economic law is to promote stability and predictability in the international economic realm, and worries that an approach such as mine, which might be seen as allowing states, at least in some situations, to "buy their way out" of the obligations imposed by treaties, will greatly reduce this stability and predictability.[70] If my proposal did greatly increase instability and unpredictability in the international trade system, it would be a significant reason to oppose it. However, I do not think this is a serious worry. First, many of the practical results that follow from my approach are similar to the current system, but with the added benefit of an expected quicker resolution. Second, by conceptualizing countervailing duties and other penalties as damages, we can increase the transparency of the system and work to develop more standardized systems of damages, perhaps drawing on the experience of contract law in various countries. We do not normally think that allowing damages other than specific performance greatly reduces the stability and predictability of the domestic economy, and I see no reason to think it would do so for the international economy. If anything, the more explicit importation of lessons learned from domestic contract law may well help promote stability and predictability, in particular by increasing transparency.

69. For useful discussion on this point, see Bix (n 8) 142–43.

70. This objection is pressed by Jackson, who suggests that it is also the opinion of many working in the WTO DSB. See Jackson (n 2) 168.

Finally, we might worry that my approach will reduce the overall amount of international cooperation by encouraging parties to "breach," thereby undermining international economic law. We might think that this approach is likely to make "breach" (and then payment of damages) more common than the traditional approach, and that this will make joining treaties less useful, perhaps leading to a downward spiral. This worry cannot be ruled out a priori, and must be taken seriously. However, I think that there is reason to think it is not the most likely outcome, even if "breach" is somewhat higher under my approach than under the traditional approach. This is so because we may reasonably expect the overall level of international economic cooperation under treaties to go up under my approach, even if there is somewhat more "breach" under any particular treaty. This result would follow if the sovereignty-enhancing aspect of my approach encourages states to enter into economic treaties that they otherwise would have found too risky under the traditional approach. If this expectation of increased activity is correct, then the total amount of beneficial cooperation will increase, even if under each treaty there is somewhat more "breach" than in the past.

XII. CONCLUSION

It would be foolish to think that all of the various difficulties that arise in relation to international economic treaties could be solved by applying ideas from domestic contract law. But, this is an as-yet underdeveloped resource for thinking about these treaties and how we might improve them. I have argued that by importing ideas from contract law we can make international economic treaties fairer and more just. In part this is done by showing how these treaties can be made sovereignty-enhancing rather than sovereignty-limiting by the use of different remedies borrowed from contract law, thereby increasing legitimacy and promoting mutually beneficial cooperation. And, I have shown how other ideas from contract law can help us understand the best way to conceptualize the potential conflicts between treaties and democracy on the one hand, and human rights on the other. Following this path, then, presents a possibility for moving toward a more just, fairer, and more prosperous world.

15

Defense and Ignorance

War, Secrecy, and the Possibility of Popular Sovereignty

ALEXANDER A. GUERRERO

It is natural to equate electoral democracy with popular sovereignty—the idea, roughly, that "we the people" govern. The main thesis of this chapter is that in the context of military and defense policy, there is a deep tension between standard electoral democratic systems of government and popular sovereignty. More bluntly: electoral democracy is incompatible with popular sovereignty, at least in the arena of national defense and military policy. We the people do not govern, we do not control what the government does; we are like dog owners holding a mile-long leash.

The first Section of this chapter will aim to get clear on the idea of popular sovereignty—what would it be for there to be popular sovereignty? Is there a realistic and attractive ideal of popular sovereignty? Should we accept popular sovereignty as a necessary condition of political legitimacy?

The second Section of the chapter will present some general problems for electoral representative systems of government in terms of popular sovereignty.

The third Section of the chapter will identify some particular problems for popular sovereignty in the defense and military context. To preview, I will suggest that four distinct but interrelated factors generate particular difficulties in the military and defense context. First, *confidentiality*: strategic requirements of confidentiality and secrecy undermine meaningful political accountability. Second, *voter ignorance*: military and defense policy is technical and complicated to an extent that the average voter lacks the information and competence required to hold elected political officials meaningfully accountable for enacting responsive policy. Third, *voter psychology and electoral pathology*: military and defense policy

Sovereignty and the New Executive Authority. Claire O. Finkelstein and Michael Skerker.

is an area—like criminal justice policy—in which low information leads to easy psychological distortion due to voters' fear, the difficulty of responding rationally to small-probability events, the conceptualization of "emergency" and "urgency," and the salience effects of bad outcomes in the military and defense context. As a result of these factors, elected officials have dramatically and inappropriately circumscribed policy options, given the electoral repercussions of appearing "weak" on military or defense (such as appearing "soft" on crime) and given that many of the most significant costs of ineffective policy are borne by others—either people in other countries or future generations of Americans. Fourth, *money*: military and defense policy is a "high financial value" policy arena—there is a lot of money to be made by a relatively small number of individuals and corporations, making lobbying and electioneering for certain political outcomes a very high value proposition for those entities. These four factors work together and overlap in complex ways, which I will discuss in this third Section.

The fourth Section of the chapter considers what might be preferable to using elected officials to enact military and defense policy from a perspective of popular sovereignty, given the real-world strategic and practical constraints. I will consider, in particular, the use of what I call "lottocratic" institutions—either in an oversight role or in a policymaking role. These institutions have been used to reform election law and voting systems in Canada and other places, and they consist of lottery-selected individuals charged with making policy and/or with policy oversight, but only after hearing from and interacting with a wide group of relevant "experts." I will consider some of the advantages and concerns about these institutions, and in particular whether they could lay claim to be institutions that would better achieve popular sovereignty than their electoral rivals.

I. THE IDEA OF POPULAR SOVEREIGNTY

Sovereignty has often been understood as referring to the property of having supreme authority within a territory or within a political community. *Popular sovereignty* is the idea that somehow the *people* (all of them together? most of them? many of them?) are the supreme authority within a territory. Popular sovereignty is often taken to be a prerequisite for political legitimacy—a necessary condition for a political system to be legitimate is that the people are the supreme authority. Putting more flesh on the bones of the idea of popular sovereignty has proven to be difficult, however.[1] What is required for the people to be the supreme authority? There are at least two dimensions that need clarification: the "people" part and the "supreme authority" part. Here are some candidate interpretations of the idea of popular sovereignty:

> FULL CONSENT: Popular sovereignty is fully consensual government: all political institutions and political actors have political power only if and only because all of the people living under those institutions have voluntarily

1. For relevant discussion, see Christopher Morris, "The Very Idea of Popular Sovereignty: 'We the People' Reconsidered," *Social Philosophy and Policy*, 17 (1) (Winter 2000): 1–26.

> consented to the existence of those political institutions and the empowerment of those political actors.

Of course, as is familiar from the literature on consent as a requirement of political legitimacy, the problem with this account is not that it fails to capture something of the ideal of popular sovereignty—doubtlessly it does. The problem, rather, is that no actual political system can satisfy this requirement, at least not if it is interpreted literally, meaning that no actual political system can claim to satisfy the demands of popular sovereignty. Not everyone has consented to the existence of the political institutions. Not everyone has consented to the empowerment of those who have political power, even in a perfectly functioning, fully inclusive democratic system. Some have argued that tacit consent—a kind of actual consent—is sufficient for legitimacy, and that tacit consent can be inferred from the fact that those living under the system continue to live under it and have not left. For a host of familiar reasons[2]—exit is costly, exit may not be possible, and there may be no better extant systems—tacit consent accounts that rely on this inference are implausible. So one direction of failure stems from construing "the people" to mean literally "all of the people."

A common weakening strategy is to require something like a *majority* of the people, rather than all of the people. So one might get something like this:

> POPULAR DEMOCRACY: Popular sovereignty is popular democracy: political power is exercised and political action is taken only if and only because a majority of the people living under the political institution consent to or support that exercise of power and the taking of that action.

This is better, in that some systems might seem close to satisfying this demand. One question is what makes it permissible to weaken the requirement from *all* of the people to just *most* of the people. Let us set that aside. A more immediate question, given the operation of modern political institutions, is that POPULAR DEMOCRACY suggests a level of detailed monitoring of and involvement with political action that is completely absent in the modern political context. Every modern democracy uses some system of electoral political representation—where some individuals are politically empowered to make binding political decisions for the rest of us. We choose legislative representatives. We choose an executive. One of way of viewing POPULAR DEMOCRACY as satisfied, even in the modern context, would be to read a vote for a political official as a tacit consent to or support of every action that official takes while in office. But that seems implausible, particularly given that elected representatives, elected executives, and appointed officials all have a great deal of leeway in terms of how they decide what they want to do once in office.[3]

2. Some pointed out by David Hume in his essay "Of the Original Contract" in 1748.

3. For relevant discussion, see Alexander A. Guerrero, "The Paradox of Voting and the Ethics of Political Representation," *Philosophy and Public Affairs* 38(3) (2010): 272–306.

Is there another interpretation of popular sovereignty that might more plausibly be satisfied, at least in some instances, by modern democratic states? One candidate ideal of popular sovereignty is "the idea that the ends of a polity should be determined by the interests or desires of its members."[4] I will recast this ideal in terms of what I will call *responsiveness.*

> RESPONSIVENESS: There is popular sovereignty in some political jurisdiction only if and only because there is responsive government in that political jurisdiction, government that generates responsive outcomes. Political outcomes are responsive to the extent that they track what the people living in the political jurisdiction believe, prefer, or value, so that if those beliefs, preferences, or values were different, the political outcomes would also be different, would be different in a similar direction, and would be different *because* the beliefs, preferences, and values were different.

Responsiveness is a multifaceted notion. And there are central complications to the basic idea. For example, the people living in a jurisdiction will not have uniform beliefs, preferences, or values—so there is a question of whether and how these are to be aggregated or measured in order to assess responsiveness. Even for a particular individual, beliefs, preferences, and values may tell in different directions. Is outcome *A* less responsive than outcome *B* because *A* tracks individuals' expressed preferences, but not their core values, while *B* does the reverse? Beliefs, preferences, and values change over time. Which are the benchmarks against which responsiveness is to be assessed? And there are many epistemic issues involved in knowing what people believe, prefer, and value, and which relate to how political problems are framed. Additionally, for some issues—ones of which the people in the jurisdiction are largely unaware—the notion of responsiveness will have to be responsiveness to implicit beliefs or plausible extensions of individuals' beliefs and values to cover issues and cases that might never have crossed their mind under those particular guises. For the purposes of this discussion, these complexities need not detain us here, although I will return to some of them below. Broadly speaking, the arguments do not turn on any particular understanding of responsiveness being the operative one, or upon any particular resolutions of these complexities.

It is worth noting that RESPONSIVENESS is a *tracking* conception of popular sovereignty. We might think that sovereignty should more immediately involve not just *tracking* of the people's beliefs, preferences, and values, but also *control* via those beliefs, preferences, and values. That is closer to what the previous two conceptions require. And it is true that RESPONSIVENESS might be satisfied by, say, an omniscient, omnipotent, benevolent dictator, who simply decided that the right way to govern was to act so as to maximally satisfy RESPONSIVENESS. It might seem strange to see this as a way of instantiating popular sovereignty. One way of seeing why this isn't so implausible, even in the case of the benevolent

4. See Morris, n. 1, p. 12.

dictator, is by noticing that there is a sense of control—counterfactual control—on which there would be control via the people's beliefs, preferences, and values. If those attitudes of the people were different, then the policy results would be different as well.

Another way of seeing this conception is as a useful *heuristic* for when popular sovereignty is present. In the actual world, in which there are no omniscient, omnipotent, benevolent dictators, if we witness responsive government over time, that is usually an excellent reason to believe that the governmental system is such that the people really are (somehow) in control. In this sense, responsiveness isn't constitutive of popular sovereignty, but it is excellent evidence of popular sovereignty.

This brings us to the general issue of why popular sovereignty is an important part of political morality. Why should we care that "we the people" are in control and that the political power is, in some sense, in our hands? There are many different arguments here, but two main routes to this conclusion are through the ideal of moral equality and the ideal of individual autonomy.

The ideal of moral equality suggests that although we are not all equally talented, attractive, strong, intelligent, kind, and so on, we are all, in some important sense, of equal moral standing or of equal moral importance. The implications of this for political institutions are controversial and contested: Does this require a literally equal say in all political decisions? Equal political power? Equal consideration or weighting of each of our interests? Equal treatment under the law? All of these? One route to popular sovereignty is through the suggestion that each of us should have equal political voice or equal political power—there should not be some people who are placed in unequal positions of power over the rest of us. Of course, many think that electoral political representation is compatible with popular sovereignty, so spelling out the precise notion of popular sovereignty required by ideals of equality may be controversial.

A second route to popular sovereignty as an ideal of political morality is through the ideal of individual autonomy, the suggestion that each of us has the ability to be autonomous, and the right to have that autonomy respected and protected. There are many debates about how exactly to understand autonomy in this context, but one way is to say that an individual is autonomous to the extent that she lives and acts in accordance with her beliefs and values, with ends that she sets for herself, rather than ends that are set for her by others. If we hold out autonomy as an ideal, then there is a question of how political and legal institutions are compatible with that ideal, as they may seem to constrain and limit how individuals may act, and to effectively set and curtail the ends that individuals can have and strive toward. So, a second route to popular sovereignty as an ideal of political morality is to suggest that there may be political and legal institutions that do less to threaten or undermine or impede individual autonomy; namely, those institutions in which it is plausible to say that *we* govern *ourselves*, rather than being governed by someone else. Of course, there are challenges to see how any actual political or legal institutions are compatible with this ideal, but we might think that at least those that can claim popular sovereignty will be better off in this regard than those that cannot.

Much more could be said about both equality and autonomy and the relationship between those aspects of political morality and requirements of popular sovereignty, but it is at least plausible that popular sovereignty as Responsiveness might be an attractive way of understanding what popular sovereignty requires in terms of respecting demands of both equality and autonomy.

It is worth noting that one way to achieve Responsiveness might be to implement popular or direct democracy or to operate only via full consent. Whether or not this is the case will depend on the resolution of some of the above complexities regarding how to best understand responsiveness. But, importantly, responsiveness as defined is institutionally neutral—many different institutional structures might achieve responsive government.[5] Additionally, we can think of responsiveness—and responsive governments—as coming in degrees, so that there might be perfectly responsive governments, somewhat responsive governments, and so on. This is plausible as an interpretation of the ideal of popular sovereignty, with that ideal more closely achieved the closer a political system is to achieving perfect responsiveness. Whether or not it captures some historical or canonical ideal of popular sovereignty, I will assume that responsiveness is an important normative ideal for political systems—at least as sketched at this very general level; obviously, there would be certain ways of filling in the details that might make it unattractive.

It is also worth stressing that responsiveness would be controversial as the *only* normative ideal for political systems, since it might be that people's beliefs, preferences, and values are terribly mistaken or heinous, or that some natural (and even egalitarian) way of aggregating those beliefs, preferences, and values generates terrible and heinous results.

Throughout the rest of the chapter, I will take Responsiveness to be an important dimension of popular sovereignty, so that systems or policy outcomes that fail to achieve or exhibit Responsiveness thereby fail along at least one significant normative dimension, a dimension that is intimately related to, if not constitutive of, popular sovereignty.

II. GENERAL PROBLEMS FOR ELECTORAL REPRESENTATIVE DEMOCRACY

In this Section, I consider a general problem for representative, electoral democratic systems of government on the grounds that they do poorly from a perspective of responsiveness, at least when dealing with certain classes of political problems. The framing is often in terms of legislative representatives, but many of the same points apply—or apply with even more force—in the case of elected executives and the political appointees of such executives.

5. For fuller discussion of the way in which social context can lead to different institutional recommendations, see Alexander A. Guerrero, "Political Functionalism and the Importance of Social Facts," *in Political Utopias* (ed. by Kevin Vallier and Michael Weber, 2017): 127–150.

The argument I offer in this Section goes against standard justifications for systems of electoral representative government. One of the main justifications for systems of democratically elected political representatives is that because representatives are in power as a result of popular election, they will be concerned to do what is in the interests of the people, rather than just what is in their own narrow interest. Systems of elected representatives achieve responsive government, the theory suggests, via mechanisms of accountability: the law they create is responsive to the beliefs and preferences of those over whom they govern. (There is also the view that voters try to elect candidates who are of a "good type"—who will act in their interests even in the absence of electoral sanction. As will become clear, I am skeptical of the viability of this strategy as a means of achieving responsive government.) Representatives may be responsive to their constituents' preferences in that representatives explicitly defer to their constituents (doing as their constituents prefer), or because they act as guardians of their constituents' interests (doing what the representative thinks is best for—and what she may hope will come to be seen as best by—her constituents).[6] In most situations, representatives will do some of both. People expect their representatives to do more than just follow their lead, but the representatives get too far ahead of their constituents at their own electoral peril. Of course, people can be wrong about what is in their interests, or they can be confused about what policy will best achieve what they prefer. In such cases, a representative might work to convince his constituents of their error, or even depart from what they presently prefer in the hope that they will eventually come around to the representative's own view of the issue. But the notion of responsiveness that is tied to popular election of representatives is, fundamentally, connected to whether constituents themselves believe that some course of action is in their interests.

The suggestion in what follows is that for electoral representative systems of government, responsiveness is tied to what I will call *meaningful* accountability. Responsiveness is tied to accountability—we expect electoral democratic systems of government to do relatively well by responsiveness *because* those systems have the particular mechanisms of accountability that they do. But responsiveness is tied only to *meaningful* accountability. Meaningful accountability is distinct from accountability simpliciter in that the former, but not the latter, is connected to *informed monitoring* and *evaluation* practices.[7]

Accountability through elections requires—at least—free, regular, competitive, and fair elections. Candidate A runs on a platform of doing X, Y, and Z, in opposition to some Candidate B, who runs on a platform that is at least somewhat different from A's. If A's platform is more popular, she will likely win the election. After being elected, she will have many decisions to make while in office. These decisions will be monitored and evaluated by her constituents and the candidate

6. For discussion of relevant complexities, see Guerrero, n. 3, pp. 272–306.

7. The argument here draws substantially on Alexander A. Guerrero, "Against Elections: The Lottocratic Alternative," *Philosophy and Public Affairs* 42 (2014):135–78.

will be held accountable for decisions made while in office when she next comes up for re-election.

If elections are not free, regular, competitive, and fair, these mechanisms of accountability will fail. Without elections of this sort, Representative A might do whatever she likes once in office without fear of electoral punishment. She would be free to act in ways that are contrary to the preferences and beliefs of her constituents. And she would be free to do whatever might be most personally beneficial to her or to the causes she cares about.

Even in well-established electoral democracies, there are familiar concerns about electoral systems on the grounds that they are not adequately free, competitive, or fair. In the United States, for example, there are financial barriers to running for office, significant electoral advantages that come with incumbency and legislative rules that favor seniority, and systemic difficulties (stemming from the use of single-member districts and first-past-the-post voting rules) that undermine the viability of third-party candidates. Corporate money and inadequately regulated television advertising play an outsized role in determining who is elected. There are hurdles in place to keep poor, marginalized, and unsophisticated citizens from successfully registering and voting. There is intentional, competition-reducing bipartisan gerrymandering of districts. And, as *Bush v. Gore* in 2000 made particularly evident, there are even inadequacies in the mechanics of casting and counting ballots.

These are serious difficulties, certainly, and they play a significant role in reducing the accountability of representatives to those over whom they govern. But even if some of these were addressed, serious problems of accountability would still arise, or so I will argue.

The central problem for systems of electoral accountability in the modern political context is deep and pervasive political ignorance. Meaningful accountability requires elections that are free, regular, competitive, and fair. But it also requires that citizens know enough about who the candidates are, what they have done, what they are likely to do, and whether what they are likely to do is a good or a bad thing—from their perspective, or more generally. Even if citizens have the mental capability to monitor their representatives, this monitoring of representatives can be thwarted by ignorance: (1) ignorance about *what one's representative is doing* ("conduct ignorance"), and (2) ignorance about a *particular political issue* ("issue ignorance"). Of course, ignorance admits of degrees: one might know something about what one's representative is doing while still remaining largely ignorant of what she is doing. And one can know something about, say, global warming (or health insurance pricing, or the regulation of financial instruments, or whatever), while still remaining largely ignorant of the details of those issues and the various policy alternatives relevant to dealing with them. In addition to conduct ignorance and issue ignorance, there is a related, third kind of ignorance that also poses a threat to accountability. Even if one knows what one's representative is doing with respect to some issue, one may have no idea (or even belief about) whether what one's representative doing is a good thing in general or whether what she is doing will be good for oneself. We can call these two kinds of ignorance "broad evaluative ignorance" and "narrow evaluative ignorance," respectively.

Conduct ignorance, issue ignorance, broad evaluative ignorance, and narrow evaluative ignorance all can thwart accountability. The way in which these kinds of ignorance can thwart accountability is straightforward: each kind of ignorance can undermine the ability of ordinary citizens to engage in meaningful *monitoring* and *evaluation* of the decisions of their representatives. If I don't know what you've done, I can't hold you accountable for it. If I don't know anything about the issues or how to evaluate what you have done, I can't hold you accountable for voting yes, rather than no, or vice versa.

One of the main themes of political science research over the past 50 years is the remarkable extent of our ignorance across almost every politically relevant domain. Ilya Somin notes that "[t]he sheer depth of most individual voters' ignorance is shocking to many observers not familiar with the research."[8] Larry Bartels says, "[t]he political ignorance of the American voter is one of the best-documented features of contemporary politics."[9] John Ferejohn writes that "[n]othing strikes the student of public opinion and democracy more forcefully than the paucity of information most people possess about politics." He continues, "[d]ecades of behavioral research have shown that most people know little about their elected officeholders, less about their opponents, and virtually nothing about the public issues that occupy officials from Washington to city hall."[10]

This ignorance is both well-documented and unsurprising. As many have noted, it is not rational for individual voters to expend time and energy in becoming well informed about politics, given how unlikely it is that any vote will be decisive.[11] These claims about ignorance are general; they do not concern military or national security policy in particular. I will focus on specific issues in those domains in the next Section.

Here I want to stress one further fact relating to ignorance that is relevant in this context. Modern policymaking in general, and national security policy and military strategy in particular, has become incredibly technical and complex. This is important because although we might be generally ignorant, there may be some issues about which people are not ignorant, at least in a broad sense. So, for example, if there is a terrorist attack in a country, people in that country may not be ignorant of that fact. Or if there is a widespread famine in a country, people may not be ignorant of that fact. Or if a decision has been made to go to war with a particular country, people may not be ignorant of that fact. The difficulty comes in knowing more than these bare facts: What ought to be done? Is this a good idea?

8. Ilya Somin, *Democracy and Political Ignorance* (2013), 17.

9. Larry Bartels, "Uninformed Votes: Information Effects in Presidential Elections," *American Journal of Political Science* 40(1) (1996): 194–230.

10. John Ferejohn, "Information and the Electoral Process," in *Information and Democratic Processes* (ed. John Ferejohn and James Kuklinski, 1990), 3.

11. For discussion and critical argument, see Guerrero, n. 3, pp. 272–275.

How should we respond? Will this be good for me, for our country, for the world? Is this the right thing to do? We need answers to all of these questions in order to hold our elected officials—the ones making these decisions—meaningfully accountable. And answering those questions is exceedingly difficult.

Here is the basic argument that electoral representative systems will fail to bring about responsive outcomes in general.[12]

> (P1) Systems of electoral representation tend to bring about outcomes that are *responsive* to the preferences of some constituency, C, with respect to some problem, P, only if C can hold their representative(s) meaningfully accountable with respect to P.

Here are some reasons to think that (P1) is true. We can begin with a question: Without meaningful accountability, why would the actions taken by representatives be responsive to the beliefs, preferences, and values of their constituents? Representatives would have no electoral incentive to act in a responsive way, and they would not even have an incentive to learn what their constituents wanted. It is true that an elected representative might try to enact responsive policy simply because she thinks it is the right thing to do. The problem is that, in the absence of meaningful accountability, it becomes electorally costly to act in certain ways—including, perhaps, responsive ways—because of the influence of certain powerful interests.

Here is the concern: elected political positions for which the elected officials are not meaningfully accountable to their constituents will be used to advance the interests of the powerful (typically the financially powerful). Let us refer to this phenomenon as *capture*: an elected official is captured if he or she uses his or her position to advance the interests of the powerful, rather than to create policy that is responsive or good (when doing so would conflict with the interests of the powerful). The suggestion is that the absence of meaningful accountability leads to an increase in capture.

Here is a plausible idea: political power is more valuable to powerful interests the more that it is untethered from the preferences and beliefs of the people. If political officials are free to take a wider range of positions—and, in particular, can take positions that are contrary to the interests of the general public—this makes the offices held by those officials more valuable. So, as representatives become less accountable, it becomes more worth the effort to control those representatives or to control who is elected. And this may be considerably easier and cheaper than trying to alter the beliefs and preferences of the majority of people in a political jurisdiction through advertising and media—particularly if the interests of the powerful are at odds with the interests of most people in a jurisdiction.

There are two main ways in which powerful interests can respond to this increased value of political positions. The first is by influencing elections: determining who can be a viable candidate. The second is by influencing those

12. A version of this argument appears, in modified form, in Guerrero (2014).

elected: determining the political positions adopted and creating directed positional shifts, particularly through lobbying. In addition to there being more incentive to take these steps in the absence of meaningful accountability, both are also easier to do in the absence of meaningful accountability. I'll say more about this in the context of national defense and military policy in the next section.

If elections are badly structured (requiring significant financial backing, allowing significant corporate/individual donations, etc.), the powerful will control who can realistically run for office, in which case even meaningful accountability post-election will come too late. If elections are badly structured *and* there is no meaningful accountability, then representatives become little more than agents of the powerful.[13]

But even if the elections are not so badly structured, there will still be serious concerns about the influence of the powerful in who can be a viable candidate. First, powerful interests can control media presentation of candidates and their positions. This can make meaningful accountability more difficult through the increase in bad or irrelevant information. And this kind of control is made easier when the issues are ones about which voters are ignorant. If voters know very little about candidates, their views, and whether these views are good or bad, it is easier to manipulate how individuals feel about the candidates. Second, if political positions are valuable, it becomes sensible to identify and groom "controllable" candidates early on, making those who end up as viable candidates likely to be those whose positions and interests are congenial to the interests of the powerful.

Even if those elected are not beholden to the powerful when elected, once they are in office, the absence of meaningful accountability will lead to positional shifts in directions that benefit the powerful. Indeed, lobbying may be much more significant than campaign spending in terms of influencing policymaking.[14] This makes sense, given that in the absence of meaningful accountability, representatives will be able to do whatever they want. The worry is that in this "free zone," powerful interests will make it so that there is at least drift, if not outright directed movement, in the direction that those interests favor. Representatives operating in this free zone will have no electoral incentives to do the right thing if it goes against the interests of the powerful (*ex hypothesi*, their constituents won't know the difference), and the powerful will provide significant incentives to do what is in their interests. Representatives will have little incentive to seek out high quality

13. Empirical work suggests that this is a significant problem. See Martin Gilens, *Affluence and Influence: Economic Inequality and Political Power in America* (2012); Jacob Hacker and Paul Pierson, In *Winner-Take-All Politics: How Washington Made the Rich Richer—and Turned Its Back on the Middle Class* (2011), Lawrence Jacobs and Robert Shapiro, *Politicians Don't Pander: Political Manipulation and the Loss of Democratic Responsiveness* (2000).

14. As noted by Ansolabehere et al., "[t]he behavior of interest groups speaks to the value of lobbying: organizations spend 10 times more on lobbying than they do on campaign contributions." Stephen Ansolabehere, John M. de Figueiredo, and James M. Snyder Jr., "Why Is There So Little Money in U.S. Politics?," *Journal of Economic Perspectives* 1(1) (2003): 105–30. They note that in 1997–1998, interest groups spent $3 billion on lobbying, compared to $300 million on PAC contributions.

information regarding what would be best, and there will be plenty of easily available bad information that makes it seem that the best thing to do is to do what is in the interests of the powerful. Thus, even if representatives aren't controlled by the powerful when elected, there is likely to be substantial influence from the powerful to adopt positions congenial to their interests, and it is reasonable to expect the "acceptable" range of policy positions to shift accordingly.

The next premise in the argument is this:

> (P2) The presence of widespread issue, conduct, or evaluative ignorance within a constituency, C, with respect to some issue, P, undermines the ability of members of C to hold their representative(s) meaningfully accountable with respect to P.

(P2) is plausible given the definition of meaningful accountability and the discussion of meaningful accountability above. If people are ignorant about some issue, or about what their representative is doing with respect to that issue, or about whether what their representative is doing is good, they cannot monitor or evaluate what their representative is doing with respect to that issue.

It has been suggested that even if people are ignorant, they can still hold one's representative meaningfully accountable by using proxies, signals, and heuristics of various kinds to overcome issue, conduct, and evaluative ignorance.[15] These strategies amount to deference to the monitoring and evaluation done by some other individual or group. For example, membership in a political party, endorsements from activist organizations or media institutions, and contributions and public endorsements from particular individuals might all seem to help individuals overcome personal ignorance to hold their representatives meaningfully accountable with respect to particular political issues.

But there are problems with strategies of this sort. First, the proxies may either be too coarse-grained to help with accountability for particular issues or too fine-grained to save individuals any effort. Membership in a political party, for example, is a very imperfect signal with respect to any particular issue. A person might be a member of a party because it aligns with their views on A, B, and C, although they departs from the party with respect to D and E. On the other hand, endorsement from an organization that focuses narrowly on a particular issue will provide information about that issue, but it will require considerable effort on the part of individuals to learn which organizations can be trusted to provide reliable assessments and what all of the issue-specific trusted organizations say about the candidates.

This highlights the second problem with the use of proxies: it can be difficult and time-consuming to determine which proxies are credible, particularly if one wants to find reliable but specific proxies for many different issues. This can take almost as much effort, and be as challenging, as doing the research oneself.

15. See, e.g., the papers in John Ferejohn and James Kuklinski, eds., *Information and Democratic Processes* (1990).

Finally, for some issues, there may not be good proxies or signals. There may be issues that are low profile or do not attract well-funded individuals or groups to do the necessary investigative work, and there may be issues for which powerful interests have a lot at stake, and do everything they can to shape the available information and to obscure the nature of their interests and efforts. And there may be issues, such as military policy, where there are organized and powerful interests on one side of an issue, but where those on the other side (for example, those who might be on the receiving end of our military equipment) might be disorganized or otherwise disempowered.

> (P3) If a political problem is *information intensive*—(a) factually complex (requiring extensive knowledge of information in order to understand the problem) or (b) technical (requiring advanced education or experience to understand and evaluate possible solutions)—then there will typically be widespread issue, conduct, and/or evaluative ignorance with respect to that problem.

The general explanation of (P3) is the standard one about rational voter ignorance (it is rational to remain ignorant given how unlikely it is that one's vote will make a difference), combined with the difficulty of staying well informed, even if one had reason or desire to do so; and the possibility of significant but effective misinformation being produced by interested parties. It would be useful to have a metric to assess how information intensive a particular problem is, but I will not attempt to offer one here. It is plausible, however, that:

> (P4) Many political problems in modern political societies are information intensive.

There will be a spectrum of how information intensive problems are. Even relatively straightforward problems may involve complex factual issues or require one to make complex assessments of the consequences of adopting some course of action. It is plausible that most political problems are information intensive, but (P4) reflects only the more modest view.

To complete the argument:

> (P5) If a political problem is information intensive, then meaningful accountability with respect to that problem will be undermined. (Follows from (P3) and (P2).)
>
> (P6) If a political problem is information intensive, then systems of electoral representation will not tend to bring about responsive outcomes with respect to that problem.
>
> (C) Therefore, for many political problems, systems of electoral representation will not tend to bring about responsive outcomes with respect to those problems.

The above argument applies in a general way to electoral systems and political decisions. In the next Section, I will supplement this general argument concerning ignorance, complexity, and the lack of meaningful accountability with specific issues that arise in the context of military and national defense policy.

Of course, the above argument might be contested at various steps, and some of the premises might be bolstered or undermined by additional empirical research. The hope, however, is that the argument articulates a familiar set of concerns about electoral representative systems. These concerns are brought to the fore when one thinks about how little one knows about most of what one's elected officials do, how little real choice went into the election of one's representative (if one is in a district like most districts), how much deference to the goodwill of one's favored political party is required, how complex some issues are, how much of what one believes about various issues is a result of information provided by a few powerful media institutions, how much money powerful interests have at stake, and how hard it is to create rules to adequately police the influence of these powerful interests.

It is not much of a surprise that electoral systems have serious problems. As I note in Guerrero (2014), these three features are enough to cause trouble:

> *Principals and Agents*: some small number of X's are chosen by a much larger number of Y's, and the X's are to act on behalf of, or for the sake of, the Y's.
>
> *Electoral Accountability*: the mechanism that is to ensure or make likely that the X's act on behalf of the Y's is twofold: (a) initial election/selection by the Y's and (b) potential for re-election/selection by the Y's after some period of time.
>
> *Complexity and Opacity*: whether the X's are or have (a) actually acted or (b) tried to act on behalf of the Y's is not obvious to the Y's in the short-term (the time between election cycles).

These three features generate problems in their own right. But they are combined with two more:

> *Significance*: what the X's do has great significance in terms of regulating (or not) the powerful members of a society.
>
> *Open Influence*: there are plausible norms that require restrictions on how much regulation of political speech and influence from one Y to another there can be, regardless of the relative power or resources of the individuals.

There are obviously ways in which things could be made better, in terms of regulating campaign finance, post-electoral employment, lobbying, media coverage of elections, and so on. The problem is that these solutions don't address the core problems stemming from complexity and opacity. Those are information asymmetry problems, and they are not easily cured.

III. POPULAR SOVEREIGNTY AND RESPONSIVENESS IN THE NATIONAL DEFENSE CONTEXT

The above concerns have been articulated about electoral systems of government in general, suggesting that, despite the common equation of electoral representative democratic government with popular sovereignty in the form of responsive government, this equation may often—or at least for a wide range of political problems—fail to hold. In this Section of the chapter, I will sharpen and narrow the focus to particular problems for responsiveness in the national defense and military context. I will suggest that four distinct but interrelated factors generate particular difficulties in this context.

A. Confidentiality

The above argument, and in particular (P3), suggested that *information intensive* political problems would lead to widespread issue, conduct, and/or evaluative ignorance with respect to that problem, that ignorance of those kinds undermines meaningful accountability, and that the absence of meaningful accountability undermines responsiveness. Problems of national security—whether dealing with the threat of domestic terrorist attacks, terrorist attacks abroad, cyberwarfare, or more conventional nation-state military threats—are undoubtedly information intensive, and so that general concern applies.

Even worse for responsiveness, however, is the fact that much of the detail of national defense policy is made in secret, shrouded from public view, for reasons of safety (of those charged with carrying out the policy) and tactical strategy (many tactics only work if hidden from view of those who pose a threat to national security).

It is plausible that much that is currently hidden from view could be made public with little or no adverse effect on safety or effectiveness. Of course, one of the difficulties I want to draw attention to is that it is hard or impossible for an ordinary citizen to know whether this is *actually* plausible or not. Why, for example, does the legal rationale offered by the Department of Justice as to the legal permissibility, under U.S. Constitutional law, of the executive summarily ordering the killing of a U.S. citizen abroad need to be confidential? Why do the details of the process by which one can come to be placed on (or removed from) a kill list need to be confidential? Why is it important that it be confidential whether we are using or would be willing to use certain "interrogation techniques" or to make use of "black sites" or "extraordinary rendition" programs? What is the objection to giving some rough quantification of the extent to which these are used (e.g., there are between 50 to 100 black sites in operation)? It is also plausible that, in general, the recent trend toward increased classification—some would say over-classification—could be reversed with little cost to safety and strategy.[16] So, too,

16. See "Why Is That a Secret?" *New York Times* (Op-Ed), Aug. 24, 2011, available at: https://www.nytimes.com/2011/08/25/opinion/why-is-that-a-secret.html?_r=1 (noting a 40 percent increase in the number of documents classified from 2009 to 2010).

it would seem that there is plenty of room to reduce the invocations of executive privilege and to rein in use (misuse) of the Espionage Act.

But even leaving what we might call "excessive secrecy" to one side, there is surely some amount of appropriate or necessary secrecy. Additionally, whatever level of secrecy might have been required historically, there is reason to think that the rise of the computer and internet, and the corresponding digital storage and transfer of information, might require an overall higher appropriate level of secrecy. Globalization and interconnectedness present opportunities, but they also present risks. The possibility of a WikiLeaks kind of breach, involving the sheer magnitude of information that those breaches have involved, is unimaginable in the brick and mortar, pen and paper, low-tech world.

So, even in the best case, it seems that many political problems in the security and military policy context will be affected by a principle such as this:

> (P-confidentiality) If a political problem, or some significant aspect of a political problem, must be addressed in a confidential manner, then there will typically be widespread issue, conduct, and/or evaluative ignorance with respect to that problem.

This premise can replace or supplement the above premise (P3), increasing the likelihood that meaningful accountability in the national defense context will be undermined.

Of course, it is hardly a new development that national defense and military policy must be conducted with significant levels of confidentiality imposed. One significant difference in the post 9/11 world (or perhaps even the post–World War II, Cold War-world), however, is that it is not just tactical strategy within a public conflict that is confidential; it is also the details of the conflicts, the nature of the threats and enemies, the broad tactics being employed to gather information about potential threats, the resources being invested, the technology being developed, and so on. There has always been—and arguably always must be—a black box, but the box is much bigger now.

B. Voter Ignorance

In the previous Section, I noted the general problem of voter ignorance. It is worth stressing its pervasiveness in particular in the context of national defense and military policy. One consequence of the widespread use of security classification and confidential policymaking is that voters are largely ignorant of the details of what is being done. One can find out some broad information about the size and scope of the relevant institutions. For example, while for the CIA "[n]either the number of employees nor the size of the Agency's budget can, at present, be publicly disclosed," one can learn that, in the 1998 fiscal year, the aggregate intelligence budget was almost $27 billion.[17] And one can learn that the Department of Defense budget for fiscal year 2011 was around $740 billion (not counting

17. CIA website FAQ: https://www.cia.gov/about-cia/faqs/index.html#employeenumbers.

spending related to Veterans Affairs or veteran's benefits), that the Department of Homeland Security spending was around $50 billion, and that FBI counterterrorism operations were around $3 billion.[18] And one could, if so inclined, learn a lot more about the details of the amount of money requested and spent on at least some of the various military programs—around $11 billion on the F-35 Joint Strike Fighter, around $5 billion on the Virginia class submarine, around $3 billion on the V-22 Osprey program, and so on.[19] And, of course, one could learn broader contextual facts, such as that during 2011 the United States spent more on its military budget than the next 13 countries combined.[20]

The problem is that, despite this, it is impossible for an average citizen to be even minimally well informed about the size and nature of the threats that we face, how significant the threats are, what measures are needed to contain or eliminate these threats, or whether what we are currently doing is at all effective or necessary to address the threats that exist. Is the world more dangerous now than it was 10 years ago, or 20 years ago, or 50 years ago? Was the significant increase in defense spending from 2001 to 2010 and beyond[21]—even leaving aside the expenses associated with wars in Iraq and Afghanistan—a response to an increase in danger or required by an increase in the costs of prevention? Would we be just as safe if we spent half of what we spend? Is our military spending—in broad strokes, or in its details—more likely to increase or decrease our long-term national security?

Perhaps no one is in a position to give particularly well-informed answers to these questions, although there are certainly many people who claim to be experts on these topics, and there are people who have much more in the way of relevant information. The suggestion here is just that voter ignorance in the context of national defense and military policy is at least as bad as it is with respect to any other category of political problem.

C. Voter Psychology and Electoral Pathology

When a person doesn't have a lot of information about a political problem, it is easier to manipulate that person into believing something through a combination of misinformation and emotional manipulation. Additionally, there are some policy problems—such as criminal justice policy and national defense policy—that generate strong emotional reactions, claim to have a certain kind of urgent or emergency status, and have truly vivid and terrible worst-case outcomes. For these problems, emotional manipulation is both particularly easy and particularly effective.

18. See OMB Fiscal Year 2012 Budget—Historical Tables, Table 3.2.

19. See United States Department of Defense Fiscal Year 2012 Budget Request, available at: http://comptroller.defense.gov/defbudget/fy2012/FY2012_Weapons.pdf.

20. Brad Plumer, "America's Staggering Defense Budget, In Charts," *Washington Post*, January 7, 2013, available at: http://www.washingtonpost.com/blogs/wonkblog/wp/2013/01/07/everything-chuck-hagel-needs-to-know-about-the-defense-budget-in-charts/.

21. See http://www.washingtonpost.com/blogs/wonkblog/wp/2012/08/28/defense-spending-in-the-u-s-in-four-charts/.

One concern about these features of national defense problems is that the idea of responsiveness can become considerably more complicated—some of the complexities elided earlier might need resolution. In particular, there might well be contradictions in an individual's expressed or superficial beliefs, preferences, and values, and that person's deeper (unmanipulated) beliefs, preferences, and values. And there is the problem of how to understand responsiveness in the face of widespread ignorance. Consider the massive amount spent on national security and defense as compared to education. In 2015, of the roughly $1.16 trillion federal discretionary spending, $640 billion was on the military, with only $72 billion spent on education, only $38 billion on energy and the environment.[22] There is no evidence that this distribution reflects responsive policy choices, rather than outcomes that have been successfully lobbied for by the corporate military industry (which will be discussed more below). The point, here, however is that the American public is remarkably ignorant regarding both the total amount that is spent on various parts of the budget, as well as relative amounts that are spent. For example, polls have shown that the average public estimate is that 28 percent of the federal budget is spent on foreign aid, when in fact the actual amount is significantly less than 1 percent of the budget. Perhaps most remarkable is how wrong most people are, with more than 20 percent of those venturing a guess estimating that the United States spends more than 40 percent of the federal budget on foreign aid (*See* Figure 15.1).

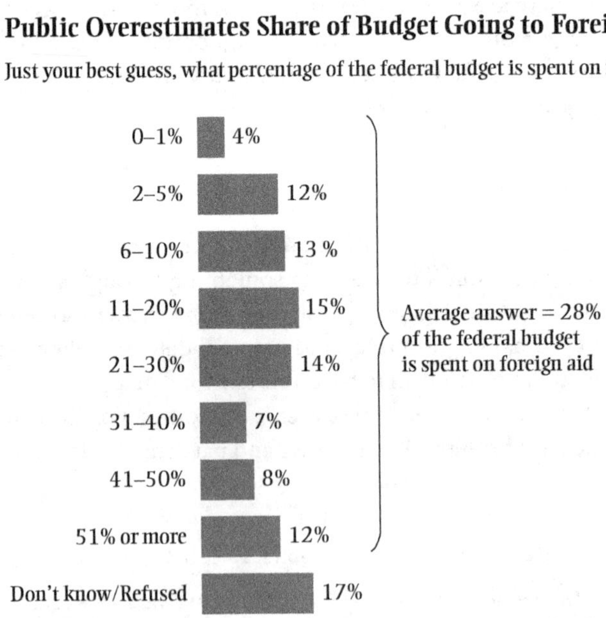

Figure 15.1 Public overestimates share of budget going to foreign aid.
SOURCE: Kaiser Family Foundation 2013 Survey of Americans on the U.S. Role in Global Health (conducted August 6–20, 2013).

22. Office of Management and Budget.

One way of understanding responsiveness in this context, then, focuses more on people's underlying values and commitments, rather than just on relatively shallow or misinformed beliefs. For example, after giving these extraordinarily high, inaccurate assessments of how much of the federal budget goes to foreign aid, people often then say they think the amount we give should be half of their very high estimate—so, 15 percent of the federal budget, rather than (what they currently think it is) 30 percent. It seems misguided to infer from that that these people would be—from a normative point of view—willing to increase the current amount of foreign aid 15–20 times what it is now, which is what an increase to 15 percent would mean. Instead, these seem well-categorized as "phantom" opinions, which would not survive presentation of all of the relevant nonmoral information. As James Fishkin puts it, reporting on Philip Converse's groundbreaking work:

> [S]ometimes the opinions reported in conventional polls do not exist. They are non-attitudes or phantom opinions because respondents almost never wish to say that they do not know. This phenomenon was originally discovered by Philip Converse.... There was a National Election Studies panel that was asked the same questions from 1956 to 1960. The questions included some low salience items such as the government's role in providing electric power. He noticed that some of the respondents offered answers that seemed to vary almost randomly over the course of the panel.... Converse concluded that there were not real opinions being reported but that a significant portion of the people were answering randomly.[23]

If we are in a situation of dealing with either absent beliefs and preferences or phantom or shallow beliefs and preferences, it will be impossible or inappropriate to measure responsiveness simply in reference to what people currently believe or prefer. Instead, it seems we will need some other means of giving people a chance to form accurate beliefs and to have policy preferences that are in line with these more accurate beliefs, given their values.

There will also be complications stemming from beliefs and values that are not simply the product of misinformation, but which the person comes to adopt for bad reasons, as a result of rationally inappropriate manipulation, rather than through some other more epistemically commendable process. Consider the belief that it was necessary to force Japanese Americans into internment camps during World War II. It is plausible that this was the result of a combination of irrational fear and manipulation into thinking that Japanese Americans posed a threat, despite the lack of evidence to support this belief. Or consider the importance placed on whether a politician is "tough on crime"—where that often means pursuing incredibly punitive criminal justice policies with almost no thought to cost. It is possible that these reflect our true beliefs and values, but there is at least

23. James Fishkin, *When the People Speak* (2009), 123.

a worry that a kind of psychological manipulation and distortion takes place: in the latter example, through the electoral process itself.

It will likely not be apparent to an individual that there are these contradictions or ignorant or poorly grounded or poorly formed attitudes, and so individuals might act based on a contradictory attitude or on a poorly formed or poorly grounded attitude Of course, it requires argument to establish that (1) some of an individual's particular beliefs, preferences, and values are "deeper" or "epistemically better" than others of that individual's beliefs, preferences, and values; and (2) that responsiveness should be responsiveness to the deeper and epistemically better attitudes rather than just whatever attitudes are expressed through votes, simple polls, or other actions. I will not provide those arguments here; I only want to note the concern that this is yet another way that responsiveness—or *real* responsiveness, as we might call it—might be undermined in the defense and military contexts.

An additional concern is that defense and military policy, like criminal justice policy, only easily moves in one direction—ratcheting up to provide more security, spending more money. There are two main reasons this might be the case. One, it is low political cost, electorally speaking, to do more, whereas it can be high cost to do less. This is so in part because emotion pushes in the direction of beefing up safety and security; the human cost is paid by others, and those others are either non-voters and even noncitizens (perhaps living in countries thousands of miles away) or politically disempowered citizens within the United States. This is particularly true given the post-conscription military era we are now living in. The financial cost—and the corresponding opportunity cost—is paid by all of us, but that has considerably less emotional resonance, particularly in a low information context such as this one; it can be completely obscure what is enough, what is necessary, and what is wasteful, even given some fixed view about the proper level of risk.

A second possible reason for concern about voter psychology and electoral pathology with respect to defense and military policy involves the relevant institutional dynamics. Bill Stuntz makes this point regarding the criminal justice context:

> A large part of the answer [to the one-way ratchet aspects of criminal law] involves not the politics of ideology and public opinion, but the politics of institutional design and incentives. Begin with the basic allocation of power over criminal law: legislators make it, prosecutors enforce it, and judges interpret it. In this system of separated powers, each branch is supposed to check the others. That does not happen. Instead, the story of American criminal law is a story of tacit cooperation between prosecutors and legislators, each of whom benefits from more and broader crimes, and growing marginalization of judges, who alone are likely to opt for narrower liability rules rather than broader ones. This dynamic does not arise out of any particular ideological stance, and does not depend on the partisan tilt of the relevant actors. Criminal law seems to expand as much, and as fast, under Democrats as under Republicans. Rather, it arises out of the incentives of the various

> actors in the system. Prosecutors are better off when criminal law is broad than when it is narrow. Legislators are better off when prosecutors are better off. The potential for alliance is strong, and obvious. And given legislative supremacy—meaning legislatures control crime definition—and prosecutorial discretion, meaning prosecutors decide whom to charge, and for what—judges cannot separate these natural allies.[24]

One can replace "prosecutors" with "the executive and military officials" and "broader crimes" with "broader military, detention, and surveillance powers and authorization." The details here are different, of course, since it is even less clear that there is legislative supremacy in this realm, given the move away from formal declarations of war, the almost complete inefficacy of the War Powers Resolution (and its questionable constitutionality[25]), and the president's standing as Commander-in-Chief of the military.

The basic point, that about institutional collusion (or, less pejoratively, cooperation), is that, if true responsiveness is eroded (as suggested above), we can expect the direction of excess to be in the direction of more expenditures on military forces and national defense and greater expansion of executive power to take steps to protect us. Why? Basically, because of the issues of confidentiality and voter ignorance described above, the only electoral benefits that elected officials can obtain in this realm are (1) being seen as doing whatever is possible—overprotecting, if necessary—to prevent a high salience, public attack, or at least not being seen as having in any way impeded such prevention; (2) being seen as pushing for aggressive policy, which plays well for the emotion/manipulation reasons described above; and (3) doing what is financially beneficial to those special interests most active in this arena—defense contractors and those who produce and invent military and surveillance technology—a point we will turn to next. As a result, it behooves elected officials to allow for more spending and more power, or at least that is the suggestion.

There are, of course, some people who care a lot about the violation of civil liberties, the possibly excessive nature of the "military industrial complex," and the devastation wrought upon distant peoples over the course of our recent military history. The suggestion is that those people have had a very uphill climb since 9/11. It is worth noting that although expense arguments have gained significant traction since the economic collapse of 2008, military spending has declined only slightly, particularly if one factors in the ends of the wars in Iraq and Afghanistan.

24. William J. Stuntz, "The Pathological Politics of Criminal Law," *Michigan Law Review* 100 (2001): 505, 510.

25. See, e.g., Philip Bobbitt, "War Powers: An Essay on John Hart Ely's *War and Responsibility: Constitutional Lessons of Vietnam and Its Aftermath*," *Michigan Law Review* 92 (1994): 1364.

D. National Defense as Big Business

Above, I noted a number of reasons to think that this premise was true:

> (P1) Systems of electoral representation tend to bring about outcomes that are *responsive* to the preferences of some constituency, C, with respect to some problem, P, only if C can hold their representative(s) meaningfully accountable with respect to P.

One reason to think this premise was true was the possibility of capture by special interests, and the suggestion that this possibility was more likely to be realized in the absence of meaningful accountability. Another factor that increases the likelihood of capture is, of course, the value to individuals of capturing the policymaking in a particular policy area.

Defense and military policy is a "high financial value" policy arena—there is an extraordinary amount of money to be made by a relatively small number of individuals and corporations, making lobbying and electioneering for certain political outcomes a very high value proposition for those entities. The sheer amount of money spent on military technology makes it an incredibly valuable area to influence. Additionally, the corporations that manufacture and develop military equipment receive a huge percentage of their revenue from defense contracts, meaning that those corporations can, and must, devote a huge percentage of their attention to lobbying and exerting political influence. It is not as if General Dynamics can sell its F-16 fighter jet to just anyone on the street. Boeing isn't running commercials advertising its Apache attack helicopter during *The Voice*. To drive the point home, consider the percentage of revenue that the largest defense corporations get from government contracts. Lockheed Martin, the corporation with the largest total defense revenue (around $44 billion in 2011), gets 94 percent of its revenue from defense contracts.[26] Boeing, the second largest corporation (around $31 billion), gets 45 percent. General Dynamics is at 78 percent, Raytheon is at 93 percent, Northrop Grumman is at 81 percent, L-3 Communications is at 83 percent, SAIC is at 80 percent, and so on. Thus, it is no surprise that 3 of the 15 largest lobbying entities in terms of total lobbying expenditures in the entire United States over the last decade are Lockheed Martin, Boeing, and Northrop Grumman (behind, among others, such giant entities as the U.S. Chamber of Commerce, AARP, and the American Medical Association).[27]

As a result, we should expect that in the defense and military policy context, if there is no meaningful accountability, then there will be an extremely significant level of capture. Arguably, the amount of money spent on lobbying by these defense corporations is simply evidence of that high level of capture.

Combining the discussion in the previous several sections, it is worth noting that these factors all work together. Confidentiality and voter ignorance work

26. See http://special.defensenews.com/top-100/charts/rank_2011.php.

27. See http://www.opensecrets.org/lobby/top.php?indexType=s.

to undermine meaningful accountability with respect to defense and military policy. The incredibly high value of being able to influence both the amount and the details of defense and military spending means that there will be overwhelming pressure exerted in one direction—to spend more, or, at least, to keep the spending levels extraordinarily high—with respect to defense and military spending. And the voter psychology and electoral pathology dimensions of military and defense policy means that it will be relatively easy for elected officials to sell more defense and military spending and engagement, when (for high salience reasons such as going to war) it becomes necessary to do so. Thus, it is no surprise when we learn that the United States spends more on its military budget than the next 13 countries combined, or that the United States is in the top-five of military expenditures per capita, along with countries that are either dictatorships or in extremely high conflict areas (or both): Saudi Arabia, Singapore, Israel, and Kuwait.[28]

IV. RECLAIMING POPULAR SOVEREIGNTY THROUGH INSTITUTIONAL REFORM: THE LOTTOCRATIC ALTERNATIVE

I hope to have made a convincing case so far for the difficulty of responsiveness and meaningful popular sovereignty in the military and defense context. There are two natural but misguided responses that might be made at this point.

The first response is to give up on the ideal of responsiveness and popular sovereignty in this context, maintaining, perhaps, that these values need not be realized in every arena, or that perhaps we should be comfortable with heightened or even complete deference in this context. That is, anyway, the line that is often pushed on us. "We are the experts, just trust us, we have to do this to keep America safe; this new military technology or equipment is essential to our safety in a modern military environment." And so on. This response has resulted in a situation in which our spending on military and defense policy is gravely out of line with our actual values and priorities, and in which much of our spending in no way makes us safer; indeed, much of it is likely to lead to needless militarization and destabilizing warmongering. At any rate, it seems worth paying close attention to whether we really think we should give up these values in this context, or whether, instead, we just see no practical way of realizing them, or, at least not any way that is better than electoral representative government and an elected president.

This brings us to the second natural response to the argument to this point: to suggest that electoral democracy of the sort found in the United States is the best that can be done with respect to popular sovereignty, even if we acknowledge it falls short of optimal levels of popular sovereignty in some (or most, or all) contexts.

28. See http://www.sipri.org/research/armaments/milex.

In this last Section, I want to briefly consider an alternative to electoral institutions as a way of achieving popular sovereignty with respect to military and defense policy. This Section introduces the idea of what I call "lottocratic" institutions,[29] and provides some reasons to think that the lottocratic government would be better than representative systems of government in terms of responsiveness, at least for some kinds of political problems, such as defense and military policy.

Before we launch into this somewhat more speculative exercise, it is worth noting that this is an area in which institutional innovation has already made some inroads. Consider, for example, the Defense Base Realignment and Closure Act of 1990, which provided "the basic framework for the transfer and disposal of military installations closed during the base realignment and closure (BRAC) process."[30] This process was introduced in response to the difficulty of reducing, realigning, or closing unnecessary or outdated military facilities due to "pork barrel politics" in which members of Congress would fight against activity reductions in military facilities in their home districts or states.[31] As some evidence of this political difficulty, it was noted that no significant military base had been closed since 1977, despite significant changes in military operations and technology in the intervening years. As a legislative assistant to then representative George E. Brown Jr. (a California Democrat) put it: "What representative up here, when confronted with two major bases closing in his or her district, wouldn't fight it?"[32]

In response to this, a process was created by which the secretary of defense would forward recommendations for realignments and closures to an "independent" nine-member panel appointed by the president, called the Base Realignment and Closure Commission (BRAC). This panel would then evaluate the recommended list of changes by taking testimony from interested parties and paying visits to affected bases. The BRAC could add bases to the list as well. Once fully evaluated by the BRAC, the list would be passed on to the president, who standardly approves the list but with the condition that the list could only be approved or disapproved in its entirety. The list is then given to Congress, with Congress enabled to enact a resolution of disapproval to the list if they do so within 45 days, but not to alter the list, and with no affirmative action required on the part of Congress.

The most recent BRAC round was in 2005. Here is an excerpt from the executive summary of that BRAC report, to give some sense of the scope of the

29. I discuss and defend these institutions at greater length in Guerrero (2014), n. 7, pp. 135–178.

30. Aaron Flynn, "Base Realignment and Closure (BRAC): Property Transfer and Disposal," *Congressional Research Service Reports* (2005).

31. For commentary, see "Base-Closing Plan Survives Assaults by Some on Hill," *Congressional Quarterly Press*, CQ Almanac 1989, 45th ed. Washington, D.C.: Congressional Quarterly). pp. 470–73. Available at: http://library.cqpress.com/cqalmanac/document.php?id=cqal89-1139303.

32. Ibid.

enterprise, and the way in which the BRAC self-conceives as an effort at instilling some popular accountability and even popular sovereignty into the process:

> In accordance with the BRAC statute, three Commissioners were directly nominated by the President and six nominated by the President after consultation with majority or minority leaders of the House and Senate. By law, and by Commission policy, the Commission's process was open, transparent, apolitical, and fair. In addition to considering certified data provided by DoD, Commissioners sought input from communities and individuals affected by the DoD recommendations. Commissioners made 182 site visits to 173 separate installations. They conducted 20 regional hearings to obtain public input and 20 deliberative hearings for input on, or discussion of, policy issues. Commissioners were accessible to communities, citizens, and to their advocates without regard to party or agenda. Commissioners participated in hundreds of meetings with public officials and received well over 200,000 pieces of mail. All documents provided to the Commission were scanned into an "e-library" and made available through the internet. The Commission's web site registered over 25 million "hits." The 2005 BRAC Commission assessed closure and realignment recommendations of unprecedented scope and complexity while setting a new standard for accessibility to the American people and transparency of deliberations.[33]

The BRAC is by no means perfect, and it is a highly technocratic body, with the nine-member panel typically composed entirely of former high-ranking military personnel and former politicians. Furthermore, it has proved incapable of continued survival in the face of some of the pressures described in Section III. It has now been over 10 years since the last BRAC, and the National Defense Authorization Act for Fiscal Year 2014 specifically prohibits authorization of future BRAC rounds. That said, it is noteworthy as an effort to move beyond normal electoral politics, and in particular as a way to circumvent some of the problems that stem from a breakdown in meaningful accountability and the overwhelming capture of defense and military policy. What I describe next can be seen as a similar kind of institutional design response to the problems identified above: confidentiality, voter ignorance, capture, and distortions due to voter psychology and electoral pathologies.

The kind of institution that I am interested in is unusual in that it employs selection of political officials by lottery, rather than by election. There is some historical precedent for this kind of method, referred to commonly as "sortition" (among other names). For example, in ancient Athens, three of the four major governmental institutions were populated by people chosen by lottery; both the brevia and the scrutiny, employed in late medieval and early Renaissance Italy, incorporated selection by lot; and, more recently, Citizens' Assemblies (in which citizens were chosen at random to serve on the assembly, and in which citizens heard from experts prior

33. Defense Base Closure and Realignment Commission, Final Report to the President (2005), Executive Summary, p. iv, available at: http://www.brac.gov/finalreport.html.

to coming up with their own proposals) in British Columbia and Ontario were used to reform election law.[34]

The kind of institution that I want to propose as a possible improvement is an instance of what I call a "lottocratic" institution. The key features of the lottocratic institutions that I will suggest might work well in this context are the following:

(1) *Single Issue*: the legislative institution focuses just on one policy area or sub-area. In this case, it could be National Defense, or there could be two such institutions, divided into, say, Domestic Defense and Global Military Policy, or there could be many such institutions that then together cover National Defense in a more elaborate network.
(2) *Lottery Selection*: the members of each single-issue legislature are chosen by *lottery* from the relevant political jurisdiction.
(3) *Learning Phase*: the members of the single-issue legislatures hear from a variety of *experts* and *stakeholders* on the relevant topic at the beginning of (and perhaps at various stages throughout) each decision-making session.
(4) *Community Engagement*: the members of the single-issue legislature spend some time talking to, interacting with, and hearing from members of the public, including activists and stakeholders affected by proposed action.
(5) *Direct Enactment*: the members of the single-issue legislature either (a) have the capacity to directly enact policy, or (b) have the capacity to enact policy if it is co-authorized by the executive branch or, in some cases, jointly with other single-issue legislatures.

More concretely, imagine that there is a network of single-issue, lottery-selected legislatures (SILLs), all focused on some aspect of National Defense, each of which consists of 300 people, chosen via random lottery from the adult citizens of the jurisdiction. One can imagine the details of the network in different ways. One version would have each SILL defined by regions—East Asia, Russia, sub-Saharan Africa, the Middle East, Latin America; or by subtopic—domestic terrorism, global terrorism, unstable states, nuclear weapons, cyberwarfare, base closings, military technology research and development, Army oversight, Air Force oversight, etc.; or by some combination of region and topic. And there could be metalevel SILLs that enabled some of these institutions to merge for discussion and policymaking when necessary, and that helped to collect input from all of thc National Defense SILLs in order to determine budget allocations.

A bit more detail about the structure of the SILLs, at least on one possible way of developing the proposal in this context. Each person chosen would serve for a four-year term. Terms would be staggered so that each year 75 new people are

34. See, e.g., Oliver Dowlen, *The Political Potential of Sortition: A Study of the Random Selection of Citizens for Public Office* (2008); Mark Warren and Hilary Pearse, eds. *Designing Deliberative Democracy: The British Columbia Citizens' Assembly* (2008).

chosen, and 75 people finish their terms. All adult citizens in the political jurisdiction would be eligible to be randomly selected, provided that (post-selection) they passed a security background check such as those required for elected officials required to deal with confidential material. People would not be legally required to serve if selected, but the financial incentives would be considerable; efforts would be made to accommodate family and work schedules (including providing relocation expenses and legal protections so that individuals or their families are not penalized professionally for serving); and the civic culture could be developed so that (unlike jury duty) serving is seen as one of the most significant civic duties and honors.[35]

In terms of decision-making, the SILLs could either be empowered to make decisions directly, or, perhaps more attractive in this context, to be in charge of vetting ideas and bringing proposals to the whole group with respect to specific areas. So, for example, the cyberwarfare SILL could hear from experts regarding the potential threats, concerns, and responses, and then develop a proposal that would then be brought to the whole group of, say, 20 SILLs, each of whom would developed expertise about some other area. This could be done as a way of assigning budget resources, or as a way of determining which areas should be prioritized. If full discussion with 6000 people was necessary but unwieldy, each of the 20 different 300-person issue-specific SILLs could choose 15 people who would represent the views of the specific SILL to the more general defense council SILL. Other structures and options are obviously possible as well. And there are questions about whether the SILLs should be given a role in making decisions directly, or whether instead they might just serve an oversight or advisory role, perhaps with the ability to veto the decisions of experts if they weren't convinced. And it could be that the SILLs need the agreement of the elected executive before doing anything, or before doing certain things (e.g., authorizing troops to go into combat, declaring war, intervening in a nation's internal conflict, etc.).

The general thought is that introducing these randomly selected citizens into some significant role in the making of defense and military policy would help generate more responsive policy, re-instilling some measure of popular sovereignty in these areas. The exact best way to do this will depend on a number of institutional, social, and political variables, and may depend on the specifics of the problems that are most significantly impairing responsiveness in a particular

35. If individuals are not required to serve, there may be a concern about disproportionality in terms of who actually ends up serving on these institutions. If that came to be a problem, one might alter the incentives for participation or make participation legally required. However, there are worries about legally required participation. First, there would have to be exceptions, and one would worry about skew being reintroduced in terms of who can take advantage of those exceptions (as in the case of military service). Second, the quality of participation may decrease if everyone is required to participate. Third, it might be objectionable to require individuals to participate in these SILLs even if they have "conscientious objections" to doing so. This might be a matter of their personal values, for example, and it might seem inappropriate to force participation. These are all reasons I prefer a system that doesn't require participation, but that makes it attractive.

political community. I don't want to attempt to set out a full case for any one particular way of using lottocratic institutions. I only want to bring them into view, so that we might consider their use, strengths, and weaknesses, particularly when thinking about alternatives such as the much more technocratic BRAC process. A full hearing is needed; here I will just present some of the more significant potential advantages and concerns of lottocratic institutions.

A few notes in advance of that. First, on the use of relatively narrow, single-issue focus, a main reason for this is that it would allow for greater learning and engagement with the particular problems. This is important given the range of backgrounds that members would bring to the institutions and concerns about decision-making competence. So, the single-issue focus is motivated by both epistemic and practical concerns.

Second, there is a question of how the randomly chosen individuals should think of their roles. Lottocratic institutions are different than electoral representative institutions, although there is a way in which some of their value comes from their representativeness. Members of the SILLs would be what Philip Pettit has called "indicative representatives." As he puts the idea of indicative representation:

> The essential difference between responsive and indicative representation is easily stated. In responsive representation, the fact that I am of a certain mind offers reason for expecting that my deputy will be of the same mind; after all, she will track what I think at the appropriate level. In indicative representation things are exactly the other way around. The fact that my proxy is of a certain mind offers reason for expecting that I will be of the same mind; that is what it means for her to serve as an indicator rather than a tracker.[36]

The thought behind lottocratic institutions is that members of the SILLs will be—at least over a long enough run—broadly descriptively and proportionately representative of the political community, simply because they have been chosen at random. But SILL members will not have in mind the idea that they are to represent some particular constituency; it is not that kind of representation. Rather, the fact that an individual member of a SILL comes to have certain views about an issue, after hearing from experts and engaging in consultation and deliberation, is a kind of evidence that members of the political community who share contextually relevant characteristics with that individual would also come to have those views, had they gone through the same experience.[37]

36. Philip Pettit, "Representation, Responsive and Indicative," *Constellations* 17 (2010): 427–28.

37. A similar idea motivates James Fishkin's "deliberative polling." On this model, those randomly chosen would be immersed in "the issues, with carefully balanced briefing materials, with intensive discussions in small groups, and with the chance to question competing experts and politicians." (This is notably similar to the "Learning Phase" of lottocratic institutions.) They would then be polled, and the results of this poll would be broadcast to the general electorate (perhaps in addition to some of the previous discussion and deliberation), prior to political primaries or elections. As Fishkin puts it, a deliberative poll is not meant to describe or predict

With these two clarifications in place, let me suggest some of the main possible advantages of lottocratic institutions in the context of national defense and military policy.

1. Possible Advantage: Combatting Ignorance without Giving Up on Popular Sovereignty

One of the most significant problems raised regarding the making of responsive policy in the defense and military policy context was that "We the People" are massively ignorant about these topics—for both familiar reasons having to do with rational voter ignorance and issue complexity, but also for reasons having to do with confidentiality and secrecy. Lottocratic institutions offer a way of combatting this problem without moving to technocratic institutions or electoral institutions that will inevitably have high degrees of capture as a result of accountability deficiencies. Lottocratic institutions take ordinary citizens and provide them with a wide range of policy-relevant information and them empower them to make decisions directly. Let me say a few words more on how this might work.

Prior to making any decisions, members of the SILL will take part in a "learning phase" during which they get general information relevant to the topic as well as more specific information relating to specific issues. As an example, in the "Learning Phase" of the BC Citizens' Assembly, experts made presentations about electoral systems, and a textbook on electoral systems was assigned as background reading. Additionally, advanced graduate students in political science from nearby universities were trained to facilitate small group discussions.[38]

There will need to be a process by which a person is allowed to speak to a SILL as an expert. This requires both a process to determine whether a person counts as an expert (the *qualification assessment* process) and a process to determine which qualified experts are given an opportunity to speak (the *expert selection* process). The point of expert presentations is to have policymaking informed by the best available knowledge relevant to the policy area at issue. One of the comparative advantages of this system is that it blends the virtues of policymaking by ordinary people with policymaking based on expertise. The hope is that by requiring experts to explain complex ideas to nonexperts, this will allow for a kind of general

public opinion; rather, "[i]t has a recommending force: these are the conclusions people would come to, were they better informed on the issues and had the opportunity and motivation to examine those issues seriously." *The Voice of the People: Public Opinion and Democracy* (1995), 162. Using "deliberative polls" of randomly selected individuals seems like an excellent idea, and it has met with some success already. My worry in this context is that they would not be enough to overcome the issues discussed in Section II, and it would be difficult to overcome confidentiality obstacles. There is also the concern that even if this led to an improvement in the quality of elected officials, those officials would still be able to pursue non-responsive policy in this context for the reasons discussed earlier.

38. For details of the BC Citizens' Assembly, from which the use of experts is borrowed, see R.B. Herath, *Real Power to the People: A Novel Approach to Electoral Reform in British Columbia* (2007) and Mark Warren and Hilary Pearse, eds., *Designing Deliberative Democracy: The British Columbia Citizens' Assembly* (2008).

comprehension, authorization, and endorsement of policy in technical and complex areas that is not present if experts are simply empowered to decide directly, while at the same time having policy that is made through epistemically responsible procedures.

It is a well-known problem with what have been called epistocratic forms of government—rule by the knowers—that for many political questions, who counts as a knower, who is an expert, is precisely what is at issue. Here, because whether an individual is an expert or not does not bear on whether that person has political power, the stakes involved in determining whether someone counts as an expert are lessened. Still, the importance of the details of the qualification assessment should be clear. For many issues, it may be relatively uncontroversial whether someone counts as an expert. For other issues, it may be controversial whether there are experts or what the bases of expertise might be. Expertise might be recognized based on advanced degrees; years of professional experience; formal professional credentials from institutions with national or international accreditation; publication of research in independent, peer-reviewed journals; and so on. A different, but also important kind of expertise is that which comes from experience, including occupational experience or lived experience, such as the experience of being a disabled person (particularly in the context of making policy that primarily affects disabled people).

Whatever process is used, experts will need to explain the basis of their expertise, describe their credentials (if relevant), and disclose any actual or possible conflicts of interest due to sources of funding or employment. A full defense of lottocratic institutions will have to do more to specify the details of the qualification assessment process, and there are significant concerns about the possibility of expert capture.[39]

Finally, it will also be important that if there are people who qualify as experts on each side of a question, then there should be substantial time for experts on each side to speak. For controversial issues, it is probably worth allowing more time for the expert presentation phase so as to allow ample time for experts to speak.

In this context, it is entirely likely that military, foreign policy, and security professionals would be among the experts presenting information and making the case to the SILLs, but they wouldn't be the only ones, and they wouldn't (at least on some versions of the idea) be making decisions directly. In this way, some measure of responsiveness might be introduced, while doing so in a way that at least lessens the ignorance of the citizens involved in making these decisions.

2. Possible Advantage: Making Capture More Difficult

As discussed above, a breakdown in meaningful accountability of elected officials and the high financial value of military and defense policy leads to a significant

39. For extended discussion of these issues regarding reliance on experts and expert testimony, see Alexander A. Guerrero, "Living with Ignorance in a World of Experts," in *Perspectives on Ignorance from Moral and Social Philosophy* (Rik Peels ed., 2016): 156–185.

level of political capture in these contexts. In general, lotteries (at least if conducted fairly) excel at preventing corruption or undue influence in the selection of representatives. This is one of several reasons to think that capture would be considerably more difficult in the SILL system. SILL members are chosen at random and don't need to run for office, so there will be no way for powerful interests to influence who becomes a SILL member or to ensure that the only viable candidates are those whose interests are congenial to their own. Because there is no need for them to raise funds for re-election, it would be easier to monitor and restrict members of the SILL to ensure that they are not having contact with or receiving funds from powerful interests either during or after their service. At least, if this is possible with juries in high profile cases, it should be possible in the case of SILLs. And since SILL membership rotates regularly, the cost of "buying off" particular SILL members would be higher, even if it could somehow be accomplished.[40] It would not be possible to capture politicians who were virtually unbeatable (from partisan districts with incumbency advantages) and count on them being an ally for 30 or more years.

There might be a worry, informed by the concerns about corporate influence over television advertising coming to dominate direct democratic institutions such as popular referenda, that in a world in which people were chosen at random to serve as political officials, the powerful interests will just shift their focus from capturing elected officials to influencing the views of the populace as a whole. This would ensure that any randomly selected individual would be likely to support the policy outcomes desired by the powerful interests. There are several things to say in response.

In a non-lottocratic political environment, the easiest, most cost-effective route of influence for powerful interests is to capture elected—but basically unaccountable—political representatives directly. The suggestion above is that this is indeed what we see in most modern political contexts. This route is the least expensive: no mass advertising or mass opinion influence necessary. And it is the most effective, being both reliable and fine-grained: one can see exactly how the supposedly captured official is behaving, and one can influence that person to do very particular things with respect to crafting and supporting (or not) particular policy decisions, even down to very specific decisions regarding particular military equipment and defense contracts, rewarding the official contingent on actual performance. A much less efficient route of influence is to affect mass opinion so as to convince ordinary citizens to vote for a particular candidate, X, where X is then expected or hoped to help enact some desired legislation. This route is likely to be much more expensive, and there is the real possibility that X will be either unable or unwilling to actually bring about the desired policy outcome.

40. This cost can be made even higher if SILL members are paid a high yearly stipend (something in the neighborhood of $500,000 or $1 million U.S. dollars each would still be within the neighborhood of the operating costs of the current U.S. Congress), but risk forfeiting that if they are discovered to have taken money or other benefits from those seeking to influence them.

Even this, however, has significant advantages over trying to affect mass opinion of the citizenry so that any randomly chosen citizen would be likely to create policy in the way desired by the powerful interests. First, there is an "information retention" limitation. As discussed above, the average voter—or, in the lottocratic context, the average potentially lottery-selected individual—is not tracking the details of political issues closely. This makes it difficult to affect that individual's views on the details of issues prior to that person's random selection—people simply aren't paying any attention. Even if someone does take note of an advertisement, it is unlikely to provide that person much in the way of detailed guidance when it comes to creating and supporting particular military or defense policy. Second, there is a "countervailing information" limitation. Whatever views a person randomly chosen to serve on a SILL had with respect to some particular issue upon being selected, it is likely that being exposed to expert presentations and considerable discussion of that issue will come to affect those initial views. Of course, effective advertising can seep into us in difficult to detect ways, but these more amorphous messages run more squarely into the previous "lack of detail" problem.

A different concern about lottocratic institutions regarding capture is that powerful interests might try to influence who is identified as a qualified expert and who is selected as an expert to speak. This is a concern. If there are nonpolitical hurdles to becoming an expert in a particular field (advanced degrees from nationally and internationally accredited educational institutions, peer-reviewed publication, and so on) and if there are disclosure requirements mandating that experts disclose sources of funding, employment, and so on, this concern might be lessened. Additionally, there can be institutional mechanisms that make capture of experts more challenging—such as having the expert identification and selection processes happen in part by the accredited community of experts nominating or certifying some individuals as candidate experts for the SILL process (in the way that, say, the American Bar Association gives ratings for proposed United States Supreme Court nominees). To achieve capture, then, would require not just buying off an individual, but an entire field.[41]

There is a worry about the politicization of expertise under a system that uses experts in this way, or in any way.[42] This is a battle that is important for any political system, whether lottocratic, electoral democratic, or technocratic. It might seem particularly dire for the lottocratic system, since the experts will be interacting with nonprofessional politicians. But the problem is just as real for elected representatives, particularly given that it might be more difficult to monitor exactly who is providing information and where they are receiving research support, and

41. For relevant further discussion, see Guerrero (2016), n. 39, pp. 178–85.

42. See, for example, the numerous books that have argued that industry and politics distort scientific practice and dissemination of information to the nonexpert public: Robert Proctor, *Cancer Wars: How Politics Shapes What We Know and Don't Know about Cancer* (1995); David Michaels, *Doubt Is Their Product: How Industry's Assault on Science Threatens Your Health* (2008).

there is a greater concern about experts being used to provide "cover" for decisions so as to thwart efforts at accountability.

Ultimately, preventing capture entirely is a difficult endeavor in a context such as military and defense policy, where powerful corporations have so much at stake financially. Our focus should be on the comparative question, then, whether introducing some lottocratic institutions into the process would improve things with respect to capture, not whether it would make capture entirely impossible or nonexistent. The suggestion here is that lottocratic institutions would do better in this regard than electoral institutions given that elected officials act untethered by any meaningful accountability in these contexts, for the reasons discussed above.

3. Possible Advantage: Improving Responsiveness and Popular Sovereignty

Another reason to think that using lottocratic institutions might be an improvement over the current system is that lottery selection is likely to result in more descriptively representative officials than elections (particularly elections such as those in the United States, employing first-past-the-post voting rules and single-member districts). Because individuals are chosen at random from the jurisdiction, they are more likely to be an ideologically, demographically, and socioeconomically representative sample of the people in the jurisdiction than those individuals who are capable of successfully running for office. As a point of comparison in the United States context, 44 percent of congresspersons have a net worth of over $1 million; 82 percent are male; 86 percent are white; and more than half are lawyers or bankers.[43]

Better descriptive representativeness doesn't ensure that SILLs will create responsive policy, but it does mean that the range of perspectives involved in making policy will be more similar to the range of perspectives of the polity as a whole, which makes responsive policy more likely.

Additionally, because SILLs focus on relatively narrower policy areas, it is less likely that non-responsive policy will result from inattention to a particular issue. With a generalist elected legislature, a few issues may draw all the attention with others left to the shadows, where policy can be created that is not responsive to the beliefs and values of the constituents without any attendant electoral consequences. (We can see various routes to reducing capture as directly improving responsiveness in this way.)

4. Possible Advantage: Avoiding Electoral Pathology and Short-Term Thinking

Another reason to think lottocratic institutions might improve policymaking in the defense and military policy context is that elections lead elected officials to focus on those problems for which they can get or claim credit for addressing or for "doing something" in the short-term, and to ignore or put on the back-burner

43. See Eric Petersen, "Representatives and Senators: Trends in Member Characteristics Since 1945," *CRS Report for Congress* (2012) at: http://www.fas.org/sgp/crs/misc/R42365.pdf.

those problems or potential solutions with a longer horizon or those solutions for which it is harder to get credit. This is related both to voter ignorance and to the perverse short-term incentives that elections provide. Since lottery-selected individuals do not have to worry about re-election or being able to claim credit, they can take a longer view and implement good ideas that might not bear fruit until 10 or 20 years later or even longer. They also don't have to worry about looking "soft" on national defense or military policy or worry about doing something—even if that something makes no sense—in response to high-salience events.

People discussing national security often stress the need for expedient decision-making in the event of emergencies. And there are definitely cases in which decisions must be made quickly, and any system that used lottocratic institutions would need to have some mechanism by which decisions could be made quickly. That said, perhaps there has been far too much focus on immediate "emergency situation" responses, responses that, in many cases, have proven to be either ineffective in addressing the problem or even counterproductive, making things worse. There is no guarantee that lottery-selected individuals wouldn't be subject to some of these same psychological pressures to do *something,* even if it wasn't obvious what ought to be done. But at least they wouldn't also have the electoral pressures bearing down on them.

As with any political institution, there are also possible concerns about lottocratic institutions. Let me briefly discuss one of these concerns and suggest some reasons to think it may be surmountable or addressable through institutional design. Throughout this discussion, it is worth noting that the severity of the concern may differ depending on the role that lottocratic institutions play—whether as an engine of direct policymaking, an advisory or supervisory institution with the power only to veto decisions, or as an institution that works in tandem with other (perhaps electoral) political institutions.

5. Possible Concern: SILL Member Competence

When the use of lottery selection of citizens is suggested, the most common worry expressed is one about the competence of the randomly chosen citizens. There is a concern—felt more powerfully by some than by others—that entrusting significant policy decisions to a randomly selected body of citizens will be a disaster, much worse than delegation to elected representatives. Perhaps electoral politics has its problems, but at least those selected have to be at least somewhat intelligent, socially competent, hard-working—or so the thought goes. This concern might be amplified in the defense and military policy context, in which the decisions made are of very high—life and death—stakes.

There are different possible responses to this concern. The extent to which one is worried about citizen competence may well depend on one's life experiences. One kind of response is to present the many institutional solutions that might increase competence: creating incentives for the full range of citizens to participate (so that one doesn't get a skewed sample as with juries), setting reasonable minimum thresholds for the particular policymaking context (e.g., requiring a high school diploma or the equivalent, or even much more education for certain technical domains), and improving public education so that the "worst off" from a competence perspective are relatively more competent.

If we have implemented improvements regarding incentives and set minimum thresholds, and the competence question remains, there are a few further possible responses. One can treat the question as a quality threshold question and argue that most citizens who might be selected actually would be competent. Or one can focus on the question as a comparative question, and attempt to highlight the incompetence of elected officials. Or one can argue that elected officials are perhaps more competent in some sense, but that this is outweighed or undermined by the ways in which they are biased as a result of being captured. All three strategies have promise, and they do not compete; indeed, the three together may be more plausible than any one in isolation. A full effort to develop these responses requires empirical investigation, but it is worth noting that it is not obvious, for example, that the average member of Congress is better able to understand technical policy issues.[44]

There are two additional reasons that suggest that randomly chosen citizens might not fair as poorly from a competence perspective as might be thought. First, the randomly chosen members of SILLs are likely to include individuals with a greater range of life experiences and vocational skills than a representative system, which may improve the quality of the outcomes due to improvements in the cognitive diversity of the group.[45] In this way, we can see the representativeness of the SILLs as a counter to the competence worry. Second, a possible side benefit of the lottery selection is what we might call the "humility of the chosen." As Barbara Goodwin puts the idea: "those allotted high office would comport themselves more humbly . . . no one could boast of his/her elevation or advancement as being personally merited."[46] This might provide a reason to think that those randomly selected feel some responsibility to demonstrate epistemic humility, to pay more attention to the issue at hand (and to leave political posturing to the side), and to engage more fully with the questions of what would be best and what people really care about. In the comparative assessment with elected officials, all of these might suggest greater relative quality in terms of the competence of the randomly chosen citizens.

Finally, a salutary side effect of using lottocratic institutions is that it makes evident the need for excellent public education for all citizens, not just for the wealthy or politically connected members of the citizenry. It may be true that, presently, a United States public high school education does not prepare one to be a helpful and engaged citizen in matters of defense and military policy. But this is something that should itself be the object of reform, not a reason to reject a proposed reform to the political system.

44. Indeed, some recent empirical work suggests otherwise. See Dana Griffin, "Citizens, Representatives, and the Myth of the Decision-Making Divide," *Political Behavior* 35 (2) (2013).

45. See Scott Page, *The Difference: How the Power of Diversity Creates Better Groups, Firms, Schools, and Societies* (2007).

46. Barbara Goodwin, *Justice by Lottery* (1992), p. 99.

There are also many more worries, of course. Worries about the legitimacy of lottocratic institutions, how they might come to be implemented (if they seemed like a good idea), how requirements of confidentiality would be enforced (although we might query whether it would need to be very different than the current system for congresspersons), whether they satisfy demands of political equality (given that not everyone is given an equal say in selecting the individuals chosen), and whether a political system could achieve adequate synchronic and diachronic policy coherence with institutions populated and empowered in this narrow and limited way.

V. CONCLUSION

In this chapter, I have raised a number of worries about standard electoral representative systems of government in terms of whether those systems can claim popular sovereignty, particularly in the realm of military and defense policy. I have suggested that an alternative kind of institution, lottocratic institutions, might do better in terms of enabling responsive policymaking. There is, of course, much more that could be said—both to defend representative systems and to raise concerns about lottocratic institutions. I leave both tasks for future work.

Index